MW00633189

WE WILL NOT BOW

Pictures of Extreme Devotion

Sacred Roots Annual 2013 - 2014

Revised Common Lectionary Year A

THE URBAN MINISTRY INSTITUTE · *a ministry of* WORLD IMPACT, INC.

This Annual is dedicated to

Mary Alice Davis

a unique and special mother of the Church,
who fought the good fight
as an African-American woman in the South,
during a season of time when conditions were vicious
and inhospitable to her and her family,
who raised eight children alone after her husband suddenly died,
who persevered through faith in the midst of
hardship, destitution, and trouble,
and yet never lost her joy in the Lord, her faith in God,
or confidence in his Word,
whose knees never bowed down
to the idols and false gods of her time,
whose entrance into glory no doubt met
with the affirmation of her Lord,
and whose life serves as a shining example of what it means
to be extremely devoted to the Savior.

His master said to him, "Well done, good and faithful servant.
You have been faithful over a little; I will set you over much.
Enter into the joy of your master."

~ Matthew 25.21

Our Prayer for Unity with the Saints: Theme Prayer for 2014

O God and Father of humankind, who has bound together the peoples of all generations; we rejoice in the communion of your saints.

We praise and bless you for all those your faithful servants whose labor in you has brought light and hope to the world. For those who were friend to the poor and the weak, defending them against outrage and oppression; for those who went forth as sheep in the midst of wolves to declare your truth and your righteousness; for those who, being in your service reviled and persecuted, did not turn back but continued steadfast to the end; for those who gave up their lives in love to you and devotion to your holy cause; for all who in ages past have helped to keep faith and hope and good will alive, we raise to you our grateful praise.

Give to us your grace, we beseech you; that we also may enter into the company of your saints, and have a part in your great redemption; and that, with those who have been given the victory over sin and death, we may dwell with you for ever and ever; through Jesus Christ our Lord.

~ Adapted from *Book of Pastor Prayers* by Ernest Freemont Tittle, p. 66.
Roger Geffen. *The Handbook of Public Prayer.*
New York, NY: The Macmillan Company, 1963. p. 95

Table of Contents

Preface

Shadrach, Meshach, and Abednego answered and said to the king, "O Nebuchadnezzar, we have no need to answer you in this matter. If this be so, our God whom we serve is able to deliver us from the burning fiery furnace, and he will deliver us out of your hand, O king. But if not, be it known to you, O king, that we will not serve your gods or worship the golden image that you have set up."

~ Daniel 3.16-18

Shared Spirituality – Religious Missionary Order Style!
All disciples of Jesus worldwide own a common stock, a mutual identity, and a shared destiny. We are saved by grace through faith in the Lord Jesus Christ, all justified by his shed blood on the Cross, and regenerated by the Holy Spirit. We have been born from above, born from Love, united to Christ in his death and resurrection, set free from the Curse and now indwelt by the Holy Spirit. As God's one undivided Church we are growing up into Christ into all things, sharing the same spiritual food, from the same Table of the Lord, baptized in the same name, inspired by the same hope. It is only right, therefore, that we strive to share a common spiritual journey, learning the same lessons, following the same Lord. We are one in the Spirit, and one in Christ Jesus, to the glory of God.

Each year, the TUMI community of missionaries deliberately join hands and hearts to share a spiritual quest and journey, to seek the Lord together in Scripture and sacrament, and to walk together in our efforts to be formed spiritually through the spiritual disciplines. All our practices, services, and activities are integrated together, informed by our commitment to walking the Christ life according to the rhythms of the Church Year. These activities are linked by a commitment to spiritual formation in sync with a biblical theme which we use to intersect and to integrate our diverse lives, numerous tasks, and ministry projects.

As members of World Impact's Religious Missionary Order, the TUMI staff takes seriously our missional identity, and seeks to translate that identity into a lifestyle that reveals us to be followers of Christ even as we seek to train leaders for Christ. We take literally our time-tested adage that *who we are in Christ is more important than what we do*. Actually, we are convinced that who we are fundamentally determines and gives rise to those things we actually represent and do.

We Will Not Bow: The Sacred Roots Annual 2013-14
Our guidebook this year is entitled *We Will Not Bow: The Sacred Roots Annual 2013-14*. This year we intend on understanding and imitating the mindset of those individuals in Scripture and throughout Church history who lived radically for God, who were willing to pay the ultimate price for their allegiance to God and to our Lord. Although we may not personally know of many martyrs, they continue to be a reality in a world lost and filled with hate for our Lord. The scope and intensity of the persecution of Christians throughout the world today is broad and deep, and we must ever be sober and alert to do all we can to stand with our brothers and sisters who are enduring suffering for the sake of Christ and his Kingdom. This year we will give special attention to understanding what it means to live lives and die deaths of extreme devotion, the kind of costly faith that honors

God and demonstrates our love for the Lord in the midst
of trials and tribulations. The power of Paul's instruction is
even more potently observed against this ever-present
background of Christian suffering in the world: "Indeed,
all who desire to live a godly life in Christ Jesus will be
persecuted" (2 Timothy 3.12).

As a community of disciples who have taken the traditional
monastic vows of obedience, chastity, and poverty, we are
interested in and committed to learning all we can about what
it means to live lives of extreme devotion. We are dedicated to
learn from the shining examples of faith both in Scripture and
in the history of the Church who honored Christ despite the
attacks of the enemy, the circumstances of persecution they
encountered, and their willingness even to die for our Lord.

Looking closely at the materials we will meditate on this
year, one would be hard pressed to find any pattern among
those who made such sacrifices for Jesus. They are from
every country, every region and clan, including men, women,
boys, and girls. They are of every age and season of life, and
are as different culturally and socially as any group could be.
Still, they all have in common a commitment to demonstrate
their love to Christ in the most unconditional, radical, and
extreme way possible. To love Jesus with one's whole heart,
it seems, is not limited to any particular color, age, gender,
or condition. Those who love the Lord prove that love,
especially during times of crisis and challenge.

Of course, our Lord Jesus himself represents the prime
example of extreme devotion. His commitment to his Father
and his dedication to testify to those in the world what he
had heard from the Father prompted people to hate him
(John 7.7). Truly, his teaching was not his own, but was from
the Father who sent him into the world. He did not seek his
own glory or speak on his own authority. He represented the
Kingdom of God in perfect harmony with God's will, and

never shrunk back from his detractors and accusers, even until the end. His devotion to the Father was extreme, unconditional, and ultimate. From his lowly birth to his horrible death by crucifixion, he never shirked or turned from his obedience to the Father. Jesus' refusal to be intimidated by evil or to change course in obeying his Father's will is the heart of all who live lives of extreme devotion. His is the true light of devotion, and ours is merely the reflection of that light. His pure heart of love and grace is the sun, and our devotion to him, the moon.

The great hymn of Philippians speaks directly to this prime example of the Lord, an expression of devotion we are called to understand and emulate:

> *Have this mind among yourselves, which is yours in Christ Jesus, who, though he was in the form of God, did not count equality with God a thing to be grasped, but emptied himself, by taking the form of a servant, being born in the likeness of men. And being found in human form, he humbled himself by becoming obedient to the point of death, even death on a cross. Therefore God has highly exalted him and bestowed on him the name that is above every name, so that at the name of Jesus every knee should bow, in heaven and on earth and under the earth, and every tongue confess that Jesus Christ is Lord, to the glory of God the Father.*

> ~ Philippians 2.5-11

Indeed, let all who love the Lord have this mind among themselves, a mind which is ours in Christ Jesus, and now, should be expressed in all facets of our devotion to God. Jesus' example of extreme humility, profound availability, and total surrender to God, even unto death, is the gold standard of what it means to be a disciple today. From total humiliation to divine vindication, we, too, must not seek our own glory, but rather, seek the glory of him who sent us, even as he sent our Lord. We belong to Christ, and God's design is to conform us to his image, to make us like him, that we might reflect his likeness in our devotion even as he did to the Father (Rom. 8.29; 2 Cor. 3.18).

Walking in the Shoes of the Persecuted
This year, we will concentrate on discovering the values, vision, and passions of those who make the extreme sacrifice of devotion to God. Throughout our days of toil and work, we will strive to keep these reflections at the primary center of our life together and shared spirituality, i.e., our reflection, devotion, discussion, and meditation. As always, we will employ an image painted by our colleague and friend Tim Ladwig, this year's amazing creation of the scene of the three Hebrew boys in the fiery furnace of the king, along with the divine visitor who saved them from death. This incident is vividly described in the Hebrew Bible, our Old Testament, in Daniel chapter 3. (Incidentally, this beautiful image on our *Annual* cover can be obtained by purchasing your own copies on our website *www.tumistore.org*). This episode of extreme devotion will be the heart of our reflection, generalizing and interpreting the nature of extreme devotion by looking at examples of it, both from Scripture and from real life through Church history. Without a doubt, knowing what it means to live a life of ultimate devotion to Jesus must be the primary concern of every disciple of Jesus, and this year we hope to be challenged to give even more of ourselves to Christ, for his glory and his Kingdom's sake.

Let God use the stories of his servants and disciples to stir your heart to offer to God and to his Son more of your love, and more of your devotion. Those who would serve as disciples of Christ must love Jesus above all marriage and family ties (Luke 14.26), take up their cross daily and follow the Lord in unconditional availability (Luke 14.27), and relinquish everything they own and have up to their Master (Luke 14.33). All of these New Testament standards simply amplify the scope and intensity of a life lived for the Lord Jesus. To him who gave up everything to his Father on behalf of his own, now, we who know him by faith, can relinquish all that we are and have up to him, for his glory.

> *Truly, truly, I say to you, unless a grain of wheat falls into the earth and dies, it remains alone; but if it dies, it bears much fruit. Whoever loves his life loses it, and whoever hates his life in this world will keep it for eternal life.*
>
> ~ John 12.24-25

It is our privilege to give up our lives to our Lord, to die to ourselves, and to hate our lives in this world in order that we may keep them for eternal life. Like our Lord, we only come to live as we learn to die. And, we can best understand what this kind of extreme devotion looks like by studying the lives of the martyrs and the saints. The cardinal virtue we will seek to demonstrate this year is empathy, i.e., our ability to put ourselves in the place of these great people, and learn vicariously from their experience.

We Will Not Bow: Pictures of Extreme Devotion, John 15.18-16.4
This year during the second, extended period of Ordinary Time during the Season after Pentecost we will go through a Who's Who list of those who offered up to God and Christ their lives in episodes of extreme devotion. We will seek to understand as best we can what kind of motives and influences impact the lives of those who offer to God unconditional surrender, and for some, even their very lives in torture, persecution, and martyrdom. This will neither be a clinical nor academic study, although we hope to do good exegesis on these events in Scripture. Rather, we will study their lives as fellow sojourners and disciples of our Lord, who desire to both revere and learn from their examples of courage and integrity. We hope to integrate into our lives the same faith, commitments, and vision that they demonstrated and so, like them, be prepared to glorify God during times of trial and crisis that we inevitably must also encounter. Listed below are the various episodes of the Scriptures we will cover during

the second period of Ordinary Time, after the celebration of Trinity Sunday:

- The Three Hebrew Boys, Dan. 3.1-30
- Jesus before Pilate, John 18.28-19.16; 1 Tim. 6.13-16
- The Innocence of Abel, Gen. 4.1-16; Heb. 11.4
- The Blood of Zechariah, 2 Chron. 24.20-22; Matt. 23.29-36
- Herod Beheads John the Baptist, Matt. 14.1-12
- Ruth's Devotion to Naomi, Ruth 1.1-18
- Daniel and the Lions' Den, Dan. 6.1-28
- Paul's Defense before Agrippa, Acts 26.1-32
- Esther Promises to Help, Esther 4.1-17
- Paul and Silas in prison, Acts 16.16-40
- Jeremiah Imprisoned for the Truth, Jer. 20.1-13
- The Stoning of Stephen, Acts 7.1-60
- Jehoshaphat Prays to God, 2 Chron. 20.1-32
- Elijah and the Prophets of Baal, 1 Kings 18. 17-46
- Elisha and the Chariots of Fire, 2 Kings 6. 8-23
- Micaiah Prophesies against Ahab, 1 Kings 22.1-40
- The Apostles Arrested and Beaten, Acts 5.12-42
- Deborah Defeats Sisera, Judg. 4.1-22
- James Is Killed with the Sword, Acts 12.1-5
- John Is Exiled to Patmos, Rev. 1.9-19
- The White-Robed Army of the Martyrs, Heb. 11.32-40, Ps. 116.10-19

We have little doubt that this close look at these amazing saints will reveal much of the life of extreme devotion that we seek to understand this year. As we learned last year, the Holy Spirit alone can help us both understand and apply God's Word in the context of our lives today. Only the Spirit of God can reproduce in us the kind of courage and passion that can allow us to glorify God in the midst of challenge as these dear saints of God did. With longing and humility, we intend to sit at their feet this year to have them instruct us in the way of discipleship.

Even If God Does Not Deliver Us – We Will Not Bow

The heart of extreme devotion is to persevere, regardless of the cost or the consequence. God's Holy Spirit has been granted to us in order that we might honor God in all that we do and all that we face. Even in the midst of the trying situation, we need not give in to doubt, fear, or intimidation. Our God is God, and he will honor the faith of him or her who stands without flinching in the face of evil. May God ever grant us this faith!

Our genuine desire is that this year's 2013-14 *Annual, We Will Not Bow*, will provide you numerous examples of men and women, as well as boys and girls who never flinched in the face of evil, but lived lives of extreme devotion at great personal cost to themselves and their families. Our love for the Lord, as Paul says, constrains and controls us (2 Cor. 5.14); our singular passion can be summarized this way: whether we are alive or dead, at home in the body or in the very presence of Jesus, to please him in all that we do and all that we are (2 Cor. 5.9). Our prayer for you and ourselves is that the texts, prayers, and readings of this *Annual* will inspire you to give all you have to the Savior, and learn to surrender with joy to the Lord Jesus as you journey with us through the calendar.

This year's *Sacred Roots Annual* invites us to sit at the feet of the saints and learn what it means to be devotees of our Lord, to empty ourselves in total surrender to Jesus in order that we may express fully his mind of dedication in our lives, right where we live, where we are. May the Lord, the Holy Spirit, fill your life with wonder and insight as you live the adventure that the saints have had in living lives of unconditional surrender to Christ, refusing to bow down to the devil's lies, the world's idols, and our sin nature's false altars. We belong to the LORD – may we express that in our devotion to him this year, for his glory alone.

~ Desirous to live a life of extreme devotion to Jesus,
Rev. Dr. Don L. Davis

We Will Not Bow

Don L. Davis, 2010

We will not bow
Won't turn around
To your empty and your vain things
We won't bow down
We won't shrink back
We'll stand our ground
To your idols and your false gods
We will not bow

Image of gold
Set up on high
All the people who don't fall down
Will be doomed to die
And as the music plays
All the peoples shout
But three boys, they refuse to bend
They will not bow

God is able to deliver
He can pry us from your hand
But if he chooses not to intervene
Our knees will never bend!

In this ol' world
Of lust and greed
Everybody tries to find a way
To meet their need
But we're not giving in
We won't bend the knee
Jesus is the Lord victorious
He's set us free

Visit *www.tumiproductions.bandcamp.com* for the musical version of this song.

How to Use This Book

The *Sacred Roots Annual* represents the devotional and liturgical structure for the Religious Missionary Order (RMO) community for TUMI International. As members of World Impact's RMO, we center our spiritual formation upon the Church Year, and share individually and corporately in the various readings, prayers, practices, and disciplines associated with it. We invite you to share this common liturgical journey with us, which is connected to the sojourn of the visible Church in the world. This wonderful spiritual trek tracks the events of biblical history with a focus on the life and ministry of Jesus. These devotions, events, emphases, and practices are designed to enhance your personal, family, small group, and congregational journeys through the living of the Christ life with the Christian calendar. Our sincere hope is that you will be greatly enriched and encouraged as you walk with us as we follow Christ.

In order to take full advantage of the *Annual's* various resources, we offer below our explanations of its critical parts, and how they are intended to function in your own spiritual formation.

Following Christ through the Church Year
As you will notice immediately, the *Sacred Roots Annual* is organized around the "Church Year." Informed by the person of Christ from his first coming to his coming in glory, the

Church Year celebrates observances, feasts, and services that allow believers all across the world to think "Christianly" about their life and times.

As a way of both worship and discipleship, the Church Year can help us put the events of our everyday lives in the context of what scholars and liturgists call the "Christ event," those promises, manifestations, and historical moments of God's saving work in the person of Jesus of Nazareth. We form our spiritual practice and discipline on our following of the Church Year, and we can attest to its ability to center worshipers and disciples on the person of Christ, and help to shape discipleship in light of the Scripture's testimony regarding his life and ministry in the world, and the hope of his return.

This year's *Sacred Roots Annual* is entitled *We Will Not Bow.* Unlike previous editions of our *Annual* and *Calendar*, this year they are themed somewhat differently. Desirous to share with our friends the photographs of our *Journey to the Holy Land,* we thought it appropriate this year to theme our *Calendar* around the land of Israel. (Of course, the surrender and devotion of the themes we highlight in the *Annual* occurred historically in the *land* of Israel, so the overlap is both obvious and clear!) Still, we will explore the *land* of Israel in our *Calendar*, while we will discuss the *life* of devotion of those who served God in Israel in our *Annual*.

Correspondingly, both the *Annual* and the calendar follow the traditional Church Year (also called the *Liturgical Year*, or *Christian Calendar*) services and observances, accompanied by references from the *Revised Common Lectionary Year A* readings. Similarly, both the *Sacred Roots Annual* and calendar interact and coordinate well with one another, with both allowing you to enrich your spiritual journey as you imagine, relive, and retell the events of Jesus in real time, re-embracing the hope of Christ, i.e., that he will soon return and transform a restored creation under God's reign.

As in previous *Annuals*, Tim Ladwig painted our *We Will Not Bow* signature graphic illustration, providing his own imaginative depiction of the three Hebrew boys of Daniel 3. Carolyn Hennings, our Curriculum and Graphic Designer, arranged the content of this year's *Annual* as well as the photographs in this year's *Calendar.* The TUMI staff took these photos during our trip to Israel in May of 2013. Carolyn's patient organization, keen eye, and brilliant design produced this year's Church Year Calendar, a major feat considering we took together more than 10,000 pictures while in Israel! Her gentle spirit and artistic skill refreshes us constantly here at the Institute, and we believe her diligent work in producing this year's calendar will also spark your own imagination as you ponder the glory of the land of Israel, the birthplace of our Lord and our faith. Of course, you can obtain copies of this year's calendar, along with various other spiritual formation resources, from our website, *www.tumi.org/annual.*

Meaning of "Proper" in the Church Year

As you follow through the Church Year Calendar, you will notice that during the Season after Pentecost (also referred to as *Ordinary Time* or *Kingdomtide*) the weeks are referred to as "Proper," followed by a particular number. This term (*Proper*) is used for all the weeks during this extended period, except special days (e.g., *Trinity Sunday, Reformation Day, All Saints Day*, and *Reign of Christ the King*). The Propers of the Church Year refer to how some church traditions assign appointed prayers (called *collects*) for specific services, along with particular Psalms and Lessons (i.e., lectionary texts) for a given week or special day. For instance, the Anglican and Episcopal traditions (among others) use these Proper references to conduct their worship services in conjunction with their books of order and books of common prayer. These are merely terms to help indicate what prayers, Scriptures, and lessons may be used during that specific week of worship.

Theme for the Week

Usually, we follow the Church Year as the guide for our weekly themes and preaching texts, drawn normally from reference outlines in the *Revised Common Lectionary*. The lectionary is a comprehensive Bible reading program drafted specifically in order to help congregations read through the major sections and stories of the Scriptures over a three-year period. The Years A, B, and C refer to the Gospel readings according to the evangelists: *Year A* referring to *Matthew*, *Year B* to *Mark*, and *Year C* to *Luke*. During these separate years which cycle the one after the other, the Gospel readings will coincide with these books. The Gospel of John is included in each of the Years A, B, and C, and is referred to liberally at various times and seasons throughout the Church Year.

The majority of this year's Gospel citations will be taken from Matthew, the designation of *Church Year A*. For most of the year, our weekly service themes are based on texts taken directly from the Lectionary, and our times of retreat, prayer, and spiritual discipline are also informed by those Scriptures as well. Within the *Annual*, you will find that our weekly themes are provided for you, along with a descriptive statement that highlights its meaning for us that week. Please check our website *www.tumi.org/annual* for an at-a-glance chart of our entire year's lectionary texts and themes.

An online version of the *Annual* is posted for you to take advantage of during those times when your soft-cover *Annual* is not available. You may find the appropriate week of devotional and liturgical reading and observance at *www.tumi.org/annual*.

Daily Devotional Guide

As a way to "pile drive" the truth of the weekly theme into our individual and corporate minds, we ponder it daily in devotional readings, meditation, and prayer. Set aside time, either in the morning or evening or both, to spend time with the Lord, reflecting on the truths learned from the text in sermon and discussion.

Structure as Servant to Spontaneity

We are convinced that the best prerequisite needed to display skill in a spontaneous environment is prolonged practice and application. Only after you follow the daily regimen of the disciplines can you be enriched in your ongoing walk and devotion to Christ. Please take note of both the order and sequence of our devotional guide, which mirrors the traditional liturgy of the Church in significant ways. First, each day is structured similarly, with a connected sequence:

Preparing Our Hearts

Invocation: Our Prayer of Acclamation
Call to Worship

Praising Our God

Te Deum Laudamus
Praise and Thanksgiving
Gloria Patri

Listening to His Voice

Chronological Bible Reading
Lectionary Readings
Reflection: Silence and/or Journaling

Responding in Faith
Recitation of the Apostles' Creed
Prayers of Confession
Assurance of Pardon
Petitions and Supplications
The Doxology

Departing to Serve
Benediction: Our Prayer of Acknowledgment
Affirmation from the Psalms
Pray without Ceasing – Flash Prayer for the Day

We do not suggest that conformity to service order is demanded in the NT for the worshiper, nor that one gets "brownie points" for following this structure. As a regimen, this is not meant to be empty and formalistic. Rather, we seek to "discipline ourselves for the purpose of godliness" (1 Tim. 4.6-7). This kind of daily focus and repetition is done, not to create mindless repetition and familiarity, but to deliberately build within us the habit of coming to God in shared process and approach.

As a worshiping, serving, and witnessing community, we have found it especially refreshing and helpful over the years to employ together the same guide – reading the same Scripture, reciting the same creed and prayers, and seeking as one body the same grace from the same Lord. We seek the Lord in our own individual ways, but strive to do so from a common prayer, devotion, and practice. Our motto in this is simple: we seek the Lord, alone together. We strive to share a spiritual journey and language with one another so we can better encourage and enrich one another.

We firmly believe that only the Holy Spirit can energize and develop true spirituality. He is our Lord and Life-giver (as the

Nicene Creed suggests), and only he can make Christ real to us in our times in the various disciplines of spiritual formation. We seek to daily give ourselves to him in this structure in order to open ourselves to his leading and teaching. The Holy Spirit is neither limited nor hindered by such a structure (notice the Jewish sacred year and its annual rhythms of Passover, Unleavened Bread, the Feast of Weeks, the Feast of Trumpets, the Day of Atonement, and the Feast of Tabernacles). Our Lord's custom was to go both to the synagogue on the Sabbath and to the great feasts in Jerusalem, and all we desire here is to be open to him in all we do.

As you employ the *Annual's* devotional order, it may be helpful to have an explanation of its parts, and what we seek to do during the various stages of our approach and indwelling of the presence of God.

Preparing Our Hearts
Invocation: Our Prayer of Acclamation
Our "Preparing Our Hearts" section begins with Invocation prayers. These are opening prayers tied directly to our weekly themes in the calendar. These are prayers of invitation (seeking the Lord's presence and blessing for our time of worship and praise), as well as prayers of acclamation (affirming the truth of God's goodness and awesome deeds on our behalf). These prayers ask the Lord to speak to us about the theme at hand through our time in praise and worship, reading, prayer, and meditation.

Call to Worship
This affirmation, taken directly from the common liturgy of the main communions of the Church, declares God as the Sovereign Lord of all creation, the receiver of our praise and worship, and acknowledges him as the sole recipient of our praise, faith, and adoration.

Praising Our God

Te Deum Laudamus: We Praise Thee, O God

We open our praise section with a familiar prayer employed now for centuries in many traditions within their morning devotional regimen, the *Te Deum Laudamus*, or translated from the Latin, "We praise Thee, O God." This prayer is an early chant of the Western Church beginning, "We praise Thee, O God, we acknowledge Thee to be the Lord." In the legend of the Church, this prayer is ascribed to an "ecstatic outburst" of St. Ambrose when he baptized St. Augustine. The prayer is now widely attributed to Bishop Nicetas of Dacia (c. 335-414). As mentioned above, the prayer is sung at morning prayer in Anglican churches and at matins in the Roman office. (It is associated with one of the order of services, Rite II, in the classic devotional guide *The Book of Common Prayer*.)

By the way, if you are not accustomed to reading your prayers of devotion and intercession, know that you are not alone! You should not be too squeamish about *reading* or *reciting* a prayer. Recall, for instance, that the Psalms are simply songs and written prayers (as are many hymns of the Church) which have been read and recited in worship for centuries. Furthermore, Christ Jesus himself told us to repeat a prayer he gave us with the Lord's prayer, and often in prayer circles the prayers of Paul, Nehemiah, Daniel, or Jehoshaphat or others are used in our supplications.

Prayer is about authentic heart conversation to God; the question is whether we are reverent, humble, and open in our address to the Lord, not whether we recite or read a prayer, or use someone else's words. Make sure your heart is right with God, and communicate through the words your own heart's desire. Focus on real prayer, not on whether you're reciting the prayers or not!

Praise and Thanksgiving

We should open our approach to God with worship, praise, song, and acclamation. God is great and greatly to be praised! Recall the words of the psalmist, "Make a joyful noise to the LORD, all the earth! Serve the LORD with gladness! Come into his presence with singing! Know that the LORD, he is God! It is he who made us, and we are his; we are his people, and the sheep of his pasture. Enter his gates with thanksgiving, and his courts with praise! Give thanks to him; bless his name!" (Ps. 110.1-4).

Feel free to bring a chorus book or hymnal to your time, and always come prepared to sing and play songs, hymns, and spiritual songs to the Lord. As members of the royal priesthood of God, remember worship of our God is both a privilege and a duty (1 Pet. 2.8-9).

Gloria Patri

> *Glory be to the Father,*
> *And to the Son and to the Holy Spirit:*
> *As it was in the beginning,*
> *Is now, and ever shall be,*
> *World without end. Amen, amen.*

This worship interlude is familiar in many traditions of the Church, and is used in a variety of services and places. For instance, Anglicans mainly use the *Gloria Patri* (Latin, "Glory to the Father") to conclude the singing or recitation of psalms and canticles at the Daily Offices (Devotions) of Morning and Evening Prayer. Lutherans historically have added it after the recitation or chanting of the Psalm during the Service of the Word and at various times in the Daily Office. Evangelical Presbyterian churches and Methodists frequently sing it to conclude the "responsive reading" at the end of the psalm readings.

In this devotional, we have placed the *Gloria Patri* at the end of our time of praise and thanksgiving, serving as a fitting closing affirmation of our triune God as the only Lord worthy of all praise, honor, and glory. In this setting it is meant to highlight our worship to the Lord, Father, Son, and Holy Spirit, as the solitary author of all life and salvation, and therefore alone worthy of our highest and best praise.

Listening to His Voice
Chronological Reading for the Day
The essential rhythm of New Testament worship is word and sacrament. Concentrating on the Word of God, listening to his voice, should be a priority in all our devotional moments in God's presence. Each year we read through the Scriptures together chronologically, gaining greater insight on the entire biblical Story of God, tracking the events of God's covenant promise in their historical order. Included in the *Sacred Roots Annual* are the texts associated with this through-the-Bible-in-one-year chronological reading process.

You can also pick up a paper guide that includes the references in brochure form. This handy guide is convenient, allowing you to place it in your favorite reading Bible. We highlight the Seasons of the Church Year in attractive colors, and key the sections to the emphases of the Church Year's time schedule. You can obtain this from our website (*www.tumistore.org*).

Reading through the Scriptures chronologically helps you see the underlying plot of the Scriptures: the salvation of God in the person of Jesus of Nazareth, the Christ. This reading provides not only richer insight into the events of Scripture, but also a greater comprehension of the whole story's meaning and movement – a story which climaxes in the Christ event; his birth, his life, his death, burial, resurrection, ascension, and return.

Lectionary Readings

As mentioned before, our reading guide is the *Revised Common Lectionary*, a Bible reading program drafted to help congregations in their public reading of Scripture. It is crafted in such a way that the vast majority of Scripture can be read together over a three-year period. It is the lectionary texts that we use to organize our worship and sermon preparation. The Years A, B, and C refer to the Gospel readings according to the evangelists: Year A referring to Matthew, Year B to Mark, and Year C to Luke's Gospel. During these separate years the Gospel readings will coincide with these books. The Gospel of John is included in each of the Years A, B, and C, and is referred to liberally at various times and seasons throughout the Church Year.

Note: In the *Annual*, the Old Testament lectionary texts are abbreviated with *OT*, and the New Testament are abbreviated with *NT*.

Reflection: Silence and/or Journaling

After hearing from God in his Word, we then respond to the voice of God with meditation, reflection, and silence. Here we would recommend that you take time to silently reflect on the meaning of the personal charge that God has spoken to you through his Word, whether a promise, a command, a teaching, or an insight. Wait in the presence of God, and be silent and patient; allow the Spirit to highlight, pinpoint, or address whatever issues and truths he wishes as you wait before the Lord.

Responding in Faith

The Apostles' Creed

In the tradition of the Church, it has been customary to follow the hearing of God's Word with the affirmation of the historic orthodox faith, in creedal form. Our daily devotional guide includes the confession of the Apostles'

Creed, the basic creed of the Reformed churches, and a significant statement still used commonly in baptism. The Apostles' Creed was used as a confessional statement at the baptism of new converts centuries ago and is still used today in that format. Reciting it each day reminds us of our "cruciform life," i.e., our baptismal covenant of allegiance to Christ, and our commitment to share his death and risen life in our daily discipleship.

The Apostles' Creed is one of the most basic statements of early Christian confession, dating from perhaps a half century or so from the time the New Testament was written. It is widely used by many denominations for both worship and Christian education purposes, its use is most prevalent in Western churches. While affirming the classic outline of the Christian faith, it does not address some Christological issues which would be later addressed in other creeds, including our oft-used "Nicene Creed" (i.e., Nicene-Constantinople Creed of C.E. 381).

Still, the Apostles' Creed represents one of the oldest, clearest, and most authoritative summaries of the faith of the ancient, undivided Church. Please note: the reference in the Creed to "catholic" refers to the universal nature of the Church's membership and makeup, i.e., the Church of all members through all ages and times, of all languages and peoples. It refers to no particular tradition or denomina- tional expression, and does not refer in particular to the Roman Catholic expression of the Church.

Prayers of Confession
Following the traditional liturgy, we include a special moment of confession and cleansing before the Lord. This response of seeking the Lord's forgiveness is an integral element in our walking with God, and maintaining an acceptable communion in Christ. It is an important part

of our faith response to the Lord. John says in his first epistle, "This is the message we have heard from him and proclaim to you, that God is light, and in him is no darkness at all. If we say we have fellowship with him while we walk in darkness, we lie and do not practice the truth. But if we walk in the light, as he is in the light, we have fellowship with one another, and the blood of Jesus his Son cleanses us from all sin. If we say we have no sin, we deceive ourselves, and the truth is not in us. If we confess our sins, he is faithful and just to forgive us our sins and to cleanse us from all unrighteousness" (1 John 1.5-9).

Assurance of Pardon
Once we have acknowledged and renounced our sins before the Lord, asking for his cleansing and forgiveness, we can know that we have been forgiven. His Word is clear: if we confess our sins, he is both faithful and just in Christ to forgive us and to cleanse us. We believe his Word, and affirm and receive his wonderful provision of daily cleansing. Be assured of your pardon today.

Petitions and Supplications Ending with The Lord's Prayer
Take time to offer prayers to God: prayers of adoration, confessions, thanks, and supplications for yourself and others. Recite the Lord's prayer or bring a prayer book and read prayers to God. Be open to the Holy Spirit as you petition the Lord, seeking his aid, grace, and help in your time of need (Heb. 4.16).

Doxology
As a part of our daily devotions we sing the *Doxology*, that wonderful, ancient, and beautiful anthem of praise to God used throughout the Church in the world. Praise the triune God for his glory and grace! (The *Doxology's* copyright is in the Public Domain [available for public usage].)

Departing to Serve

Benediction: Our Prayer of Acknowledgment

We encourage you to formally close your time of meditation, prayer, and worship with God with a formal benediction. These prayers are expressions of our understanding and devotion to God in light of the truths he has imprinted upon us during our time with him. They are short prayers that acknowledge God as our Source and life, that ask him for his aid to make his truth our own, and that focus on God's person and work. They often summarize the theme of the Scripture for the week or the special day of commemoration, and usually close our communion with God with a specific request to him tied directly to our weekly theme. In all things we desire the Lord to be acknowledged for who he truly is: the true and living God, and God and Father of our Lord Jesus Christ.

Of course, as with all the prayers of the *Sacred Roots Annual*, these need not be tied merely to your time alone or together with God. These prayers (invocations, benedictions) may also be recited throughout the day, encouraging us to seek God's favor on a particular request we received through the Spirit's teaching from the Word.

Affirmation from the Psalms

Each devotional session ends with an affirmation from the Psalms which can also be used as "flash prayers" to focus our minds and hearts upon the Lord, who is the aim and goal of all our devotion and service in our spiritual formation disciplines. Let us obey James where he instructs us to pray and praise for spiritual edification: "Is anyone among you suffering? Let him pray. Is anyone cheerful? Let him sing praise" (James 5.13). In everything, too, let us give thanks to God through Christ: "And whatever you do, in word or deed, do everything in the name of the Lord Jesus, giving thanks to God the Father through him" (Col. 3.17).

Pray without Ceasing

This prayer is also another "flash prayer," as Frank Laubach called it, to be used whenever and wherever throughout the day and for the week. We encourage you to stay focused on the theme of the week each day. Concentrating on a single main idea each day throughout the entire week can enable us to bring together our various meditations, prayers, and dialogues, helping us stay focused on one big idea. This prayer encourages you to recall the theme as often as you can. Repeat this short prayer throughout your day to help you stay attuned to the meaning of our weekly theme.

For Your Weekly Journey

In addition to the daily devotional guide, we also provide weekly practices associated with our theme. Other disciplines we share come into play here: additional readings, Scripture memorization, times of retreat, fasting, and prayer, and readings of select books also connect to our themes. Such a rich listing of observances and disciplines requires much adjustment; some weeks, for instance, we find our disciplines easier to accomplish than others! In all things we seek to follow the mind of the Spirit in the rhythm of our lives. Find your own group's unique capacity and availability, and strive to walk together focused on the same spiritual themes and practices. Such a shared walk will strengthen you together in your corporate journey in faith.

Prayer, Fasting, Solitude and Silence Days

As believers committed to living and serving in community, we seek to share our spiritual journeys together in prayer, fasting, silence, and retreat. Set aside time regularly to decompress your life, to give the Lord extended periods of focus and time. Below are some ways you might follow us as we practice these disciplines both alone and together each quarter.

Intercessory Prayer Concerts: Let God Arise! Prayer Movement
We employ our Let God Arise! prayer guide to pray for
the urban church and the great cities of the world. You can
obtain many resources connected with this movement from
our website (*www.tumi.org/LetGodArise*), including our *Let
God Arise! Prayer Booklet* which leads through the seven A's
of effective prayer concerts in the church. Also, watch each
Church Year season on our website for our *Let God Arise!*
devotional materials and videos.

Fasting, Solitude, and Silence
In obedience to the biblical injunction to fast, we set aside
regular times together to fast and pray each quarter, fasting
from food for 1-3 meals, and spending time in prayer during
the fast period. We also set aside time alone with the Lord
in isolation and in silence, for the purpose of listening to him
and opening ourselves up to his Word and his Spirit. We
seek neither to be wooden nor legalistic in our practice of
these disciplines. Our sole desire is to see and touch the Lord
during these times of spiritual seeking. We vary these times
(e.g., spending time together or alone, adjust how long they
are or how often) depending on our schedule, or our shared
sense for retreat with the Lord.

Celebrations and Observances: Special Days of the Church Year
In regard to special days for spiritual purposes, Paul affirmed
our freedom in Christ to use observances of days as a means
of enhancing our walk with him. Look at his counsel to the
Romans on this issue (Rom. 14.5-7):

One person esteems one day as better than another, while
another esteems all days alike. Each one should be fully
convinced in his own mind. [6] The one who observes the
day, observes it in honor of the Lord. The one who eats, eats
in honor of the Lord, since he gives thanks to God, while the
one who abstains, abstains in honor of the Lord and gives
thanks to God. [7] For none of us lives to himself, and none
of us dies to himself.

Paul went on to instruct us that if we live or die we are the Lord's, and should do all things with his glory and honor in mind.

Led, counseled, and disciplined by this freedom in Christ, we employ the Church Year. Of course, we also recognize that there is neither merit nor righteousness imputed in the keeping of the Christian calendar! Righteousness is from God through faith in our Lord Jesus Christ (Phil. 3.9). Nevertheless, we observe the Christ journey of the Church Year with its seasons and special days not as days which are sacred in and of themselves, but as a helpful means by which we can remember and reflect on the mystery and wonder of Christ's work in the world, and his soon and coming Kingdom.

As those committed to following and being conformed to the person of Christ, we find the Church Year invaluable. It allows us to follow the life of Jesus in real time in our worship and discipleship context. For us, it is about our commitment, adoration, and delight in the person of Christ and our desire to be identified with his life, death, and resurrection.

So, as we celebrate the Church Year together, we begin with the promise and fulfillment of the incarnation of Christ (*Advent* to *Epiphany*). Next, in our worship and reflection we focus on the revelation of Christ's mission to the world (*Epiphany* and *Transfiguration*). We then journey with our Lord to his Passion, being reminded through the Church Year that Jesus set his face toward Jerusalem and the cross (*Ash Wednesday* and *Lent*). We follow the historical events of Christ's work as it climaxes in his final week – his entry into Jerusalem, his confrontation with his enemies, his Supper with his disciples, his sham trial, his crucifixion, his burial (*Holy Week*), and his resurrection (*Easter*). We affirm in celebration his ascension to the Father's right hand in glory (*Ascension Day*), and remember the birth of his Church through the outpouring of his Spirit on the people (*Pentecost*).

We continue our observances as we acknowledge his active presence in the Church, remembering his headship, his mandate to the harvest, and the hope of his Church throughout the ages (*Season after Pentecost*). On October 31 we commemorate the protestant reformation of the Church (*Reformation Day*), and on November 1 we anticipate the gathering of all believers together at his throne, while remembering his martyrs and generations gone by (*All Saints Day*). Finally, we anticipate and await his return, and acknowledge in worship and service that Christ will soon reign supreme as Lord and King over all (*Reign of Christ the King*).

In our celebrations, we notice the "rhythms" of worship and doctrine in the Church Year. Advent both ends the cycle and begins it again. It looks forward to his Second Coming as the conclusion of the Church Year but also prepares to remember again his First Coming and thus starts the Church Year afresh.

The Church Year is our reflection, participation, enactment, and embodiment of the Christ story in the midst of our personal and community lives. Join us as we walk afresh through the major milestones of our Lord's life and ministry, seeking to become like him in his incarnation, death, and resurrection!

Feast Day Invocation and Benediction Prayers
We have included select ancient believers' prayers on each special day and commemoration of the Church Year. As those who deeply cherish the communion of all Christians throughout all the ages we believe it is important to affirm our union with the Church through the ages, whose legacy we defend and follow. Through their prayers we can identify with their longings, and, in them, see our own for the coming of our Lord's Kingdom.

Bibliographic Information for Prayers of the Saints

Bright, William. *Ancient Collects and Other Prayers: Selected for Devotional Use from Various Rituals*, 8th ed. Oxford and London: James Parker, 1908.

Ferguson, James and Charles L. Wallis, eds. *Prayers for Public Worship: A Service Book of Morning and Evening Prayers Following the Course of the Christian Year*. New York, NY: Harper & Brothers, 1958.

Fox, Selina Fitzherbert. *A Chain of Prayer across the Ages: Forty Centuries of Prayer from 2000 B.C.-A.D. 1916*. New York, NY: E. P. Dutton, 1943.

Geffen, Roger. *The Handbook of Public Prayer*. New York, NY: The Macmillan Company, 1963.

Lindemann, Fred H. *The Sermon and the Propers: Volume I, Advent and Epiphany*. St. Louis, MO: Concordia Publishing House, 1958.

Oden, Thomas C. *Ancient Christian Devotional*. Downers Grove, IL: IVP Books, 2007.

Suter, John Wallace, Jr., ed. *The Book of English Collects*. New York, NY: Harper, 1940.

Tickle, Phyllis. *The Divine Hours: Prayers for Autumn and Wintertime*. New York, NY: Image Books, 2000.

Book Reading

This year we will be reading four texts designed to enrich our dialogue and meditation on the beauty and challenge of extreme devotion to God. These texts are easy to read and challenging, filled with inspiring stories of men, women, boys, and girls who expressed their devotion to God in perseverance and, in some cases, martyrdom. The diversity and richness of these books will spark important thinking and dialogue among us, providing a lively ongoing intellectual and spiritual challenge for our missionary community, and we hope, for you as well as you join us on our journey of discovery. The bibliographic information for each text is given below in the order of our reading through the course of the year:

Extreme Devotion Writing Team (Editor). *Extreme Devotion: The Voice of the Martyrs.* Nashville, TN: W Publishing Group, 2001.

Marvin J. Newell. *A Martyr's Grace: Stories of Those Who Gave All for Christ and His Cause.* Chicago, IL: Moody Publishers, 2006.

D. C. Talk, The Voice of the Martyrs. *Jesus Freaks: Stories of Those Who Stood for Jesus, the Ultimate Jesus Freaks.* Bloomington, MN: Bethany House Publishers, 1999.

James C. Howell. *Servants, Misfits, and Martyrs: Saints and Their Stories.* Nashville, TN. Upper Room Books, 1999.

On-Line Sacred Roots Annual

As an added benefit, the devotional content from this year's *Sacred Roots Annual 2013-14* is also available online for your perusal and use. In addition to these rich spiritual devotional guides you will find many other helpful materials designed to help you grow spiritually in Christ, formed through the Church Year. Visit *www.tumi.org/annual*, and click on "On-line Annual" to find the *Sacred Roots Annual's* devotional content as well as convenient links to Dr. Davis's teaching and outlines for each week's theme. We have also linked you to the ESV Bible's audio recording of the Daily Chronological Reading Guide, which we follow each year. Click on the specific "Week" link to view its devotional guide and resources!

The Sacred Roots Annual:
A Swiss Army Knife of Spiritual Formation

Nothing is more powerful in times of preparation, crisis, and opportunity than having the right tool for the right job at the right moment.

The *Sacred Roots Annual* is intended to be such a tool, one that can serve us at every phase or stage of our spiritual formation, as member or minister, whether in devotion, discipleship, or pastoral care. Like a Swiss Army knife, an implement filled with assorted tools for particular tasks, we are convinced that the *Sacred Roots Annual* is appropriate for various levels of spiritual growth and in a variety of venues. We believe it can be a great resource for the Christian seeker, the discipler, and the pastor alike. Over the years, we have entertained and answered numerous questions on the issue of who is best suited for the *Annual* – individuals, small groups, or congregations. Our answers to these questions have become ever more simple and clear: we believe that the *Sacred Roots Annual* can be used by a wide range of people and groups, and that it is a great tool for small groups and congregations interested in sharing a spiritual journey together!

Suitable for the Individual, Family, or Small Group
The *Sacred Roots Annual* is designed for multiple users: individuals wanting to grow in Christ, families hoping to

start regular times of seeking God, or cells or small groups desiring to track with one another in spiritual formation.

Individuals will benefit from a disciplined approach to spiritual formation with Christ at the center. Its clear focus on personal devotion and personal walk makes it an ideal choice for anyone interested in beginning a structured yet flexible regimen of the spiritual disciplines for spiritual growth. Likewise, the exercises, readings, and suggestions of the *Sacred Roots Annual* are also easily employed within a group context. You can practice the disciplines together, or do them separately alone, and come together to share your insights, questions, and ideas. A threefold cord is not easily broken, nor is a tight-knit spiritual formation cell likely to fail in its quest to grow in Christ. We recommend that you practice the disciplines both *alone* and *together with others*. The rhythm of a personal journey and shared spirituality will provide you with greater richness and insight into the wonder and mystery that Christ Jesus is to you, his disciple, and to us, his people.

On this note, the journey and walk motif we use throughout the *Sacred Roots Annual* is done deliberately. Having sought God together rigorously as a community for years now, we understand how powerful and meaningful that shared spirituality can be when we devote ourselves together to mature in Christ. Our hope is that whether you use the *Annual* as an individual, as a family, or as a small group you will begin to practice the disciplines *regularly* and *together*, that you will strive to walk in community in spiritual formation sharing a spirituality, and learning of Christ and his ways as a group.

A Strategic Tool for the Teacher, Discipler, Spiritual Director, or Pastor
Perhaps the greatest added benefit of the *Sacred Roots Annual* is the help it can provide to those who are in roles of spiritual

direction and discipling others. If you are a pastor, shepherding others, or if you are responsible for others' spiritually, i.e., the "care of souls," the *Sacred Roots Annual* allows you a wonderful and efficient way to organize your shared journey with those you lead. If you embrace the *Annual's* "spiritual logic," that is, if you determine that following the Christ life through the Church Year has merit, you can structure your preaching, teaching, Christian education, and service and missions projects all in conjunction with the schedule within the *Annual*.

For instance, for you as a busy pastor, seeing Christ formed in you and your congregation can readily occur if you embrace the Church Year as your overall worship and discipleship structure. With a clear, deliberate focus on Christ Jesus in all dimensions of your life together, it is both profitable and effective to order your services, your preaching and teaching, your Christian education (at various levels), and your service and outreach in connection to the themes included. Know too that, if you choose this discipline and regimen, you will certainly not be alone! Literally, hundreds of thousands of congregations order their spiritual formation around the celebration of the Christ life in the Church Year, and the resources for preaching, teaching, and Christian education are voluminous for those who use it. There are a number of practical ideas for you to apply the insights of the *Sacred Roots Annual* to your strategy of spiritual formation:

- Use the *Revised Common Lectionary (RCL) to identify specific texts and themes for preaching and teaching series, and themes for worship service.* For instance, the texts provided in the Lectionary Year A readings allows for you to consistently teach and preach from texts being read throughout the churches worldwide. Often, churches and preachers will opt to go through a series, book, or topical focus during the extended Ordinary Time period, which occurs later in the year.

This year, with our focus on the saints and martyrs of Scripture, we have chosen particular texts not found in the Year A textual list. Use freedom during this extended time to concentrate on those areas of need the Holy Spirit leads you to address, for your own sake and/or the sake of those whom you lead.

- Structure your *weekly worship themes in conjunction with the images, stories, and seasons reflected in the Church Year* (many thousands of churches do this, although most evangelical churches are barely acquainted with such applications of the Church Year, celebrating only Christmas and Easter!)

- Incorporate select *Scripture readings of the Lectionary to be included in the worship experience* of the church, as responsive readings or separate Bible readings.

- *Highlight the feast days or seasons of the Church Year* for special times of worship, training, celebration, or outreach (Christmas, Easter, Pentecost, Reign of Christ the King).

- Organize your *Christian education and Sunday School programs* around seasons, concentrating on a particular season of Christ's life and ministry. For various seasons or series synchronize all your Sunday School, small group, and pulpit ministry themes together in order to consider a singular integrated theme and direction for the entire church. Although this is not done often, it pays huge dividends, not only in terms of connecting all members of the body to a single theme (enabling us to walk together spiritually more coherently), it also pile drives the theme home by helping families, whatever the members' age or station, center down on one big, significant idea.

- Think through your entire Church Year calendar, *using it to map out your weekly and seasonal themes* for the entire church body for the year. You might choose (as we have done) to *draft an annual theme for your church based on a selected focus you wish to emphasize or highlight for the Church Year* (remember, the Church Year is from December through November!)

- Use the general structure of the Church Year, *highlighting each of the special seasons as focus for a series or emphasis in your worship or spiritual training* (the "Cycle of Light": Advent, Christmas, Epiphany, and the "Cycle of Life": Lent, Easter, Pentecost. For the purpose of thematic focus we break up the single "Season after Pentecost" into select sections of emphasis, *The Coming of the Holy Spirit*, *A Season of Christ's Headship*, *A Season of Christ's Harvest*, *A Season of Christ's Hope*, and *Remembering the Saints/Exalting the King*.)

- *Create your own special series for the two seasons of "Ordinary Time" in the calendar* (after Epiphany, and after Pentecost). There is great flexibility here, for during these weeks there is no special theme emphasized in the Church Year.

The possibilities of using the Church Year as a key structural tool for you as a spiritual leader are endless. Visit our website, *www.tumi.org/annual*, to discover more exciting ways to incorporate and integrate your spiritual formation efforts with the Church Year.

This *Sacred Roots Annual* is the formal blueprint for our community's shared spiritual journey, and we invite you to join us as we read Scripture, seek God's face, and use this travel log to be conformed to the image of our dear Savior,

Jesus of Nazareth. In seeking him, we desire to walk in his steps, to share his journey, and to become like him in his humiliation and exaltation, for the Father's glory. We use this *Sacred Roots Annual* to tread the same path that has been traversed by pilgrims, disciples, and followers of Jesus through the ages – remembering, rehearsing, and reenacting the greatest Tale ever told or retold.

Since our earliest records, the Church has made it a point to remember and celebrate the events of Jesus' life, death, burial, and resurrection, ascension, session, and return. Come along with us as we share our lives together, walking with our Lord as he forms his life in us.

Door of Humility
Church of the Nativity, Bethlehem

THE SEASON OF ADVENT ✠ THE COMING OF CHRIST

THE SEASON OF ADVENT: THE COMING OF CHRIST
DECEMBER 1 - 23, 2013

Advent is a season of anticipation and repentance which focuses on the First and Second Comings of Christ. The dual focus means that Advent both begins and ends the Christian Year (Isa. 9.1-7, 11.1-16; Mark 1.1-8).

The Coming of Christ
Advent anticipates the First and Second Comings of our Lord. God's prophets foretold his Coming, and angels announced his birth to Mary and the shepherds. We affirm God's promise fulfilled in the arrival of Messiah in Bethlehem.

Week 1: Anticipation
The Advent wreath reminds us of God's eternal love, without a beginning, without an end. The candles remind us of Christ's light coming into the world. We light the first candle looking forward to the coming of the Messiah, Immanuel, God-with-us.

Week 2: Annunciation
We light the second candle to announce the birth of the Savior King, as the angel Gabriel announced to Mary, and the angels announced to the shepherds.

Week 3: Affirmation
We light the third candle recognizing the fulfillment of God's promise of our salvation.

Week 4: Arrival
We light the fourth candle in celebration of the arrival of the baby, born in a stable at Bethlehem, whose name is Immanuel, God-with-us.

Celebrating Advent

Advent season is the start of the Church Year calendar. By observing the Church Year, we remind ourselves that we do not belong to this world but operate in the earth as a peculiar people whose citizenship is in the New Jerusalem. The word Advent means "coming" or "arrival" and the season has a dual focus of remembering the first coming of Christ and looking forward to his second coming.

Theologically speaking, the season of Advent signifies a time of both preparation and hope. Therefore, preaching during Advent has traditionally emphasized both repentance and joy.

Like other seasons in the Church Year, at Advent we use colors to remind us of theological truths. The primary color of Advent is purple (the color of royalty) which is used to remind us that we are awaiting the coming of a king. The secondary color of Advent is green (the color of life) used to remind us that God is sending the One who will make all things new.

The Advent candles consist of five candles: three purple, one pink, and one white candle. The purple candles (lit on the Sundays of week one, two, and four) remind us that we are awaiting royalty, and the sole pink candle (which is lit on the third week), affirms God's intent to eliminate all fear and restore creation through the coming Messiah. The final white center candle (called the Christ Candle), is lit on Christmas Day, and calls us to rejoice in the incarnation of the Son of God into the world. The greenery around the candle reminds us that we are proclaiming the promise of new life that Messiah brings. The flames of the candles remind us that Jesus is the light of the world who shines in the darkness and that the darkness cannot overcome the light. By lighting one new candle each week we remind ourselves that God is doing something in the world and that more is yet to come.

- The first candle is the Anticipation candle which remembers the prophecies made about the Messiah who was to come.

- The second candle is the Annunciation (i.e. announcement) candle which remembers the announcement made by Gabriel to Mary and by the angels to the shepherds.

- The third candle is the Affirmation candle which recognizes that by sending the Messiah, God has affirmed and fulfilled the promises that he made to humanity.

- The fourth candle is the Arrival candle which celebrates the birth of Christ.

- The center white candle, called the Christ Candle, is lit on Christmas Day – "Joy to the world, the Lord is come!"

Come, Thou Long Expected Jesus!
Let us all together with one voice join together with Charles Wesley (1744) and Rowland Hugh Prichard (1855) in singing:

Come, thou long expected Jesus, born to set Thy people free.
From our fears and sins release us; let us find our rest in Thee.
Israel's strength and consolation, hope of all the earth Thou art;
Dear Desire of ev'ry nation, joy of ev'ry longing heart.

Born Thy people to deliver, born a Child and yet a King.
Born to reign in us forever, now Thy gracious kingdom bring.
By Thine own eternal Spirit, rule in all our hearts alone;
By Thine all-sufficient merit, raise us to Thy glorious throne.

✠

FIRST SUNDAY OF ADVENT: ANTICIPATION

December 1 - 7, 2013

Advent joyously affirms the First and Second comings of our Lord. Through the prophets, God foretold the Messiah's appearing to his people, Israel. Through the angels, he announced his birth to Zechariah, Mary, and the shepherds. Let us reverently ponder the sure promise of God – the Deliverer will come and ransom captive Israel and the world.

THIS WEEK'S THEME
No One Knows the Day, Matthew 24.36-44

Jesus told his disciples that no one (including the angels!) knows either the day or the hour of the return of the Son of Man to earth. Only the Father knows what day and what the precise moment he has reserved for our Lord Jesus to return to earth. We must, therefore, be ready, for the Son of Man will come at a time that no one is expecting. Let us be watching and waiting, for soon and very soon the Lord will come, with his reward with him, to give to each one what they deserve. We will be attentive and alert, sober and ready, for we do not know when our Lord Jesus will arrive. Still we cry, *Maranatha!*

DAILY DEVOTIONAL GUIDE

PREPARING OUR HEARTS

Invocation: Our Prayer of Acclamation

O LORD, for whose advent thy Church has waited long: save us lest the hope of thee grow dim, and we say: Where is the promise of his coming? And lest we, forgetting to watch with lamps trimmed and loins girded, be found unprepared to meet thee, when thou comest at such an hour as we think not. But grant that we be numbered with the wise, who, looking to thy promises, prepare the way for the Son of Man to come in his glory. Amen.

~ W. E. Orchard (Ferguson, p. 7)

Call to Worship

Blessed are you, O God: Father, Son, and Holy Spirit. And blessed is your Kingdom, both now and forever, Amen.

PRAISING OUR GOD

Te Deum Laudamus

You are God: we praise you; you are the Lord; we acclaim you; you are the eternal Father: All creation worships you. To you all angels, all the powers of heaven, Cherubim and Seraphim, sing in endless praise: Holy, holy, holy Lord, God of power and might, heaven and earth are full of your glory.

The glorious company of apostles praise you. The noble fellowship of prophets praise you. The white-robed army of martyrs praise you. Throughout the world the holy Church acclaims you; Father, of majesty unbounded, your true and only Son, worthy of all worship, and the Holy Spirit, advocate and guide.

You, Christ, are the king of glory, the eternal Son of the Father. When you became man to set us free you did not shun the Virgin's womb. You overcame the sting of death and opened the kingdom of heaven to all believers. You are seated at God's right hand in glory. We believe that you will come and be our judge. Come then, Lord, and help your people, bought with the price of your own blood, and bring us with your saints to glory everlasting.

Praise and Thanksgiving (Songs and Prayers)

Gloria Patri

Glory be to the Father,
And to the Son and to the Holy Spirit:
As it was in the beginning,
Is now, and ever shall be,
World without end. Amen, amen.

LISTENING TO HIS VOICE

Chronological Reading for the Day
Sunday: Gen. 1-3 ✤ *Monday:* Gen. 4-6; 1 Chron. 1.1-4 ✤
Tuesday: Gen. 7-10; 1 Chron. 1.5-23 ✤ *Wednesday:* Gen. 11-14;
1 Chron. 1.24-27 ✤ *Thursday:* Gen. 15-17 ✤ *Friday:* Gen.
18-20 ✤ *Saturday:* Gen. 21-24

Lectionary Readings
Psalm: Ps. 122   *OT:* Isa. 2.1-5
Gospel: Matt. 24.36-44   *NT:* Rom. 13.11-14

Reflection: Silence and/or Journaling

RESPONDING IN FAITH

The Apostles' Creed
*I believe in God, the Father Almighty, Maker of heaven and earth;
and in Jesus Christ, his only Son, our Lord, who was conceived by the
Holy Spirit, born of the Virgin Mary, suffered under Pontius Pilate,
was crucified, dead, and buried; he descended into hell; the third day
he arose again from the dead; he ascended into heaven and sits on
the right hand of God the Father Almighty; from thence he shall come
to judge the quick and the dead.*

I believe in the Holy Spirit, the holy catholic church, the communion
of saints, the forgiveness of sins, the resurrection of the body, and the
life everlasting. Amen.*

* In the Apostles' and Nicene Creeds, the term catholic refers to the Church's
universality, through all ages and times, of all languages and peoples. It refers to no
particular tradition or denominational expression (e.g., as in Roman Catholic).

Prayers of Confession
Let us now confess our sins to God and receive mercy and
grace to help in our time of need.

Assurance of Pardon
Having faithfully confessed and renounced your sin, Christ also has been faithful to forgive your sins and to purify you from all unrighteousness. It is certain, that there is One who has spoken to the Father in your defense, Jesus Christ, the Righteous One who is the atoning sacrifice for our sins and for the sins of the whole world. His grace and peace are with you now. Amen.

Petitions and Supplications, Ending with The Lord's Prayer
Our Father which art in heaven, Hallowed be thy name. Thy kingdom come, Thy will be done in earth, as it is in heaven. Give us this day our daily bread. And forgive us our debts, as we forgive our debtors. And lead us not into temptation, but deliver us from evil: For thine is the kingdom, and the power, and the glory, for ever. Amen.

~ Matthew 6.9-13 (KJV)

Doxology (and/or closing song)
Praise God from whom all blessings flow;
Praise Him all creatures here below;
Praise Him above ye heavenly host;
Praise Father, Son and Holy Ghost. Amen.

DEPARTING TO SERVE

Benediction
Abide with us, O Lord, for it is toward evening, and the day is far spent. Abide with us, for the days are hastening on, and we hasten with them, and our life is short and transient as a dream. Abide with us, for we are weak and helpless, and if thou abide not with us, we perish by the way. Abide with us until the Day-star ariseth, and the morning light appeareth, when we shall abide forever with thee. Amen.

~ James Burns (Ferguson, p. 13)

Affirmation from the Psalms

Pray for the peace of Jerusalem! "May they be secure who love you! Peace be within your walls and security within your towers!" For my brothers and companions' sake I will say, "Peace be within you!" For the sake of the house of the LORD our God, I will seek your good.

~ Psalm 122.6-9

Pray without Ceasing – Flash Prayer for the Day

Keep us ready, dear Savior, for you are coming at an hour that we cannot know and will not expect.

FOR YOUR WEEKLY JOURNEY

Let God Arise! Seasonal Focus

The Word Became Flesh, John 1.1-14

Book Reading

DAILY: Extreme Devotion Writing Team, *Extreme Devotion*

Newell, *A Martyr's Grace*

December 8 - 14, 2013

Advent joyously affirms the First and Second comings of our Lord. Through the prophets, God foretold the Messiah's appearing to his people, Israel. Through the angels, he announced his birth to Zechariah, Mary, and the shepherds. Let us reverently ponder the sure promise of God – the Deliverer will come and ransom captive Israel and the world.

THIS WEEK'S THEME
The Righteous Reign of the Branch, Isaiah 11.1-10

From the stump (lineage) of Jesse will come the Messiah, he who will be filled with the Spirit of the LORD, the Spirit of wisdom and understanding, counsel and might, and the knowledge and fear of the LORD. He will reign over the nations of the world with righteousness, and during his rule all creation shall be transformed. The wolf will dwell with the lamb, the leopard with the young goat, and the calf and the lion together. Nothing will hurt or destroy in all the holy mountain of the LORD, for the reign of Jesse's branch will bring everlasting peace and joy. As those whose entire lives are anchored in the promise of the Messiah's return, let us announce his Kingdom to come, and yearn for his righteous reign, the authority and rule of the great King, Son of Jesse, Son of David, and Lord of all.

DAILY DEVOTIONAL GUIDE

PREPARING OUR HEARTS

Invocation: Our Prayer of Acclamation

O LORD our God, who has bidden the light to shine out of darkness, who hast again wakened us to praise thy goodness, and ask for thy grace: accept now in thine endless mercy the sacrifice of our worship and thanksgiving, and grant unto us all such requests as may be wholesome for us. Make us to be children of the light and of the day, and heirs of thy everlasting inheritance. Pour out upon us the riches

SECOND SUNDAY OF ADVENT: ANNUNCIATION

*of thy mercy, so that we, redeemed in soul and body, and steadfast in
faith, may ever praise thy wonderful and holy name; through Jesus
Christ our Lord. Amen.*

~ Liturgy of the Greek Church (Ferguson, p. 1)

Call to Worship

Blessed are you, O God: Father, Son, and Holy Spirit. And
blessed is your Kingdom, both now and forever, Amen.

PRAISING OUR GOD

Te Deum Laudamus

*You are God: we praise you; you are the Lord; we acclaim you; you are
the eternal Father: All creation worships you. To you all angels, all the
powers of heaven, Cherubim and Seraphim, sing in endless praise:
Holy, holy, holy Lord, God of power and might, heaven and earth are
full of your glory.*

*The glorious company of apostles praise you. The noble fellowship
of prophets praise you. The white-robed army of martyrs praise you.
Throughout the world the holy Church acclaims you; Father, of
majesty unbounded, your true and only Son, worthy of all worship,
and the Holy Spirit, advocate and guide.*

*You, Christ, are the king of glory, the eternal Son of the Father. When
you became man to set us free you did not shun the Virgin's womb.
You overcame the sting of death and opened the kingdom of heaven
to all believers. You are seated at God's right hand in glory. We believe
that you will come and be our judge. Come then, Lord, and help your
people, bought with the price of your own blood, and bring us with
your saints to glory everlasting.*

Praise and Thanksgiving (Songs and Prayers)

Gloria Patri

Glory be to the Father,
And to the Son and to the Holy Spirit:
As it was in the beginning,
Is now, and ever shall be,
World without end. Amen, amen.

LISTENING TO HIS VOICE

Chronological Reading for the Day

Sunday: Gen. 25.1-26; 1 Chron. 1.28-34 ✠ *Monday:* Gen. 25.27-28.5 ✠ *Tuesday:* Gen. 28.6-30.24 ✠ *Wednesday:* Gen. 30.25-31.55 ✠ *Thursday:* Gen. 32.1-35.27 ✠ *Friday:* Gen. 36; 1 Chron. 1.35-2.2 ✠ *Saturday:* Gen. 37-39; 1 Chron. 2.3-6, v.8

Lectionary Readings

Psalm: Ps. 72.1-7, 18-19   *OT:* Isa. 11.1-10
Gospel: Matt. 3.1-12   *NT:* Rom. 15.4-13

Reflection: Silence and/or Journaling

RESPONDING IN FAITH

The Apostles' Creed

I believe in God, the Father Almighty, Maker of heaven and earth;
and in Jesus Christ, his only Son, our Lord, who was conceived by the
Holy Spirit, born of the Virgin Mary, suffered under Pontius Pilate,
was crucified, dead, and buried; he descended into hell; the third day
he arose again from the dead; he ascended into heaven and sits on
the right hand of God the Father Almighty; from thence he shall come
to judge the quick and the dead.

I believe in the Holy Spirit, the holy catholic* church, the communion
of saints, the forgiveness of sins, the resurrection of the body, and the
life everlasting. Amen.

* In the Apostles' and Nicene Creeds, the term catholic refers to the Church's universality, through all ages and times, of all languages and peoples. It refers to no particular tradition or denominational expression (e.g., as in Roman Catholic).

Prayers of Confession

Let us now confess our sins to God and receive mercy and grace to help in our time of need.

Assurance of Pardon

Having faithfully confessed and renounced your sin, Christ also has been faithful to forgive your sins and to purify you from all unrighteousness. It is certain, that there is One who has spoken to the Father in your defense, Jesus Christ, the Righteous One who is the atoning sacrifice for our sins and for the sins of the whole world. His grace and peace are with you now. Amen.

Petitions and Supplications, Ending with The Lord's Prayer

Our Father which art in heaven, Hallowed be thy name. Thy kingdom come, Thy will be done in earth, as it is in heaven. Give us this day our daily bread. And forgive us our debts, as we forgive our debtors. And lead us not into temptation, but deliver us from evil: For thine is the kingdom, and the power, and the glory, for ever. Amen.

~ Matthew 6.9-13 (KJV)

Doxology (and/or closing song)

Praise God from whom all blessings flow;
Praise Him all creatures here below;
Praise Him above ye heavenly host;
Praise Father, Son and Holy Ghost. Amen.

DEPARTING TO SERVE

Benediction

Merciful God, who sent your messengers the prophets to preach repentance and prepare the way for our salvation: Grant us grace to heed their warnings and forsake our sins, that we may greet with joy

the coming of Jesus Christ our Redeemer; who lives and reigns with
you and the Holy Spirit, one God, now and for ever. Amen.

~ Book of Common Prayer (Tickle, p. 331)

Affirmation from the Psalms
*Give the king your justice, O God, and your righteousness to the royal
son! May he judge your people with righteousness, and your poor with
justice! Let the mountains bear prosperity for the people, and the hills,
in righteousness! May he defend the cause of the poor of the people,
give deliverance to the children of the needy, and crush the oppressor!
May they fear you while the sun endures, and as long as the moon,
throughout all generations! May he be like rain that falls on the mown
grass, like showers that water the earth! In his days may the righteous
flourish, and peace abound, till the moon be no more!*

~ Psalm 72.1-7 (ESV)

Pray without Ceasing – Flash Prayer for the Day
Come, dear Messiah of Jesse's branch and line, and establish
your forever kingdom of justice and peace.

FOR YOUR WEEKLY JOURNEY

Let God Arise! Seasonal Focus
The Word Became Flesh, John 1.1-14

Book Reading
DAILY: Extreme Devotion Writing Team, *Extreme Devotion*

Newell, *A Martyr's Grace*

THIRD SUNDAY OF ADVENT: AFFIRMATION

December 15 - 21, 2013

Advent joyously affirms the First and Second comings of our Lord. Through the prophets, God foretold the Messiah's appearing to his people, Israel. Through the angels, he announced his birth to Zechariah, Mary, and the shepherds. Let us reverently ponder the sure promise of God – the Deliverer will come and ransom captive Israel and the world.

THIS WEEK'S THEME
May the Lord Be Magnified, Luke 1.46b-55

During Mary's visit to the pregnant Elizabeth, Mary burst into an affirmation of praise to God. This wonderful song, called the Magnificat, expressed Mary's magnification of the Lord, and the rejoicing in her heart regarding his blessing of her humble estate, his mighty deeds on her behalf, and the mercy he had given to his people over the generations – to Abraham and his offspring. She acknowledged God's scattering of the proud, his blessing of the lowly and the humble, and the help he had given to Israel. She remembered his mercy and covenant, the same spoken to Abraham and his people forever. In all things, the God of Abraham and Israel is a God of covenant faithfulness, who is worthy to be magnified!

DAILY DEVOTIONAL GUIDE

PREPARING OUR HEARTS

Invocation: Our Prayer of Acclamation
Replenish our hearts, O Lord, with the oil of a true faith in thy coming; and grant us vigilance in the dark night, whilst thou art longsuffering and waiting that all should come to repentance; so that, when there shall be a cry, Behold the Bridegroom! we may be found ready for his appearing, and by thy mercy fit to enter into his joy; through the same

Jesus Christ our Lord, unto whom, with thee and the Holy Ghost, be glory and praise, ever world without end. Amen.

~ James Ferguson (Ferguson, p. 19-20)

Call to Worship

Blessed are you, O God: Father, Son, and Holy Spirit. And blessed is your Kingdom, both now and forever, Amen.

PRAISING OUR GOD

Te Deum Laudamus

You are God: we praise you; you are the Lord; we acclaim you; you are the eternal Father: All creation worships you. To you all angels, all the powers of heaven, Cherubim and Seraphim, sing in endless praise: Holy, holy, holy Lord, God of power and might, heaven and earth are full of your glory.

The glorious company of apostles praise you. The noble fellowship of prophets praise you. The white-robed army of martyrs praise you. Throughout the world the holy Church acclaims you; Father, of majesty unbounded, your true and only Son, worthy of all worship, and the Holy Spirit, advocate and guide.

You, Christ, are the king of glory, the eternal Son of the Father. When you became man to set us free you did not shun the Virgin's womb. You overcame the sting of death and opened the kingdom of heaven to all believers. You are seated at God's right hand in glory. We believe that you will come and be our judge. Come then, Lord, and help your people, bought with the price of your own blood, and bring us with your saints to glory everlasting.

Praise and Thanksgiving (Songs and Prayers)

Gloria Patri
Glory be to the Father,
And to the Son and to the Holy Spirit:
As it was in the beginning,
Is now, and ever shall be,
World without end. Amen, amen.

LISTENING TO HIS VOICE

Chronological Reading for the Day
Sunday: Gen. 35.28-29; ch.40-41 ✣ *Monday:* Gen. 42.1-45.15
✣ *Tuesday:* Gen. 45.16-47.27 ✣ *Wednesday:* Gen. 47.28-50.26
✣ *Thursday:* Job 1-4 ✣ *Friday:* Job 5-7 ✣ *Saturday:* Job 8-11

Lectionary Readings
Psalm: Ps. 146.5-10   *OT:* Isa. 35.1-10
Gospel: Luke 1.46b-55   *NT:* James 5.7-10

Reflection: Silence and/or Journaling

RESPONDING IN FAITH

The Apostles' Creed
I believe in God, the Father Almighty, Maker of heaven and earth; and in Jesus Christ, his only Son, our Lord, who was conceived by the Holy Spirit, born of the Virgin Mary, suffered under Pontius Pilate, was crucified, dead, and buried; he descended into hell; the third day he arose again from the dead; he ascended into heaven and sits on the right hand of God the Father Almighty; from thence he shall come to judge the quick and the dead.

I believe in the Holy Spirit, the holy catholic* church, the communion of saints, the forgiveness of sins, the resurrection of the body, and the life everlasting. Amen.

* In the Apostles' and Nicene Creeds, the term catholic refers to the Church's universality, through all ages and times, of all languages and peoples. It refers to no particular tradition or denominational expression (e.g., as in Roman Catholic).

Prayers of Confession
Let us now confess our sins to God and receive mercy and grace to help in our time of need.

Assurance of Pardon
Having faithfully confessed and renounced your sin, Christ also has been faithful to forgive your sins and to purify you from all unrighteousness. It is certain, that there is One who has spoken to the Father in your defense, Jesus Christ, the Righteous One who is the atoning sacrifice for our sins and for the sins of the whole world. His grace and peace are with you now. Amen.

Petitions and Supplications, Ending with The Lord's Prayer
Our Father which art in heaven, Hallowed be thy name. Thy kingdom come, Thy will be done in earth, as it is in heaven. Give us this day our daily bread. And forgive us our debts, as we forgive our debtors. And lead us not into temptation, but deliver us from evil: For thine is the kingdom, and the power, and the glory, for ever. Amen.

~ Matthew 6.9-13 (KJV)

Doxology (and/or closing song)
Praise God from whom all blessings flow;
Praise Him all creatures here below;
Praise Him above ye heavenly host;
Praise Father, Son and Holy Ghost. Amen.

Departing to Serve

Benediction
O LORD, who has put in our hearts the desire to please thee; help our endeavors this and every day, so that in the face of all that is contrary, we may be able to finish that good work of faith, which thou has caused us to begin; through Jesus Christ our Lord. Amen.

~ James Ferguson (Ferguson, p. 4)

Affirmation from the Psalms

Blessed is he whose help is the God of Jacob, whose hope is in the LORD his God, who made heaven and earth, the sea, and all that is in them, who keeps faith forever; who executes justice for the oppressed, who gives food to the hungry. The LORD sets the prisoners free; the LORD opens the eyes of the blind. The LORD lifts up those who are bowed down; the LORD loves the righteous. The LORD watches over the sojourners; he upholds the widow and the fatherless, but the way of the wicked he brings to ruin. The LORD will reign forever, your God, O Zion, to all generations. Praise the LORD!

~ Psalm 146.5-10

Pray without Ceasing – Flash Prayer for the Day

O God, we bless you for the mighty deeds you have done, and your eternal promise to save a people for yourself who believe like faithful Abraham.

FOR YOUR WEEKLY JOURNEY

Let God Arise! Seasonal Focus

The Word Became Flesh, John 1.1-14

Book Reading

DAILY: Extreme Devotion Writing Team, *Extreme Devotion*

Newell, *A Martyr's Grace*

December 22 - 28, 2013

Advent joyously affirms the First and Second comings of our Lord. Through the prophets, God foretold the Messiah's appearing to his people, Israel. Through the angels, he announced his birth to Zechariah, Mary, and the shepherds. Let us reverently ponder the sure promise of God – the Deliverer will come and ransom captive Israel and the world.

THIS WEEK'S THEME
Immanuel Has Come, Matthew 1.18-25

During the season of Mary's betrothal to Joseph, she was found to be with child from the Holy Spirit. Although Joseph considered the possibility of privately divorcing Mary (lest she be exposed to shame), the angel of the Lord appeared to him in a dream, assuring him that the baby conceived in Mary was from the Holy Spirit. The angel told Joseph that Mary would bear a son, and they would call his name Jesus, for he would save his people from their sins. This fulfilled God's prophecy in Isaiah, which said that a virgin would conceive and bear a son whose name would be called Immanuel – God with us. In the incarnation of Jesus, God has come to earth, and visited his people.

DAILY DEVOTIONAL GUIDE

PREPARING OUR HEARTS

Invocation: Our Prayer of Acclamation

Almighty God, who has kept us in life, and wakened us to the light and hope of a new day; drive from our hearts all sloth and gloom by the beams of thy lovingkindness. And since our life is thy gift, defend that which thou hast given; preserve and increase us in all health; that when the evening comes, we may thankfully say: The Lord is the

SECOND SUNDAY OF ADVENT: ANNUNCIATION

strength of my life; the Lord is my light and salvation. According to this our faith, be it done unto us; through Jesus Christ our Lord. Amen.

~ James Ferguson (Ferguson, p. 14)

Call to Worship
Blessed are you, O God: Father, Son, and Holy Spirit. And blessed is your Kingdom, both now and forever, Amen.

PRAISING OUR GOD

Te Deum Laudamus
You are God: we praise you; you are the Lord; we acclaim you; you are the eternal Father: All creation worships you. To you all angels, all the powers of heaven, Cherubim and Seraphim, sing in endless praise: Holy, holy, holy Lord, God of power and might, heaven and earth are full of your glory.

The glorious company of apostles praise you. The noble fellowship of prophets praise you. The white-robed army of martyrs praise you. Throughout the world the holy Church acclaims you; Father, of majesty unbounded, your true and only Son, worthy of all worship, and the Holy Spirit, advocate and guide.

You, Christ, are the king of glory, the eternal Son of the Father. When you became man to set us free you did not shun the Virgin's womb. You overcame the sting of death and opened the kingdom of heaven to all believers. You are seated at God's right hand in glory. We believe that you will come and be our judge. Come then, Lord, and help your people, bought with the price of your own blood, and bring us with your saints to glory everlasting.

Praise and Thanksgiving (Songs and Prayers)

Gloria Patri

Glory be to the Father,
And to the Son and to the Holy Spirit:
As it was in the beginning,
Is now, and ever shall be,
World without end. Amen, amen.

LISTENING TO HIS VOICE

Chronological Reading for the Day

Sunday: Job 12-14 ✦ *Monday:* Job 15-18 ✦ *Tuesday:* Job 19-21 ✦ *Wednesday:* Job 22-25 ✦ *Thursday:* Job 26-29 ✦ *Friday:* Job 30-31 ✦ *Saturday:* Job 32-34

Lectionary Readings

Psalm: Ps. 80.1-7, 17-19   *OT:* Isa. 7.10-16
Gospel: Matt. 1.18-25   *NT:* Rom. 1.1-7

Reflection: Silence and/or Journaling

RESPONDING IN FAITH

The Apostles' Creed

I believe in God, the Father Almighty, Maker of heaven and earth; and in Jesus Christ, his only Son, our Lord, who was conceived by the Holy Spirit, born of the Virgin Mary, suffered under Pontius Pilate, was crucified, dead, and buried; he descended into hell; the third day he arose again from the dead; he ascended into heaven and sits on the right hand of God the Father Almighty; from thence he shall come to judge the quick and the dead.

I believe in the Holy Spirit, the holy catholic* church, the communion of saints, the forgiveness of sins, the resurrection of the body, and the life everlasting. Amen.

* In the Apostles' and Nicene Creeds, the term catholic refers to the Church's universality, through all ages and times, of all languages and peoples. It refers to no particular tradition or denominational expression (e.g., as in Roman Catholic).

Prayers of Confession

Let us now confess our sins to God and receive mercy and grace to help in our time of need.

Assurance of Pardon

Having faithfully confessed and renounced your sin, Christ also has been faithful to forgive your sins and to purify you from all unrighteousness. It is certain, that there is One who has spoken to the Father in your defense, Jesus Christ, the Righteous One who is the atoning sacrifice for our sins and for the sins of the whole world. His grace and peace are with you now. Amen.

Petitions and Supplications, Ending with The Lord's Prayer

Our Father which art in heaven, Hallowed be thy name. Thy kingdom come, Thy will be done in earth, as it is in heaven. Give us this day our daily bread. And forgive us our debts, as we forgive our debtors. And lead us not into temptation, but deliver us from evil: For thine is the kingdom, and the power, and the glory, for ever. Amen.

~ Matthew 6.9-13 (KJV)

Doxology (and/or closing song)

Praise God from whom all blessings flow;
Praise Him all creatures here below;
Praise Him above ye heavenly host;
Praise Father, Son and Holy Ghost. Amen.

Departing to Serve

Benediction

O Son of God, who once camest in weakness to restore us: free us from all remaining bonds of our error and unbelief, that we may await thy mighty Advent without fear. And when thou comest, seeking thy kingdom within us, constrain us, O Christ, to open wide the gates, and to yield up the keys of our life unto thee; that thy power may be our power, and our wills be thine, and thy will be done, O Jesus Christ, Son of God, our Saviour. Amen.

~ *The Priest's Prayer Book* (Ferguson, p. 20)

Affirmation from the Psalms
Give ear, O Shepherd of Israel, you who lead Joseph like a flock. You who are enthroned upon the cherubim, shine forth. Before Ephraim and Benjamin and Manasseh, stir up your might and come to save us! Restore us, O God; let your face shine, that we may be saved!

~ Psalm 80.1-3

Pray without Ceasing – Flash Prayer for the Day
Immanuel, God with us, thank you for descending from your heavenly home and dwelling among us.

FOR YOUR WEEKLY JOURNEY

Let God Arise! Seasonal Focus
The Word Became Flesh, John 1.1-14

Book Reading
DAILY: Extreme Devotion Writing Team, *Extreme Devotion*

Newell, *A Martyr's Grace*

Special Church Year Services
Christmas Eve: Tuesday, December 24, 2013
Christmas Day: Wednesday, December 25, 2013

Olive wood nativity scene, Bethlehem

Christmas is a celebration of the mystery of the incarnation of the Son of God, the Word made flesh in the world. It celebrates the birth of Christ.

In those days a decree went out from Caesar Augustus that all the world should be registered. [2] This was the first registration when Quirinius was governor of Syria. [3] And all went to be registered, each to his own town. [4] And Joseph also went up from Galilee, from the town of Nazareth, to Judea, to the city of David, which is called Bethlehem, because he was of the house and lineage of David, [5] to be registered with Mary, his betrothed, who was with child.

[6] And while they were there, the time came for her to give birth. [7] And she gave birth to her firstborn son and wrapped him in swaddling cloths and laid him in a manger, because there was no place for them in the inn. [8] And in the same region there were shepherds out in the field, keeping watch over their flock by night. [9] And an angel of the Lord appeared to them, and the glory of the Lord shone around them, and they were filled with fear. [10] And the angel said to them, "Fear not, for behold, I bring you good news of a great joy that will be for all the people. [11] For unto you is born this day in the city of David a Savior, who is Christ the Lord. [12] And this will be a sign for you: you will find a baby wrapped in swaddling cloths and lying in a manger." [13] And suddenly there was with the angel a multitude of the heavenly host praising God and saying, [14] "Glory to God in the highest, and on earth peace among those with whom he is pleased!" [15] When the angels went away from them into heaven, the shepherds said to one another, "Let us go over to Bethlehem and see this thing that has happened, which the Lord has made known to us."

[16] And they went with haste and found Mary and Joseph, and the baby lying in a manger. [17] And when they saw it, they made known the saying that had been told them concerning this child. [18] And all who heard it wondered at what the shepherds told them. [19] But Mary treasured up all these things, pondering them in her heart. [20] And the shepherds returned, glorifying and praising God for all they had heard and seen, as it had been told them.

~ Luke 2.1-20 (ESV)

Christmas celebrates the mystery of the incarnation of the Son of God, the Word made flesh. He enters the world to reveal the Father's love to humankind, to destroy the devil's work, and to redeem his people from their sins. Although the highest Christological reflection has sought to plumb the depths of this mystery, only faith, awe, and worship can draw near to its richness. In order to redeem humankind from its waywardness, to reconcile creation that was cursed at the Fall, to destroy the enemies of God, and to reveal the Father's glory to the world, the eternal Word became a human being. The One through whom the Father created trillions of galaxies by his omnipotent, creative Word, was joined to human likeness, and entered the world as a baby boy. And all this for love and grace.

This grand celebration and time of remembrance is an invitation to wonder, to meditate upon a truth that can easily be recited in the dry theological language of the schools, but can never be fathomed fully. Who can possibly grasp the total meaning of the Christ-child, the One sent and anointed by God to reign forever after he conquered sin and death through his passion? As Christians, we join the shepherds and the Magi at the foot of the baby boy, and quietly, reverently bow with Mary and Joseph under the gleam of the star that rested above him who would one day become King of kings and Lord of lords. His coming is soon, and we eagerly wait still for that time when the prophets' foretellings will become true. Yes, the kingdoms of this world will become the kingdoms of our Lord and of this child, and he will reign forever and ever.

At Christmas, believers worldwide celebrate the birth of the Messiah in Bethlehem, the Lord Jesus Christ. Together we affirm that Jesus was – and is – God's only begotten Son, the Word made flesh, and the human son of the Virgin Mary. In him we see the love of God revealed for all humankind. He is God's mystery that causes broken hearts to marvel and rejoice. This little child would fulfill the prophecy of a Savior who, by dying and rising, would conquer humanity's mortal enemy, the devil, free us from sin's bondage and curse, and restore creation under the reign of God. "Joy to the world, the Lord has come! Let earth receive her King!"

~ Rev. Dr. Don L. Davis

Hark, the Herald Angels Sing

Hark! the herald angels sing, "Glory to the newborn King;
Peace on earth and mercy mild, God and sinners reconciled."
Joyful, all ye nations, rise, join the triumph of the skies;
With th' angelic host proclaim, "Christ is born in Bethlehem!"
Hark! the herald angels sing, "Glory to the newborn King."

Christ, by highest heav'n adored, Christ, the everlasting Lord;
Late in time behold Him come, offspring of a virgin's womb.
Veiled in flesh the Godhead see, hail, the incarnate Deity!
Pleased as man with men to dwell, Jesus our Emmanuel.
Hark! the herald angels sing, "Glory to the newborn King."

Hail the heav'n born Prince of Peace! Hail the Sun of righteousness!
Light and life to all He brings, ris'n with healing in His wings.
Mild He lays His glory by, born that man no more may die.
Born to raise the sons of earth, born to give them second birth.
Hark! the herald angels sing, "Glory to the newborn King!"

Come, Desire of nations, come! Fix in us Thy humble home.
Rise, the woman's conqu'ring seed, bruise in us the serpent's head;
Adam's likeness now efface, stamp Thine image in its place;
Second Adam from above, reinstate us in Thy love.
Hark! the herald angels sing, "Glory to the newborn King."

December 24, 2013

Christmas celebrates the birth of Messiah, Jesus, who is the incarnation of the Son of God, Mary's child. He is the Word made flesh, the conqueror who enters this fallen world to reveal to us the Father's love, to destroy the devil's work, and to redeem his people from their sins.

TODAY'S THEME
O Come Let Us Adore Him, Luke 2.1-20

During the time when Caesar Augustus issued a decree for the inhabitants of his empire to be registered, Joseph went up from Nazareth of Galilee to the city of David, Bethlehem, with his betrothed Mary who was with child. While they were there, she gave birth to her firstborn son, Jesus. In that region, shepherds were out in the field, keeping watch over their flocks by night, and an angel of the Lord appeared to them, with God's glory surrounding them.

The angel announced the good news of the birth of the baby as the Christ, the Lord, who could be found wrapped in swaddling clothes in a manger. After hearing a multitude of the heavenly host praise God, the shepherds determined to go over to Bethlehem and see the child. They went in haste, found Mary and Joseph, and the baby lying in a manger. They testified to those around what God had made known to them, and glorified God for all they had heard and seen. This Christmastide, along with the angels and the shepherds, let us kneel before the Baby Jesus, the Christ-child, and come, and adore him.

CHRISTMAS EVE

DAILY DEVOTIONAL GUIDE

PREPARING OUR HEARTS

Invocation: Our Prayer of Acclamation

O Eternal God, Father Almighty, Who, as at this time, didst give Thine only Son to be born of a woman and to be made the Son of man, that we might be made the sons of God, grant to us to be indeed Thy children; and be Thou now and ever our Father, through the same Jesus Christ our Lord. Amen.

~ Rev. H. Stobart, Nineteenth Century (Fox, p. 213)

Call to Worship

Blessed are you, O God: Father, Son, and Holy Spirit. And blessed is your Kingdom, both now and forever, Amen.

PRAISING OUR GOD

Te Deum Laudamus

You are God: we praise you; you are the Lord; we acclaim you; you are the eternal Father: All creation worships you. To you all angels, all the powers of heaven, Cherubim and Seraphim, sing in endless praise: Holy, holy, holy Lord, God of power and might, heaven and earth are full of your glory.

The glorious company of apostles praise you. The noble fellowship of prophets praise you. The white-robed army of martyrs praise you. Throughout the world the holy Church acclaims you; Father, of majesty unbounded, your true and only Son, worthy of all worship, and the Holy Spirit, advocate and guide.

You, Christ, are the king of glory, the eternal Son of the Father. When you became man to set us free you did not shun the Virgin's womb. You overcame the sting of death and opened the kingdom of heaven to all believers. You are seated at God's right hand in glory. We believe that you will come and be our judge. Come then, Lord, and help your

people, bought with the price of your own blood, and bring us with your saints to glory everlasting.

Praise and Thanksgiving (Songs and Prayers)

Gloria Patri
Glory be to the Father,
And to the Son and to the Holy Spirit:
As it was in the beginning,
Is now, and ever shall be,
World without end. Amen, amen.

LISTENING TO HIS VOICE

Chronological Reading for the Day
Job 19-21

Lectionary Readings
Psalm: Ps. 96   *OT:* Isa. 9.2-7
Gospel: Luke 2.1-20   *NT:* Titus 2.11-14

Reflection: Silence and/or Journaling

RESPONDING IN FAITH

The Apostles' Creed
I believe in God, the Father Almighty, Maker of heaven and earth; and in Jesus Christ, his only Son, our Lord, who was conceived by the Holy Spirit, born of the Virgin Mary, suffered under Pontius Pilate, was crucified, dead, and buried; he descended into hell; the third day he arose again from the dead; he ascended into heaven and sits on the right hand of God the Father Almighty; from thence he shall come to judge the quick and the dead.

I believe in the Holy Spirit, the holy catholic* church, the communion of saints, the forgiveness of sins, the resurrection of the body, and the life everlasting. Amen.

* In the Apostles' and Nicene Creeds, the term catholic refers to the Church's universality, through all ages and times, of all languages and peoples. It refers to no particular tradition or denominational expression (e.g., as in Roman Catholic).

Prayers of Confession
Let us now confess our sins to God and receive mercy and grace to help in our time of need.

Assurance of Pardon
Having faithfully confessed and renounced your sin, Christ also has been faithful to forgive your sins and to purify you from all unrighteousness. It is certain, that there is One who has spoken to the Father in your defense, Jesus Christ, the Righteous One who is the atoning sacrifice for our sins and for the sins of the whole world. His grace and peace are with you now. Amen.

Petitions and Supplications, Ending with The Lord's Prayer
Our Father which art in heaven, Hallowed be thy name. Thy kingdom come, Thy will be done in earth, as it is in heaven. Give us this day our daily bread. And forgive us our debts, as we forgive our debtors. And lead us not into temptation, but deliver us from evil: For thine is the kingdom, and the power, and the glory, for ever. Amen.

~ Matthew 6.9-13 (KJV)

Doxology (and/or closing song)
Praise God from whom all blessings flow;
Praise Him all creatures here below;
Praise Him above ye heavenly host;
Praise Father, Son and Holy Ghost. Amen.

Departing to Serve

Benediction
May God Almighty, Who by the Incarnation of His only begotten Son drove away the darkness of the world, and by His glorious Birth enlightened this day, drive away from us the darkness of sins, and

enlighten our hearts with the light of Christian graces. And may He who willed that the great day of His most holy Birth should be told to the shepherds by an angel, pour upon us the refreshing shower of His blessing, and guide us, Himself being our Shepherd, to the pastures of everlasting joy. And may He, Who through His Incarnation united earthly things with heavenly, fill us with the sweetness of inward peace and goodwill, and make us partakers with the heavenly host; for the glory of His great Name. Amen.

~ *Treasury of Devotion*, AD 1869 (Fox, p. 213)

Affirmation from the Psalms
Oh sing to the Lord a new song; sing to the Lord, all the earth! Sing to the Lord, bless his name; tell of his salvation from day to day. Declare his glory among the nations, his marvelous works among all the peoples!

~ Psalm 96.1-3

Pray without Ceasing – Flash Prayer for the Day
May we, like the angels and the shepherds, acknowledge the birth of Jesus as the birth of the Messiah, the Lord – let us come and adore the King of Israel and the world!

FOR YOUR WEEKLY JOURNEY

Let God Arise! Seasonal Focus
The Word Became Flesh, John 1.1-14

Book Reading
DAILY: Extreme Devotion Writing Team, *Extreme Devotion*

Newell, *A Martyr's Grace*

CHRISTMAS DAY: NATIVITY OF THE LORD

December 25, 2013

Christmas celebrates the birth of Messiah, Jesus, who is the incarnation of the Son of God, Mary's child. He is the Word made flesh, the conqueror who enters this fallen world to reveal to us the Father's love, to destroy the devil's work, and to redeem his people from their sins.

TODAY'S THEME

The Word Became Flesh, John 1.1-14

Jesus of Nazareth is the incarnation of the Word of God, who became flesh and was seen in the world. He was in the beginning with God, and was God. All things were made through him, in him was life, and that life was the light of humankind. He enlightens everyone coming into the world, and although he was in the world, and though the world did not know him, he still grants life to all who receive him, to all who believe. In Jesus, the Word became flesh and dwelt among us all, the glory of the Father's only Son, full of grace and truth.

DAILY DEVOTIONAL GUIDE

PREPARING OUR HEARTS

Invocation: Our Prayer of Acclamation

Grant, O Lord, we beseech Thee, to Thy people firmness of faith, that as we confess Thine only begotten Son, the everlasting partaker of Thy glory, to have been born in our very flesh of the Virgin Mother, we may be delivered from present adversities, and admitted into joys that shall abide; through the same Jesus Christ Thy Son, our Lord and Saviour. Amen.

~ St. Leo, AD 440 (Fox, p. 213)

Call to Worship

Blessed are you, O God: Father, Son, and Holy Spirit. And blessed is your Kingdom, both now and forever, Amen.

PRAISING OUR GOD

Te Deum Laudamus

You are God: we praise you; you are the Lord; we acclaim you; you are the eternal Father: All creation worships you. To you all angels, all the powers of heaven, Cherubim and Seraphim, sing in endless praise: Holy, holy, holy Lord, God of power and might, heaven and earth are full of your glory.

The glorious company of apostles praise you. The noble fellowship of prophets praise you. The white-robed army of martyrs praise you. Throughout the world the holy Church acclaims you; Father, of majesty unbounded, your true and only Son, worthy of all worship, and the Holy Spirit, advocate and guide.

You, Christ, are the king of glory, the eternal Son of the Father. When you became man to set us free you did not shun the Virgin's womb. You overcame the sting of death and opened the kingdom of heaven to all believers. You are seated at God's right hand in glory. We believe that you will come and be our judge. Come then, Lord, and help your people, bought with the price of your own blood, and bring us with your saints to glory everlasting.

Praise and Thanksgiving (Songs and Prayers)

Gloria Patri

Glory be to the Father,
And to the Son and to the Holy Spirit:
As it was in the beginning,
Is now, and ever shall be,
World without end. Amen, amen.

LISTENING TO HIS VOICE

Chronological Reading for the Day

Job 22-25

Lectionary Readings

Psalm: Ps. 98	*OT:* Isa. 52.7-10
Gospel: John 1.1-14	*NT:* Heb. 1.1-12

Reflection: Silence and/or Journaling

RESPONDING IN FAITH

The Apostles' Creed

I believe in God, the Father Almighty, Maker of heaven and earth; and in Jesus Christ, his only Son, our Lord, who was conceived by the Holy Spirit, born of the Virgin Mary, suffered under Pontius Pilate, was crucified, dead, and buried; he descended into hell; the third day he arose again from the dead; he ascended into heaven and sits on the right hand of God the Father Almighty; from thence he shall come to judge the quick and the dead.

I believe in the Holy Spirit, the holy catholic* church, the communion of saints, the forgiveness of sins, the resurrection of the body, and the life everlasting. Amen.

* In the Apostles' and Nicene Creeds, the term catholic refers to the Church's universality, through all ages and times, of all languages and peoples. It refers to no particular tradition or denominational expression (e.g., as in Roman Catholic).

Prayers of Confession

Let us now confess our sins to God and receive mercy and grace to help in our time of need.

Assurance of Pardon

Having faithfully confessed and renounced your sin, Christ also has been faithful to forgive your sins and to purify you from all unrighteousness. It is certain, that there is One who has spoken to the Father in your defense, Jesus Christ, the Righteous One who is the atoning sacrifice for our sins and for the sins of the whole world. His grace and peace are with you now. Amen.

Petitions and Supplications, Ending with The Lord's Prayer

Our Father which art in heaven, Hallowed be thy name. Thy kingdom come, Thy will be done in earth, as it is in heaven. Give us this day our daily bread. And forgive us our debts, as we forgive our debtors. And lead us not into temptation, but deliver us from evil: For thine is the kingdom, and the power, and the glory, for ever. Amen.

~ Matthew 6.9-13 (KJV)

Doxology (and/or closing song)

Praise God from whom all blessings flow;
Praise Him all creatures here below;
Praise Him above ye heavenly host;
Praise Father, Son and Holy Ghost. Amen.

Departing to Serve

Benediction

Glory be to God in the highest, and on earth peace, goodwill towards men: for unto us is born this day a Saviour, Who is Christ the Lord. We praise Thee, we bless Thee, we glorify Thee, we give thanks unto Thee, for this greatest of Thy mercies, O Lord God, Heavenly King, God the Father Almighty. O Lord, the only begotten Son Jesus Christ, O Lord God, Lamb of God, Son of the Father, Who wast made man to take away the sins of the world, have mercy upon us by turning us from our iniquities. Thou Who wast manifested to destroy the works of the devil, have mercy upon us by enabling us to renounce and forsake them. Thou Who art the great Advocate with the Father, receive our prayer, we humbly beseech Thee. Amen.

~ Bishop Ken, AD 1637 (Fox, p. 213)

Affirmation from the Psalms

Oh sing to the Lord a new song, for he has done marvelous things! His right hand and his holy arm have worked salvation for him. The Lord has made known his salvation; he has revealed his righteousness in the sight of the nations. He has remembered his steadfast love and faithfulness to the house of Israel. All the ends of the earth have seen the salvation of our God.

~ Psalm 98.1-3

Pray without Ceasing – Flash Prayer for the Day
Dear Savior and Lord, Jesus, son of Mary, thank you for coming to earth, the Word who became flesh, and accomplishing your great work of salvation for the world.

FOR YOUR WEEKLY JOURNEY

Let God Arise! Seasonal Focus
The Word Became Flesh, John 1.1-14

Book Reading
DAILY: Extreme Devotion Writing Team, *Extreme Devotion*

Newell, *A Martyr's Grace*

December 29, 2013 - January 4, 2014

Christmas celebrates the birth of Messiah, Jesus, who is the incarnation of the Son of God, Mary's child. He is the Word made flesh, the conqueror who enters this fallen world to reveal to us the Father's love, to destroy the devil's work, and to redeem his people from their sins.

THIS WEEK'S THEME
The Flight to Egypt, the Return to Nazareth, Matthew 2.13-23

After the Magi had departed from their trip to see the Messiah child, an angel of the Lord appeared to Joseph and told him to rise and take Mary and the child to Egypt and remain there, for Herod was about to search for the child to destroy him. Joseph departed and came to Egypt and remained there until Herod's death.

When Herod saw that the Magi did not return after seeing the child, he was furious and ordered all male children in Bethlehem and the region who were two years and under to be killed, according to the time specified by the wise men. Joseph, Mary and our Lord avoided the brutal slaughter of the innocents by fleeing to Egypt. After Herod died, an angel of the Lord again appeared to Joseph in a dream commanding him to return to the land of Israel. On returning, being warned about Herod's son in Judea, Joseph withdrew to Galilee, and settled in a city called Nazareth. In this lowly place, our Lord would grow to manhood, and be prepared for his great work as Messiah of God.

DAILY DEVOTIONAL GUIDE

PREPARING OUR HEARTS

Invocation: Our Prayer of Acclamation
Almighty God, who hast poured upon us the new light of thine incarnate Word: Grant that the same light, enkindled in our hearts, may shine forth in our lives; through Jesus Christ our Lord. Amen.

~ Book of Common Prayer (U.S.) (Suter, p. 6)

Call to Worship
Blessed are you, O God: Father, Son, and Holy Spirit. And blessed is your Kingdom, both now and forever, Amen.

PRAISING OUR GOD

Te Deum Laudamus
You are God: we praise you; you are the Lord; we acclaim you; you are the eternal Father: All creation worships you. To you all angels, all the powers of heaven, Cherubim and Seraphim, sing in endless praise: Holy, holy, holy Lord, God of power and might, heaven and earth are full of your glory.

The glorious company of apostles praise you. The noble fellowship of prophets praise you. The white-robed army of martyrs praise you. Throughout the world the holy Church acclaims you; Father, of majesty unbounded, your true and only Son, worthy of all worship, and the Holy Spirit, advocate and guide.

You, Christ, are the king of glory, the eternal Son of the Father. When you became man to set us free you did not shun the Virgin's womb. You overcame the sting of death and opened the kingdom of heaven to all believers. You are seated at God's right hand in glory. We believe that you will come and be our judge. Come then, Lord, and help your people, bought with the price of your own blood, and bring us with your saints to glory everlasting.

Praise and Thanksgiving (Songs and Prayers)

Gloria Patri
Glory be to the Father,
And to the Son and to the Holy Spirit:
As it was in the beginning,
Is now, and ever shall be,
World without end. Amen, amen.

LISTENING TO HIS VOICE

Chronological Reading for the Day
Sunday: Job 35-37 ✥ *Monday:* Job 38-39 ✥ *Tuesday:* Job 40-42 ✥ *Wednesday:* Exod. 1-4; 1 Chron. 6.1-3a ✥ *Thursday:* Exod. 5-7 ✥ *Friday:* Exod. 8-9 ✥ *Saturday:* Exod. 10-12

Lectionary Readings
Psalm: Ps. 148   *OT:* Isa. 63.7-9
Gospel: Matt. 2.13-23   *NT:* Heb. 2.10-18

Reflection: Silence and/or Journaling

RESPONDING IN FAITH

The Apostles' Creed
I believe in God, the Father Almighty, Maker of heaven and earth; and in Jesus Christ, his only Son, our Lord, who was conceived by the Holy Spirit, born of the Virgin Mary, suffered under Pontius Pilate, was crucified, dead, and buried; he descended into hell; the third day he arose again from the dead; he ascended into heaven and sits on the right hand of God the Father Almighty; from thence he shall come to judge the quick and the dead.

I believe in the Holy Spirit, the holy catholic* church, the communion of saints, the forgiveness of sins, the resurrection of the body, and the life everlasting. Amen.

* In the Apostles' and Nicene Creeds, the term catholic refers to the Church's universality, through all ages and times, of all languages and peoples. It refers to no particular tradition or denominational expression (e.g., as in Roman Catholic).

Prayers of Confession

Let us now confess our sins to God and receive mercy and grace to help in our time of need.

Assurance of Pardon

Having faithfully confessed and renounced your sin, Christ also has been faithful to forgive your sins and to purify you from all unrighteousness. It is certain, that there is One who has spoken to the Father in your defense, Jesus Christ, the Righteous One who is the atoning sacrifice for our sins and for the sins of the whole world. His grace and peace are with you now. Amen.

Petitions and Supplications, Ending with The Lord's Prayer

Our Father which art in heaven, Hallowed be thy name. Thy kingdom come, Thy will be done in earth, as it is in heaven. Give us this day our daily bread. And forgive us our debts, as we forgive our debtors. And lead us not into temptation, but deliver us from evil: For thine is the kingdom, and the power, and the glory, for ever. Amen.

~ Matthew 6.9-13 (KJV)

Doxology (and/or closing song)

Praise God from whom all blessings flow;
Praise Him all creatures here below;
Praise Him above ye heavenly host;
Praise Father, Son and Holy Ghost. Amen.

Departing to Serve

Benediction

O God, who hast made this most holy night to shine with the brightness of the true Light, grant, we beseech Thee, that as we have known on earth the mysteries of that Light, we may also come to the fullness of His joys in heaven. Through Jesus Christ, Thy Son, our Lord, who liveth and reigneth with Thee and the Holy Ghost, ever one God, world without end. Amen.

~ *The Common Service Book* (Lindemann, p. 69)

Affirmation from the Psalms
Let them praise the name of the Lord, for his name alone is exalted; his majesty is above earth and heaven. He has raised up a horn for his people, praise for all his saints, for the people of Israel who are near to him. Praise the Lord!

~ Psalm 148.13-14

Pray without Ceasing – Flash Prayer for the Day
Dear Jesus, who was led to live in Nazareth of Galilee, lead us into your perfect will, to live with honor in the place where you direct, that we might bring glory and honor to your name there, glorifying you alone. In your name we pray, amen.

FOR YOUR WEEKLY JOURNEY

Let God Arise! Seasonal Focus
The Word Became Flesh, John 1.1-14

Book Reading
DAILY: Extreme Devotion Writing Team, *Extreme Devotion*

Newell, *A Martyr's Grace*

Special Church Year Services
New Year's Day/Holy Name of Jesus: Wednesday, January 1, 2014

January 1, 2014

Christmas celebrates the birth of Messiah, Jesus, who is the incarnation of the Son of God, Mary's child. He is the Word made flesh, the conqueror who enters this fallen world to reveal to us the Father's love, to destroy the devil's work, and to redeem his people from their sins.

TODAY'S THEME
The Dwelling Place of God, Revelation 21.1-6a

During his vision of the end times, the apostle John saw a new heaven and new earth, and the holy city, the new Jerusalem coming down out of heaven from God. This glorious city, the place where the saints will dwell with the Lord, was adorned as a bride for her husband. John heard a loud voice from the throne declare that the dwelling place of God is with man, that God would dwell with them, and they would be his people. God himself would be their God, and he would wipe away every tear from their eyes. Death would be no more, and with the descent of this city, mourning, crying, and pain would forever be banished, for all the former things would pass away.

The one who sits on the throne exclaimed that he would make all things new, that this vision was trustworthy and true, and he as Alpha and Omega, the beginning and the end, would give to the thirsty the water of life without payment. Let us believe this word, and commit our entire lives to become residents of this glorious city and destiny, at the time of Jesus' return.

DAILY DEVOTIONAL GUIDE

PREPARING OUR HEARTS

Invocation: Our Prayer of Acclamation
Almighty God, who hast given unto thy Son Jesus Christ the Name which is above every name, and hast taught us that there is none

other whereby we may be saved: Mercifully grant that as thy faithful people have comfort and peace in his Name, so they may ever labour to proclaim it unto all nations; through the same Jesus Christ our Lord. Amen.

~ Book of Common Prayer, Scotland (Suter, p. 58)

Call to Worship
Blessed are you, O God: Father, Son, and Holy Spirit. And blessed is your Kingdom, both now and forever, Amen.

PRAISING OUR GOD

Te Deum Laudamus
You are God: we praise you; you are the Lord; we acclaim you; you are the eternal Father: All creation worships you. To you all angels, all the powers of heaven, Cherubim and Seraphim, sing in endless praise: Holy, holy, holy Lord, God of power and might, heaven and earth are full of your glory.

The glorious company of apostles praise you. The noble fellowship of prophets praise you. The white-robed army of martyrs praise you. Throughout the world the holy Church acclaims you; Father, of majesty unbounded, your true and only Son, worthy of all worship, and the Holy Spirit, advocate and guide.

You, Christ, are the king of glory, the eternal Son of the Father. When you became man to set us free you did not shun the Virgin's womb. You overcame the sting of death and opened the kingdom of heaven to all believers. You are seated at God's right hand in glory. We believe that you will come and be our judge. Come then, Lord, and help your people, bought with the price of your own blood, and bring us with your saints to glory everlasting.

Praise and Thanksgiving (Songs and Prayers)

Gloria Patri

Glory be to the Father,
And to the Son and to the Holy Spirit:
As it was in the beginning,
Is now, and ever shall be,
World without end. Amen, amen.

LISTENING TO HIS VOICE

Chronological Reading for the Day

Exod. 1-4; 1 Chron. 6.1-3a

Lectionary Readings for *Holy Name of Jesus*

Psalm: Ps. 8   *OT:* Num. 6.22-27
Gospel: Luke 2.15-21   *NT:* Gal. 4.4-7

Lectionary Readings for *New Year's Day*

Psalm: Ps. 8   *OT:* Eccles. 3.1-13
Gospel: Matt. 25.31-46   *NT:* Rev. 21.1-6a

Reflection: Silence and/or Journaling

RESPONDING IN FAITH

The Apostles' Creed

I believe in God, the Father Almighty, Maker of heaven and earth;
and in Jesus Christ, his only Son, our Lord, who was conceived by the
Holy Spirit, born of the Virgin Mary, suffered under Pontius Pilate,
was crucified, dead, and buried; he descended into hell; the third day
he arose again from the dead; he ascended into heaven and sits on
the right hand of God the Father Almighty; from thence he shall come
to judge the quick and the dead.

I believe in the Holy Spirit, the holy catholic* church, the communion
of saints, the forgiveness of sins, the resurrection of the body, and the
life everlasting. Amen.

* In the Apostles' and Nicene Creeds, the term catholic refers to the Church's universality, through all ages and times, of all languages and peoples. It refers to no particular tradition or denominational expression (e.g., as in Roman Catholic).

Prayers of Confession

Let us now confess our sins to God and receive mercy and grace to help in our time of need.

Assurance of Pardon

Having faithfully confessed and renounced your sin, Christ also has been faithful to forgive your sins and to purify you from all unrighteousness. It is certain, that there is One who has spoken to the Father in your defense, Jesus Christ, the Righteous One who is the atoning sacrifice for our sins and for the sins of the whole world. His grace and peace are with you now. Amen.

Petitions and Supplications, Ending with The Lord's Prayer

Our Father which art in heaven, Hallowed be thy name. Thy kingdom come, Thy will be done in earth, as it is in heaven. Give us this day our daily bread. And forgive us our debts, as we forgive our debtors. And lead us not into temptation, but deliver us from evil: For thine is the kingdom, and the power, and the glory, for ever. Amen.

~ Matthew 6.9-13 (KJV)

Doxology (and/or closing song)

Praise God from whom all blessings flow;
Praise Him all creatures here below;
Praise Him above ye heavenly host;
Praise Father, Son and Holy Ghost. Amen.

Departing to Serve

Benediction

May Christ our Lord, Who is the Head of every beginning, grant us so to pass through the coming year with faithful hearts, that we may be able in all things to please His loving eyes. O God, Who art the Self-

same, Whose years shall not fail, grant us to spend this year as Thy devoted servants, according to Thy good pleasure. Fill the earth with fruit, grant our bodies to be free from disease, our souls from offences; take away scandals, and keep far from our borders all manner of calamitous events; through Jesus Christ Thy Son our Lord, Amen.

~ *The Mozarabic Missal and Breviary* (Bright, p. 164)

Affirmation from the Psalms

O LORD, our Lord, how majestic is your name in all the earth! You have set your glory above the heavens. Out of the mouth of babies and infants, you have established strength because of your foes, to still the enemy and the avenger. When I look at your heavens, the work of your fingers, the moon and the stars, which you have set in place, what is man that you are mindful of him, and the son of man that you care for him? Yet you have made him a little lower than the heavenly beings and crowned him with glory and honor. You have given him dominion over the works of your hands; you have put all things under his feet, all sheep and oxen, and also the beasts of the field, the birds of the heavens, and the fish of the sea, whatever passes along the paths of the seas. O LORD, our Lord, how majestic is your name in all the earth!

~ Psalm 8.1-9

Pray without Ceasing – Flash Prayer for the Day

O God, who has built a city for all those who trust in you, prepare us that we might through your Son be found worthy to dwell with you, in the eternal dwelling place of God, the New Jerusalem. In Christ's name we pray, amen.

FOR YOUR WEEKLY JOURNEY

Let God Arise! Seasonal Focus
The Word Became Flesh, John 1.1-14

Book Reading
DAILY: Extreme Devotion Writing Team, *Extreme Devotion*

Newell, *A Martyr's Grace*

✠

SECOND SUNDAY AFTER CHRISTMAS DAY

January 5 - 11, 2014

Christmas celebrates the birth of Messiah, Jesus, who is the incarnation of the Son of God, Mary's child. He is the Word made flesh, the conqueror who enters this fallen world to reveal to us the Father's love, to destroy the devil's work, and to redeem his people from their sins.

THIS WEEK'S THEME
Spiritual Blessings in Heavenly Places, Ephesians 1.3-14

Summary of theme–Blessed be the God and Father of our Lord Jesus Christ who has blessed those who believe with every spiritual blessing in the heavenly places. In Jesus we have been chosen before the world began to be holy and without fault in God's eyes; we were purchased by the Son, redeemed by his blood, forgiven that we might praise God, preserved by the Holy Spirit, who guarantees our eternal security. This great salvation was planned by the Father, purchased by the Son, and preserved by the Holy Spirit.

DAILY DEVOTIONAL GUIDE

PREPARING OUR HEARTS

Invocation: Our Prayer of Acclamation
We beseech Thee, O Lord, bestow on Thy servants the increase of faith, hope, and charity; that as they glory in the Nativity of Thy Son our Lord, they may, by Thy governance, not feel the adversitied of this world; and also that what they desire to celebrate in time, they may enjoy to all eternity; through the same Jesus Christ our Lord. Amen.

~ Leonine Sacramentary (Bright, p. 22)

Call to Worship

Blessed are you, O God: Father, Son, and Holy Spirit. And blessed is your Kingdom, both now and forever, Amen.

PRAISING OUR GOD

Te Deum Laudamus

You are God: we praise you; you are the Lord; we acclaim you; you are the eternal Father: All creation worships you. To you all angels, all the powers of heaven, Cherubim and Seraphim, sing in endless praise: Holy, holy, holy Lord, God of power and might, heaven and earth are full of your glory.

The glorious company of apostles praise you. The noble fellowship of prophets praise you. The white-robed army of martyrs praise you. Throughout the world the holy Church acclaims you; Father, of majesty unbounded, your true and only Son, worthy of all worship, and the Holy Spirit, advocate and guide.

You, Christ, are the king of glory, the eternal Son of the Father. When you became man to set us free you did not shun the Virgin's womb. You overcame the sting of death and opened the kingdom of heaven to all believers. You are seated at God's right hand in glory. We believe that you will come and be our judge. Come then, Lord, and help your people, bought with the price of your own blood, and bring us with your saints to glory everlasting.

Praise and Thanksgiving (Songs and Prayers)

Gloria Patri

Glory be to the Father,
And to the Son and to the Holy Spirit:
As it was in the beginning,
Is now, and ever shall be,
World without end. Amen, amen.

LISTENING TO HIS VOICE

Chronological Reading for the Day

Sunday: Exod. 13-15 ⊕ *Monday:* Exod. 16-19 ⊕ *Tuesday:* Exod. 20-21 ⊕ *Wednesday:* Exod. 22-24 ⊕ *Thursday:* Exod. 25-28 ⊕ *Friday:* Exod. 29-31 ⊕ *Saturday:* Exod. 32-34

Lectionary Readings

Psalm: Ps. 147.12-20   *OT:* Jer. 31.7-14
Gospel: John 1.1-18   *NT:* Eph. 1.3-14

Reflection: Silence and/or Journaling

RESPONDING IN FAITH

The Apostles' Creed

I believe in God, the Father Almighty, Maker of heaven and earth; and in Jesus Christ, his only Son, our Lord, who was conceived by the Holy Spirit, born of the Virgin Mary, suffered under Pontius Pilate, was crucified, dead, and buried; he descended into hell; the third day he arose again from the dead; he ascended into heaven and sits on the right hand of God the Father Almighty; from thence he shall come to judge the quick and the dead.

I believe in the Holy Spirit, the holy catholic* church, the communion of saints, the forgiveness of sins, the resurrection of the body, and the life everlasting. Amen.

* In the Apostles' and Nicene Creeds, the term catholic refers to the Church's universality, through all ages and times, of all languages and peoples. It refers to no particular tradition or denominational expression (e.g., as in Roman Catholic).

Prayers of Confession

Let us now confess our sins to God and receive mercy and grace to help in our time of need.

Assurance of Pardon

Having faithfully confessed and renounced your sin, Christ also has been faithful to forgive your sins and to purify you from all unrighteousness. It is certain, that there is One who has spoken to the Father in your defense, Jesus Christ, the Righteous One who is the atoning sacrifice for our sins and for the sins of the whole world. His grace and peace are with you now. Amen.

Petitions and Supplications, Ending with The Lord's Prayer

Our Father which art in heaven, Hallowed be thy name. Thy kingdom come, Thy will be done in earth, as it is in heaven. Give us this day our daily bread. And forgive us our debts, as we forgive our debtors. And lead us not into temptation, but deliver us from evil: For thine is the kingdom, and the power, and the glory, for ever. Amen.

~ Matthew 6.9-13 (KJV)

Doxology (and/or closing song)

Praise God from whom all blessings flow;
Praise Him all creatures here below;
Praise Him above ye heavenly host;
Praise Father, Son and Holy Ghost. Amen.

Departing to Serve

Benediction

Grant, O Lord, we beseech Thee, to Thy people an inviolable firmness of faith; that as they confess Thine Only-begotten Son, the everlasting partaker of Thy glory, to have been born in our very flesh, of the Virgin Mother, they may be delivered from present adversities, and admitted into joys that shall abide; through the same Jesus Christ our Lord. Amen.

~ *Leonine Sacramentary* (Bright, p. 23)

Affirmation from the Psalms

Praise the Lord, O Jerusalem! Praise your God, O Zion! For he strengthens the bars of your gates; he blesses your children within you.

~ Psalm 147.12-13

Pray without Ceasing – Flash Prayer for the Day

Blessed be the Father for his plan, the Son for his sacrifice, and the Spirit for his pledge of salvation, and to our God who has blessed us in the heavenly places, soon to be revealed.

FOR YOUR WEEKLY JOURNEY

Let God Arise! Seasonal Focus

The Word Became Flesh, John 1.1-14

Book Reading

DAILY: Extreme Devotion Writing Team, *Extreme Devotion*

Newell, *A Martyr's Grace*

Special Church Year Services

The Epiphany of the Lord: Monday, January 6, 2014

Ruins at Capernaum

The Season after Epiphany: The Manifestation of Christ
January 6 - March 4, 2014

The *Feast of Epiphany* on January 6 commemorates the coming of the Magi which reveals Christ's mission to the world. The entire season of Epiphany then emphasizes the way in which Christ revealed himself to the world as the Son of God (Luke 2.32; Matt. 17.1-6; John 12.32).

Again, *Epiphany* remembers the Magi's arrival, those remarkable seekers who followed the star in search of the Christ child. The season emphasizes Christ's mission to and for the entire world, including the Gentile nations. The light of God's salvation is revealed to all peoples in the person of Jesus, the Son of God.

The Season after Epiphany begins with the celebration of the *Epiphany of the Lord* on January 6 each year, and is celebrated until the Lenten season begins on *Ash Wednesday*.

Epiphany means "manifestation" and teaches us that God revealed himself in Christ Jesus.

We celebrate *Epiphany* remembering our Lord Jesus Christ as light to the Gentiles, who was revealed to the non-Jewish Magi (wise ones) who themselves symbolize that God's salvation is available to all people.

The "Season after Epiphany" is the time between *Epiphany* and *Transfiguration Day* in which we remember how Christ was revealed as God in the world.

How was Christ revealed as God? Through the Magi, through his presentation at the Temple, through John the Baptist's testimony, through the Voice at his baptism, through the

miracle at Cana, through his healings, through Peter's
confession, and through the Transfiguration.

Epiphany is known as the season of light because we
remember the words of the prophet: "The people walking
in darkness have seen a great light; on those living in the
land of the shadow of death a light has dawned" (Isa. 9.2,
Isa. 2.5, John 1.5).

- The *Baptism of the Lord* (the first Sunday after the
  Epiphany of the Lord): This special day commemorates
  the baptism of the Lord. On it we reflect on and
  remember Jesus' baptism by John the Baptizer at the
  beginning of his public ministry. Jesus' true identity
  as Messiah and Lord was revealed by the Holy Spirit's
  descent upon him in the form of a dove, and the
  Father's testimony concerning him, "This is my beloved
  Son, with whom I am well pleased" (Matt. 3.17).

- The *Presentation of the Lord*: The Presentation at the
  Temple is a feast celebrated forty days after Christmas.
  The event is described in Luke 2.22-40 where Mary
  and Joseph presented Jesus as their firstborn to God,
  as required by the Law. All firstborn males were
  required not only to be circumcised on the eighth
  day following their birth (Lev. 12.3), but also to be
  presented to God thirty-three days later, along with an
  offering for the mother's purification after childbirth
  (Lev. 12.1-8; Exod. 13.2, 12). Upon bringing Jesus to
  the Temple, they met godly Simeon, who had been
  promised by the LORD that that he would not die till
  he saw the Lord's Messiah (Luke 2.26). Simeon's
  prayer prophesied regarding the ministry of Jesus, who
  would become a light to the nations, and the glory
  of Israel (Luke 2.29-32). Anna, an elderly widow and
  prophetess, also acknowledged the baby Jesus' upcoming role in the salvation of Israel (Luke 2.36-38).

- *Transfiguration Sunday*: This feast day "recalls the Transfiguration of Christ on the last Sunday of Epiphany (which is the Sunday before *Ash Wednesday*, the beginning of our Lenten journey)" (Robert Webber). The glory of Christ manifest in this world – to us and through us.

The first period of Ordinary Time (meaning *ordinal* [*numbered*] *time*, not *plain* or *common time*) begins in many Western liturgical settings on the day after the feast of the *Baptism of the Lord* (which normally falls on the Sunday after Epiphany). This period continues to the Season of Lent, which begins on *Ash Wednesday*. While there is some variation among traditions as to when the *Baptism of the Lord* is celebrated, this first cycle of Ordinary Time begins in many Western churches on the day after the *Epiphany of the Lord*.

In a spiritual sense, the Church Year's weeks are "numbered," counted in anticipation (in the first cycle) toward our journey to the Cross, and in the second period of Ordinary Time, from the coming of the Holy Spirit to the return of Christ in glory.

THE EPIPHANY OF THE LORD

January 6, 2014

Epiphany commemorates the coming of the Magi, the wise men from the East who followed the star in search of the Christ child. This season emphasizes Christ's mission to the Gentiles and his claim of salvation for the world.

TODAY'S THEME

The Magi Find and Worship the Messiah, Matthew 2.1-12

After our Lord was born in Bethlehem in Judea in the days of Herod the king, Magi (wise men) from the east traveled to Jerusalem and inquired where the king of the Jews had been born. They announced that they had seen his star when it rose, and they had come to worship him. Herod inquired of the priests who said that the Governor to come would be born in Bethlehem, as the prophets foretold.

Herod found out from the Magi when the star appeared, and sent them to Bethlehem to search for the child, and when found, to return to him so he could join them in worship. They went on their way to the place over which the star rested, and they went into the house where Mary and the child were. Before the child, they fell down, worshiped him, and offered him gifts of gold, frankincense, and myrrh. After being warned in a dream not to connect again with the devious Herod, they returned home by another route.

Like the Magi, let us seek the child who is destined to govern the world forever, and once we have found him, let us too fall down, worship him, and offer him all that we are and have, for his glory.

DAILY DEVOTIONAL GUIDE

PREPARING OUR HEARTS

Invocation: Our Prayer of Acclamation

Almighty God, who has poured upon us the new light of thine incarnate Word: Grant that the same light, enkindled in our hearts, may shine forth in our lives; through Jesus Christ our Lord.

~ 1549. *Book of English Collects*, No. 102 (Geffen, p. 74)

Call to Worship

Blessed are you, O God: Father, Son, and Holy Spirit. And blessed is your Kingdom, both now and forever, Amen.

PRAISING OUR GOD

Te Deum Laudamus

You are God: we praise you; you are the Lord; we acclaim you; you are the eternal Father: All creation worships you. To you all angels, all the powers of heaven, Cherubim and Seraphim, sing in endless praise: Holy, holy, holy Lord, God of power and might, heaven and earth are full of your glory.

The glorious company of apostles praise you. The noble fellowship of prophets praise you. The white-robed army of martyrs praise you. Throughout the world the holy Church acclaims you; Father, of majesty unbounded, your true and only Son, worthy of all worship, and the Holy Spirit, advocate and guide.

You, Christ, are the king of glory, the eternal Son of the Father. When you became man to set us free you did not shun the Virgin's womb. You overcame the sting of death and opened the kingdom of heaven to all believers. You are seated at God's right hand in glory. We believe that you will come and be our judge. Come then, Lord, and help your people, bought with the price of your own blood, and bring us with your saints to glory everlasting.

Praise and Thanksgiving (Songs and Prayers)

Gloria Patri
Glory be to the Father,
And to the Son and to the Holy Spirit:
As it was in the beginning,
Is now, and ever shall be,
World without end. Amen, amen.

LISTENING TO HIS VOICE

Chronological Reading for the Day
Exod. 16-19

Lectionary Readings
Psalm: Ps. 72.1-7, 10-14   *OT:* Isa. 60.1-6
Gospel: Matt. 2.1-12   *NT:* Eph. 3.1-12

Reflection: Silence and/or Journaling

RESPONDING IN FAITH

The Apostles' Creed
I believe in God, the Father Almighty, Maker of heaven and earth;
and in Jesus Christ, his only Son, our Lord, who was conceived by the
Holy Spirit, born of the Virgin Mary, suffered under Pontius Pilate,
was crucified, dead, and buried; he descended into hell; the third day
he arose again from the dead; he ascended into heaven and sits on
the right hand of God the Father Almighty; from thence he shall come
to judge the quick and the dead.

I believe in the Holy Spirit, the holy catholic* church, the communion
of saints, the forgiveness of sins, the resurrection of the body, and the
life everlasting. Amen.

* In the Apostles' and Nicene Creeds, the term catholic refers to the Church's
universality, through all ages and times, of all languages and peoples. It refers to no
particular tradition or denominational expression (e.g., as in Roman Catholic).

Prayers of Confession
Let us now confess our sins to God and receive mercy and grace to help in our time of need.

Assurance of Pardon
Having faithfully confessed and renounced your sin, Christ also has been faithful to forgive your sins and to purify you from all unrighteousness. It is certain, that there is One who has spoken to the Father in your defense, Jesus Christ, the Righteous One who is the atoning sacrifice for our sins and for the sins of the whole world. His grace and peace are with you now. Amen.

Petitions and Supplications, Ending with The Lord's Prayer
Our Father which art in heaven, Hallowed be thy name. Thy kingdom come, Thy will be done in earth, as it is in heaven. Give us this day our daily bread. And forgive us our debts, as we forgive our debtors. And lead us not into temptation, but deliver us from evil: For thine is the kingdom, and the power, and the glory, for ever. Amen.

~ Matthew 6.9-13 (KJV)

Doxology (and/or closing song)
Praise God from whom all blessings flow;
Praise Him all creatures here below;
Praise Him above ye heavenly host;
Praise Father, Son and Holy Ghost. Amen.

DEPARTING TO SERVE

Benediction
We beseech Thee, O Lord, in Thy loving-kindness, to pour Thy holy light into our souls; that we may ever be devoted to Thee, by Whose wisdom we were created, and by Whose providence we are governed: through Jesus Christ our Lord. Amen.

~ Gelasian Sacramentary, AD 494 (Fox, p. 47)

Affirmation from the Psalms

Give the king your justice, O God, and your righteousness to the royal son! May he judge your people with righteousness, and your poor with justice! Let the mountains bear prosperity for the people, and the hills, in righteousness! May he defend the cause of the poor of the people, give deliverance to the children of the needy, and crush the oppressor!

~ Psalm 72.1-4

Pray without Ceasing – Flash Prayer for the Day

Dear Savior and King, may we in humility and calm, like the wise men from the east, seek you out with all our hearts until we find you, and, once found, fall down, worship, and offer you our best. For Christ's sake, amen.

FOR YOUR WEEKLY JOURNEY

Let God Arise! Seasonal Focus

The Beloved Son of the Father, Matt. 3.13-17

Book Reading

DAILY: Extreme Devotion Writing Team, *Extreme Devotion*

Newell, *A Martyr's Grace*

January 12 - 18, 2014

Epiphany commemorates the coming of the Magi, the wise men from the East who followed the star in search of the Christ child. This season emphasizes Christ's mission to the Gentiles and his claim of salvation for the world.

THIS WEEK'S THEME

The Beloved Son of the Father, Matthew 3.13-17

When Jesus came from Galilee to the Jordan, he approached John to be baptized by him. John found Christ's request unacceptable, saying that he was the one who needed to be baptized by Jesus. Jesus answered John that they should go ahead and do it, so as to fulfill all righteousness. So John went ahead and baptized the Lord, and when Jesus came up out of the waters, the skies opened up and John saw the Holy Spirit descending like a dove and coming to rest on him. And a voice from heaven said, "This is my beloved Son, with whom I am well pleased." Jesus is the true beloved Son of the Father.

DAILY DEVOTIONAL GUIDE

PREPARING OUR HEARTS

Invocation: Our Prayer of Acclamation

Keep us, O Lord, from the vain strife of words, and grant to us a constant profession of the truth. Preserve us in the Faith, true and undefiled; so that we may ever hold fast that which we professed when we were baptized into the Name of the Father, and of the Son, and of the Holy Ghost; that we may have Thee for our Father, that we abide in Thy Son, and in the fellowship of the Holy Ghost; through the same Jesus Christ our Lord. Amen.

~ S. Hilary, Bishop of Poitiers, AD 300 (Fox, p. 233)

BAPTISM OF THE LORD, FIRST SUNDAY AFTER THE EPIPHANY

Call to Worship

Blessed are you, O God: Father, Son, and Holy Spirit. And blessed is your Kingdom, both now and forever, Amen.

PRAISING OUR GOD

Te Deum Laudamus

You are God: we praise you; you are the Lord; we acclaim you; you are the eternal Father: All creation worships you. To you all angels, all the powers of heaven, Cherubim and Seraphim, sing in endless praise: Holy, holy, holy Lord, God of power and might, heaven and earth are full of your glory.

The glorious company of apostles praise you. The noble fellowship of prophets praise you. The white-robed army of martyrs praise you. Throughout the world the holy Church acclaims you; Father, of majesty unbounded, your true and only Son, worthy of all worship, and the Holy Spirit, advocate and guide.

You, Christ, are the king of glory, the eternal Son of the Father. When you became man to set us free you did not shun the Virgin's womb. You overcame the sting of death and opened the kingdom of heaven to all believers. You are seated at God's right hand in glory. We believe that you will come and be our judge. Come then, Lord, and help your people, bought with the price of your own blood, and bring us with your saints to glory everlasting.

Praise and Thanksgiving (Songs and Prayers)

Gloria Patri

Glory be to the Father,
And to the Son and to the Holy Spirit:
As it was in the beginning,
Is now, and ever shall be,
World without end. Amen, amen.

LISTENING TO HIS VOICE

Chronological Reading for the Day
Sunday: Exod. 35-36 ✤ *Monday:* Exod. 37-38 ✤ *Tuesday:* Exod. 39-40; Num. 9.15-23 ✤ *Wednesday:* Num. 7 ✤ *Thursday:* Num. 8.1-9.14; Lev. 1-3 ✤ *Friday:* Lev. 4-6 ✤ *Saturday:* Lev. 7-8

Lectionary Readings
Psalm: Ps. 29   *OT:* Isa. 42.1-9
Gospel: Matt. 3.13-17   *NT:* Acts 10.34-43

Reflection: Silence and/or Journaling

RESPONDING IN FAITH

The Apostles' Creed
I believe in God, the Father Almighty, Maker of heaven and earth; and in Jesus Christ, his only Son, our Lord, who was conceived by the Holy Spirit, born of the Virgin Mary, suffered under Pontius Pilate, was crucified, dead, and buried; he descended into hell; the third day he arose again from the dead; he ascended into heaven and sits on the right hand of God the Father Almighty; from thence he shall come to judge the quick and the dead.

I believe in the Holy Spirit, the holy catholic* church, the communion of saints, the forgiveness of sins, the resurrection of the body, and the life everlasting. Amen.

* In the Apostles' and Nicene Creeds, the term catholic refers to the Church's universality, through all ages and times, of all languages and peoples. It refers to no particular tradition or denominational expression (e.g., as in Roman Catholic).

Prayers of Confession
Let us now confess our sins to God and receive mercy and grace to help in our time of need.

Assurance of Pardon

Having faithfully confessed and renounced your sin, Christ also has been faithful to forgive your sins and to purify you from all unrighteousness. It is certain, that there is One who has spoken to the Father in your defense, Jesus Christ, the Righteous One who is the atoning sacrifice for our sins and for the sins of the whole world. His grace and peace are with you now. Amen.

Petitions and Supplications, Ending with The Lord's Prayer

Our Father which art in heaven, Hallowed be thy name. Thy kingdom come, Thy will be done in earth, as it is in heaven. Give us this day our daily bread. And forgive us our debts, as we forgive our debtors. And lead us not into temptation, but deliver us from evil: For thine is the kingdom, and the power, and the glory, for ever. Amen.

~ Matthew 6.9-13 (KJV)

Doxology (and/or closing song)

Praise God from whom all blessings flow;
Praise Him all creatures here below;
Praise Him above ye heavenly host;
Praise Father, Son and Holy Ghost. Amen.

Departing to Serve

Benediction

O God, Who by the Baptism of Thine Only-begotten Son hast been pleased to sanctify the streams of water; grant that we who are born again of Water and the Spirit may attain an entrance into eternal joys; through the same Jesus Christ our Lord.

~ Gregorian, as edited by Pamelius (Bright, p. 161)

Affirmation from the Psalms
Ascribe to the LORD, O heavenly beings, ascribe to the LORD glory and strength. Ascribe to the LORD the glory due his name; worship the LORD in the splendor of holiness.

~ Psalm 29.1-2

Pray without Ceasing – Flash Prayer for the Day
Lord of light and love, Jesus of Nazareth, thank you for identifying with us in your baptism, fulfilling all righteousness before the Father. You are the beloved, true Son of the Father. Be glorified today. In your name we pray, amen.

FOR YOUR WEEKLY JOURNEY

Let God Arise! Seasonal Focus
The Beloved Son of the Father, Matt. 3.13-17

Book Reading
DAILY: Extreme Devotion Writing Team, *Extreme Devotion*

Newell, *A Martyr's Grace*

Our Corporate Disciplines
Prayer and Fasting, ending with Book Review:
Wednesday, January 15, 2014

Concert of Prayer:
Saturday, January 18, 2014

WEEK

8

✠

January 19 - 25, 2014

Epiphany commemorates the coming of the Magi, the wise men from the East who followed the star in search of the Christ child. This season emphasizes Christ's mission to the Gentiles and his claim of salvation for the world.

THIS WEEK'S THEME

Sustained to the End, 1 Corinthians 1.1-9

In writing to the Corinthians, Paul wrote that all who call upon Jesus, wherever they are, have been set apart by him for a new, God-centered life. He affirmed the working of God in their midst, especially highlighting the evidence of Christ's goodness and salvation demonstrated in their belief in the Gospel. He affirmed that through God's grace his gifts were abundantly theirs, as they confidently waited for the Master to return for the consummation of all things. Paul assured them that the Lord would be present himself right alongside them, in all their journeys and challenges, to keep them steady and on track until he returned to complete his full salvation. The Lord himself would sustain them to the very end; he would never abandon or give up on them. God is faithful who called them (and us!) into fellowship with his Son, Jesus Christ our Lord.

DAILY DEVOTIONAL GUIDE

PREPARING OUR HEARTS

Invocation: Our Prayer of Acclamation

Great God of our Lord Jesus Christ, thank you for calling us into communion with you and your Son. Thank you for the promise of your provision and presence till the day that your Son returns to redeem us finally at the End. Open our eyes to see the wonderful things you have provided for us as we wait in your presence here now. Come, and speak to our hearts as we wait before you. In Christ's name, amen.

Call to Worship

Blessed are you, O God: Father, Son, and Holy Spirit. And blessed is your Kingdom, both now and forever, Amen.

PRAISING OUR GOD

Te Deum Laudamus

You are God: we praise you; you are the Lord; we acclaim you; you are the eternal Father: All creation worships you. To you all angels, all the powers of heaven, Cherubim and Seraphim, sing in endless praise: Holy, holy, holy Lord, God of power and might, heaven and earth are full of your glory.

The glorious company of apostles praise you. The noble fellowship of prophets praise you. The white-robed army of martyrs praise you. Throughout the world the holy Church acclaims you; Father, of majesty unbounded, your true and only Son, worthy of all worship, and the Holy Spirit, advocate and guide.

You, Christ, are the king of glory, the eternal Son of the Father. When you became man to set us free you did not shun the Virgin's womb. You overcame the sting of death and opened the kingdom of heaven to all believers. You are seated at God's right hand in glory. We believe that you will come and be our judge. Come then, Lord, and help your people, bought with the price of your own blood, and bring us with your saints to glory everlasting.

Praise and Thanksgiving (Songs and Prayers)

Gloria Patri

Glory be to the Father,
And to the Son and to the Holy Spirit:
As it was in the beginning,
Is now, and ever shall be,
World without end. Amen, amen.

Listening to His Voice

Chronological Reading for the Day
Sunday: Lev. 9-11 ✠ *Monday:* Lev. 12-14 ✠ *Tuesday:* Lev. 15-16 ✠ *Wednesday:* Lev. 17-19 ✠ *Thursday:* Lev. 20-22 ✠ *Friday:* Lev. 23-24 ✠ *Saturday:* Lev. 25-26

Lectionary Readings
Psalm: Ps. 40.1-11   *OT:* Isa. 49.1-7
Gospel: John 1.29-42   *NT:* 1 Cor. 1.1-9

Reflection: Silence and/or Journaling

Responding in Faith

The Apostles' Creed
I believe in God, the Father Almighty, Maker of heaven and earth; and in Jesus Christ, his only Son, our Lord, who was conceived by the Holy Spirit, born of the Virgin Mary, suffered under Pontius Pilate, was crucified, dead, and buried; he descended into hell; the third day he arose again from the dead; he ascended into heaven and sits on the right hand of God the Father Almighty; from thence he shall come to judge the quick and the dead.

I believe in the Holy Spirit, the holy catholic* church, the communion of saints, the forgiveness of sins, the resurrection of the body, and the life everlasting. Amen.

* In the Apostles' and Nicene Creeds, the term catholic refers to the Church's universality, through all ages and times, of all languages and peoples. It refers to no particular tradition or denominational expression (e.g., as in Roman Catholic).

Prayers of Confession
Let us now confess our sins to God and receive mercy and grace to help in our time of need.

Assurance of Pardon

Having faithfully confessed and renounced your sin, Christ also has been faithful to forgive your sins and to purify you from all unrighteousness. It is certain, that there is One who has spoken to the Father in your defense, Jesus Christ, the Righteous One who is the atoning sacrifice for our sins and for the sins of the whole world. His grace and peace are with you now. Amen.

Petitions and Supplications, Ending with The Lord's Prayer

Our Father which art in heaven, Hallowed be thy name. Thy kingdom come, Thy will be done in earth, as it is in heaven. Give us this day our daily bread. And forgive us our debts, as we forgive our debtors. And lead us not into temptation, but deliver us from evil: For thine is the kingdom, and the power, and the glory, for ever. Amen.

~ Matthew 6.9-13 (KJV)

Doxology (and/or closing song)

Praise God from whom all blessings flow;
Praise Him all creatures here below;
Praise Him above ye heavenly host;
Praise Father, Son and Holy Ghost. Amen.

Departing to Serve

Benediction

Thank you Lord Jesus, for the testimony about your finished work has been confirmed among us. We do not lack a single gift, for you have been gracious to us. We with joyful hearts wait for your revelation, and we are confident that you will sustain us to the very end and present us faultless and guiltless in your amazing day to come. We affirm your faithfulness and love, and thank you for our wonderful fellowship with you, granted to us through your Father. We love you and praise you. In your name, Jesus Christ our Lord, we pray, amen.

Affirmation from the Psalms

*Blessed is the man who makes the Lord his trust, who does not turn
to the proud, to those who go astray after a lie! You have multiplied,
O Lord my God, your wondrous deeds and your thoughts toward us;
none can compare with you! I will proclaim and tell of them, yet they
are more than can be told.*

~ Psalm 40.4-5

Pray without Ceasing – Flash Prayer for the Day

Assure our hearts, O Lamb and King, that you will never
leave us, and sustain us to the very end, till the day you
appear to take us away from the world of sin.

FOR YOUR WEEKLY JOURNEY

Let God Arise! Seasonal Focus

The Beloved Son of the Father, Matt. 3.13-17

Book Reading

DAILY: Extreme Devotion Writing Team, *Extreme Devotion*

Newell, *A Martyr's Grace*

Our Corporate Disciplines

Concert of Prayer:
     Tuesday, January 21, 2014

January 26 - February 1, 2014

Epiphany commemorates the coming of the Magi, the wise men from the East who followed the star in search of the Christ child. This season emphasizes Christ's mission to the Gentiles and his claim of salvation for the world.

THIS WEEK'S THEME
The Messiah Commences His Ministry, Matthew 4.12-23
After his baptism by John, Jesus was led up by the Holy Spirit into the wilderness to be tempted by the devil. After fasting for forty days and nights, he was hungry. Although tempted three times by the twisting of Scripture by Satan, the Lord triumphed over him, quoting God's holy Scripture and refuting the devil's lies and attacks. Having withstood the devil's assaults and temptations, our Lord returned to Galilee in the power of the Holy Spirit and began his ministry of kingdom proclamation and demonstration. It was there, in Galilee, that he called his first four disciples, gathering to his side those apostles who would accompany him throughout his earthly ministry. Jesus of Nazareth is the Messiah of God, who fulfilled the Scripture's prophecy, proclaiming the Kingdom come throughout the land.

DAILY DEVOTIONAL GUIDE

PREPARING OUR HEARTS

Invocation: Our Prayer of Acclamation
Eternal God, our Father, grant us spiritual eyes to see and spiritual wisdom to comprehend the majesty and glory of the person of your Son, our dear Savior, who triumphed over the devil, taught and proclaimed the gospel of the Kingdom in his words and deeds, and healed every disease and oppression of the devil. He did this precisely as you foretold in your holy Scriptures. Accomplish your will in us and through us, as you did with our Lord. In his name we pray, amen.

Call to Worship
Blessed are you, O God: Father, Son, and Holy Spirit. And blessed is your Kingdom, both now and forever, Amen.

PRAISING OUR GOD

Te Deum Laudamus
You are God: we praise you; you are the Lord; we acclaim you; you are the eternal Father: All creation worships you. To you all angels, all the powers of heaven, Cherubim and Seraphim, sing in endless praise: Holy, holy, holy Lord, God of power and might, heaven and earth are full of your glory.

The glorious company of apostles praise you. The noble fellowship of prophets praise you. The white-robed army of martyrs praise you. Throughout the world the holy Church acclaims you; Father, of majesty unbounded, your true and only Son, worthy of all worship, and the Holy Spirit, advocate and guide.

You, Christ, are the king of glory, the eternal Son of the Father. When you became man to set us free you did not shun the Virgin's womb. You overcame the sting of death and opened the kingdom of heaven to all believers. You are seated at God's right hand in glory. We believe that you will come and be our judge. Come then, Lord, and help your people, bought with the price of your own blood, and bring us with your saints to glory everlasting.

Praise and Thanksgiving (Songs and Prayers)

Gloria Patri
Glory be to the Father,
And to the Son and to the Holy Spirit:
As it was in the beginning,
Is now, and ever shall be,
World without end. Amen, amen.

LISTENING TO HIS VOICE

Chronological Reading for the Day
Sunday: Lev. 27; Num. 1 ✦ *Monday:* Num. 2-3 ✦ *Tuesday:* Num. 4-5 ✦ *Wednesday:* Num. 6; 10 ✦ *Thursday:* Num. 11-13 ✦ *Friday:* Num. 14-15 ✦ *Saturday:* Num. 16-18

Lectionary Readings
Psalm: Ps. 27.1, 4-9   *OT:* Isa. 9.1-4
Gospel: Matt. 4.12-23   *NT:* 1 Cor. 1.10-18

Reflection: Silence and/or Journaling

RESPONDING IN FAITH

The Apostles' Creed
I believe in God, the Father Almighty, Maker of heaven and earth; and in Jesus Christ, his only Son, our Lord, who was conceived by the Holy Spirit, born of the Virgin Mary, suffered under Pontius Pilate, was crucified, dead, and buried; he descended into hell; the third day he arose again from the dead; he ascended into heaven and sits on the right hand of God the Father Almighty; from thence he shall come to judge the quick and the dead.

I believe in the Holy Spirit, the holy catholic* church, the communion of saints, the forgiveness of sins, the resurrection of the body, and the life everlasting. Amen.

* In the Apostles' and Nicene Creeds, the term catholic refers to the Church's universality, through all ages and times, of all languages and peoples. It refers to no particular tradition or denominational expression (e.g., as in Roman Catholic).

Prayers of Confession
Let us now confess our sins to God and receive mercy and grace to help in our time of need.

Assurance of Pardon

Having faithfully confessed and renounced your sin, Christ also has been faithful to forgive your sins and to purify you from all unrighteousness. It is certain, that there is One who has spoken to the Father in your defense, Jesus Christ, the Righteous One who is the atoning sacrifice for our sins and for the sins of the whole world. His grace and peace are with you now. Amen.

Petitions and Supplications, Ending with The Lord's Prayer

Our Father which art in heaven, Hallowed be thy name. Thy kingdom come, Thy will be done in earth, as it is in heaven. Give us this day our daily bread. And forgive us our debts, as we forgive our debtors. And lead us not into temptation, but deliver us from evil: For thine is the kingdom, and the power, and the glory, for ever. Amen.

~ Matthew 6.9-13 (KJV)

Doxology (and/or closing song)

Praise God from whom all blessings flow;
Praise Him all creatures here below;
Praise Him above ye heavenly host;
Praise Father, Son and Holy Ghost. Amen.

DEPARTING TO SERVE

Benediction

Lord Jesus, who resisted the deception of the enemy with the Word of the Father, and who faithfully carried out your ministry as led by the Holy Spirit, please grant us the strength and commitment to stay true to you in all the temptations we face. Grant us the same heart and mind that you had as you obeyed the Father's command, called to yourself your own disciples, and proclaimed in word and deed the power of the Kingdom. Without you, we are both lost and hopeless. Come, and work through us for your name's sake. Amen.

Affirmation from the Psalms

One thing have I asked of the LORD, that will I seek after: that I may dwell in the house of the LORD all the days of my life, to gaze upon the beauty of the LORD and to inquire in his temple. For he will hide me in his shelter in the day of trouble; he will conceal me under the cover of his tent; he will lift me high upon a rock.

~ Psalm 27.4-5

Pray without Ceasing – Flash Prayer for the Day

Eternal God, grant us grace through your Spirit to stand our ground in the face of evil and deception as our Lord did during the temptation in the wilderness.

FOR YOUR WEEKLY JOURNEY

Let God Arise! Seasonal Focus

The Beloved Son of the Father, Matt. 3.13-17

Book Reading

DAILY: Extreme Devotion Writing Team, *Extreme Devotion*

Newell, *A Martyr's Grace*

✠

PRESENTATION OF THE LORD, FOURTH SUNDAY AFTER THE EPIPHANY

February 2 - 8, 2014

Epiphany affirms Jesus' presence in the world as hope for all peoples. In him alone, God provides the light of his salvation, making known God's grace to all peoples, even to the farthest corners of the earth.

THIS WEEK'S THEME

In the Presence of the Peoples, Luke 2.22-40

When the time came for purification according to the Law of Moses, Joseph and Mary brought Jesus to Jerusalem to present him to the Lord as commanded in the Scripture. There was a righteous and devout man in Jerusalem, Simeon by name, who waited for the revealing of the Messiah, to whom it was revealed by the Spirit that he would see the Messiah before he died.

After coming into the temple in the Spirit he saw Jesus' parents with him to do as the Law required. Simeon took the baby Jesus in his arms and blessed the Lord, saying, "Lord, now you are letting your servant depart in peace, according to your word; for my eyes have seen your salvation that you have prepared in the presence of all peoples, a light for revelation to the Gentiles, and for glory to your people Israel." The child Jesus was the salvation of God in the presence of all peoples, the light of the nations and the glory of Israel.

DAILY DEVOTIONAL GUIDE

PREPARING OUR HEARTS

Invocation: Our Prayer of Acclamation

O Lord God, who for our sakes hast made thy blessed Son, our Saviour, subject to the Law, and caused Him to endure the circumcision of the flesh, grant us the true circumcision of the Spirit, that our hearts may be pure from all sinful desire and lusts; through the same thy Son Jesus Christ our Lord.

~1549, Cranmer. *The Sermon and the Propers*, p. 106 (Geffen, p. 72)

Call to Worship

Blessed are you, O God: Father, Son, and Holy Spirit. And blessed is your Kingdom, both now and forever, Amen.

PRAISING OUR GOD

Te Deum Laudamus

You are God: we praise you; you are the Lord; we acclaim you; you are the eternal Father: All creation worships you. To you all angels, all the powers of heaven, Cherubim and Seraphim, sing in endless praise: Holy, holy, holy Lord, God of power and might, heaven and earth are full of your glory.

The glorious company of apostles praise you. The noble fellowship of prophets praise you. The white-robed army of martyrs praise you. Throughout the world the holy Church acclaims you; Father, of majesty unbounded, your true and only Son, worthy of all worship, and the Holy Spirit, advocate and guide.

You, Christ, are the king of glory, the eternal Son of the Father. When you became man to set us free you did not shun the Virgin's womb. You overcame the sting of death and opened the kingdom of heaven to all believers. You are seated at God's right hand in glory. We believe that you will come and be our judge. Come then, Lord, and help your people, bought with the price of your own blood, and bring us with your saints to glory everlasting.

Praise and Thanksgiving (Songs and Prayers)

Gloria Patri

Glory be to the Father,
And to the Son and to the Holy Spirit:
As it was in the beginning,
Is now, and ever shall be,
World without end. Amen, amen.

Listening to His Voice

Chronological Reading for the Day
Sunday: Num. 19-21 ✤ *Monday:* Num. 22-24 ✤ *Tuesday:* Num. 25-26 ✤ *Wednesday:* Num. 27-29 ✤ *Thursday:* Num. 30-31 ✤ *Friday:* Num. 32-33 ✤ *Saturday:* Num. 34-36

Lectionary Readings
Psalm: Ps. 84   *OT:* Mal. 3.1-4
Gospel: Luke 2.22-40   *NT:* Heb. 2.14-18

Reflection: Silence and/or Journaling

Responding in Faith

The Apostles' Creed
I believe in God, the Father Almighty, Maker of heaven and earth; and in Jesus Christ, his only Son, our Lord, who was conceived by the Holy Spirit, born of the Virgin Mary, suffered under Pontius Pilate, was crucified, dead, and buried; he descended into hell; the third day he arose again from the dead; he ascended into heaven and sits on the right hand of God the Father Almighty; from thence he shall come to judge the quick and the dead.

I believe in the Holy Spirit, the holy catholic* church, the communion of saints, the forgiveness of sins, the resurrection of the body, and the life everlasting. Amen.

* In the Apostles' and Nicene Creeds, the term catholic refers to the Church's universality, through all ages and times, of all languages and peoples. It refers to no particular tradition or denominational expression (e.g., as in Roman Catholic).

Prayers of Confession
Let us now confess our sins to God and receive mercy and grace to help in our time of need.

Assurance of Pardon
Having faithfully confessed and renounced your sin, Christ also has been faithful to forgive your sins and to purify you from all unrighteousness. It is certain, that there is One who has spoken to the Father in your defense, Jesus Christ, the Righteous One who is the atoning sacrifice for our sins and for the sins of the whole world. His grace and peace are with you now. Amen.

Petitions and Supplications, Ending with The Lord's Prayer
Our Father which art in heaven, Hallowed be thy name. Thy kingdom come, Thy will be done in earth, as it is in heaven. Give us this day our daily bread. And forgive us our debts, as we forgive our debtors. And lead us not into temptation, but deliver us from evil: For thine is the kingdom, and the power, and the glory, for ever. Amen.

~ Matthew 6.9-13 (KJV)

Doxology (and/or closing song)
Praise God from whom all blessings flow;
Praise Him all creatures here below;
Praise Him above ye heavenly host;
Praise Father, Son and Holy Ghost. Amen.

DEPARTING TO SERVE

Benediction
O GOD, whose blessed Son was manifested that he might destroy the works of the devil, and make us the sons of God and heirs of eternal life: grant us, we beseech thee, that, having this hope, we may purify ourselves, even as he is pure; that when he shall appear again, with power and great glory, we may be made like unto him in his eternal and glorious kingdom; where with thee, O Father, and thee, O Holy Ghost, he liveth and reigneth ever, one God world without end. Amen.

~ *Book of Common Prayer*, England Revised (1928) (Suter, p. 8)

Affirmation from the Psalms

O LORD God of hosts, hear my prayer; give ear, O God of Jacob! Selah. Behold our shield, O God; look on the face of your anointed! For a day in your courts is better than a thousand elsewhere. I would rather be a doorkeeper in the house of my God than dwell in the tents of wickedness. For the LORD God is a sun and shield; the LORD bestows favor and honor. No good thing does he withhold from those who walk uprightly. O LORD of hosts, blessed is the one who trusts in you!

~ Psalm 84.8-12

Pray without Ceasing – Flash Prayer for the Day

Dear Master and Lord, Simeon confirmed that truth about you which we hold dear – you are the light for the nations, you are the glory of your people, Israel.

FOR YOUR WEEKLY JOURNEY

Let God Arise! Seasonal Focus

Listen to the Son, Matt. 17.1-9

Book Reading

Daily: Extreme Devotion Writing Team, *Extreme Devotion*

Newell, *A Martyr's Grace*

February 9 - 15, 2014

Epiphany affirms Jesus' presence in the world as hope for all peoples. In him alone, God provides the light of his salvation, making known God's grace to all peoples, even to the farthest corners of the earth.

THIS WEEK'S THEME
Living as Salt and Light, Matthew 5.13-20

During the Sermon on the Mount, Jesus affirmed that those who believe in him are the salt of the earth. Yet, he affirmed, if that salt loses its taste, its saltiness could not be restored. It would become useless, only to be thrown out and trampled under people's feet. He said that we are the light of the world, and that a city set on a hill could not be hidden. He emphasized that people do not light a lamp and put it under a basket. Rather, they put it on a stand where it can illumine everyone and all that is in the house. Jesus affirmed that, in the same way, we must let our light shine before others, so that they might see our good works and give glory to our Father who is in heaven.

He declared that until heaven and earth pass away, not an iota or a dot would pass from the Law until all is accomplished. Those who relax the commandment would be least in the Kingdom, and those who taught and did them would be great in the Kingdom of heaven. Our righteousness must exceed that of the scribes and Pharisees in order to enter the Kingdom of heaven.

FIFTH SUNDAY AFTER THE EPIPHANY

DAILY DEVOTIONAL GUIDE

PREPARING OUR HEARTS

Invocation: Our Prayer of Acclamation

Eternal Father, our Maker and Defender, give to us the power to be both salt and light in the midst of a lost and evil world which desperately needs the spice and preservation of your saltiness and the illumination and glory of your light. Make us that city on a hill that cannot be hidden, that through our good works people may see evidence of your Kingdom, and be drawn to you and give you glory. In the name of our Lord we pray, amen.

Call to Worship

Blessed are you, O God: Father, Son, and Holy Spirit. And blessed is your Kingdom, both now and forever, Amen.

PRAISING OUR GOD

Te Deum Laudamus

You are God: we praise you; you are the Lord; we acclaim you; you are the eternal Father: All creation worships you. To you all angels, all the powers of heaven, Cherubim and Seraphim, sing in endless praise: Holy, holy, holy Lord, God of power and might, heaven and earth are full of your glory.

The glorious company of apostles praise you. The noble fellowship of prophets praise you. The white-robed army of martyrs praise you. Throughout the world the holy Church acclaims you; Father, of majesty unbounded, your true and only Son, worthy of all worship, and the Holy Spirit, advocate and guide.

You, Christ, are the king of glory, the eternal Son of the Father. When you became man to set us free you did not shun the Virgin's womb. You overcame the sting of death and opened the kingdom of heaven to all believers. You are seated at God's right hand in glory. We believe that you will come and be our judge. Come then, Lord, and help your people, bought with the price of your own blood, and bring us with your saints to glory everlasting.

Praise and Thanksgiving (Songs and Prayers)

Gloria Patri

Glory be to the Father,
And to the Son and to the Holy Spirit:
As it was in the beginning,
Is now, and ever shall be,
World without end. Amen, amen.

LISTENING TO HIS VOICE

Chronological Reading for the Day

Sunday: Deut. 1-3 ✤ *Monday:* Deut. 4-5 ✤ *Tuesday:* Deut. 6-9
✤ *Wednesday:* Deut. 10-12 ✤ *Thursday:* Deut. 13-16 ✤
Friday: Deut. 17-20 ✤ *Saturday:* Deut. 21-25

Lectionary Readings

Psalm: Ps. 112.1-10   *OT:* Isa. 58.1-9a
Gospel: Matt. 5.13-20   *NT:* 1 Cor. 2.1-12

Reflection: Silence and/or Journaling

RESPONDING IN FAITH

The Apostles' Creed

I believe in God, the Father Almighty, Maker of heaven and earth;
and in Jesus Christ, his only Son, our Lord, who was conceived by the
Holy Spirit, born of the Virgin Mary, suffered under Pontius Pilate,
was crucified, dead, and buried; he descended into hell; the third day
he arose again from the dead; he ascended into heaven and sits on
the right hand of God the Father Almighty; from thence he shall come
to judge the quick and the dead.

I believe in the Holy Spirit, the holy catholic* church, the communion
of saints, the forgiveness of sins, the resurrection of the body, and the
life everlasting. Amen.

* In the Apostles' and Nicene Creeds, the term catholic refers to the Church's
universality, through all ages and times, of all languages and peoples. It refers to no
particular tradition or denominational expression (e.g., as in Roman Catholic).

Prayers of Confession
Let us now confess our sins to God and receive mercy and grace to help in our time of need.

Assurance of Pardon
Having faithfully confessed and renounced your sin, Christ also has been faithful to forgive your sins and to purify you from all unrighteousness. It is certain, that there is One who has spoken to the Father in your defense, Jesus Christ, the Righteous One who is the atoning sacrifice for our sins and for the sins of the whole world. His grace and peace are with you now. Amen.

Petitions and Supplications, Ending with The Lord's Prayer
Our Father which art in heaven, Hallowed be thy name. Thy kingdom come, Thy will be done in earth, as it is in heaven. Give us this day our daily bread. And forgive us our debts, as we forgive our debtors. And lead us not into temptation, but deliver us from evil: For thine is the kingdom, and the power, and the glory, for ever. Amen.

~ Matthew 6.9-13 (KJV)

Doxology (and/or closing song)
Praise God from whom all blessings flow;
Praise Him all creatures here below;
Praise Him above ye heavenly host;
Praise Father, Son and Holy Ghost. Amen.

Departing to Serve

Benediction
Great God and Father of our Lord Jesus Christ, make us channels of your truth and your light, that those who live in deception and in darkness may observe our works and hear our words, and be won into the Kingdom of your dear Son, Jesus. Reveal your glory through us, that we may reflect for

all to see that glory and majesty belong to you alone. Make us like your Son. In his name we pray, amen.

Affirmation from the Psalms

Light dawns in the darkness for the upright; he is gracious, merciful, and righteous. It is well with the man who deals generously and lends; who conducts his affairs with justice. For the righteous will never be moved; he will be remembered forever. He is not afraid of bad news; his heart is firm, trusting in the LORD. His heart is steady; he will not be afraid, until he looks in triumph on his adversaries.

~ Psalm 112.4-8

Pray without Ceasing – Flash Prayer for the Day

Living Savior and Christ, our Lord Jesus, make us light in you, that those who see us today may be drawn to your holiness and joy.

FOR YOUR WEEKLY JOURNEY

Let God Arise! Seasonal Focus

Listen to the Son, Matt. 17.1-9

Book Reading

DAILY: Extreme Devotion Writing Team, *Extreme Devotion*

Newell, *A Martyr's Grace*

February 16 - 22, 2014

Epiphany affirms Jesus' presence in the world as hope for all peoples. In him alone, God provides the light of his salvation, making known God's grace to all peoples, even to the farthest corners of the earth.

THIS WEEK'S THEME
The High Standard of the Kingdom, Matthew 5.21-37
As Lord of the Kingdom and Rabbi of God, Jesus not only highlighted the Old Testament truth but broadened and intensified it to reflect the holiness his Kingdom required. While the Law said you should not murder another person, the King said that hating someone is the same as murder. While the Law said do not commit adultery, the King said that looking lustfully at someone is the same as adultery. While the Law said a man can divorce his wife by giving a letter of divorce, the King said that unlawful divorce and remarriage is the same as adultery. While the Law said you must carry out your oaths, the King said don't make any vows, but a simple yes or no is sufficient. The Kingdom of God and its righteousness intensifies the Law and reveals a high standard that none can keep – without Christ's forgiveness and the Holy Spirit, God's gift to those who believe.

DAILY DEVOTIONAL GUIDE

PREPARING OUR HEARTS

Invocation: Our Prayer of Acclamation
Thank you, heavenly Father, for your righteous and holy will, your pure Word and holy standard which is good, true, and right. Your law reveals to us our own lawlessness and calls us to cry out to you for both mercy and help. Grant us through the gift of your Spirit the power that the righteousness of the Law can be fulfilled in us (not by our own strength) as we trust and wait on you. In Jesus' name, amen.

Call to Worship

Blessed are you, O God: Father, Son, and Holy Spirit. And blessed is your Kingdom, both now and forever, Amen.

Te Deum Laudamus

You are God: we praise you; you are the Lord; we acclaim you; you are the eternal Father: All creation worships you. To you all angels, all the powers of heaven, Cherubim and Seraphim, sing in endless praise: Holy, holy, holy Lord, God of power and might, heaven and earth are full of your glory.

The glorious company of apostles praise you. The noble fellowship of prophets praise you. The white-robed army of martyrs praise you. Throughout the world the holy Church acclaims you; Father, of majesty unbounded, your true and only Son, worthy of all worship, and the Holy Spirit, advocate and guide.

You, Christ, are the king of glory, the eternal Son of the Father. When you became man to set us free you did not shun the Virgin's womb. You overcame the sting of death and opened the kingdom of heaven to all believers. You are seated at God's right hand in glory. We believe that you will come and be our judge. Come then, Lord, and help your people, bought with the price of your own blood, and bring us with your saints to glory everlasting.

Praise and Thanksgiving (Songs and Prayers)

Gloria Patri

Glory be to the Father,
And to the Son and to the Holy Spirit:
As it was in the beginning,
Is now, and ever shall be,
World without end. Amen, amen.

LISTENING TO HIS VOICE

Chronological Reading for the Day
Sunday: Deut. 26-28 ✤ *Monday:* Deut. 29-30 ✤ *Tuesday:* Deut. 31-32; Ps. 90 ✤ *Wednesday:* Deut. 33-34; Josh. 1-2 ✤ *Thursday:* Josh. 3-6 ✤ *Friday:* Josh. 7-9; 1 Chron. 2.7 ✤ *Saturday:* Josh. 10-11

Lectionary Readings
Psalm: Ps. 119.1-8   *OT:* Deut. 30.15-20
Gospel: Matt. 5.21-37   *NT:* 1 Cor. 3.1-9

Reflection: Silence and/or Journaling

RESPONDING IN FAITH

The Apostles' Creed
I believe in God, the Father Almighty, Maker of heaven and earth; and in Jesus Christ, his only Son, our Lord, who was conceived by the Holy Spirit, born of the Virgin Mary, suffered under Pontius Pilate, was crucified, dead, and buried; he descended into hell; the third day he arose again from the dead; he ascended into heaven and sits on the right hand of God the Father Almighty; from thence he shall come to judge the quick and the dead.

I believe in the Holy Spirit, the holy catholic* church, the communion of saints, the forgiveness of sins, the resurrection of the body, and the life everlasting. Amen.

* In the Apostles' and Nicene Creeds, the term catholic refers to the Church's universality, through all ages and times, of all languages and peoples. It refers to no particular tradition or denominational expression (e.g., as in Roman Catholic).

Prayers of Confession
Let us now confess our sins to God and receive mercy and grace to help in our time of need.

Assurance of Pardon

Having faithfully confessed and renounced your sin, Christ also has been faithful to forgive your sins and to purify you from all unrighteousness. It is certain, that there is One who has spoken to the Father in your defense, Jesus Christ, the Righteous One who is the atoning sacrifice for our sins and for the sins of the whole world. His grace and peace are with you now. Amen.

Petitions and Supplications, Ending with The Lord's Prayer

Our Father which art in heaven, Hallowed be thy name. Thy kingdom come, Thy will be done in earth, as it is in heaven. Give us this day our daily bread. And forgive us our debts, as we forgive our debtors. And lead us not into temptation, but deliver us from evil: For thine is the kingdom, and the power, and the glory, for ever. Amen.

~ Matthew 6.9-13 (KJV)

Doxology (and/or closing song)

Praise God from whom all blessings flow;
Praise Him all creatures here below;
Praise Him above ye heavenly host;
Praise Father, Son and Holy Ghost. Amen.

Departing to Serve

Benediction

Lord Jesus, your holy teaching and commands are right and good, and we desire to please you by obeying your will. We understand and know that, apart from the gift of your Holy Spirit and the power of your nature within us, we cannot fulfill your high standard and will. Grant us the mind and heart to depend on you, to look to your Spirit for the power to fulfill your commandments. In your name we pray, amen.

Affirmation from the Psalms

Oh give thanks to the LORD, for he is good; for his steadfast love
endures forever! Let Israel say, "His steadfast love endures forever."
Let the house of Aaron say, "His steadfast love endures forever." Let
those who fear the LORD say, "His steadfast love endures forever."
Out of my distress I called on the LORD; the LORD answered me and
set me free. The LORD is on my side; I will not fear. What can man
do to me?

~ Psalm 118.1-6

Pray without Ceasing – Flash Prayer for the Day

Righteous Lord and Rabbi, teach us what it means to keep
your commandments and please you in all that we say and
do, for your sake.

FOR YOUR WEEKLY JOURNEY

Let God Arise! Seasonal Focus

Listen to the Son, Matt. 17.1-9

Book Reading

DAILY: Extreme Devotion Writing Team, *Extreme Devotion*

Newell, *A Martyr's Grace*

February 23 - March 1, 2014

Epiphany affirms Jesus' presence in the world as hope for all peoples. In him alone, God provides the light of his salvation, making known God's grace to all peoples, even to the farthest corners of the earth.

THIS WEEK'S THEME
Retaliation and Loving One's Enemies, Matthew 5.38-48
The heart of the ethic of the Kingdom of God is non-retaliation and love for one's neighbor. While the basic Old Testament concept regarding retaliation anchored righteous acts on an eye for an eye and a tooth for a tooth. Jesus declared that we should turn the other cheek to those who struck one, and do abundantly beyond what we were asked or was demanded. In connection to love, the Law said love your neighbor and hate your enemy, but Jesus declared that we should love our enemies, pray for those who persecute us, and bless those who curse us. In saying this, he made his own perfect life and pattern the standard of all true kingdom living.

DAILY DEVOTIONAL GUIDE

PREPARING OUR HEARTS

Invocation: Our Prayer of Acclamation
Almighty Father, maker of all things, grant us the spiritual eyesight to see how your beloved Son intensified and interpreted truly your will regarding retaliation and loving our enemies. In his deeds and reactions, we have come to see the nature of your love and Father heart: you truly are a God who blesses all humankind, the just and the unjust, and are kind and considerate to all, even those who neither know or believe in you. Make our heart like your own great heart, for Jesus' sake. Amen.

SEVENTH SUNDAY AFTER THE EPIPHANY

Call to Worship

Blessed are you, O God: Father, Son, and Holy Spirit. And blessed is your Kingdom, both now and forever, Amen.

PRAISING OUR GOD

Te Deum Laudamus

You are God: we praise you; you are the Lord; we acclaim you; you are the eternal Father: All creation worships you. To you all angels, all the powers of heaven, Cherubim and Seraphim, sing in endless praise: Holy, holy, holy Lord, God of power and might, heaven and earth are full of your glory.

The glorious company of apostles praise you. The noble fellowship of prophets praise you. The white-robed army of martyrs praise you. Throughout the world the holy Church acclaims you; Father, of majesty unbounded, your true and only Son, worthy of all worship, and the Holy Spirit, advocate and guide.

You, Christ, are the king of glory, the eternal Son of the Father. When you became man to set us free you did not shun the Virgin's womb. You overcame the sting of death and opened the kingdom of heaven to all believers. You are seated at God's right hand in glory. We believe that you will come and be our judge. Come then, Lord, and help your people, bought with the price of your own blood, and bring us with your saints to glory everlasting.

Praise and Thanksgiving (Songs and Prayers)

Gloria Patri

Glory be to the Father,
And to the Son and to the Holy Spirit:
As it was in the beginning,
Is now, and ever shall be,
World without end. Amen, amen.

LISTENING TO HIS VOICE

Chronological Reading for the Day
Sunday: Josh. 12-14 ✠ *Monday:* Josh. 15-17 ✠ *Tuesday:* Josh. 18-19 ✠ *Wednesday:* Josh. 20-21; 1 Chron. 6.54-81 ✠ *Thursday:* Josh. 22-24 ✠ *Friday:* Judg. 1-3 ✠ *Saturday:* Judg. 4-6

Lectionary Readings
Psalm: Ps. 119.33-40   *OT:* Lev. 19.1-2, 9-18
Gospel: Matt. 5.38-48   *NT:* 1 Cor. 3.10-11, 16-23

Reflection: Silence and/or Journaling

RESPONDING IN FAITH

The Apostles' Creed
I believe in God, the Father Almighty, Maker of heaven and earth; and in Jesus Christ, his only Son, our Lord, who was conceived by the Holy Spirit, born of the Virgin Mary, suffered under Pontius Pilate, was crucified, dead, and buried; he descended into hell; the third day he arose again from the dead; he ascended into heaven and sits on the right hand of God the Father Almighty; from thence he shall come to judge the quick and the dead.

I believe in the Holy Spirit, the holy catholic* church, the communion of saints, the forgiveness of sins, the resurrection of the body, and the life everlasting. Amen.

* In the Apostles' and Nicene Creeds, the term catholic refers to the Church's universality, through all ages and times, of all languages and peoples. It refers to no particular tradition or denominational expression (e.g., as in Roman Catholic).

Prayers of Confession
Let us now confess our sins to God and receive mercy and grace to help in our time of need.

Assurance of Pardon

Having faithfully confessed and renounced your sin, Christ also has been faithful to forgive your sins and to purify you from all unrighteousness. It is certain, that there is One who has spoken to the Father in your defense, Jesus Christ, the Righteous One who is the atoning sacrifice for our sins and for the sins of the whole world. His grace and peace are with you now. Amen.

Petitions and Supplications, Ending with The Lord's Prayer

Our Father which art in heaven, Hallowed be thy name. Thy kingdom come, Thy will be done in earth, as it is in heaven. Give us this day our daily bread. And forgive us our debts, as we forgive our debtors. And lead us not into temptation, but deliver us from evil: For thine is the kingdom, and the power, and the glory, for ever. Amen.

~ Matthew 6.9-13 (KJV)

Doxology (and/or closing song)

Praise God from whom all blessings flow;
Praise Him all creatures here below;
Praise Him above ye heavenly host;
Praise Father, Son and Holy Ghost. Amen.

Departing to Serve

Benediction

Lord Jesus, our dear Lord who suffered for us, you left us your own perfect example, so that we might follow in your steps. You committed no sin, and no deceit was found in your mouth. When you were reviled, you did not revile in return; when you suffered, you did not threaten, but continued entrusting yourself to the Father who judges justly. Make us like you, the kind of disciples who do not retaliate. Help us to love our enemies from the heart. In your name we pray, amen.

Affirmation from the Psalms

Teach me, O LORD, the way of your statutes; and I will keep it to the end. Give me understanding, that I may keep your law and observe it with my whole heart. Lead me in the path of your commandments, for I delight in it. Incline my heart to your testimonies, and not to selfish gain! Turn my eyes from looking at worthless things; and give me life in your ways.

~ Psalm 119.33-37

Pray without Ceasing – Flash Prayer for the Day

Dear gentle Savior, grant us that we may carry your light burden and wear your light yoke, in order that, in all things, we can express to others your lowliness and gentleness.

FOR YOUR WEEKLY JOURNEY

Let God Arise! Seasonal Focus

Listen to the Son, Matt. 17.1-9

Book Reading

DAILY: Extreme Devotion Writing Team, *Extreme Devotion*

Newell, *A Martyr's Grace*

Our Corporate Disciplines

Retreat, ending with Book Review:
Wednesday, February 26, 2014

Concert of Prayer:
Saturday, March 1, 2014

TRANSFIGURATION SUNDAY, LAST SUNDAY BEFORE LENT ✤

March 2 - 8, 2014

Epiphany affirms Jesus' presence in the world as hope for all peoples. In him alone, God provides the light of his salvation, making known God's grace to all peoples, even to the farthest corners of the earth.

THIS WEEK'S THEME
Listen to the Son, Matthew 17.1-9

On the occasion of our Lord's transfiguration, he took with himself Peter and James, and John his brother, and led them up a high mountain by themselves. While on top of that mountain, our Lord was transfigured before them – his face shone like the sun, and his clothes became white as light. Accompanying Jesus there were Moses and Elijah, talking with him. Overwhelmed by the entire experience, Peter requested to erect three tents – one for Jesus, one for Moses, and one for Elijah – there, on the mount.

While Peter was yet speaking, a bright cloud overshadowed them, and a voice from the cloud said, "This is my beloved Son, with whom I am well pleased; listen to him." Hearing this voice, the disciples fell on their faces with fear. Jesus, however, came, touched them, and told them to rise without fear. The disciples lifted their eyes up, and saw only Jesus, and no one else. On descending from the mount, Jesus commanded them to tell no one of this incident until he had risen from the dead.

We should respond in faith and obedience to the voice that called out on the mount: Jesus of Nazareth is the beloved Son of the Father, with whom he is well pleased. In all things, let us listen to him.

DAILY DEVOTIONAL GUIDE

PREPARING OUR HEARTS

Invocation: Our Prayer of Acclamation

O God, who in the glorious Transfiguration of Thine only-begotten Son hast confirmed the mysteries of the faith by the testimony of the fathers and who, in the voice that came from the bright cloud, didst in a wonderful manner foreshow the adoption of sons, mercifully vouchsafe to make us coheirs with the King of His glory, and bring us to the enjoyment of the same; through Jesus Christ, Thy Son, our Lord, who liveth and reigneth with Thee and the Holy Ghost, ever one God, world without end. Amen.

~ *The Common Service Book* (Lindemann, p. 184-185)

Call to Worship

Blessed are you, O God: Father, Son, and Holy Spirit. And blessed is your Kingdom, both now and forever, Amen.

PRAISING OUR GOD

Te Deum Laudamus

You are God: we praise you; you are the Lord; we acclaim you; you are the eternal Father: All creation worships you. To you all angels, all the powers of heaven, Cherubim and Seraphim, sing in endless praise: Holy, holy, holy Lord, God of power and might, heaven and earth are full of your glory.

The glorious company of apostles praise you. The noble fellowship of prophets praise you. The white-robed army of martyrs praise you. Throughout the world the holy Church acclaims you; Father, of majesty unbounded, your true and only Son, worthy of all worship, and the Holy Spirit, advocate and guide.

You, Christ, are the king of glory, the eternal Son of the Father. When you became man to set us free you did not shun the Virgin's womb.

You overcame the sting of death and opened the kingdom of heaven to all believers. You are seated at God's right hand in glory. We believe that you will come and be our judge. Come then, Lord, and help your people, bought with the price of your own blood, and bring us with your saints to glory everlasting.

Praise and Thanksgiving (Songs and Prayers)

Gloria Patri
Glory be to the Father,
And to the Son and to the Holy Spirit:
As it was in the beginning,
Is now, and ever shall be,
World without end. Amen, amen.

LISTENING TO HIS VOICE

Chronological Reading for the Day
Sunday: Judg. 7-9 ✤ *Monday:* Judg. 10-12 ✤ *Tuesday:* Judg. 13-15 ✤ *Wednesday:* Judg. 16-18 ✤ *Thursday:* Judg. 19-21 ✤ *Friday:* Ruth 1-4 ✤ *Saturday:* 1 Chron. 2.9-55; 4.1-23; 1 Sam. 1

Lectionary Readings
Psalm: Ps. 2   *OT:* Exod. 24.12-18
Gospel: Matt. 17.1-9   *NT:* 2 Pet. 1.16-21

Reflection: Silence and/or Journaling

RESPONDING IN FAITH

The Apostles' Creed
I believe in God, the Father Almighty, Maker of heaven and earth; and in Jesus Christ, his only Son, our Lord, who was conceived by the Holy Spirit, born of the Virgin Mary, suffered under Pontius Pilate, was crucified, dead, and buried; he descended into hell; the third day he arose again from the dead; he ascended into heaven and sits on

the right hand of God the Father Almighty; from thence he shall come to judge the quick and the dead.

I believe in the Holy Spirit, the holy catholic* church, the communion of saints, the forgiveness of sins, the resurrection of the body, and the life everlasting. Amen.

* In the Apostles' and Nicene Creeds, the term catholic refers to the Church's universality, through all ages and times, of all languages and peoples. It refers to no particular tradition or denominational expression (e.g., as in Roman Catholic).

Prayers of Confession
Let us now confess our sins to God and receive mercy and grace to help in our time of need.

Assurance of Pardon
Having faithfully confessed and renounced your sin, Christ also has been faithful to forgive your sins and to purify you from all unrighteousness. It is certain, that there is One who has spoken to the Father in your defense, Jesus Christ, the Righteous One who is the atoning sacrifice for our sins and for the sins of the whole world. His grace and peace are with you now. Amen.

Petitions and Supplications, Ending with The Lord's Prayer
Our Father which art in heaven, Hallowed be thy name. Thy kingdom come, Thy will be done in earth, as it is in heaven. Give us this day our daily bread. And forgive us our debts, as we forgive our debtors. And lead us not into temptation, but deliver us from evil: For thine is the kingdom, and the power, and the glory, for ever. Amen.

~ Matthew 6.9-13 (KJV)

Doxology (and/or closing song)
Praise God from whom all blessings flow;
Praise Him all creatures here below;
Praise Him above ye heavenly host;
Praise Father, Son and Holy Ghost. Amen.

Benediction

O GOD, who on the holy mount didst reveal to chosen witnesses thy well-beloved Son wonderfully transfigured: Mercifully grant unto us such a vision of his divine Majesty that we, being purified and strengthened by thy grace, may be transformed into his likeness from glory to glory; through the same thy Son Jesus Christ our Lord. Amen.

~ *Book of Common Prayer*, Canada (Suter, p. 57)

Affirmation from the Psalms

Ask of me, and I will make the nations your heritage, and the ends of the earth your possession. You shall break them with a rod of iron and dash them in pieces like a potter's vessel." Now therefore, O kings, be wise; be warned, O rulers of the earth. Serve the LORD with fear, and rejoice with trembling. Kiss the Son, lest he be angry, and you perish in the way, for his wrath is quickly kindled. Blessed are all who take refuge in him.

~ Psalm 2.8-12

Pray without Ceasing – Flash Prayer for the Day

Messiah who was transfigured on the mountain with his disciples, we hear afresh the voice of the One who called out in the cloud, declared you to be his beloved Son, in whom was all his delight. The voice commanded us to listen to you, and we do so. Be our Teacher and Rabbi, our Prophet and Lord, and lead us in your holy way through your living word which we hear through the promptings of your Holy Spirit. You are the Son, and we will listen to you. In your name we pray, amen.

FOR YOUR WEEKLY JOURNEY

Let God Arise! Seasonal Focus
Listen to the Son, Matt. 17.1-9

Book Reading
DAILY: Extreme Devotion Writing Team, *Extreme Devotion*

Newell, *A Martyr's Grace*

Special Church Year Service
Ash Wednesday: Wednesday, March 5, 2014

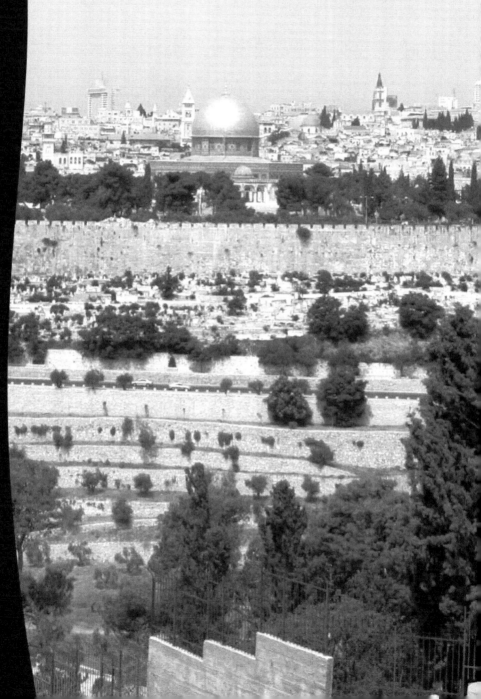
Jerusalem from the Mount of Olives

The Lenten season is that forty-day period of the Church Year which starts on *Ash Wednesday* and ends on Saturday of Holy Week. It calls the faithful community to reflect on Jesus' suffering, crucifixion, and death. Following our Lord in his preparation for his Passion, we prepare ourselves on the way of the Cross for full obedience to God. The season of Lent is, therefore, as one commentator put it, a season of "preparation, accompaniment, and journey." As followers of Jesus of Nazareth, the Church finds its life in his sacrifice on the Cross, his victory over evil, chaos, sin, and death, and his restoration of all things through his resurrection, his ascension, and soon return.

Beginning with the recognition of *Ash Wednesday*, we accompany our Lord on his journey to the Cross, humbling ourselves before him who gave his all for us in order that we might be set free from sin, Satan, and the grave. *Ash Wednesday* historically has been observed as a day of fasting and repentance that reminds us that as disciples our journey with Jesus ends with him at the Cross (Luke 9.51). *Ash Wednesday* begins the observance of Lent.

Welcoming New Converts, Restoring Backsliders, Strengthening Disciples: Lent in the Ancient Church

Modeling our spiritual passion after the candidates for baptism of the ancient church, so we too strive during our observance of the Lenten season to be faithful with Jesus on our way to the Cross and the Tomb. This is the heart of our participation and witness of the covenant of faith confirmed in our baptism. Even as Jesus died upon the Cross, so we too, by faith, have died with him to sin, and even as he lives forevermore, so too we live in newness of life (Rom. 6.4-6). In all phases of our personal and private worship, in our small groups, our congregational times, and all our disciplined seeking of the Lord, we acknowledge our Lord's lowliness, humiliation, and sacrifice on our behalf, and ask for his grace to become more like him in his death. Only through this humbling, this brokenness, and openness to his Spirit, can we as followers of Jesus come to fully know the freedom and life that he alone can provide.

In the ancient Church, this season was a dedicated time of preparation for those seeking baptism and incorporation into the Church. This was a season of profound soul-searching and preparation. In a striking display of allegiance to Christ and departure from worldliness, candidates for baptism experienced a formal service of exorcism, one final act of supreme separation from the world in preparation for their incorporation into the Church.

After undergoing an extended vigil on holy Saturday, all new converts were welcomed into the Church on Easter morning through their confession at baptism! The Lenten season, too, was a time to reclaim the penitent – it was a time when back-sliders who had returned to the Church were encouraged to join in these observances and ready themselves for a fresh start as re-committed disciples. Over time, the whole Church joined these converts and penitents in this season of readiness, with all believers affirming together their desire to flesh out in tangible and compelling ways their discipleship. Discipleship is not merely for those seeking baptism or to be restored after sin; rather, it is also for all who love the Lord Jesus and who strive to honor him in truth and deed. During this season, we all accompany these seekers and together follow the journey of our Lord as he traveled to the Tree where our redemption was won.

Through God's gracious act of God's revelation, Peter acknowledged Jesus of Nazareth as the Messiah and Son of the Living God. Immediately after this, the disciples

were warned to tell no one of this truth. It was then that
our Lord began to teach the disciples of his impending death,
and the resurrection to come. It was then that he challenged
them to take up their crosses and follow him. It was then
that he revealed God's full plan for his entering into sufferings
in order that he might be glorified later:

> *Luke 9.22-26 – saying, "The Son of Man must suffer many things
> and be rejected by the elders and chief priests and scribes, and be
> killed, and on the third day be raised." [23] And he said to all, "If
> anyone would come after me, let him deny himself and take up his
> cross daily and follow me. [24] For whoever would save his life will
> lose it, but whoever loses his life for my sake will save it. [25] For
> what does it profit a man if he gains the whole world and loses or
> forfeits himself? [26] For whoever is ashamed of me and of my
> words, of him will the Son of Man be ashamed when he comes in
> his glory and the glory of the Father and of the holy angels."*

Lent is our resounding "Yes!" to follow our Lord to the
Cross. During this season we take up our crosses and follow
him. This journey is recognized in different ways by different
traditions and churches. Using ashes made of the previous
year's palm leaves from *Palm Sunday* celebrations, many
congregations start the journey on *Ash Wednesday*, signifying
their commitment to brokenness with the mark of ashes on
their foreheads on that day. Others begin with special times
of discipline, reading, and practice of spiritual and ministry
disciplines to show their solidarity with all other believing
congregations who spiritually accompany our Lord to the
Cross once more during the Lenten season. However you
choose to begin your journey and recognize our Lord's
humility and availability, stay focused on the challenge and
blessing of identifying with our Lord in his death. Let your
tradition, context, and situation guide you as you explore
ways to tangibly demonstrate your identification with our
Lord and his people as they journey to Calvary.

Incorporating Believers into the Church
through Baptism: Following the Way of Jesus

Restoring the ancient Church's focus on preparation for incorporation into the Church through baptism can be a wonderful way to renew one's faith and discipleship. The *Revised Common Lectionary* readings emphasize this focus.

Placing the observance of Lent in its ancient and historical context enables us to see how significant this season of the Church Year was for penitents and new converts then, and for our spiritual formation now. This entire season was known as a time of preparation and readiness, climaxing for candidates for baptism in an Easter baptism and celebration of the Lord's Supper. Backsliders who had repented and were coming back to the Church used this season to reorient their lives under the lordship of Christ, and sought to forsake the world and its pollution, and be re-incorporated into the family of God. Through the teaching on the Creed, the cleansings and the rites, and the tutoring and training, the new converts and penitents prepared with the entire congregation for a new level of spiritual life and growth.

Truly, Lent was not merely a time of giving up a few delicacies or habits; rather, Lent became associated with a re-ordering of one's priorities and direction, all under the long-casting shadow of the Cross of Calvary. Jesus' story of submission and humility, then, is offered to us as our own personal journey of transformation as we prepare to die to ourselves in order to live anew with the risen Christ.

Walking the Way of the Cross:
Remembering the Passion of Jesus of Nazareth

The Lenten season, then, is a time for reflection on the suffering and death of Jesus. During this time we emphasize our own dying with him, and so, like Jesus, we must prepare ourselves to obey God no matter what sacrifice it involves.

Lenten observance calls for people to fast as a way of affirming this attitude of obedience (Luke 5.35; 1 Cor. 9.27; 2 Tim. 2.4; Heb. 11.1-3). Let us then humble ourselves, inviting one another to new levels of identifying with our Lord in his death through times of fasting, sacrifice, and prayer.

Some traditions challenge their members to engage in tangible acts of "self-denial," in order to visibly make oneself more open to God's leading. Others invite members, couples, and families to deny themselves of things which hinder or distract during this season, and to serve in ways that reflect obedience to God and love to neighbor. As those made free through the shed blood of Christ (Gal. 5.1), we ought to emphasize that, whatever our observances during the season of Lent, we are free in Christ to respond as he leads us. We ought neither to mandate nor insist that we fast during this season; such practice cannot be seen as an emblem of spiritual superiority or uniqueness.

On the contrary, Lenten observance has been viewed as a journey where the Christian community joins its candidates for baptism and reconciled believers in following Christ into a life of repentance and faith. Let us encourage and bless one another in all areas of our responses, and insist only that each follows that which the Holy Spirit has prompted them to do in solidarity with God's people.

However you may specifically reflect and respond to our Lord's suffering and death, let your meditation and practice individually and corporately affirm your participation in the humility of Christ, and your longing together to be one with him in his death and risen life.

~ Rev. Dr. Don L. Davis

ASH WEDNESDAY

March 5, 2014

The Lenten Season, a forty-day period starting on Ash Wednesday and ending on Holy Saturday of Holy Week, calls us to reflect on Jesus' suffering, crucifixion, and death. As disciples of the humble Nazarene, we embrace his lowliness and humility, seeking to share the mind of him who was obedient to death, even death on a cross.

TODAY'S THEME
Now Is the Favorable Time, 2 Corinthians 5.20b-6.10
Paul interprets to the Corinthians God's appeal to all humankind through the prophet Isaiah's call to Israel to both repent and persevere in light of the coming Day of God's visitation. Paul identifies our new covenant message of grace with this appeal, quoting Isaiah's call within the favorable time and the day of salvation. Rather than put off any decision regarding God's offer of grace and forgiveness, Paul challenges the Corinthians (and us) to realize that now, at this hour and in this place, is the favorable time of God's gracious offer and help. Let us start our Lenten journey by recognizing the opportune moment this is to open our hearts up to God in a new way, for a new working of his Spirit and move of his power.

DAILY DEVOTIONAL GUIDE

PREPARING OUR HEARTS

Invocation: Our Prayer of Acclamation
Almighty Father, Lord of heaven and earth, we confess that we have often sinned against Thee in thought, word, and deed. Have mercy upon us, O Lord; have mercy upon us, after Thy great goodness; according to the multitude of Thy mercies, put away our offences and cleanse us from our sins; through Jesus Christ Thy Son, our Lord. Amen.

~ Ps. 1i., adapted. (Fox, p. 39)

Call to Worship

Blessed are you, O God: Father, Son, and Holy Spirit. And blessed is your Kingdom, both now and forever, Amen.

PRAISING OUR GOD

Te Deum Laudamus

You are God: we praise you; you are the Lord; we acclaim you; you are the eternal Father: All creation worships you. To you all angels, all the powers of heaven, Cherubim and Seraphim, sing in endless praise: Holy, holy, holy Lord, God of power and might, heaven and earth are full of your glory.

The glorious company of apostles praise you. The noble fellowship of prophets praise you. The white-robed army of martyrs praise you. Throughout the world the holy Church acclaims you; Father, of majesty unbounded, your true and only Son, worthy of all worship, and the Holy Spirit, advocate and guide.

You, Christ, are the king of glory, the eternal Son of the Father. When you became man to set us free you did not shun the Virgin's womb. You overcame the sting of death and opened the kingdom of heaven to all believers. You are seated at God's right hand in glory. We believe that you will come and be our judge. Come then, Lord, and help your people, bought with the price of your own blood, and bring us with your saints to glory everlasting.

Praise and Thanksgiving (Songs and Prayers)

Gloria Patri

Glory be to the Father,
And to the Son and to the Holy Spirit:
As it was in the beginning,
Is now, and ever shall be,
World without end. Amen, amen.

LISTENING TO HIS VOICE

Chronological Reading for the Day
Judg. 16-18

Lectionary Readings

Psalm: Ps. 51.1-17   *OT:* Joel 2.1-2, 12-17
Gospel: Matt. 6.1-6, 16-21   *NT:* 2 Cor. 5.20b-6.10

Reflection: Silence and/or Journaling

RESPONDING IN FAITH

The Apostles' Creed
*I believe in God, the Father Almighty, Maker of heaven and earth;
and in Jesus Christ, his only Son, our Lord, who was conceived by the
Holy Spirit, born of the Virgin Mary, suffered under Pontius Pilate,
was crucified, dead, and buried; he descended into hell; the third day
he arose again from the dead; he ascended into heaven and sits on
the right hand of God the Father Almighty; from thence he shall come
to judge the quick and the dead.*

I believe in the Holy Spirit, the holy catholic church, the communion
of saints, the forgiveness of sins, the resurrection of the body, and the
life everlasting. Amen.*

* In the Apostles' and Nicene Creeds, the term catholic refers to the Church's
universality, through all ages and times, of all languages and peoples. It refers to no
particular tradition or denominational expression (e.g., as in Roman Catholic).

Prayers of Confession
Let us now confess our sins to God and receive mercy and
grace to help in our time of need.

Assurance of Pardon
Having faithfully confessed and renounced your sin, Christ
also has been faithful to forgive your sins and to purify you

from all unrighteousness. It is certain, that there is One who has spoken to the Father in your defense, Jesus Christ, the Righteous One who is the atoning sacrifice for our sins and for the sins of the whole world. His grace and peace are with you now. Amen.

Petitions and Supplications, Ending with The Lord's Prayer
Our Father which art in heaven, Hallowed be thy name. Thy kingdom come, Thy will be done in earth, as it is in heaven. Give us this day our daily bread. And forgive us our debts, as we forgive our debtors. And lead us not into temptation, but deliver us from evil: For thine is the kingdom, and the power, and the glory, for ever. Amen.

~ Matthew 6.9-13 (KJV)

Doxology (and/or closing song)
Praise God from whom all blessings flow;
Praise Him all creatures here below;
Praise Him above ye heavenly host;
Praise Father, Son and Holy Ghost. Amen.

DEPARTING TO SERVE

Benediction
O God, whose blessed Son did overcome death for our salvation: Mercifully grant that we, who have his glorious passion in remembrance, may take up our cross daily and follow him; through the same thy Son Jesus Christ our Lord.

~ *Book of English Collects*, No. 31 (Geffen, p. 78)

Affirmation from the Psalms
Have mercy on me, O God, according to your steadfast love; according to your abundant mercy blot out my transgressions. Wash me thoroughly from my iniquity, and cleanse me from my sin!

~ Psalm 51.1-2

Pray without Ceasing – Flash Prayer for the Day

Help me to realize, O God of all love and purpose, that now is the favorable time to respond to your grace, and today, this day, is the day of salvation.

FOR YOUR WEEKLY JOURNEY

Let God Arise! Seasonal Focus

That the Blind May See, John 9.1-41

Book Reading

DAILY: Extreme Devotion Writing Team, *Extreme Devotion*

DC Talk, The Voice of the Martyrs, *Jesus Freaks*

March 9 - 15, 2014

The Lenten Season, a forty-day period starting on Ash Wednesday and ending on Holy Saturday of Holy Week, calls us to reflect on Jesus' suffering, crucifixion, and death. As disciples of the humble Nazarene, we embrace his lowliness and humility, seeking to share the mind of him who was obedient to death, even death on a cross.

THIS WEEK'S THEME
It Is Written, Matthew 4.1-11

After the Lord Jesus was baptized by John in the Jordan river, the Spirit of God immediately led him into the desert (traditionally considered to be near the region of Jericho) to be tested by the devil. After fasting forty days, the Scripture testifies that our Lord became hungry, and at that moment of vulnerability and exhaustion, the temptations started. The tempter sought to undermine our Lord's trust in the Father by tempting him to turn stones into bread, to cast himself down from the pinnacle of the temple so angels could rescue him, and to bow down and worship him, the tempter, in exchange for possession of the world's kingdoms. In every case our Lord resisted the temptation, quoting God's Word and standing true to the Father. Our Lord's stamina and steadfastness reveals his heart for the Father, and serves as a pattern for us as we walk with him during our journey through the season of Lent (and life).

DAILY DEVOTIONAL GUIDE

PREPARING OUR HEARTS

Invocation: Our Prayer of Acclamation

Eternal God our Father, who sustained your Son during his fasting and temptations in the wilderness, reveal yourself to us today, and show us how through faith and perseverance we, like our Lord, can stand up for you in the midst of trial. Reproduce in us the humility, valor, and patience of the Savior, who through all trials honored you and learned obedience through the things he suffered. In his name we pray, amen.

Call to Worship

Blessed are you, O God: Father, Son, and Holy Spirit. And blessed is your Kingdom, both now and forever, Amen.

PRAISING OUR GOD

Te Deum Laudamus

You are God: we praise you; you are the Lord; we acclaim you; you are the eternal Father: All creation worships you. To you all angels, all the powers of heaven, Cherubim and Seraphim, sing in endless praise: Holy, holy, holy Lord, God of power and might, heaven and earth are full of your glory.

The glorious company of apostles praise you. The noble fellowship of prophets praise you. The white-robed army of martyrs praise you. Throughout the world the holy Church acclaims you; Father, of majesty unbounded, your true and only Son, worthy of all worship, and the Holy Spirit, advocate and guide.

You, Christ, are the king of glory, the eternal Son of the Father. When you became man to set us free you did not shun the Virgin's womb. You overcame the sting of death and opened the kingdom of heaven to all believers. You are seated at God's right hand in glory. We believe that you will come and be our judge. Come then, Lord, and help your people, bought with the price of your own blood, and bring us with your saints to glory everlasting.

Praise and Thanksgiving (Songs and Prayers)

Gloria Patri

Glory be to the Father,
And to the Son and to the Holy Spirit:
As it was in the beginning,
Is now, and ever shall be,
World without end. Amen, amen.

LISTENING TO HIS VOICE

Chronological Reading for the Day

Sunday: 1 Sam. 2-4 ✦ *Monday:* 1 Sam. 5-8 ✦ *Tuesday:*
1 Sam. 9-12 ✦ *Wednesday:* 1 Chron. 9.35-39; 1 Sam. 13-14
✦ *Thursday:* 1 Sam. 15-17 ✦ *Friday:* 1 Sam. 18-19; Ps. 59 ✦
Saturday: 1 Sam. 20-21; Ps. 34

Lectionary Readings

Psalm: Ps. 32   *OT:* Gen. 2.15-17; 3.1-7
Gospel: Matt. 4.1-11   *NT:* Rom. 5.12-19

Reflection: Silence and/or Journaling

RESPONDING IN FAITH

The Apostles' Creed

I believe in God, the Father Almighty, Maker of heaven and earth;
and in Jesus Christ, his only Son, our Lord, who was conceived by the
Holy Spirit, born of the Virgin Mary, suffered under Pontius Pilate,
was crucified, dead, and buried; he descended into hell; the third day
he arose again from the dead; he ascended into heaven and sits on
the right hand of God the Father Almighty; from thence he shall come
to judge the quick and the dead.

I believe in the Holy Spirit, the holy catholic* church, the communion
of saints, the forgiveness of sins, the resurrection of the body, and the
life everlasting. Amen.

* In the Apostles' and Nicene Creeds, the term catholic refers to the Church's universality, through all ages and times, of all languages and peoples. It refers to no particular tradition or denominational expression (e.g., as in Roman Catholic).

Prayers of Confession

Let us now confess our sins to God and receive mercy and grace to help in our time of need.

Assurance of Pardon

Having faithfully confessed and renounced your sin, Christ also has been faithful to forgive your sins and to purify you from all unrighteousness. It is certain, that there is One who has spoken to the Father in your defense, Jesus Christ, the Righteous One who is the atoning sacrifice for our sins and for the sins of the whole world. His grace and peace are with you now. Amen.

Petitions and Supplications, Ending with The Lord's Prayer

Our Father which art in heaven, Hallowed be thy name. Thy kingdom come, Thy will be done in earth, as it is in heaven. Give us this day our daily bread. And forgive us our debts, as we forgive our debtors. And lead us not into temptation, but deliver us from evil: For thine is the kingdom, and the power, and the glory, for ever. Amen.

~ Matthew 6.9-13 (KJV)

Doxology (and/or closing song)

Praise God from whom all blessings flow;
Praise Him all creatures here below;
Praise Him above ye heavenly host;
Praise Father, Son and Holy Ghost. Amen.

Departing to Serve

Benediction

Lord Jesus, who faithfully withstood the onslaught of lies and deception hurled at you by the tempter, now through your Spirit fortify our hearts in order that we, like you, can stand in the evil day, resist the lies and deception of the enemy, and glorify you as we walk with you in this sin-cursed, and soon-to-end world system. Be glorified in all we are and do, for your glory's sake. Amen.

Affirmation from the Psalms

For when I kept silent, my bones wasted away through my groaning all day long. For day and night your hand was heavy upon me; my strength was dried up as by the heat of summer. Selah. I acknowledged my sin to you, and I did not cover my iniquity; I said, "I will confess my transgressions to the LORD," and you forgave the iniquity of my sin. Selah. Therefore let everyone who is godly offer prayer to you at a time when you may be found; surely in the rush of great waters, they shall not reach him. You are a hiding place for me; you preserve me from trouble; you surround me with shouts of deliverance. Selah.

~ Psalm 32.3-7

Pray without Ceasing – Flash Prayer for the Day

Help us remember, Lord and King, that no temptation we face can overwhelm or overcome us if we cling to you in faith and simple obedience.

FOR YOUR WEEKLY JOURNEY

Let God Arise! Seasonal Focus
That the Blind May See, John 9.1-41

Book Reading
DAILY: Extreme Devotion Writing Team, *Extreme Devotion*

DC Talk, The Voice of the Martyrs, *Jesus Freaks*

✤

SECOND SUNDAY IN LENT

March 16 - 22, 2014

The Lenten Season, a forty-day period starting on Ash Wednesday and ending on Holy Saturday of Holy Week, calls us to reflect on Jesus' suffering, crucifixion, and death. As disciples of the humble Nazarene, we embrace his lowliness and humility, seeking to share the mind of him who was obedient to death, even death on a cross.

THIS WEEK'S THEME
You Must Be Born Again, John 3.1-17
One of the teachers of Israel, Nicodemus, both a Pharisee and member of the Jewish Council, the Sanhedrin, came to Jesus at night. Jesus proclaimed to him that unless one is born again they can neither see nor enter the Kingdom of God. Nicodemus was puzzled, asking whether one who is old cannot enter into the womb a second time to be born. Jesus again asserted that unless one is born of the water and the Holy Spirit they cannot enter the Kingdom of God. Only the Spirit can redeem us.

Jesus further assured Nicodemus that God's motivation in sending him down from heaven was a demonstration of his great love. In fact, he loved us so much he offered his only Son as a ransom for the world. Everyone who believes will never perish, but inherit eternal life. Jesus assured Nicodemus that his mission was not to judge the world, but rather, to save it through God's expression of love.

DAILY DEVOTIONAL GUIDE

PREPARING OUR HEARTS

Invocation: Our Prayer of Acclamation
Great God and Creator of all things, Father of our Lord Jesus Christ, help us to see that our own human strivings and religious efforts can never please you or make us acceptable

in your sight. Reveal to us the true meaning of the Lord's teaching, that we must be born again, truly born from above, in order to become your child, to be saved from the penalty of our sin, and to be redeemed and reconciled to you. We trust in your Son, Jesus Christ, and look to him as our life and light. In his name we pray, amen.

Call to Worship
Blessed are you, O God: Father, Son, and Holy Spirit. And blessed is your Kingdom, both now and forever, Amen.

PRAISING OUR GOD

Te Deum Laudamus
You are God: we praise you; you are the Lord; we acclaim you; you are the eternal Father: All creation worships you. To you all angels, all the powers of heaven, Cherubim and Seraphim, sing in endless praise: Holy, holy, holy Lord, God of power and might, heaven and earth are full of your glory.

The glorious company of apostles praise you. The noble fellowship of prophets praise you. The white-robed army of martyrs praise you. Throughout the world the holy Church acclaims you; Father, of majesty unbounded, your true and only Son, worthy of all worship, and the Holy Spirit, advocate and guide.

You, Christ, are the king of glory, the eternal Son of the Father. When you became man to set us free you did not shun the Virgin's womb. You overcame the sting of death and opened the kingdom of heaven to all believers. You are seated at God's right hand in glory. We believe that you will come and be our judge. Come then, Lord, and help your people, bought with the price of your own blood, and bring us with your saints to glory everlasting.

Praise and Thanksgiving (Songs and Prayers)

Gloria Patri
Glory be to the Father,
And to the Son and to the Holy Spirit:
As it was in the beginning,
Is now, and ever shall be,
World without end. Amen, amen.

LISTENING TO HIS VOICE

Chronological Reading for the Day
Sunday: 1 Sam. 22-23; Pss. 52; 57; 142; 1 Chron. 12.8-18 ✦
Monday: 1 Sam. 24-25; Ps. 54 ✦ *Tuesday:* 1 Sam. 26-29;
1 Chron. 12.1-7, v.19; Ps. 56 ✦ *Wednesday:* 1 Sam. 30-31;
1 Chron. 9.40-10.14; 12.20-22; 2 Sam. 1 ✦ *Thursday:*
2 Sam. 2.1-3.5; 23.8-39; 1 Chron. 3.1-4a; 11.10-47 ✦
Friday: 2 Sam. 3.6-4.12 ✦ *Saturday:* 2 Sam. 5.1-13, vv.17-25;
6.1-11; 1 Chron. 3.4b; 11.1-9; 12.23-14.2; 14.8-17

Lectionary Readings
Psalm: Ps. 121 *OT:* Gen. 12.1-4a
Gospel: John 3.1-17 *NT:* Rom. 4.1-5, 13-17

Reflection: Silence and/or Journaling

RESPONDING IN FAITH

The Apostles' Creed
I believe in God, the Father Almighty, Maker of heaven and earth; and in Jesus Christ, his only Son, our Lord, who was conceived by the Holy Spirit, born of the Virgin Mary, suffered under Pontius Pilate, was crucified, dead, and buried; he descended into hell; the third day he arose again from the dead; he ascended into heaven and sits on the right hand of God the Father Almighty; from thence he shall come to judge the quick and the dead.

I believe in the Holy Spirit, the holy catholic* church, the communion of saints, the forgiveness of sins, the resurrection of the body, and the life everlasting. Amen.

* In the Apostles' and Nicene Creeds, the term catholic refers to the Church's universality, through all ages and times, of all languages and peoples. It refers to no particular tradition or denominational expression (e.g., as in Roman Catholic).

Prayers of Confession
Let us now confess our sins to God and receive mercy and grace to help in our time of need.

Assurance of Pardon
Having faithfully confessed and renounced your sin, Christ also has been faithful to forgive your sins and to purify you from all unrighteousness. It is certain, that there is One who has spoken to the Father in your defense, Jesus Christ, the Righteous One who is the atoning sacrifice for our sins and for the sins of the whole world. His grace and peace are with you now. Amen.

Petitions and Supplications, Ending with The Lord's Prayer
Our Father which art in heaven, Hallowed be thy name. Thy kingdom come, Thy will be done in earth, as it is in heaven. Give us this day our daily bread. And forgive us our debts, as we forgive our debtors. And lead us not into temptation, but deliver us from evil: For thine is the kingdom, and the power, and the glory, for ever. Amen.

~ Matthew 6.9-13 (KJV)

Doxology (and/or closing song)
Praise God from whom all blessings flow;
Praise Him all creatures here below;
Praise Him above ye heavenly host;
Praise Father, Son and Holy Ghost. Amen.

DEPARTING TO SERVE

Benediction

Thank you, Lord Most High, that you have redeemed us by faith in your Son, the Lord Jesus Christ, and have born us anew. We now have a new nature, a new future, and a new management. Grant us a desire to live true to that new nature, and live as your very own children in the midst of this lost and declining world. We are yours by faith in your only Son. In his name we pray, amen.

Affirmation from the Psalms

I lift up my eyes to the hills. From where does my help come? My help comes from the Lord, who made heaven and earth. He will not let your foot be moved; he who keeps you will not slumber. Behold, he who keeps Israel will neither slumber nor sleep.

~ Psalm 121.1-4

Pray without Ceasing – Flash Prayer for the Day

Thank you, Father, that you have born us again by a living hope through faith in the Lord Jesus Christ. In him we are no longer sons of disobedience, but children of Abraham by faith in him.

FOR YOUR WEEKLY JOURNEY

Let God Arise! Seasonal Focus
That the Blind May See, John 9.1-41

Book Reading
DAILY: Extreme Devotion Writing Team, *Extreme Devotion*

DC Talk, The Voice of the Martyrs, *Jesus Freaks*

Our Corporate Disciplines
Solitude and Silence, ending with Book Review:
    Wednesday, March 19, 2014

✤

THIRD SUNDAY IN LENT

March 23 - 29, 2014

The Lenten Season, a forty-day period starting on Ash Wednesday and ending on Holy Saturday of Holy Week, calls us to reflect on Jesus' suffering, crucifixion, and death. As disciples of the humble Nazarene, we embrace his lowliness and humility, seeking to share the mind of him who was obedient to death, even death on a cross.

THIS WEEK'S THEME
Water from the Rock, Exodus 17.1-7

After the people of Israel moved on from the wilderness of Sin by stages, according to God's commandment, they settled at Rephidim. The people found no water there to drink, and they subsequently quarreled with Moses. Frustrated and angry, they demanded water, and grumbled against Moses for even taking them out of Egypt. Incredibly, they actually accused the LORD and Moses of leading them out of Egypt for the purpose of killing them, their children, and their livestock through thirst. Moses cried to the LORD, and the LORD commanded him to stand before the rock at Horeb with his staff, and when he struck the rock water would come out of it, and the people would drink. It occurred just as the Lord said, and so God provided for his people yet another time on their journey. Moses called the place by two names: Massah ("testing") and Meribah ("quarreling"), for the people never seemed to trust the Lord, in spite of his many rescues and miracles of supply on their account.

DAILY DEVOTIONAL GUIDE

PREPARING OUR HEARTS

Invocation: Our Prayer of Acclamation

Great God and Father, the same God who supplied his people with water from the Rock at Horeb, teach us to depend on your grace and mercy, especially in the midst of a dry and thirsty land (time). Teach us to be grateful, to neither grumble nor quarrel with your timing and method, but rather to wait patiently on you as you lead us. You will supply us with all we need to accomplish your will, till the end. In Jesus' name, amen.

Call to Worship
Blessed are you, O God: Father, Son, and Holy Spirit. And blessed is your Kingdom, both now and forever, Amen.

PRAISING OUR GOD

Te Deum Laudamus
You are God: we praise you; you are the Lord; we acclaim you; you are the eternal Father: All creation worships you. To you all angels, all the powers of heaven, Cherubim and Seraphim, sing in endless praise: Holy, holy, holy Lord, God of power and might, heaven and earth are full of your glory.

The glorious company of apostles praise you. The noble fellowship of prophets praise you. The white-robed army of martyrs praise you. Throughout the world the holy Church acclaims you; Father, of majesty unbounded, your true and only Son, worthy of all worship, and the Holy Spirit, advocate and guide.

You, Christ, are the king of glory, the eternal Son of the Father. When you became man to set us free you did not shun the Virgin's womb. You overcame the sting of death and opened the kingdom of heaven to all believers. You are seated at God's right hand in glory. We believe that you will come and be our judge. Come then, Lord, and help your people, bought with the price of your own blood, and bring us with your saints to glory everlasting.

Praise and Thanksgiving (Songs and Prayers)

Gloria Patri
Glory be to the Father,
And to the Son and to the Holy Spirit:
As it was in the beginning,
Is now, and ever shall be,
World without end. Amen, amen.

LISTENING TO HIS VOICE

Chronological Reading for the Day
Sunday: 2 Sam. 6.12-23; 1 Chron. 15-16 ✢ *Monday:* 2 Sam.
7-8; 1 Chron. 17-18; Ps. 60 ✢ *Tuesday:* 2 Sam. 9-10; 1 Chron.
6.16-48, vv.50-53; ch.19 ✢ *Wednesday:* 1 Chron. 3.5-9;
14.3-7; 20.1-3; 2 Sam. 11.1-12.25; 5.14-16; Ps. 51 ✢
Thursday: 2 Sam. 12.26-14.33 ✢ *Friday:* 2 Sam. 15-17 ✢
Saturday: 2 Sam. 18-19; Pss. 3; 63

Lectionary Readings

Psalm: Ps. 95   *OT:* Exod. 17.1-7
Gospel: John 4.5-42   *NT:* Rom. 5.1-11

Reflection: Silence and/or Journaling

RESPONDING IN FAITH

The Apostles' Creed
I believe in God, the Father Almighty, Maker of heaven and earth;
and in Jesus Christ, his only Son, our Lord, who was conceived by the
Holy Spirit, born of the Virgin Mary, suffered under Pontius Pilate,
was crucified, dead, and buried; he descended into hell; the third day
he arose again from the dead; he ascended into heaven and sits on
the right hand of God the Father Almighty; from thence he shall come
to judge the quick and the dead.

I believe in the Holy Spirit, the holy catholic* church, the communion
of saints, the forgiveness of sins, the resurrection of the body, and the
life everlasting. Amen.

* In the Apostles' and Nicene Creeds, the term catholic refers to the Church's universality, through all ages and times, of all languages and peoples. It refers to no particular tradition or denominational expression (e.g., as in Roman Catholic).

Prayers of Confession

Let us now confess our sins to God and receive mercy and grace to help in our time of need.

Assurance of Pardon

Having faithfully confessed and renounced your sin, Christ also has been faithful to forgive your sins and to purify you from all unrighteousness. It is certain, that there is One who has spoken to the Father in your defense, Jesus Christ, the Righteous One who is the atoning sacrifice for our sins and for the sins of the whole world. His grace and peace are with you now. Amen.

Petitions and Supplications, Ending with The Lord's Prayer

Our Father which art in heaven, Hallowed be thy name. Thy kingdom come, Thy will be done in earth, as it is in heaven. Give us this day our daily bread. And forgive us our debts, as we forgive our debtors. And lead us not into temptation, but deliver us from evil: For thine is the kingdom, and the power, and the glory, for ever. Amen.

~ Matthew 6.9-13 (KJV)

Doxology (and/or closing song)

Praise God from whom all blessings flow;
Praise Him all creatures here below;
Praise Him above ye heavenly host;
Praise Father, Son and Holy Ghost. Amen.

DEPARTING TO SERVE

Benediction

Eternal God, whose name is Jehovah-jireh, enable us to rely on your mercy and grace, and to trust your hand of provision while we journey through this life. Forgive us for the many times we have failed to trust you, those times when we grumbled at your provision and quarreled with your leaders. Teach us to quietly and confidently rest in you, looking to your hand to supply our need, and to wait patiently until you reveal your will to us. You are our Source and life. In Jesus' name, amen.

Affirmation from the Psalms
Oh come, let us sing to the LORD; let us make a joyful noise to the rock of our salvation! Let us come into his presence with thanksgiving; let us make a joyful noise to him with songs of praise! For the LORD is a great God, and a great King above all gods.

~ Psalm 95.1-3

Pray without Ceasing – Flash Prayer for the Day
Dear Savior, enable us to rely on your provision, to trust you both in your methods and timing, and to never doubt, regardless of how things may appear to us.

FOR YOUR WEEKLY JOURNEY

Let God Arise! Seasonal Focus
That the Blind May See, John 9.1-41

Book Reading
DAILY: Extreme Devotion Writing Team, *Extreme Devotion*

DC Talk, The Voice of the Martyrs, *Jesus Freaks*

March 30 - April 5, 2014

The Lenten Season, a forty-day period starting on Ash Wednesday and ending on Holy Saturday of Holy Week, calls us to reflect on Jesus' suffering, crucifixion, and death. As disciples of the humble Nazarene, we embrace his lowliness and humility, seeking to share the mind of him who was obedient to death, even death on a cross.

THIS WEEK'S THEME
That the Blind May See, John 9.1-41

Having taught his disciples he was truly the light of the world, Jesus passed a man who had been blind from birth, and, after making mud pies with his spittle and rubbing them on the blind man's eyes, he commanded him to go to the pool of Siloam and wash. The man returned seeing, providing a clear sign that Jesus indeed is the light of the world. The Pharisees accused the healing to be illegitimate, since it occurred on the Sabbath, and questioned the man.

Although the blind man could not testify of Jesus' origins and identity, he did testify that he indeed had been born blind, that now he could see. He asserted that Jesus could do nothing if he had not been of God. Incensed at the bravado of the man healed from his blindness, the Pharisees cast him out of their presence, and presumably, out of the synagogue.

Jesus condemned the Pharisees, accusing them of claiming to see but actually being blind. Being both blind and unwilling to submit to him as the light of the world, they would tragically remain in their blindness. Their condition was far worse than those who were blind, and yet admitted their blindness. Jesus came that those who are blind might be given sight again, and those claiming to see, might remain in their state of spiritual blindness.

DAILY DEVOTIONAL GUIDE

PREPARING OUR HEARTS

Invocation: Our Prayer of Acclamation

God of all creation, who made the eyes and ears of humankind, cause us who have been blinded by sin to see the light through the gift you have given to us through the Lord Jesus Christ. In him, we who have been born spiritually blind can see again, and we who have walked our whole lives in darkness may receive the light of life. Shine through us today. In Jesus' name we pray, amen.

Call to Worship

Blessed are you, O God: Father, Son, and Holy Spirit. And blessed is your Kingdom, both now and forever, Amen.

PRAISING OUR GOD

Te Deum Laudamus

You are God: we praise you; you are the Lord; we acclaim you; you are the eternal Father: All creation worships you. To you all angels, all the powers of heaven, Cherubim and Seraphim, sing in endless praise: Holy, holy, holy Lord, God of power and might, heaven and earth are full of your glory.

The glorious company of apostles praise you. The noble fellowship of prophets praise you. The white-robed army of martyrs praise you. Throughout the world the holy Church acclaims you; Father, of majesty unbounded, your true and only Son, worthy of all worship, and the Holy Spirit, advocate and guide.

You, Christ, are the king of glory, the eternal Son of the Father. When you became man to set us free you did not shun the Virgin's womb. You overcame the sting of death and opened the kingdom of heaven to all believers. You are seated at God's right hand in glory. We believe that you will come and be our judge. Come then, Lord, and help your

people, bought with the price of your own blood, and bring us with your saints to glory everlasting.

Praise and Thanksgiving (Songs and Prayers)

Gloria Patri
Glory be to the Father,
And to the Son and to the Holy Spirit:
As it was in the beginning,
Is now, and ever shall be,
World without end. Amen, amen.

LISTENING TO HIS VOICE

Chronological Reading for the Day
Sunday: 2 Sam. 20-21; Ps. 7; 1 Chron. 20.4-8 ✠ *Monday:* 2 Sam. 22; Ps. 18 ✠ *Tuesday:* 2 Sam. 24; 1 Chron. 21-22 ✠ *Wednesday:* 1 Chron. 23-25 ✠ *Thursday:* 1 Chron. 26-28 ✠ *Friday:* 1 Chron. 29.1-22; 1 Kings 1 ✠ *Saturday:* 1 Kings 2.1-12; 2 Sam. 23.1-7; 1 Chron. 29.26-30; Pss. 4-6; 8; 9; 11

Lectionary Readings
Psalm: Ps. 23   *OT:* 1 Sam. 16.1-13
Gospel: John 9.1-41   *NT:* Eph. 5.8-14

Reflection: Silence and/or Journaling

RESPONDING IN FAITH

The Apostles' Creed
I believe in God, the Father Almighty, Maker of heaven and earth; and in Jesus Christ, his only Son, our Lord, who was conceived by the Holy Spirit, born of the Virgin Mary, suffered under Pontius Pilate, was crucified, dead, and buried; he descended into hell; the third day he arose again from the dead; he ascended into heaven and sits on the right hand of God the Father Almighty; from thence he shall come to judge the quick and the dead.

I believe in the Holy Spirit, the holy catholic* church, the communion of saints, the forgiveness of sins, the resurrection of the body, and the life everlasting. Amen.

* In the Apostles' and Nicene Creeds, the term catholic refers to the Church's universality, through all ages and times, of all languages and peoples. It refers to no particular tradition or denominational expression (e.g., as in Roman Catholic).

Prayers of Confession
Let us now confess our sins to God and receive mercy and grace to help in our time of need.

Assurance of Pardon
Having faithfully confessed and renounced your sin, Christ also has been faithful to forgive your sins and to purify you from all unrighteousness. It is certain, that there is One who has spoken to the Father in your defense, Jesus Christ, the Righteous One who is the atoning sacrifice for our sins and for the sins of the whole world. His grace and peace are with you now. Amen.

Petitions and Supplications, Ending with The Lord's Prayer
Our Father which art in heaven, Hallowed be thy name. Thy kingdom come, Thy will be done in earth, as it is in heaven. Give us this day our daily bread. And forgive us our debts, as we forgive our debtors. And lead us not into temptation, but deliver us from evil: For thine is the kingdom, and the power, and the glory, for ever. Amen.

~ Matthew 6.9-13 (KJV)

Doxology (and/or closing song)
Praise God from whom all blessings flow;
Praise Him all creatures here below;
Praise Him above ye heavenly host;
Praise Father, Son and Holy Ghost. Amen.

DEPARTING TO SERVE

Benediction

Lord Jesus Christ, Lord and King of all creation, thank you for proclaiming yourself to be the light of the world. We have come to know and believe that you are the light of life. Now, through your Holy Spirit, cause our spiritual eyes to be blessed with wisdom and revelation that we can come to understand all things, as it were, from your point of view. Only in your light can we see light, and only by your grace can we see. Thank you for giving us back our spiritual sight. We love you and praise you. In your name we pray, amen.

Affirmation from the Psalms

The LORD is my shepherd; I shall not want. He makes me lie down in green pastures. He leads me beside still waters. He restores my soul. He leads me in paths of righteousness for his name's sake. Even though I walk through the valley of the shadow of death, I will fear no evil, for you are with me; your rod and your staff, they comfort me. You prepare a table before me in the presence of my enemies; you anoint my head with oil; my cup overflows. Surely goodness and mercy shall follow me all the days of my life, and I shall dwell in the house of the LORD forever.

~ Psalm 23.1-6

Pray without Ceasing – Flash Prayer for the Day

Dear Lord Jesus, who came that the blind might see, and those who claim to see might be made blind, open our eyes that we may behold all things through your eyes of truth.

FOR YOUR WEEKLY JOURNEY

Let God Arise! Seasonal Focus
That the Blind May See, John 9.1-41

Book Reading
DAILY: Extreme Devotion Writing Team, *Extreme Devotion*

DC Talk, The Voice of the Martyrs, *Jesus Freaks*

April 6 - 12, 2014

The Lenten Season, a forty-day period starting on Ash Wednesday and ending on Holy Saturday of Holy Week, calls us to reflect on Jesus' suffering, crucifixion, and death. As disciples of the humble Nazarene, we embrace his lowliness and humility, seeking to share the mind of him who was obedient to death, even death on a cross.

THIS WEEK'S THEME
That the Doubting May Believe, Romans 8.6-11

Paul instructed the Roman Christians concerning the power of the mind, and what it happens to settle itself upon. He said that to set the mind on the flesh would bring death, but to set the mind on the Spirit would be both life and peace. Anyone who sets his mind on the flesh is in hostility with God, since a fleshly mind neither submits to God's law, nor is it able to do so. Those who live according to their fleshly nature simply cannot please God.

On the other hand, Paul said that if we are in the Spirit we are not in the flesh, for the Spirit of God indwells us. If we do not have God's Spirit, we do not belong to Christ. And, if Christ indwells us by his Spirit, our body has been rendered dead to sin, and now the Holy Spirit leads us into life because of righteousness. Because the Spirit of God dwells in us, the same Spirit which raised Jesus from the dead, he will also give life to our mortal bodies – we will be raised to life by the same Spirit that lives in us.

DAILY DEVOTIONAL GUIDE

PREPARING OUR HEARTS

Invocation: Our Prayer of Acclamation

Holy Spirit of God, Lord and Life-giver, he who indwells all who believe by faith in the Lord Jesus, fill us and complete us in the will of God. Reveal the things of Christ to us, and conform our will to his holy pattern that in all things we may glorify the Father. We yield ourselves to you in order that your power and life might be seen in us and through us, for Christ's sake. Amen.

Call to Worship
Blessed are you, O God: Father, Son, and Holy Spirit. And blessed is your Kingdom, both now and forever, Amen.

PRAISING OUR GOD

Te Deum Laudamus
You are God: we praise you; you are the Lord; we acclaim you; you are the eternal Father: All creation worships you. To you all angels, all the powers of heaven, Cherubim and Seraphim, sing in endless praise: Holy, holy, holy Lord, God of power and might, heaven and earth are full of your glory.

The glorious company of apostles praise you. The noble fellowship of prophets praise you. The white-robed army of martyrs praise you. Throughout the world the holy Church acclaims you; Father, of majesty unbounded, your true and only Son, worthy of all worship, and the Holy Spirit, advocate and guide.

You, Christ, are the king of glory, the eternal Son of the Father. When you became man to set us free you did not shun the Virgin's womb. You overcame the sting of death and opened the kingdom of heaven to all believers. You are seated at God's right hand in glory. We believe that you will come and be our judge. Come then, Lord, and help your people, bought with the price of your own blood, and bring us with your saints to glory everlasting.

Praise and Thanksgiving (Songs and Prayers)

Gloria Patri
Glory be to the Father,
And to the Son and to the Holy Spirit:
As it was in the beginning,
Is now, and ever shall be,
World without end. Amen, amen.

LISTENING TO HIS VOICE

Chronological Reading for the Day
Sunday: Pss. 12-17; 19-21 ✠ *Monday:* Pss. 22-26 ✠ *Tuesday:* Pss. 27-32 ✠ *Wednesday:* Pss. 35-38 ✠ *Thursday:* Pss. 39-41; 53; 55; 58 ✠ *Friday:* Pss. 61-62; 64-67 ✠ *Saturday:* Pss. 68-70; 86; 101

Chronological Holy Week Readings
Saturday: Matt. 26.6-13; Mark 14.3-9; John 12.1-8

Lectionary Readings
Psalm: Ps. 130   *OT:* Ezek. 37.1-14
Gospel: John 11.1-45   *NT:* Rom. 8.6-11

Reflection: Silence and/or Journaling

RESPONDING IN FAITH

The Apostles' Creed
I believe in God, the Father Almighty, Maker of heaven and earth;
and in Jesus Christ, his only Son, our Lord, who was conceived by the
Holy Spirit, born of the Virgin Mary, suffered under Pontius Pilate,
was crucified, dead, and buried; he descended into hell; the third day
he arose again from the dead; he ascended into heaven and sits on
the right hand of God the Father Almighty; from thence he shall come
to judge the quick and the dead.

I believe in the Holy Spirit, the holy catholic* church, the communion of saints, the forgiveness of sins, the resurrection of the body, and the life everlasting. Amen.

* In the Apostles' and Nicene Creeds, the term catholic refers to the Church's universality, through all ages and times, of all languages and peoples. It refers to no particular tradition or denominational expression (e.g., as in Roman Catholic).

Prayers of Confession

Let us now confess our sins to God and receive mercy and grace to help in our time of need.

Assurance of Pardon

Having faithfully confessed and renounced your sin, Christ also has been faithful to forgive your sins and to purify you from all unrighteousness. It is certain, that there is One who has spoken to the Father in your defense, Jesus Christ, the Righteous One who is the atoning sacrifice for our sins and for the sins of the whole world. His grace and peace are with you now. Amen.

Petitions and Supplications, Ending with The Lord's Prayer

Our Father which art in heaven, Hallowed be thy name. Thy kingdom come, Thy will be done in earth, as it is in heaven. Give us this day our daily bread. And forgive us our debts, as we forgive our debtors. And lead us not into temptation, but deliver us from evil: For thine is the kingdom, and the power, and the glory, for ever. Amen.

~ Matthew 6.9-13 (KJV)

Doxology (and/or closing song)

Praise God from whom all blessings flow;
Praise Him all creatures here below;
Praise Him above ye heavenly host;
Praise Father, Son and Holy Ghost. Amen.

DEPARTING TO SERVE

Benediction

Thank you heavenly Father, giver of the Holy Spirit, for sending down to us the gift of your indwelling Spirit. We now know that by faith you have come and indwelt us, that we are not alone, that all we need for life and godliness you have provided for us in your Spirit. Make us like Christ, and conform our lives to his, in every way, shape, and form. We want to be like him, and to accomplish your will in all things, just as he did. We wait on you alone. In Jesus' name we pray, amen.

Affirmation from the Psalms

Out of the depths I cry to you, O LORD! O Lord, hear my voice! Let your ears be attentive to the voice of my pleas for mercy! If you, O LORD, should mark iniquities, O Lord, who could stand? But with you there is forgiveness, that you may be feared. I wait for the LORD, my soul waits, and in his word I hope; my soul waits for the Lord more than watchmen for the morning, more than watchmen for the morning.

~ Psalm 130.1-6

Pray without Ceasing – Flash Prayer for the Day

Come, Holy Spirit, and show us the way to the Father's heart. Reproduce in us the life of Jesus, that all may see our works come from you alone.

FOR YOUR WEEKLY JOURNEY

Let God Arise! Seasonal Focus
That the Blind May See, John 9.1-41

Book Reading
DAILY: Extreme Devotion Writing Team, *Extreme Devotion*

DC Talk, The Voice of the Martyrs, *Jesus Freaks*

Our Corporate Disciplines
In-Service, ending with Book Review:
    Wednesday, April 9, 2014

Supposed site of the Garden of Gethsemane

Holy Week: Sharing His Death to Rise with Him

**Palms of Welcome, the Passion of Suffering,
the Pain of Crucifixion, and the Power of Resurrection**
For believers, Christ crucified is both the power and wisdom
of God. This is the period where followers of Jesus enter the
high point of our spiritual formation in observance of the
Church Year: our participation by faith in the Passion of our
Lord.

Holy Week is the last week of the Lenten season. Beginning
with our *Palm Sunday Celebration*, and through the various
activities of the week, we join with believers worldwide to
recall and be transformed by the story of Jesus of Nazareth –
his trial, suffering, and death which occurred so many
centuries ago in Jerusalem. The three days at the end of this
week represent the most serious and solemn days of the
Church calendar, focusing as they do on the events of Jesus'
final hours before his death on the Cross.

> *In the ancient church the three days [of the Paschal Triduum]
> started on Thursday evening and ended with the great Paschal
> vigil of Saturday night. These services are called the Paschal
> Triduum [or, the Three Great Days] . . . They are the most holy,
> solemn, and serious days of the entire year. For in these days we
> experience and encounter our own destiny in the destiny of
> Christ's ignominious death and burial and in his triumphant
> resurrection from the dead.*
>
> ~ Robert Webber. *Ancient Future Time.*
> Grand Rapids: Baker Books, 2004, p. 125.

During Holy Week we recall the events of our Lord's trial,
suffering, and death. We ponder with joy and anticipation his

triumphant entry into Jerusalem on *Palm Sunday*, listen to his matchless teaching through the week, and huddle with his disciples in the Upper Room as he gives the new commandment of love on *Maundy Thursday*. We hang our heads in shame and regret as we recall his crucifixion on *Good Friday*, and finally we end the week with the solemn vigil of Saturday night before *Easter Sunday*.

Holy Week Observances
Below is a short description of some of the highlights we observe and celebrate during this upcoming week:

> *Palm Sunday*
> The Sunday before Easter which commemorates the Triumphal Entry of Jesus of Nazareth into Jerusalem, his public proclamation of his identity as Messiah and Lord (John 12.12-18).

> *Maundy Thursday*
> The Thursday before Easter which commemorates the giving of the New Commandment and the Lord's Supper prior to Christ's Death (Mark 14.12-26; John 13). [From the Latin mandatum novarum which means "new commandment" (John 13.34)]

> *Good Friday*
> The Friday before Easter which commemorates the crucifixion of Christ (John 18-19).

> *Holy Saturday*
> The day before Easter which commemorates the burial of Jesus before his resurrection on Sunday (John 18-19).

Again, *Holy Week* is Lent's final week. As a season, Lent starts on *Ash Wednesday* and ends Saturday of Holy Week, with the vigil on *Holy Saturday*. As a time of soul-searching and preparation in the ancient Church, so today we ought to let this week be our own personal journey to the Cross, spending time reflecting on the lowliness and humiliation of our Lord. Here we clearly see the meaning of our baptism in Christ – being united with him in his suffering, death, burial, and resurrection from the dead.

When We Survey the Wondrous Cross:
Pondering the Passion of Jesus Christ
During Holy Week we invite you to join with us and the millions of disciples of Jesus worldwide who will remember and seek to be transformed by a fresh experience of the meaning of Jesus' suffering and death on the Cross. For those who believe, he is the slain Lamb of God who takes the world's sin away (John 1.29), our glorious Conqueror who leads us in his triumph (2 Cor. 2.14), and the scorned Messiah who bore the curse for us on the Tree (Gal. 3.13). We seek to die daily with him in order that his life might be manifested in us (2 Cor. 4.10-11). He is Lord of all.

Come with us, and kneel at the Cross of him who alone can transform the lives of the millions languishing in oppression and poverty in the inner cities of America. He bids you to come.

~ A fellow traveler on the way,
Rev. Dr. Don L. Davis

WEEK
20

✠

PALM SUNDAY, SIXTH SUNDAY IN LENT

April 13 - 19, 2014

Holy Week recalls the events of our Lord's suffering and death. We recall his triumphant entry into Jerusalem on Palm Sunday, his giving of the commandments on Maundy Thursday, his crucifixion and burial on Good Friday, and the solemn vigil of Saturday night before Easter Sunday.

THIS WEEK'S THEME
The Messiah Enters the Holy City, Matthew 21.1-11

As Jesus and his apostolic company approached Jerusalem on the last week of his life, he sent two disciples into the city to find a donkey to carry him into Jerusalem. This took place in order to fulfill Zechariah's prophecy, "Say to the daughter of Zion, 'Behold, your king is coming to you, humble, and mounted on a donkey, on a colt, the foal of a beast of burden.'" The disciples obeyed the Lord's directions, brought the donkey along with its colt, put their cloaks on the animals, and Jesus sat on them.

Most of the crowd spread their cloaks on the road, and others cut branches from the trees and laid them on the road. The people that went before him and behind him shouted "Hosanna to the Son of David! Blessed is he who comes in the name of the Lord! Hosanna in the highest!" And as the Lord entered the holy city, the whole place was stirred up, asking "Who is this?" And the crowds said, "This is the prophet Jesus, from Nazareth of Galilee." Jesus of Nazareth is the Son of Man, the Son of David, the promised King of Israel.

DAILY DEVOTIONAL GUIDE

PREPARING OUR HEARTS

Invocation: Our Prayer of Acclamation

O Lord God, who takest pleasure in thy people: inflame our hearts with the thought of thy goodness and send upon us the spirit of prayer and devotion, that we may worthily praise him who suffered and went down to death, that he might open for us the gates of everlasting life; our Lord and Saviour Jesus Christ. Amen.

~ James Ferguson (Ferguson, p. 134)

Call to Worship

Blessed are you, O God: Father, Son, and Holy Spirit. And blessed is your Kingdom, both now and forever, Amen.

PRAISING OUR GOD

Te Deum Laudamus

You are God: we praise you; you are the Lord; we acclaim you; you are the eternal Father: All creation worships you. To you all angels, all the powers of heaven, Cherubim and Seraphim, sing in endless praise: Holy, holy, holy Lord, God of power and might, heaven and earth are full of your glory.

The glorious company of apostles praise you. The noble fellowship of prophets praise you. The white-robed army of martyrs praise you. Throughout the world the holy Church acclaims you; Father, of majesty unbounded, your true and only Son, worthy of all worship, and the Holy Spirit, advocate and guide.

You, Christ, are the king of glory, the eternal Son of the Father. When you became man to set us free you did not shun the Virgin's womb. You overcame the sting of death and opened the kingdom of heaven to all believers. You are seated at God's right hand in glory. We believe that you will come and be our judge. Come then, Lord, and help your people, bought with the price of your own blood, and bring us with your saints to glory everlasting.

Praise and Thanksgiving (Songs and Prayers)

Gloria Patri

Glory be to the Father,
And to the Son and to the Holy Spirit:
As it was in the beginning,
Is now, and ever shall be,
World without end. Amen, amen.

LISTENING TO HIS VOICE

Chronological Reading for the Day

Sunday: Pss. 103; 108-110; 122; 124 ✤ *Monday:* Pss. 131;
133; 138-141; 143 ✤ *Tuesday:* Pss. 144-145; 88-89 ✤
Wednesday: Pss. 50; 73-74 ✤ *Thursday:* Pss. 75-78 ✤
Friday: Pss. 79-82 ✤ *Saturday:* Ps. 83; 1 Chron. 29.23-25;
2 Chron. 1.1-13; 1 Kings 2.13-3.28

Chronological Holy Week Readings

Palm Sunday: Matt. 21.1-17; Mark 11.1-11; Luke 19.28-48;
John 12.12-50

Lectionary Readings for *Liturgy of the Palms*

Psalm: Ps. 118.1-2, 19-29   *OT:* Isa. 50.4-9
Gospel: Matt. 21.1-11   *NT:* Phil. 2.5-11

Reflection: Silence and/or Journaling

RESPONDING IN FAITH

The Apostles' Creed

I believe in God, the Father Almighty, Maker of heaven and earth;
and in Jesus Christ, his only Son, our Lord, who was conceived by the
Holy Spirit, born of the Virgin Mary, suffered under Pontius Pilate,
was crucified, dead, and buried; he descended into hell; the third day
he arose again from the dead; he ascended into heaven and sits on
the right hand of God the Father Almighty; from thence he shall come
to judge the quick and the dead.

I believe in the Holy Spirit, the holy catholic* church, the communion of saints, the forgiveness of sins, the resurrection of the body, and the life everlasting. Amen.

* In the Apostles' and Nicene Creeds, the term catholic refers to the Church's universality, through all ages and times, of all languages and peoples. It refers to no particular tradition or denominational expression (e.g., as in Roman Catholic).

Prayers of Confession
Let us now confess our sins to God and receive mercy and grace to help in our time of need.

Assurance of Pardon
Having faithfully confessed and renounced your sin, Christ also has been faithful to forgive your sins and to purify you from all unrighteousness. It is certain, that there is One who has spoken to the Father in your defense, Jesus Christ, the Righteous One who is the atoning sacrifice for our sins and for the sins of the whole world. His grace and peace are with you now. Amen.

Petitions and Supplications, Ending with The Lord's Prayer
Our Father which art in heaven, Hallowed be thy name. Thy kingdom come, Thy will be done in earth, as it is in heaven. Give us this day our daily bread. And forgive us our debts, as we forgive our debtors. And lead us not into temptation, but deliver us from evil: For thine is the kingdom, and the power, and the glory, for ever. Amen.

~ Matthew 6.9-13 (KJV)

Doxology (and/or closing song)
Praise God from whom all blessings flow;
Praise Him all creatures here below;
Praise Him above ye heavenly host;
Praise Father, Son and Holy Ghost. Amen.

DEPARTING TO SERVE

Benediction

Almighty and Everlasting God, who hast sent thy Son, our Saviour Jesus Christ, to take upon him our flesh and suffer death upon the cross that all mankind should follow the example of his great humility, mercifully grant that we may both follow the example of his patience and also be made partakers of his resurrection; through the same Jesus Christ our Lord.

~ Gregorian Sacramentary, altered by Cranmer.
The Sermon and the Propers II, p. 92 (Geffen, p. 79)

Affirmation from the Psalms

Oh give thanks to the LORD, for he is good; for his steadfast love endures forever! Let Israel say, "His steadfast love endures forever."

Open to me the gates of righteousness, that I may enter through them and give thanks to the LORD. This is the gate of the LORD; the righteous shall enter through it. I thank you that you have answered me and have become my salvation. The stone that the builders rejected has become the cornerstone. This is the LORD's doing; it is marvelous in our eyes. This is the day that the LORD has made; let us rejoice and be glad in it. Save us, we pray, O LORD! O LORD, we pray, give us success! Blessed is he who comes in the name of the LORD! We bless you from the house of the LORD.

~ Psalm 118.1-2, 19-26

Pray without Ceasing – Flash Prayer for the Day

Lord Jesus Christ, prophet from Nazareth and King of Israel, we believe in you and shout our hosannas of praise and worship to you alone.

FOR YOUR WEEKLY JOURNEY

Let God Arise! Seasonal Focus
Lift Up the Son of Man, John 12.20-36

Book Reading
DAILY: Extreme Devotion Writing Team, *Extreme Devotion*

DC Talk, The Voice of the Martyrs, *Jesus Freaks*

Special Church Year Services
Maundy Thursday: Thursday, April 17, 2014
Good Friday: Friday, April 18, 2014
Holy Saturday: Saturday, April 19, 2014

MONDAY OF HOLY WEEK

April 14, 2014

Holy Week recalls the events of our Lord's suffering and death. We recall his triumphant entry into Jerusalem on Palm Sunday, his giving of the commandments on Maundy Thursday, his crucifixion and burial on Good Friday, and the solemn vigil of Saturday night before Easter Sunday.

TODAY'S THEME

Redeemed through the Blood of Jesus, Hebrews 9.11-15

The writer of the Hebrews teaches us that when Christ appeared as a high priest of the good things that have come, he entered once for all into the holy places, not by means of the blood of goats and calves but by means of his own blood, thus securing an eternal redemption. The author declares that if the blood of goats and bulls, and the sprinkling of defiled persons with the ashes of a heifer could actually set someone apart and, sanctify them for the purification of the flesh, how much more, then, will Christ's blood purify our conscience from dead works to serve the living and true God.

Jesus offered himself as our sacrifice through the eternal Spirit without blemish to God. In so doing he has become the mediator of a new covenant, one in which all who are called can now receive the promised eternal inheritance, having been redeemed from the transgressions committed under the first covenant.

DAILY DEVOTIONAL GUIDE

PREPARING OUR HEARTS

Invocation: Our Prayer of Acclamation

Eternal God and our Creator, who received the sacrifice of your Son on our behalf to redeem us from our sins, thank you for your redemption and grace. Through your Son's offering of himself you have washed and redeemed us and given us the right to receive the promised eternal inheritance reserved for all who cling to your Son in faith. We honor you for your grace, thank you for our High Priest, and for the blood that he shed for the forgiveness of our sins. In his name we offer these thanks, amen.

Call to Worship
Blessed are you, O God: Father, Son, and Holy Spirit. And blessed is your Kingdom, both now and forever, Amen.

PRAISING OUR GOD

Te Deum Laudamus
You are God: we praise you; you are the Lord; we acclaim you; you are the eternal Father: All creation worships you. To you all angels, all the powers of heaven, Cherubim and Seraphim, sing in endless praise: Holy, holy, holy Lord, God of power and might, heaven and earth are full of your glory.

The glorious company of apostles praise you. The noble fellowship of prophets praise you. The white-robed army of martyrs praise you. Throughout the world the holy Church acclaims you; Father, of majesty unbounded, your true and only Son, worthy of all worship, and the Holy Spirit, advocate and guide.

You, Christ, are the king of glory, the eternal Son of the Father. When you became man to set us free you did not shun the Virgin's womb. You overcame the sting of death and opened the kingdom of heaven to all believers. You are seated at God's right hand in glory. We believe that you will come and be our judge. Come then, Lord, and help your people, bought with the price of your own blood, and bring us with your saints to glory everlasting.

Praise and Thanksgiving (Songs and Prayers)

Gloria Patri
Glory be to the Father,
And to the Son and to the Holy Spirit:
As it was in the beginning,
Is now, and ever shall be,
World without end. Amen, amen.

LISTENING TO HIS VOICE

Chronological Reading for the Day
Pss. 131; 133; 138-141; 143

Chronological Holy Week Readings
Monday of Holy Week: Matt. 21.18-19; Mark 11.12-19

Lectionary Readings
Psalm: Ps. 36.5-11   *OT:* Isa. 42.1-9
Gospel: John 12.1-11   *NT:* Heb. 9.11-15

Reflection: Silence and/or Journaling

RESPONDING IN FAITH

The Apostles' Creed
I believe in God, the Father Almighty, Maker of heaven and earth;
and in Jesus Christ, his only Son, our Lord, who was conceived by the
Holy Spirit, born of the Virgin Mary, suffered under Pontius Pilate,
was crucified, dead, and buried; he descended into hell; the third day
he arose again from the dead; he ascended into heaven and sits on
the right hand of God the Father Almighty; from thence he shall come
to judge the quick and the dead.

I believe in the Holy Spirit, the holy catholic* church, the communion
of saints, the forgiveness of sins, the resurrection of the body, and the
life everlasting. Amen.

* In the Apostles' and Nicene Creeds, the term catholic refers to the Church's universality, through all ages and times, of all languages and peoples. It refers to no particular tradition or denominational expression (e.g., as in Roman Catholic).

Prayers of Confession

Let us now confess our sins to God and receive mercy and grace to help in our time of need.

Assurance of Pardon

Having faithfully confessed and renounced your sin, Christ also has been faithful to forgive your sins and to purify you from all unrighteousness. It is certain, that there is One who has spoken to the Father in your defense, Jesus Christ, the Righteous One who is the atoning sacrifice for our sins and for the sins of the whole world. His grace and peace are with you now. Amen.

Petitions and Supplications, Ending with The Lord's Prayer

Our Father which art in heaven, Hallowed be thy name. Thy kingdom come, Thy will be done in earth, as it is in heaven. Give us this day our daily bread. And forgive us our debts, as we forgive our debtors. And lead us not into temptation, but deliver us from evil: For thine is the kingdom, and the power, and the glory, for ever. Amen.

~ Matthew 6.9-13 (KJV)

Doxology (and/or closing song)

Praise God from whom all blessings flow;
Praise Him all creatures here below;
Praise Him above ye heavenly host;
Praise Father, Son and Holy Ghost. Amen.

DEPARTING TO SERVE

Benediction

Lord Jesus, who stands before God as both our High Priest and Paschal Sacrifice, thank you for shedding your blood on the cross, for making payment for our sin and washing us clean from the guilt which has plagued us our whole lives long. Grant us humility to remember that it is through your blood alone that we have entrance into the Father's presence, and can be forgiven for our transgression of your law and your will. In your name we pray, amen.

Affirmation from the Psalms
Your steadfast love, O LORD, extends to the heavens, your faithfulness to the clouds. Your righteousness is like the mountains of God; your judgments are like the great deep; man and beast you save, O LORD. How precious is your steadfast love, O God! The children of mankind take refuge in the shadow of your wings. They feast on the abundance of your house, and you give them drink from the river of your delights. For with you is the fountain of life; in your light do we see light. Oh, continue your steadfast love to those who know you, and your righteousness to the upright of heart! Let not the foot of arrogance come upon me, nor the hand of the wicked drive me away.

~ Psalm 36.5-11

Pray without Ceasing – Flash Prayer for the Day
Thank you Lord Jesus, for being our High Priest and the Paschal sacrifice, whose blood has redeemed us to God and saved us from the penalty and guilt of our sins.

FOR YOUR WEEKLY JOURNEY

Let God Arise! Seasonal Focus
Lift Up the Son of Man, John 12.20-36

Book Reading
DAILY: Extreme Devotion Writing Team, *Extreme Devotion*

DC Talk, The Voice of the Martyrs, *Jesus Freaks*

April 15, 2014

Holy Week recalls the events of our Lord's suffering and death. We recall his triumphant entry into Jerusalem on Palm Sunday, his giving of the commandments on Maundy Thursday, his crucifixion and burial on Good Friday, and the solemn vigil of Saturday night before Easter Sunday.

TODAY'S THEME
Lift Up the Son of Man, John 12.20-36

During the last week of Jesus' life, some Greeks (God-fearing Gentiles) were present at the feast, and asked Philip if they could see Jesus. Philip and Andrew went to Jesus, telling him of their request. Jesus answered that his hour, the hour for the Son of Man to be glorified, had now come. He affirmed that unless a grain of wheat falls into the earth and dies, it remains alone; but if it dies, it bears much fruit. He said that whoever loves his life will lose it, and whoever would hate his life in this world would keep it for eternal life. Those who served him would follow him, and wherever he, the Christ, was, so they too would also be there. All those who serve Jesus the Father would honor.

After testifying that his soul was deeply troubled, Jesus affirmed that for this purpose he had come to this very hour. A voice from heaven answered Jesus' words to the Father to glorify his name, and the people heard it. Jesus affirmed that now the judgment of this world was to occur, and the ruler of this world would be cast out, and when he would be lifted up from the earth, he would draw all people to himself. The Savior of the world knew that his time was short, and commanded the people to remain in the light while they had the light, and to believe in the light, in order that they might be the children of light.

TUESDAY OF HOLY WEEK

DAILY DEVOTIONAL GUIDE

PREPARING OUR HEARTS

Invocation: Our Prayer of Acclamation

Eternal God, who is light and in whom there is no darkness at all, thank you for the courage of your Son during his time of sojourn on earth. Although he was troubled and persecuted, his resolve to obey you never wavered, and he knew that only in dying would he be able to grant life to others. Teach us this pattern, so that in losing our lives we might find them, and in dying to this world we might live to the next one. In his name we pray, amen.

Call to Worship

Blessed are you, O God: Father, Son, and Holy Spirit. And blessed is your Kingdom, both now and forever, Amen.

PRAISING OUR GOD

Te Deum Laudamus

You are God: we praise you; you are the Lord; we acclaim you; you are the eternal Father: All creation worships you. To you all angels, all the powers of heaven, Cherubim and Seraphim, sing in endless praise: Holy, holy, holy Lord, God of power and might, heaven and earth are full of your glory.

The glorious company of apostles praise you. The noble fellowship of prophets praise you. The white-robed army of martyrs praise you. Throughout the world the holy Church acclaims you; Father, of majesty unbounded, your true and only Son, worthy of all worship, and the Holy Spirit, advocate and guide.

You, Christ, are the king of glory, the eternal Son of the Father. When you became man to set us free you did not shun the Virgin's womb. You overcame the sting of death and opened the kingdom of heaven to all believers. You are seated at God's right hand in glory. We believe

that you will come and be our judge. Come then, Lord, and help your
people, bought with the price of your own blood, and bring us with
your saints to glory everlasting.

Praise and Thanksgiving (Songs and Prayers)

Gloria Patri
Glory be to the Father,
And to the Son and to the Holy Spirit:
As it was in the beginning,
Is now, and ever shall be,
World without end. Amen, amen.

LISTENING TO HIS VOICE

Chronological Reading for the Day
Pss. 144-145; 88-89

Chronological Holy Week Readings
Tuesday of Holy Week: Matt. 21.20-26.13; Mark 11.20-13.37;
Luke 2021

Lectionary Readings
Psalm: Ps. 71.1-14   *OT:* Isa. 49.1-7
Gospel: John 12.20-36   *NT:* 1 Cor. 1.18-31

Reflection: Silence and/or Journaling

RESPONDING IN FAITH

The Apostles' Creed
I believe in God, the Father Almighty, Maker of heaven and earth;
and in Jesus Christ, his only Son, our Lord, who was conceived by the
Holy Spirit, born of the Virgin Mary, suffered under Pontius Pilate,
was crucified, dead, and buried; he descended into hell; the third day
he arose again from the dead; he ascended into heaven and sits on

the right hand of God the Father Almighty; from thence he shall come to judge the quick and the dead.

I believe in the Holy Spirit, the holy catholic* church, the communion of saints, the forgiveness of sins, the resurrection of the body, and the life everlasting. Amen.

* In the Apostles' and Nicene Creeds, the term catholic refers to the Church's universality, through all ages and times, of all languages and peoples. It refers to no particular tradition or denominational expression (e.g., as in Roman Catholic).

Prayers of Confession
Let us now confess our sins to God and receive mercy and grace to help in our time of need.

Assurance of Pardon
Having faithfully confessed and renounced your sin, Christ also has been faithful to forgive your sins and to purify you from all unrighteousness. It is certain, that there is One who has spoken to the Father in your defense, Jesus Christ, the Righteous One who is the atoning sacrifice for our sins and for the sins of the whole world. His grace and peace are with you now. Amen.

Petitions and Supplications, Ending with The Lord's Prayer
Our Father which art in heaven, Hallowed be thy name. Thy kingdom come, Thy will be done in earth, as it is in heaven. Give us this day our daily bread. And forgive us our debts, as we forgive our debtors. And lead us not into temptation, but deliver us from evil: For thine is the kingdom, and the power, and the glory, for ever. Amen.

~ Matthew 6.9-13 (KJV)

Doxology (and/or closing song)
Praise God from whom all blessings flow;
Praise Him all creatures here below;
Praise Him above ye heavenly host;
Praise Father, Son and Holy Ghost. Amen.

DEPARTING TO SERVE

Benediction

Dear Lord Jesus, who taught us that whoever loves his life loses it, and whoever hates his life in this world keeps it for eternal life, protect us from every urge and whim to live for fleeting pleasures and empty concerns. Drive from our hearts all pettiness and waste, and teach us to focus our hearts on you, on the things that truly matter, and on the eternal life to come. Help us to be drawn to you, for you were lifted up, and now our hearts are yours alone. In your name we pray, amen.

Affirmation from the Psalms

O LORD my God, in you do I take refuge; save me from all my pursuers and deliver me, lest like a lion they tear my soul apart, rending it in pieces, with none to deliver. O LORD my God, if I have done this, if there is wrong in my hands, if I have repaid my friend with evil or plundered my enemy without cause, let the enemy pursue my soul and overtake it, and let him trample my life to the ground and lay my glory in the dust. Selah. Arise, O LORD, in your anger; lift yourself up against the fury of my enemies; awake for me; you have appointed a judgment.

~ Psalm 7.1-6

Pray without Ceasing – Flash Prayer for the Day

Eternal Father, Lord God Almighty, who sent your Son to earth to die in the stead and for the sake of us all, train us to have the same mind and heart as our Lord. Produce in us the same burden, the same sense of urgency, the same sacrificial spirit that would allow our Lord Jesus to give up all that he had for us, unworthy sinners. He was lifted up from the earth as a sacrifice for sin, and we have been drawn to him as his very own. Help us to die in order that others might live through us. In Jesus' name, amen.

FOR YOUR WEEKLY JOURNEY

Let God Arise! Seasonal Focus
Lift Up the Son of Man, John 12.20-36

Book Reading
DAILY: Extreme Devotion Writing Team, *Extreme Devotion*

DC Talk, The Voice of the Martyrs, *Jesus Freaks*

April 16, 2014

Holy Week recalls the events of our Lord's suffering and death. We recall his triumphant entry into Jerusalem on Palm Sunday, his giving of the commandments on Maundy Thursday, his crucifixion and burial on Good Friday, and the solemn vigil of Saturday night before Easter Sunday.

TODAY'S THEME
For the Joy Set before Him, Hebrews 12.1-3

We present-day followers of Christ are surrounded by such a great cloud of witnesses, all the saints, both ancient and contemporary, who have offered themselves up to God in extreme devotion and service. With them surrounding us as a gallery of victorious saints, we now today should also lay aside every weight, and the sin which clings so closely, and run with endurance the race that is set before us. As we run, we should keep our eyes upon the Lord Jesus, who is both the founder and perfecter of our faith. For the joy that was set before him he endured the cross, despised its shame, and now, as a result of his obedience and victory, has been exalted by God; he is seated at the right hand of the throne of God. In all our sacrifice we ought to consider Jesus who himself endured from sinners such hostility against himself. Keeping our eyes on him, and the joy set before us, we will not then grow weary or fainthearted.

DAILY DEVOTIONAL GUIDE

PREPARING OUR HEARTS

Invocation: Our Prayer of Acclamation

Sovereign God, Lord Most High, thank you for the examples given to us of your saints who withstood the world and proved faithful to the end. We especially thank you for the Lord Jesus, our faith's author and end, who for the joy set before him endured it all to win for us the victory, and obeyed your mandate in this world. Teach us to lay aside all sin, to consider him, and never to grow weary or fainthearted in accomplishing your will. In your name, amen.

Call to Worship

Blessed are you, O God: Father, Son, and Holy Spirit. And blessed is your Kingdom, both now and forever, Amen.

PRAISING OUR GOD

Te Deum Laudamus

You are God: we praise you; you are the Lord; we acclaim you; you are the eternal Father: All creation worships you. To you all angels, all the powers of heaven, Cherubim and Seraphim, sing in endless praise: Holy, holy, holy Lord, God of power and might, heaven and earth are full of your glory.

The glorious company of apostles praise you. The noble fellowship of prophets praise you. The white-robed army of martyrs praise you. Throughout the world the holy Church acclaims you; Father, of majesty unbounded, your true and only Son, worthy of all worship, and the Holy Spirit, advocate and guide.

You, Christ, are the king of glory, the eternal Son of the Father. When you became man to set us free you did not shun the Virgin's womb. You overcame the sting of death and opened the kingdom of heaven to all believers. You are seated at God's right hand in glory. We believe that you will come and be our judge. Come then, Lord, and help your people, bought with the price of your own blood, and bring us with your saints to glory everlasting.

Praise and Thanksgiving (Songs and Prayers)

Gloria Patri

Glory be to the Father,
And to the Son and to the Holy Spirit:
As it was in the beginning,
Is now, and ever shall be,
World without end. Amen, amen.

LISTENING TO HIS VOICE

Chronological Reading for the Day

Pss. 50; 73-74

Chronological Holy Week Readings

Wednesday of Holy Week: Matt. 26.1-16; Mark 14.1-2, 10-11;
Luke 22.1-6

Lectionary Readings

Psalm: Ps. 70   *OT:* Isa. 50.4-9a
Gospel: John 13.21-32   *NT:* Heb. 12.1-3

Reflection: Silence and/or Journaling

RESPONDING IN FAITH

The Apostles' Creed

I believe in God, the Father Almighty, Maker of heaven and earth;
and in Jesus Christ, his only Son, our Lord, who was conceived by the
Holy Spirit, born of the Virgin Mary, suffered under Pontius Pilate,
was crucified, dead, and buried; he descended into hell; the third day
he arose again from the dead; he ascended into heaven and sits on
the right hand of God the Father Almighty; from thence he shall come
to judge the quick and the dead.

I believe in the Holy Spirit, the holy catholic* church, the communion
of saints, the forgiveness of sins, the resurrection of the body, and the
life everlasting. Amen.

* In the Apostles' and Nicene Creeds, the term catholic refers to the Church's universality, through all ages and times, of all languages and peoples. It refers to no particular tradition or denominational expression (e.g., as in Roman Catholic).

Prayers of Confession
Let us now confess our sins to God and receive mercy and grace to help in our time of need.

Assurance of Pardon
Having faithfully confessed and renounced your sin, Christ also has been faithful to forgive your sins and to purify you from all unrighteousness. It is certain, that there is One who has spoken to the Father in your defense, Jesus Christ, the Righteous One who is the atoning sacrifice for our sins and for the sins of the whole world. His grace and peace are with you now. Amen.

Petitions and Supplications, Ending with The Lord's Prayer
Our Father which art in heaven, Hallowed be thy name. Thy kingdom come, Thy will be done in earth, as it is in heaven. Give us this day our daily bread. And forgive us our debts, as we forgive our debtors. And lead us not into temptation, but deliver us from evil: For thine is the kingdom, and the power, and the glory, for ever. Amen.

~ Matthew 6.9-13 (KJV)

Doxology (and/or closing song)
Praise God from whom all blessings flow;
Praise Him all creatures here below;
Praise Him above ye heavenly host;
Praise Father, Son and Holy Ghost. Amen.

DEPARTING TO SERVE

Benediction
Lord Jesus Christ, who for the joy set before you refused to bow or give in to the temptations of the world or the urge to quit, produce in our hearts and mind the same resolve and

commitment you had to the Father. Cause your Spirit to create in us a clean heart, and give us the kind of commitment that honors you in all things, despite all the provocation and temptation that will seek to undermine our faith. Make us like you. In your name we pray, amen.

Affirmation from the Psalms
Make haste, O God, to deliver me! O LORD, make haste to help me! Let them be put to shame and confusion who seek my life! Let them be turned back and brought to dishonor who delight in my hurt! Let them turn back because of their shame who say, "Aha, Aha!" May all who seek you rejoice and be glad in you! May those who love your salvation say evermore, "God is great!" But I am poor and needy; hasten to me, O God! You are my help and my deliverer; O LORD, do not delay!

~ Psalm 70.1-5

Pray without Ceasing – Flash Prayer for the Day
Lord Jesus, remind us that we are surrounded by such a great arena of witnesses, and imprint your example on our hearts, that we neither quit or become fainthearted.

FOR YOUR WEEKLY JOURNEY

Let God Arise! Seasonal Focus
Lift Up the Son of Man, John 12.20-36

Book Reading
DAILY: Extreme Devotion Writing Team, *Extreme Devotion*

DC Talk, The Voice of the Martyrs, *Jesus Freaks*

MAUNDY THURSDAY

April 17, 2014

Holy Week recalls the events of our Lord's suffering and death. We recall his triumphant entry into Jerusalem on Palm Sunday, his giving of the commandments on Maundy Thursday, his crucifixion and burial on Good Friday, and the solemn vigil of Saturday night before Easter Sunday.

TODAY'S THEME
The Table of the Lord, 1 Corinthians 11.23-26
In speaking of the Lord's Supper to the Corinthians, Paul affirms that he received from the Lord what he also delivered to them. The tradition he received was that the Lord Jesus, on the night when he was betrayed, took bread, gave thanks, then broke it, and said, "This is my body which is for you. Do this in remembrance of me." In the same way, the Lord Jesus also took the cup, after supper, and said, "This cup is the new covenant in my blood. Do this, as often as you drink it, in remembrance of me." This re-enactment of his death was his gift to his people throughout all generations. Paul affirmed to the Corinthians, also, that as often as you eat this bread and drink the cup, you proclaim the Lord's death until he comes. This is the Table of the Lord.

DAILY DEVOTIONAL GUIDE

PREPARING OUR HEARTS

Invocation: Our Prayer of Acclamation
Almighty Father, whose dear Son on the night before he suffered did institute the Sacrament of his Body and Blood: Mercifully grant that we may thankfully receive the same, in remembrance of him who in these holy mysteries giveth us a pledge of life eternal, the same thy Son Jesus Christ our Lord; who now liveth and reigneth with thee and the Holy Spirit, ever one God, world without end.

~ 1928 American Prayer Book Revision Commission.
Book of English Collects, No. 38 (Geffen, p. 80)

Call to Worship

Blessed are you, O God: Father, Son, and Holy Spirit. And blessed is your Kingdom, both now and forever, Amen.

PRAISING OUR GOD

Te Deum Laudamus

You are God: we praise you; you are the Lord; we acclaim you; you are the eternal Father: All creation worships you. To you all angels, all the powers of heaven, Cherubim and Seraphim, sing in endless praise: Holy, holy, holy Lord, God of power and might, heaven and earth are full of your glory.

The glorious company of apostles praise you. The noble fellowship of prophets praise you. The white-robed army of martyrs praise you. Throughout the world the holy Church acclaims you; Father, of majesty unbounded, your true and only Son, worthy of all worship, and the Holy Spirit, advocate and guide.

You, Christ, are the king of glory, the eternal Son of the Father. When you became man to set us free you did not shun the Virgin's womb. You overcame the sting of death and opened the kingdom of heaven to all believers. You are seated at God's right hand in glory. We believe that you will come and be our judge. Come then, Lord, and help your people, bought with the price of your own blood, and bring us with your saints to glory everlasting.

Praise and Thanksgiving (Songs and Prayers)

Gloria Patri

Glory be to the Father,
And to the Son and to the Holy Spirit:
As it was in the beginning,
Is now, and ever shall be,
World without end. Amen, amen.

LISTENING TO HIS VOICE

Chronological Reading for the Day
Pss. 75-78

Chronological Holy Week Readings
Maundy Thursday: Matt. 26.17-75; Mark 14.12-42; Luke 22.7-65; John 13.1-18.27

Lectionary Readings
Psalm: Ps. 116.1-2, 12-19   *OT:* Exod. 12.1-14
Gospel: John 13.1-17, 31b-35   *NT:* 1 Cor. 11.23-26

Reflection: Silence and/or Journaling

RESPONDING IN FAITH

The Apostles' Creed
I believe in God, the Father Almighty, Maker of heaven and earth; and in Jesus Christ, his only Son, our Lord, who was conceived by the Holy Spirit, born of the Virgin Mary, suffered under Pontius Pilate, was crucified, dead, and buried; he descended into hell; the third day he arose again from the dead; he ascended into heaven and sits on the right hand of God the Father Almighty; from thence he shall come to judge the quick and the dead.

I believe in the Holy Spirit, the holy catholic* church, the communion of saints, the forgiveness of sins, the resurrection of the body, and the life everlasting. Amen.

* In the Apostles' and Nicene Creeds, the term catholic refers to the Church's universality, through all ages and times, of all languages and peoples. It refers to no particular tradition or denominational expression (e.g., as in Roman Catholic).

Prayers of Confession
Let us now confess our sins to God and receive mercy and grace to help in our time of need.

Assurance of Pardon

Having faithfully confessed and renounced your sin, Christ also has been faithful to forgive your sins and to purify you from all unrighteousness. It is certain, that there is One who has spoken to the Father in your defense, Jesus Christ, the Righteous One who is the atoning sacrifice for our sins and for the sins of the whole world. His grace and peace are with you now. Amen.

Petitions and Supplications, Ending with The Lord's Prayer
Our Father which art in heaven, Hallowed be thy name. Thy kingdom come, Thy will be done in earth, as it is in heaven. Give us this day our daily bread. And forgive us our debts, as we forgive our debtors. And lead us not into temptation, but deliver us from evil: For thine is the kingdom, and the power, and the glory, for ever. Amen.

~ Matthew 6.9-13 (KJV)

Doxology (and/or closing song)
Praise God from whom all blessings flow;
Praise Him all creatures here below;
Praise Him above ye heavenly host;
Praise Father, Son and Holy Ghost. Amen.

DEPARTING TO SERVE

Benediction
Almighty and Everlasting God, who of thy tender love toward mankind, hast sent thy Son, our Saviour Jesus Christ, to take upon him our flesh, and to suffer death upon the Cross, that all mankind should follow the example of his great humility: mercifully grant that we may both follow the example of his patience, and also be made partakers of his resurrection; through the same Jesus Christ our Lord. Amen.

~ *Book of Common Prayer* (Ferguson, p. 143)

Affirmation from the Psalms
I love the LORD, because he has heard my voice and my pleas for mercy. Because he inclined his ear to me, therefore I will call on him as long as I live.

~ Psalm 116.1-2

Pray without Ceasing – Flash Prayer for the Day
Thank you Lord Jesus Christ, for your living presence among us whenever we partake of the bread and the wine at the Table of the Lord.

FOR YOUR WEEKLY JOURNEY

Let God Arise! Seasonal Focus
Lift Up the Son of Man, John 12.20-36

Book Reading
DAILY: Extreme Devotion Writing Team, *Extreme Devotion*

DC Talk, The Voice of the Martyrs, *Jesus Freaks*

April 18, 2014

Holy Week recalls the events of our Lord's suffering and death. We recall his triumphant entry into Jerusalem on Palm Sunday, his giving of the commandments on Maundy Thursday, his crucifixion and burial on Good Friday, and the solemn vigil of Saturday night before Easter Sunday.

TODAY'S THEME

Hold Fast Your Confession, Hebrews 4.14-16; 5.7-9

We know that our Lord Jesus was our high priest who offered himself up to God as our paschal sacrifice, as our Passover lamb. And so, since then we have him now as our great high priest who has passed through the heavens, Jesus, the Son of God, let us hold fast our confession. Our Lord Jesus offered up prayers and supplications during the days of his flesh, and did so with loud crying and tears. He entrusted himself to him who was able to save him from death, and he was heard because of his reverence. And though a son, he learned obedience through what he suffered, was made perfect, and thus became the source of eternal salvation to all who obey him.

Let us remember that we do not have a high priest who cannot sympathize with our weaknesses. Rather yet, we have one who in every respect was tempted even as we are today, with the exception that he (unlike us) never sinned once. We ought to draw near to the throne of grace with confidence and boldness, and readily receive both the mercy and grace to help in time of need.

DAILY DEVOTIONAL GUIDE

PREPARING OUR HEARTS

Invocation: Our Prayer of Acclamation

O Lord God, Who didst send down Thine only Son to redeem the world by His obedience unto death; grant, we humbly beseech Thee, that the continual memory of His bitter Cross and Passion may teach us so to crucify the flesh with the affections and lusts thereof that, dying unto sin and living unto Thee, we may, in the union and merits of His Cross and Passion, die with Him, and rest with Him, and rise again with Him, and live with Him forever; to Whom with Thee and the Holy Ghost be all honour and glory, world without end. Amen.

~ Archbishop Hamilton, AD 1511 (Fox, p. 224)

Call to Worship

Blessed are you, O God: Father, Son, and Holy Spirit. And blessed is your Kingdom, both now and forever, Amen.

PRAISING OUR GOD

Te Deum Laudamus

You are God: we praise you; you are the Lord; we acclaim you; you are the eternal Father: All creation worships you. To you all angels, all the powers of heaven, Cherubim and Seraphim, sing in endless praise: Holy, holy, holy Lord, God of power and might, heaven and earth are full of your glory.

The glorious company of apostles praise you. The noble fellowship of prophets praise you. The white-robed army of martyrs praise you. Throughout the world the holy Church acclaims you; Father, of majesty unbounded, your true and only Son, worthy of all worship, and the Holy Spirit, advocate and guide.

You, Christ, are the king of glory, the eternal Son of the Father. When you became man to set us free you did not shun the Virgin's womb.

*You overcame the sting of death and opened the kingdom of heaven
to all believers. You are seated at God's right hand in glory. We believe
that you will come and be our judge. Come then, Lord, and help your
people, bought with the price of your own blood, and bring us with
your saints to glory everlasting.*

Praise and Thanksgiving (Songs and Prayers)

Gloria Patri
*Glory be to the Father,
And to the Son and to the Holy Spirit:
As it was in the beginning,
Is now, and ever shall be,
World without end. Amen, amen.*

LISTENING TO HIS VOICE

Chronological Reading for the Day
Pss. 79-82

Chronological Holy Week Readings
Good Friday: Matt. 27.1-61; Mark 15.1-47; Luke 22.66-23.56a;
John 18.28-19.42

Lectionary Readings
Psalm: Ps. 22   *OT:* Isa. 52.13-53.12
Gospel: John 18.1-19.42   *NT:* Heb. 4.14-16; 5.7-9

Reflection: Silence and/or Journaling

RESPONDING IN FAITH

The Apostles' Creed
*I believe in God, the Father Almighty, Maker of heaven and earth;
and in Jesus Christ, his only Son, our Lord, who was conceived by the
Holy Spirit, born of the Virgin Mary, suffered under Pontius Pilate,
was crucified, dead, and buried; he descended into hell; the third day*

he arose again from the dead; he ascended into heaven and sits on the right hand of God the Father Almighty; from thence he shall come to judge the quick and the dead.

I believe in the Holy Spirit, the holy catholic* church, the communion of saints, the forgiveness of sins, the resurrection of the body, and the life everlasting. Amen.

* In the Apostles' and Nicene Creeds, the term catholic refers to the Church's universality, through all ages and times, of all languages and peoples. It refers to no particular tradition or denominational expression (e.g., as in Roman Catholic).

Prayers of Confession
Let us now confess our sins to God and receive mercy and grace to help in our time of need.

Assurance of Pardon
Having faithfully confessed and renounced your sin, Christ also has been faithful to forgive your sins and to purify you from all unrighteousness. It is certain, that there is One who has spoken to the Father in your defense, Jesus Christ, the Righteous One who is the atoning sacrifice for our sins and for the sins of the whole world. His grace and peace are with you now. Amen.

Petitions and Supplications, Ending with The Lord's Prayer
Our Father which art in heaven, Hallowed be thy name. Thy kingdom come, Thy will be done in earth, as it is in heaven. Give us this day our daily bread. And forgive us our debts, as we forgive our debtors. And lead us not into temptation, but deliver us from evil: For thine is the kingdom, and the power, and the glory, for ever. Amen.

~ Matthew 6.9-13 (KJV)

Doxology (and/or closing song)
Praise God from whom all blessings flow;
Praise Him all creatures here below;
Praise Him above ye heavenly host;
Praise Father, Son and Holy Ghost. Amen.

Benediction
Almighty and Everlasting God, who hast willed that thy Son should bear for us the pains of the Cross that thou mightest remove from us the power of the adversary, help us so to remember and give thanks for our Lord's Passion that we may obtain remission of sins and redemption from everlasting death; through the same Jesus Christ our Lord.

~ *The Sermon and the Propers II*, p. 124 (Geffen, p. 81)

Affirmation from the Psalms
My God, my God, why have you forsaken me? Why are you so far from saving me, from the words of my groaning? O my God, I cry by day, but you do not answer, and by night, but I find no rest. Yet you are holy, enthroned on the praises of Israel. In you our fathers trusted; they trusted, and you delivered them. To you they cried and were rescued; in you they trusted and were not put to shame.

~ Psalm 22.1-5

Pray without Ceasing – Flash Prayer for the Day
Great High Priest and Passover sacrifice, save us from sin and receive our souls to yourself. Grant us the eternal life promised to all who cling to you in faith.

FOR YOUR WEEKLY JOURNEY

Let God Arise! Seasonal Focus
Lift Up the Son of Man, John 12.20-36

Book Reading
DAILY: Extreme Devotion Writing Team, *Extreme Devotion*

DC Talk, The Voice of the Martyrs, *Jesus Freaks*

April 19, 2014

Holy Week recalls the events of our Lord's suffering and death. We recall his triumphant entry into Jerusalem on Palm Sunday, his giving of the commandments on Maundy Thursday, his crucifixion and burial on Good Friday, and the solemn vigil of Saturday night before Easter Sunday.

TODAY'S THEME

The Mercies of the Lord, Lamentations 3.1-9, 19-24

We have seen affliction under the Lord's rod, and felt his judgments and discipline. Though it appears as if our call and cry for help are ignored, and our prayers are shut out and unanswered, he has not abandoned his people; he will not forsake his own. We plead to God to remember our affliction and wanderings, the wormwood and the gall! Although our souls are bowed down within us, this we can call to mind and have hope: the steadfast love of the LORD never ceases; his mercies never come to an end; they are new every morning; great is your faithfulness. So, even on this day, let us cry out in faith, "The LORD is my portion," says my soul, "therefore I will hope in him."

DAILY DEVOTIONAL GUIDE

PREPARING OUR HEARTS

Invocation: Our Prayer of Acclamation

Grant, O Lord, that as we are baptized into the death of thy blessed Son our Saviour Jesus Christ, so by continual mortifying our corrupt affections we may be buried with him; and that through the grave, and gate of death, we may pass to our joyful resurrection; for his merits who died, and was buried, and rose again for us, the same thy Son Jesus Christ our Lord. Amen.

~ 1662 from 1637 *Scottish Prayer Book*, attributed to Laud and Cosin.
Book of English Collects, No. 43 (Geffen, p. 82)

Call to Worship
Blessed are you, O God: Father, Son, and Holy Spirit. And blessed is your Kingdom, both now and forever, Amen.

PRAISING OUR GOD

Te Deum Laudamus
You are God: we praise you; you are the Lord; we acclaim you; you are the eternal Father: All creation worships you. To you all angels, all the powers of heaven, Cherubim and Seraphim, sing in endless praise: Holy, holy, holy Lord, God of power and might, heaven and earth are full of your glory.

The glorious company of apostles praise you. The noble fellowship of prophets praise you. The white-robed army of martyrs praise you. Throughout the world the holy Church acclaims you; Father, of majesty unbounded, your true and only Son, worthy of all worship, and the Holy Spirit, advocate and guide.

You, Christ, are the king of glory, the eternal Son of the Father. When you became man to set us free you did not shun the Virgin's womb. You overcame the sting of death and opened the kingdom of heaven to all believers. You are seated at God's right hand in glory. We believe that you will come and be our judge. Come then, Lord, and help your people, bought with the price of your own blood, and bring us with your saints to glory everlasting.

Praise and Thanksgiving (Songs and Prayers)

Gloria Patri
Glory be to the Father,
And to the Son and to the Holy Spirit:
As it was in the beginning,
Is now, and ever shall be,
World without end. Amen, amen.

LISTENING TO HIS VOICE

Chronological Reading for the Day
Ps. 83; 1 Chron. 29.23-25; 2 Chron. 1.1-13; 1 Kings 2.13-3.28

Chronological Holy Week Readings
Holy Saturday: Matt. 27.62-66; Luke 23.56b

Lectionary Readings
Psalm: Ps. 31.1-4, 15-16   *OT:* Lam. 3.1-9, 19-24
Gospel: Matt. 27.57-66   *NT:* 1 Pet. 4.1-8

Easter Vigil Readings
- Gen. 1.1-2.4a; Ps. 136.1-9, 23-26
- Gen. 7.1-5, 11-18; 8.6-18; 9.8-13; Ps. 46
- Gen. 22.1-18; Ps. 16
- Exod. 14.10-31; 15.20-21; 15.1b-13, 17-18
- Isa. 55.1-11; 12.2-6
- Prov. 8.1-8, 19-21; 9.4b-6; Ps. 19
- Ezek. 36.24-28; Ps. 42, 43
- Ezek. 37.1-14; Ps. 143
- Zeph. 3.14-20; Ps. 98
- Rom. 6.3-11; Ps. 114
- Matt. 28.1-10

Reflection: Silence and/or Journaling

RESPONDING IN FAITH

The Apostles' Creed
I believe in God, the Father Almighty, Maker of heaven and earth;
and in Jesus Christ, his only Son, our Lord, who was conceived by the
Holy Spirit, born of the Virgin Mary, suffered under Pontius Pilate,
was crucified, dead, and buried; he descended into hell; the third day
he arose again from the dead; he ascended into heaven and sits on
the right hand of God the Father Almighty; from thence he shall come
to judge the quick and the dead.

I believe in the Holy Spirit, the holy catholic* church, the communion of saints, the forgiveness of sins, the resurrection of the body, and the life everlasting. Amen.

* In the Apostles' and Nicene Creeds, the term catholic refers to the Church's universality, through all ages and times, of all languages and peoples. It refers to no particular tradition or denominational expression (e.g., as in Roman Catholic).

Prayers of Confession

Let us now confess our sins to God and receive mercy and grace to help in our time of need.

Assurance of Pardon

Having faithfully confessed and renounced your sin, Christ also has been faithful to forgive your sins and to purify you from all unrighteousness. It is certain, that there is One who has spoken to the Father in your defense, Jesus Christ, the Righteous One who is the atoning sacrifice for our sins and for the sins of the whole world. His grace and peace are with you now. Amen.

Petitions and Supplications, Ending with The Lord's Prayer

Our Father which art in heaven, Hallowed be thy name. Thy kingdom come, Thy will be done in earth, as it is in heaven. Give us this day our daily bread. And forgive us our debts, as we forgive our debtors. And lead us not into temptation, but deliver us from evil: For thine is the kingdom, and the power, and the glory, for ever. Amen.

~ Matthew 6.9-13 (KJV)

Doxology (and/or closing song)

Praise God from whom all blessings flow;
Praise Him all creatures here below;
Praise Him above ye heavenly host;
Praise Father, Son and Holy Ghost. Amen.

DEPARTING TO SERVE

Benediction
O God, who didst enlighten this most holy night with the glory of the Lord's resurrection, preserve in all thy people the spirit of adoption which thou hast given, so that, renewed in body and soul, they may perform unto thee a pure service; through the same Jesus Christ our Lord. Amen.

~ *The Sermon and the Propers II*, p. 125 (Geffen, p. 82)

Affirmation from the Psalms
In you, O LORD, do I take refuge; let me never be put to shame; in your righteousness deliver me! Incline your ear to me; rescue me speedily! Be a rock of refuge for me, a strong fortress to save me! For you are my rock and my fortress; and for your name's sake you lead me and guide me; you take me out of the net they have hidden for me, for you are my refuge.

~ Psalm 31.1-4

Pray without Ceasing – Flash Prayer for the Day
Your steadfast love, O Lord, is never-ending, and your mercies are fresh and new each morning. Your faithfulness is great, and we praise you for your love.

FOR YOUR WEEKLY JOURNEY

Let God Arise! Seasonal Focus
Lift Up the Son of Man, John 12.20-36

Book Reading
DAILY: Extreme Devotion Writing Team, *Extreme Devotion*

DC Talk, The Voice of the Martyrs, *Jesus Freaks*

"Feed My Sheep"
Outside the Church of Peter's Primacy, Tabgha

The Tomb Is Empty, and the Lord Lives!

The exclamation "Christ is risen! He is risen, indeed!" is as old as the Church itself. It testifies to the central, controlling belief of believers in Jesus of Nazareth worldwide as they celebrate his victory over the grave in his bodily resurrection from the dead. As was prophesied in Scripture, and foreseen by our Lord himself, he suffered on the Tree bearing our sins in his body and overcoming the guilt and power of the grave and the curse. Yet, on the third day down he rose triumphant from the grave, and is alive now forevermore! His resurrection serves as the pinnacle of all Christian belief, and is itself the ground for all biblical revelation on the redemption won for us through the Father's love.

The apostles taught that the resurrection of Jesus represents the central doctrine in all Christian faith and belief. Paul told the Corinthians that if the resurrection did not occur, then not even Christ has been raised, their apostolic preaching was worthless, and their faith would be futile. The apostles themselves would be found to be misrepresenting God, having borne witness that Christ has risen, when he did not (1 Cor. 15.12-15).

The Resurrection as the Centerpiece of Our Doctrine and the Heart of Christian Faith

The fact is, however, that Jesus did not simply teach the resurrection; he claimed to be, in fact, the Resurrection and the Life itself (John 11.25-26)! As such, his rising confirms God's veracity and truthfulness, authenticating the testimony of the Scriptures. From its earliest worship, the Church made the resurrection the centerpiece of its worship and community. As the living Savior he is with us to the end of this age (Matt. 28.20). Even his "going away" (in suffering

and death) did not prevent him from coming to us again in
his resurrected glory, leading to his gift of the Holy Spirit to
all believers (John 14.28). By faith we died with him, have
been made alive together with him, are raised with him
through baptism, and even have ascended and sit with him
in heavenly places (Rom. 6.1-4; Eph. 2.5).

Clearly, it is in Jesus' resurrection that *Christus Victor*
becomes most convincing (Gal. 1.4; Col. 2.15; 1 John 4.40).
In the person of Jesus Christ, and through his resurrection,
the Age to Come has broken into this present age, with our
Lord becoming the firstfruits of those who sleep. Christ is
the first fruits of the eschatological harvest of souls destined
to live in the fully consummated Age to come (1 Cor. 15.20).
Moreover, he is the "firstborn" from among the dead, i.e., the
primary one, the preeminent one, and the pattern of all who
with him will rise from the dead and inherit eternal life in the
new heavens and earth (Col. 1.18; Rev. 1.5-6). By the power
of his resurrection, God has birthed us to a living hope,
rooted in God's mercy and an inheritance that will never
perish or fade away (1 Pet. 1.3-5).

Surely then, it makes sense that the early Church chose
Easter as the singular event to welcome new converts into
the Church, to restore backsliders and penitents, and to
convocate in joyous gatherings of remembrance and worship. Christ's resurrection does not merely guarantee the life
of the Age to Come for a future time; rather, it provides us
with hope, power, and confidence to live a new life today,
right here, right now in him. Truly, if anyone is in Christ, s/he
is a new creation. The old has passed away; behold, the new
has come (2 Cor. 5.17).

He Is Risen, Indeed!
Come, celebrate this Easter season with glad shouts of
victory and honor to Jesus, our risen Lord! His resurrection
serves as the absolute proof of the coming consummation

of the plan of God, the coming resurrection of the dead, the gift of the Holy Spirit, and the promise of eternal life for those who believe. Let us gladly stir up pure longings for his return, and the end of this present fleeting age of darkness and sin. Join us in confessing that Jesus is Lord, and that God has raised him from the dead. This same Jesus of Nazareth, who was crucified and killed by lawless men is no longer dead. God has raised him up as victorious conqueror, and being loosed from the chains of death, he can secure all who believe by the same power. Because he lives, we can live today and face tomorrow.

"Christ is risen! He is risen, indeed!"

~ Rev. Dr. Don L. Davis

✠

EASTER SUNDAY, RESURRECTION OF THE LORD

April 20 - 26, 2014

> On Easter Sunday we celebrate the bodily resurrection of Jesus. The same lowly Nazarene -- he who was betrayed by his own disciple, who suffered under Pilate's cruel gaze, who was crucified on a Roman cross, and who was buried in a borrowed tomb -- the same Lord rose triumphantly on the third day. Jesus has risen from death to life through the power of God. "Christ is risen! He is risen, indeed!"

THIS WEEK'S THEME
The Tomb Is Empty, John 20.1-18

On the first day of the week, Mary Magdalene came early to the tomb, while it was still dark, and saw that the stone had been taken away from the tomb. She ran and told Simon Peter and John that the Lord had been taken out of the tomb, and that she did not know where he was laid. They went to the tomb, Peter before John, entered the tomb, found it empty, as Mary said, and went back to their homes.

Mary continued, standing and weeping outside the tomb, and as she wept she stooped to look into the tomb. She saw two angels in white, sitting where the body of Jesus had lain, one at the head and one at the feet. They asked her why she was weeping, and she answered, "They have taken away my Lord, and I do not know where they have laid him."

Having said this, Mary turned around and saw Jesus standing there, but she did not know that it was him. Jesus said to her, "Woman, why are you weeping? Whom are you seeking?" Thinking he was the gardener, she said, "Sir, if you have carried him away, tell me where you have laid him, and I will take him away." Then Jesus said to her, "Mary." She turned and said to him in Aramaic, "Rabboni!" (which means Teacher). The Lord then said to her, "Do not cling to me, for I have not yet ascended to the Father; but go to my brothers and say to them, 'I am ascending to my Father and your Father, to my God and your God.'" Mary then went and announced to the disciples, "I have seen the Lord" and that he had said these things to her.

DAILY DEVOTIONAL GUIDE

PREPARING OUR HEARTS

Invocation: Our Prayer of Acclamation
O God, who for our redemption didst give thine only-begotten Son to the death of the cross, and by his glorious resurrection hast delivered us from the power of our enemy: Grant us so to die daily from sin, that we may evermore live with him in the joy of his resurrection; through the same Jesus Christ our Lord.

~ John Wallace Suter, Jr.
Book of English Collects, No. 45 (Geffen, p. 83)

Call to Worship
Blessed are you, O God: Father, Son, and Holy Spirit. And blessed is your Kingdom, both now and forever, Amen.

PRAISING OUR GOD

Te Deum Laudamus
You are God: we praise you; you are the Lord; we acclaim you; you are the eternal Father: All creation worships you. To you all angels, all the powers of heaven, Cherubim and Seraphim, sing in endless praise: Holy, holy, holy Lord, God of power and might, heaven and earth are full of your glory.

The glorious company of apostles praise you. The noble fellowship of prophets praise you. The white-robed army of martyrs praise you. Throughout the world the holy Church acclaims you; Father, of majesty unbounded, your true and only Son, worthy of all worship, and the Holy Spirit, advocate and guide.

You, Christ, are the king of glory, the eternal Son of the Father. When you became man to set us free you did not shun the Virgin's womb.

You overcame the sting of death and opened the kingdom of heaven to all believers. You are seated at God's right hand in glory. We believe that you will come and be our judge. Come then, Lord, and help your people, bought with the price of your own blood, and bring us with your saints to glory everlasting.

Praise and Thanksgiving (Songs and Prayers)

Gloria Patri
Glory be to the Father,
And to the Son and to the Holy Spirit:
As it was in the beginning,
Is now, and ever shall be,
World without end. Amen, amen.

LISTENING TO HIS VOICE

Chronological Reading for the Day
Sunday: 1 Kings 5-6; 2 Chron. 2.1-3.14 ✛ *Monday:* 1 Kings 7; 2 Chron. 3.15-4.22 ✛ *Tuesday:* 1 Kings 8; 2 Chron. 5-6 ✛ *Wednesday:* 2 Chron. 7; 1 Kings 9.1-14 ✛ *Thursday:* 2 Chron. 1.14-17; 8.1-9.28; 1 Kings 9.15-10.29 ✛ *Friday:* 1 Kings 4; Pss. 72; 127 ✛ *Saturday:* Prov. 1-4

Chronological Holy Week Readings
Easter Sunday: Mark 16.1-20; Luke 24.1-53; John 20.1-25

Lectionary Readings for *Easter Morning*
Psalm: Ps. 118.1-2, 14-24   *Acts*:* Acts 10.34-43
Gospel: John 20.1-18   *NT:* Col. 3.1-4

* During Eastertide, a reading from Acts is often sustituted for the lesson from the Hebrew Bible.

Lectionary Readings for *Easter Evening*
Psalm: Ps. 114   *OT:* Isa. 25.6-9
Gospel: Luke 24.13-49   *NT:* 1 Cor. 5.6b-8

Reflection: Silence and/or Journaling

<u>RESPONDING IN FAITH</u>

The Apostles' Creed
*I believe in God, the Father Almighty, Maker of heaven and earth;
and in Jesus Christ, his only Son, our Lord, who was conceived by the
Holy Spirit, born of the Virgin Mary, suffered under Pontius Pilate,
was crucified, dead, and buried; he descended into hell; the third day
he arose again from the dead; he ascended into heaven and sits on
the right hand of God the Father Almighty; from thence he shall come
to judge the quick and the dead.*

I believe in the Holy Spirit, the holy catholic church, the communion
of saints, the forgiveness of sins, the resurrection of the body, and the
life everlasting. Amen.*

* In the Apostles' and Nicene Creeds, the term catholic refers to the Church's
universality, through all ages and times, of all languages and peoples. It refers to no
particular tradition or denominational expression (e.g., as in Roman Catholic).

Prayers of Confession
Let us now confess our sins to God and receive mercy and
grace to help in our time of need.

Assurance of Pardon
Having faithfully confessed and renounced your sin, Christ
also has been faithful to forgive your sins and to purify you
from all unrighteousness. It is certain, that there is One who
has spoken to the Father in your defense, Jesus Christ, the
Righteous One who is the atoning sacrifice for our sins and
for the sins of the whole world. His grace and peace are with
you now. Amen.

Petitions and Supplications, Ending with The Lord's Prayer
*Our Father which art in heaven, Hallowed be thy name. Thy kingdom
come, Thy will be done in earth, as it is in heaven. Give us this day our
daily bread. And forgive us our debts, as we forgive our debtors. And*

lead us not into temptation, but deliver us from evil: For thine is the kingdom, and the power, and the glory, for ever. Amen.

~ Matthew 6.9-13 (KJV)

Doxology (and/or closing song)
Praise God from whom all blessings flow;
Praise Him all creatures here below;
Praise Him above ye heavenly host;
Praise Father, Son and Holy Ghost. Amen.

DEPARTING TO SERVE

Benediction
O Lord God Almighty, whose blessed Son our Saviour Jesus Christ did on the third day rise triumphant over death: Raise us, we beseech thee, from the death of sin unto the life of righteousness, that we may seek those things which are above, where he sitteth on thy right hand in glory; and this we beg for the sake of the same thy Son Jesus Christ our Lord.

~ *Book of English Collects*, No. 46 (Geffen, p. 83)

Affirmation from the Psalms
The LORD is my strength and my song; he has become my salvation. Glad songs of salvation are in the tents of the righteous: "The right hand of the LORD does valiantly, the right hand of the LORD exalts, the right hand of the LORD does valiantly!" I shall not die, but I shall live, and recount the deeds of the LORD.

~ Psalm 118.14-17

Pray without Ceasing – Flash Prayer for the Day
Thank you, Lord Jesus, that your tomb is forever empty; you have conquered death, ended the curse, and banished all fear of the grave. In you alone, we are free.

FOR YOUR WEEKLY JOURNEY

Let God Arise! Seasonal Focus
On the Road to Emmaus, Luke 24.13-35

Book Reading
DAILY: Extreme Devotion Writing Team, *Extreme Devotion*

DC Talk, The Voice of the Martyrs, *Jesus Freaks*

SECOND SUNDAY OF EASTER

April 27 - May 3, 2014

On Easter Sunday we celebrate the bodily resurrection of Jesus. The same lowly Nazarene -- he who was betrayed by his own disciple, who suffered under Pilate's cruel gaze, who was crucified on a Roman cross, and who was buried in a borrowed tomb -- the same Lord rose triumphantly on the third day. Jesus has risen from death to life through the power of God. "Christ is risen! He is risen, indeed!"

THIS WEEK'S THEME
Jesus Appears to the Apostles, John 20.19-31
On the evening of Christ's resurrection day, the first day of the week, the doors were locked and the disciples were hiding inside for fear of the Jews. Amazingly, Jesus came and stood in the midst of them. He showed the disciples his hands and his side, and the disciples were glad when they saw the Lord.

The Lord pronounced his peace upon them, commissioned them to go as apostles, and entrusted them with authority to represent him and his forgiveness in the world. Thomas, one of the Twelve, called the Twin, was not with them when Jesus came, and refused to believe in the risen Jesus unless he personally saw the mark of the nails and placed his finger into those marks, both in his hands and side.

Eight days later, his disciples were inside again, with Thomas present, and then Jesus came and stood among them with the doors locked as before. After blessing them with peace, he said to Thomas, "Put your finger here, and see my hands; and put out your hand, and place it in my side. Do not disbelieve, but believe." Thomas answered him, "My Lord and my God!" Jesus said to him, "Have you believed because you have seen me? Blessed are those who have not seen and yet have believed." Jesus did many other signs in the presence of the disciples, not written in John's gospel, but the ones written are provided so that all may believe that Jesus is the Christ, the Son of God, and that by believing, have life in his name.

DAILY DEVOTIONAL GUIDE

PREPARING OUR HEARTS

Invocation: Our Prayer of Acclamation
Eternal God our Father, thank you for giving clear, infallible, and convincing proofs to the disciples that our Lord truly rose from the dead. You chose them to be witnesses to the Word made flesh, and they bore witness to his resurrection after your Spirit raised Jesus' body from the dead. Thank you for their testimony, and the truth of it. We believe in your Son through their word. In Jesus' name we pray, amen.

Call to Worship
Blessed are you, O God: Father, Son, and Holy Spirit. And blessed is your Kingdom, both now and forever, Amen.

PRAISING OUR GOD

Te Deum Laudamus
You are God: we praise you; you are the Lord; we acclaim you; you are the eternal Father: All creation worships you. To you all angels, all the powers of heaven, Cherubim and Seraphim, sing in endless praise: Holy, holy, holy Lord, God of power and might, heaven and earth are full of your glory.

The glorious company of apostles praise you. The noble fellowship of prophets praise you. The white-robed army of martyrs praise you. Throughout the world the holy Church acclaims you; Father, of majesty unbounded, your true and only Son, worthy of all worship, and the Holy Spirit, advocate and guide.

You, Christ, are the king of glory, the eternal Son of the Father. When you became man to set us free you did not shun the Virgin's womb. You overcame the sting of death and opened the kingdom of heaven to all believers. You are seated at God's right hand in glory. We believe that you will come and be our judge. Come then, Lord, and help your

people, bought with the price of your own blood, and bring us with
your saints to glory everlasting.

Praise and Thanksgiving (Songs and Prayers)

Gloria Patri
Glory be to the Father,
And to the Son and to the Holy Spirit:
As it was in the beginning,
Is now, and ever shall be,
World without end. Amen, amen.

LISTENING TO HIS VOICE

Chronological Reading for the Day
Sunday: Prov. 5-7 ✤ *Monday:* Prov. 8-10 ✤ *Tuesday:* Prov.
11-13 ✤ *Wednesday:* Prov. 14-16 ✤ *Thursday:* Prov. 17-19 ✤
Friday: Prov. 20.1-22.16 ✤ *Saturday:* Prov. 22.17-24.34

Lectionary Readings
Psalm: Ps. 16   *Acts*:* Acts 2.14a, 22-32
Gospel: John 20.19-31   *NT:* 1 Pet. 1.3-9

* During Eastertide, a reading from Acts is often sustituted for the lesson from the
Hebrew Bible.

Reflection: Silence and/or Journaling

RESPONDING IN FAITH

The Apostles' Creed
I believe in God, the Father Almighty, Maker of heaven and earth;
and in Jesus Christ, his only Son, our Lord, who was conceived by the
Holy Spirit, born of the Virgin Mary, suffered under Pontius Pilate,
was crucified, dead, and buried; he descended into hell; the third day
he arose again from the dead; he ascended into heaven and sits on

the right hand of God the Father Almighty; from thence he shall come to judge the quick and the dead.

I believe in the Holy Spirit, the holy catholic* church, the communion of saints, the forgiveness of sins, the resurrection of the body, and the life everlasting. Amen.

* In the Apostles' and Nicene Creeds, the term catholic refers to the Church's universality, through all ages and times, of all languages and peoples. It refers to no particular tradition or denominational expression (e.g., as in Roman Catholic).

Prayers of Confession

Let us now confess our sins to God and receive mercy and grace to help in our time of need.

Assurance of Pardon

Having faithfully confessed and renounced your sin, Christ also has been faithful to forgive your sins and to purify you from all unrighteousness. It is certain, that there is One who has spoken to the Father in your defense, Jesus Christ, the Righteous One who is the atoning sacrifice for our sins and for the sins of the whole world. His grace and peace are with you now. Amen.

Petitions and Supplications, Ending with The Lord's Prayer

Our Father which art in heaven, Hallowed be thy name. Thy kingdom come, Thy will be done in earth, as it is in heaven. Give us this day our daily bread. And forgive us our debts, as we forgive our debtors. And lead us not into temptation, but deliver us from evil: For thine is the kingdom, and the power, and the glory, for ever. Amen.

~ Matthew 6.9-13 (KJV)

Doxology (and/or closing song)

Praise God from whom all blessings flow;
Praise Him all creatures here below;
Praise Him above ye heavenly host;
Praise Father, Son and Holy Ghost. Amen.

DEPARTING TO SERVE

Benediction

Lord Jesus, you came and showed yourself to your disciples
after you were raised from the dead. They examined you,
heard your voice, received your teaching and commission,
and bore witness that the Father brought you to life again
through the Holy Spirit. They are witnesses to the resurrection;
you appeared to them, and we believe in you through their
word. Thank you for their witness, and for their faithful
testimony regarding the truth. In your name we pray, amen.

Affirmation from the Psalms

*Therefore my heart is glad, and my whole being rejoices; my flesh also
dwells secure. For you will not abandon my soul to Sheol, or let your
holy one see corruption. You make known to me the path of life; in
your presence there is fullness of joy; at your right hand are pleasures
forevermore.*

~ Psalm 16.9-11

Pray without Ceasing – Flash Prayer for the Day

Dear Father, thank you for the apostles, those who saw the
Lord after his resurrection, whose hearts were glad when
they saw the risen Lord.

FOR YOUR WEEKLY JOURNEY

Let God Arise! Seasonal Focus
On the Road to Emmaus, Luke 24.13-35

Book Reading
Daily: Extreme Devotion Writing Team, *Extreme Devotion*

DC Talk, The Voice of the Martyrs, *Jesus Freaks*

Our Corporate Disciplines
Concert of Prayer:
    Tuesday, April 29, 2014

✙

THIRD SUNDAY OF EASTER

May 4 - 10, 2014

On Easter Sunday we celebrate the bodily resurrection of Jesus. The same lowly Nazarene -- he who was betrayed by his own disciple, who suffered under Pilate's cruel gaze, who was crucified on a Roman cross, and who was buried in a borrowed tomb -- the same Lord rose triumphantly on the third day. Jesus has risen from death to life through the power of God. "Christ is risen! He is risen, indeed!"

THIS WEEK'S THEME
On the Road to Emmaus, Luke 24.13-35

On the first day of the week, when our Lord had appeared to Mary and the disciples, two of the disciples were going to a village named Emmaus, about seven miles from Jerusalem. As they journeyed, they were talking with one another about all the happenings of those recent days. While they were talking and discussing, Jesus himself drew near, and went with them (although their eyes were kept from recognizing him). In answer to Jesus' question about their conversation, they spoke of Jesus of Nazareth, the mighty prophet, who was delivered to the rulers, condemned to death, and crucified. But they thought he was the one to redeem Israel. Further, they spoke of the testimony of the women concerning his appearance that the women had witnessed, and others who visited the tomb and found it empty.

Jesus rebuked the two, saying, "O foolish ones, and slow of heart to believe all that the prophets have spoken! Was it not necessary that the Christ should suffer these things and enter into his glory?" And then, starting from the book of Moses and the Prophets, Jesus interpreted to the two in all the Scriptures the things concerning himself.

After they drew near to the village, the two urged Jesus strongly to stay with them, and so he did. When they were at table with them, he took the bread, blessed it, and broke it, and gave it to them. Suddenly, their eyes were opened to see that, in fact, their traveler, the stranger, was the risen Jesus of Nazareth! After Jesus had vanished from their sight, they spoke to each other concerning how their hearts burned within them as he talked on the road and opened the Scriptures to them. They then returned to Jerusalem, reported to the company of disciples what happened on the road, and how he was known to them in the breaking of the bread.

DAILY DEVOTIONAL GUIDE

PREPARING OUR HEARTS

Invocation: Our Prayer of Acclamation

Great Father, who raised our Lord from the grave on the third day, thank you that the risen Lord is open to walking with us on the road of our lives, that as we walk with each other in the faith that he is willing to join our journey, explain to us his truth on the way, and to make himself known to us in the breaking of the bread. Let the risen Lord come to us in the midst of our walk, and speak to us, even as he did with those of old. In Jesus' name we pray, amen.

Call to Worship

Blessed are you, O God: Father, Son, and Holy Spirit. And blessed is your Kingdom, both now and forever, Amen.

PRAISING OUR GOD

Te Deum Laudamus

You are God: we praise you; you are the Lord; we acclaim you; you are the eternal Father: All creation worships you. To you all angels, all the powers of heaven, Cherubim and Seraphim, sing in endless praise: Holy, holy, holy Lord, God of power and might, heaven and earth are full of your glory.

The glorious company of apostles praise you. The noble fellowship of prophets praise you. The white-robed army of martyrs praise you. Throughout the world the holy Church acclaims you; Father, of majesty unbounded, your true and only Son, worthy of all worship, and the Holy Spirit, advocate and guide.

You, Christ, are the king of glory, the eternal Son of the Father. When you became man to set us free you did not shun the Virgin's womb. You overcame the sting of death and opened the kingdom of heaven to all believers. You are seated at God's right hand in glory. We believe that you will come and be our judge. Come then, Lord, and help your people, bought with the price of your own blood, and bring us with your saints to glory everlasting.

Praise and Thanksgiving (Songs and Prayers)

Gloria Patri
Glory be to the Father,
And to the Son and to the Holy Spirit:
As it was in the beginning,
Is now, and ever shall be,
World without end. Amen, amen.

LISTENING TO HIS VOICE

Chronological Reading for the Day
Sunday: Song of Sol. 1-8 ✤ *Monday:* 1 Kings 11; 2 Chron. 9.29-31 ✤ *Tuesday:* Eccles. 1-6 ✤ *Wednesday:* Eccles. 7-12 ✤ *Thursday:* 1 Kings 12; 2 Chron. 10.1-11.17 ✤ *Friday:* 1 Kings 13.1-15.15, vv.25-34; 2 Chron. 11.18-15.19 ✤ *Saturday:* 1 Kings 15.16-24; 16.1-17.7; 2 Chron. 16-17

Lectionary Readings
Psalm: Ps. 116.1-4, 12-19   *Acts*:* Acts 2.14a, 36-41
Gospel: Luke 24.13-35   *NT:* 1 Pet. 1.17-23

* During Eastertide, a reading from Acts is often sustituted for the lesson from the Hebrew Bible.

Reflection: Silence and/or Journaling

RESPONDING IN FAITH

The Apostles' Creed
I believe in God, the Father Almighty, Maker of heaven and earth; and in Jesus Christ, his only Son, our Lord, who was conceived by the Holy Spirit, born of the Virgin Mary, suffered under Pontius Pilate, was crucified, dead, and buried; he descended into hell; the third day he arose again from the dead; he ascended into heaven and sits on the right hand of God the Father Almighty; from thence he shall come to judge the quick and the dead.

I believe in the Holy Spirit, the holy catholic* church, the communion of saints, the forgiveness of sins, the resurrection of the body, and the life everlasting. Amen.

* In the Apostles' and Nicene Creeds, the term catholic refers to the Church's universality, through all ages and times, of all languages and peoples. It refers to no particular tradition or denominational expression (e.g., as in Roman Catholic).

Prayers of Confession
Let us now confess our sins to God and receive mercy and grace to help in our time of need.

Assurance of Pardon
Having faithfully confessed and renounced your sin, Christ also has been faithful to forgive your sins and to purify you from all unrighteousness. It is certain, that there is One who has spoken to the Father in your defense, Jesus Christ, the Righteous One who is the atoning sacrifice for our sins and for the sins of the whole world. His grace and peace are with you now. Amen.

Petitions and Supplications, Ending with The Lord's Prayer
Our Father which art in heaven, Hallowed be thy name. Thy kingdom come, Thy will be done in earth, as it is in heaven. Give us this day our daily bread. And forgive us our debts, as we forgive our debtors. And

lead us not into temptation, but deliver us from evil: For thine is the kingdom, and the power, and the glory, for ever. Amen.

~ Matthew 6.9-13 (KJV)

Doxology (and/or closing song)

Praise God from whom all blessings flow;
Praise Him all creatures here below;
Praise Him above ye heavenly host;
Praise Father, Son and Holy Ghost. Amen.

DEPARTING TO SERVE

Benediction

Lord Jesus, thank you for the testimony of your walk with the two disciples on the road to Emmaus, how you joined them on their walk and entered into their conversation. You listened to them and responded, and instructed them into a deeper vision of your mission and work as you walked with them on the Way. In the same way, we ask that you come and meet us here in the midst of our journeys, wherever we are, right where we sojourn, and enter into our conversations and teach us, too. Make yourself known to us in the breaking of the bread, and we will worship you alone. Cause our hearts to burn, even as theirs did, for your sake. In your name we pray, amen.

Affirmation from the Psalms

O LORD, I am your servant; I am your servant, the son of your maidservant. You have loosed my bonds. I will offer to you the sacrifice of thanksgiving and call on the name of the LORD. I will pay my vows to the LORD in the presence of all his people, in the courts of the house of the LORD, in your midst, O Jerusalem. Praise the LORD!

~ Psalm 116.16-19

Pray without Ceasing – Flash Prayer for the Day
Gentle Savior, who joined the journey and conversation of
the two disciples so long ago, come and join us, walk with
us, as we learn more of you together, for your sake.

FOR YOUR WEEKLY JOURNEY

Let God Arise! Seasonal Focus
On the Road to Emmaus, Luke 24.13-35

Book Reading
Daily: Extreme Devotion Writing Team, *Extreme Devotion*

DC Talk, The Voice of the Martyrs, *Jesus Freaks*

May 11 - 17, 2014

On Easter Sunday we celebrate the bodily resurrection of Jesus. The same lowly Nazarene -- he who was betrayed by his own disciple, who suffered under Pilate's cruel gaze, who was crucified on a Roman cross, and who was buried in a borrowed tomb -- the same Lord rose triumphantly on the third day. Jesus has risen from death to life through the power of God. "Christ is risen! He is risen, indeed!"

THIS WEEK'S THEME
The Good Shepherd, John 10.1-10

Jesus of Nazareth explained his relationship to his true disciples as the Good Shepherd. He used this figure of speech, although many did not understand what he was saying to them. As rabbi, he taught his disciples that the one who does not enter the sheepfold by the door but climbs in by another way is a thief and a robber. The one, however, who enters by the door is the shepherd of the sheep. Jesus said that to the shepherd the gatekeeper opens, and that the sheep hear his voice, he calls his own sheep by name, and then leads them out.

The true shepherd, according to Jesus, brings out all his own, goes before them, and the sheep follow him, for they know his voice. The sheep will not follow strangers, but will rather flee from them, for they do not know the voice of strangers. To help them better understand, Jesus again said to them, "Truly, truly, I say to you, I am the door of the sheep. All who came before me are thieves and robbers, but the sheep did not listen to them. I am the door. If anyone enters by me, he will be saved and will go in and out and find pasture. The thief comes only to steal and kill and destroy. I came that they may have life and have it abundantly." Jesus of Nazareth is truly the Good Shepherd, who laid down his life for his sheep.

DAILY DEVOTIONAL GUIDE

PREPARING OUR HEARTS

Invocation: Our Prayer of Acclamation

Eternal God our Father, whose only Son declared himself to be the Good Shepherd who laid down his life for his own, thank you for your love and compassion. Your great love allowed you to give him a commandment to come and ransom us, and he, without fail or condition, agreed. We are yours because of your love and his obedience. We bask in your great love, and thank you for all you are to us, and all you have done for us. In Jesus' name we pray, amen.

Call to Worship

Blessed are you, O God: Father, Son, and Holy Spirit. And blessed is your Kingdom, both now and forever, Amen.

PRAISING OUR GOD

Te Deum Laudamus

You are God: we praise you; you are the Lord; we acclaim you; you are the eternal Father: All creation worships you. To you all angels, all the powers of heaven, Cherubim and Seraphim, sing in endless praise: Holy, holy, holy Lord, God of power and might, heaven and earth are full of your glory.

The glorious company of apostles praise you. The noble fellowship of prophets praise you. The white-robed army of martyrs praise you. Throughout the world the holy Church acclaims you; Father, of majesty unbounded, your true and only Son, worthy of all worship, and the Holy Spirit, advocate and guide.

You, Christ, are the king of glory, the eternal Son of the Father. When you became man to set us free you did not shun the Virgin's womb. You overcame the sting of death and opened the kingdom of heaven to all believers. You are seated at God's right hand in glory. We believe

that you will come and be our judge. Come then, Lord, and help your people, bought with the price of your own blood, and bring us with your saints to glory everlasting.

Praise and Thanksgiving (Songs and Prayers)

Gloria Patri
Glory be to the Father,
And to the Son and to the Holy Spirit:
As it was in the beginning,
Is now, and ever shall be,
World without end. Amen, amen.

LISTENING TO HIS VOICE

Chronological Reading for the Day
Sunday: 1 Kings 17.8-20.22 ⊕ *Monday:* 1 Kings 20.23-22.9; 2 Chron. 18.1-8 ⊕ *Tuesday:* 1 Kings 22.10-40, vv.51-53; 2 Chron. 18.9-20.37 ⊕ *Wednesday:* 2 Kings 1; 3; 8.16-22; 1 Kings 22.41-50; 2 Chron. 21.1-7 ⊕ *Thursday:* 2 Kings 2; ch.4 ⊕ *Friday:* 2 Kings 5.1-8.15 ⊕ *Saturday:* 2 Chron. 21.8-22.9; 2 Kings 8.23-10.31

Lectionary Readings
Psalm: Ps. 23   *Acts*:* Acts 2.42-47
Gospel: John 10.1-10   *NT:* 1 Pet. 2.19-25

* During Eastertide, a reading from Acts is often sustituted for the lesson from the Hebrew Bible.

Reflection: Silence and/or Journaling

RESPONDING IN FAITH

The Apostles' Creed
I believe in God, the Father Almighty, Maker of heaven and earth; and in Jesus Christ, his only Son, our Lord, who was conceived by the

Holy Spirit, born of the Virgin Mary, suffered under Pontius Pilate, was crucified, dead, and buried; he descended into hell; the third day he arose again from the dead; he ascended into heaven and sits on the right hand of God the Father Almighty; from thence he shall come to judge the quick and the dead.

I believe in the Holy Spirit, the holy catholic* church, the communion of saints, the forgiveness of sins, the resurrection of the body, and the life everlasting. Amen.

* In the Apostles' and Nicene Creeds, the term catholic refers to the Church's universality, through all ages and times, of all languages and peoples. It refers to no particular tradition or denominational expression (e.g., as in Roman Catholic).

Prayers of Confession

Let us now confess our sins to God and receive mercy and grace to help in our time of need.

Assurance of Pardon

Having faithfully confessed and renounced your sin, Christ also has been faithful to forgive your sins and to purify you from all unrighteousness. It is certain, that there is One who has spoken to the Father in your defense, Jesus Christ, the Righteous One who is the atoning sacrifice for our sins and for the sins of the whole world. His grace and peace are with you now. Amen.

Petitions and Supplications, Ending with The Lord's Prayer

Our Father which art in heaven, Hallowed be thy name. Thy kingdom come, Thy will be done in earth, as it is in heaven. Give us this day our daily bread. And forgive us our debts, as we forgive our debtors. And lead us not into temptation, but deliver us from evil: For thine is the kingdom, and the power, and the glory, for ever. Amen.

~ Matthew 6.9-13 (KJV)

Doxology (and/or closing song)
Praise God from whom all blessings flow;
Praise Him all creatures here below;
Praise Him above ye heavenly host;
Praise Father, Son and Holy Ghost. Amen.

DEPARTING TO SERVE

Benediction
Lord Jesus, who is the door of the sheep, the good shepherd who laid his life down for the sheep, thank you for making a way for us to relate to and enjoy your Father, the Lord God Almighty. All who came before you we declare to be both thieves and robbers, and we as your sheep will listen to no one else but you. You are the door, and we enter by faith through you alone. Save us, let us go in and out and find pasture, and protect us from the thief who seeks to steal and kill and destroy. We entrust ourselves to you, for you came that we might have life, and have it abundantly. Lead us into your perfect will. In your name we pray, amen.

Affirmation from the Psalms
The LORD is my shepherd; I shall not want. He makes me lie down in green pastures. He leads me beside still waters. He restores my soul. He leads me in paths of righteousness for his name's sake. Even though I walk through the valley of the shadow of death, I will fear no evil, for you are with me; your rod and your staff, they comfort me. You prepare a table before me in the presence of my enemies; you anoint my head with oil; my cup overflows. Surely goodness and mercy shall follow me all the days of my life, and I shall dwell in the house of the LORD forever.

~ Psalm 23.1-6

Pray without Ceasing – Flash Prayer for the Day
Lord Jesus, Savior and Lord, like a shepherd lead us into your pastures green, protect us from those who would prey upon us, and gather us all into one flock and fold.

FOR YOUR WEEKLY JOURNEY

Let God Arise! Seasonal Focus
On the Road to Emmaus, Luke 24.13-35

Book Reading
DAILY: Extreme Devotion Writing Team, *Extreme Devotion*

DC Talk, The Voice of the Martyrs, *Jesus Freaks*

Our Corporate Disciplines
Prayer and Fasting, ending with Book Review:
    Wednesday, May 14, 2014
Concert of Prayer:
    Saturday, May 17, 2014

Russian Orthodox Church of the Ascension, Mount of Olives

The Risen Lord Has Ascended to the Right Hand of God

The Ascension of Christ to heaven refers to that event where the risen Jesus, after 40 days of confirming his resurrection to his disciples, ascended to the Father. On his arrival, God "seated him at his right hand in the heavenly realms, far above all rule and authority, power and dominion, and every title that can be given, not only in the present age but also in the one to come" (Eph. 1.20b-21; 1 Pet. 3.22; Luke 24.17-53). On Thursday, May 17, we celebrate with Christians all over the world the Ascension of our Lord to God's right hand. Glorified by the Father as Head of the Church (cf. Eph. 1.15-23), our Lord has sent his Spirit into the world, intercedes for his own before God, and reigns above in a position of glory and power awaiting the coming judgment.

As one commentator put it, there is "no incident in the life of Jesus at one and the same time so beset with difficulties and so essential as the Ascension" (William Barclay as quoted in Norman Gulley, "The Ascension of Christ" in *The Anchor Bible Dictionary*, Vol. 1, p. 472). Others have referred to this important doctrine of the Church and Creed as the "most neglected doctrine of the church." Still, the Ascension of Jesus is one of the New Testament's central themes. Without it, we cannot understand the sending of the Spirit into the world, Jesus' high priestly ministry for the Church, the harvesting of souls during this age "between the times," or the blessed hope of Jesus' return. The claim of God's exaltation of Jesus to his right hand was a staple in the apostles' preaching and teaching, and it must become a central theme in our worship and mission if we are to be true witnesses of the Gospel.

Proofs of the Resurrection, Promises of the Spirit's Coming

For forty days following his resurrection from the dead, the risen Jesus provided the apostles with a number of convincing proofs of his return from death, and taught them concerning the Kingdom of God (Acts 1.3). He commanded them to stay in Jerusalem until the promise of the Father (i.e., the Holy Spirit) would be granted to them (cf. Acts 1.5; John 14.16; 15.26; 16.7). They questioned him concerning the timing of God's restoration of the Kingdom, revealing the close connection in their minds of the promised outpouring of the Holy Spirit and the end of the age, climaxed with the coming of the promised Kingdom of the Father (cf. Isa. 32.15-20; 44.3-5; Ezek. 39.28-29; Joel 2.28-3.1; Zech. 12.8-10).

After commanding his apostles to share the Good News to the ends of the earth, starting at Jerusalem, Jesus ascended as they looked on, and was lifted up with a cloud taking him out of their sight (Acts 1.9). As firsthand witnesses, the apostles saw the risen Christ ascend. According to Luke's account,"two men in white robes" [i.e., angels of God] made the following affirmation: "Men of Galilee, why do you stand looking into heaven? This Jesus, who was taken up from you into heaven, will come in the same way as you saw him go into heaven," (Acts 1.10-11).

This doctrine is critical for Christian worship, spiritual warfare, and fruitful mission. Christ ascended to the Father's right hand in order to fulfill his promise of his return to the Father (John 6.62; 14.2, 12; 16.5, 10, 28; 20.17), to vindicate his messiahship and sonship, and to pour out the Holy Spirit upon the Church for worship and witness (cf. John 16.7 with Acts 1.8; Acts 2.33). As conquering Lord, Christ now spreads abroad the "spoils" of his divine triumph over the devil and the forces of evil (Eph. 4.8-10), and he now prepares a place (i.e., the New Jerusalem) for his redeemed company and body, the Church (John 14.2-3; Acts 3.21). Because he has ascended, he can now empower all members of his Church with his divine presence through the Spirit (Matt. 28.20, cf. John 16.7-15), and ensure that soon and very soon, he will

return and restore creation under his reign (Acts 1.9-11).
This central doctrine calls for our shouts of praise, affirmations of faith, and acts of courage in witness. Jesus is risen
and ascended to the Father for his own glory, and for us!

Because Jesus our Lord is ascended, exalted, and glorified
at the Father's right hand, let us affirm him to be the Head of
the Church, the Lord of the Harvest, and the High Priest
of the Lord. Let us acknowledge him to be *Christus Victor*,
supreme sovereign to whom all authority has been entrusted.

Truly, let us submit our wills to him as our exalted Head, and
bear bold witness of his saving work to the world. Above all,
let us stir up our hearts in anticipation of his return as the
coming Judge of all and our coming King. With all believers,
we affirm together the great anthem of the Church: "All hail
the power of Jesus' name, let angels prostrate fall! Bring forth
the royal diadem, and crown him Lord of all!"

Bring Forth the Royal Diadem, and Crown Jesus Lord of All!
Come, let us continue our Easter celebration with praise and
thanksgiving as we remember the Ascension of Jesus Christ.
With Christians around the world, let us glory in the exalted
status of our Champion and Victor. Having destroyed death,
defeated evil and the powers, rescinded the curse, and
established the future recreation of all things, he has been
enthroned at the Father's right hand as Lord. The crucified
One has indeed been given all power, and he must reign
until all his enemies are subdued and conquered under his
feet. Let us glory in our Lord Jesus, whom the Father has
made both Lord and Christ, who has ascended to the Father's
presence to intercede on our behalf. From the Father's side,
we await the coming of our Savior and Lord. Jesus Christ is
Lord, to the glory of God the Father!

~ Celebrating the exaltation of the Master,
Rev. Dr. Don L. Davis

✚

FIFTH SUNDAY OF EASTER

May 18 - 24, 2014

For forty days after his resurrection, Jesus revealed himself alive to his disciples. On the fortieth day, he ascended to heaven to take his place as Lord and Christ at God's right hand. Ten days after this, on the fiftieth day after his resurrection, he would send to us the promise of the Father -- the Holy Spirit, the pledge of our salvation. Here we ponder the wonder of God's working, from Easter Sunday to the Spirit's descent at Pentecost.

THIS WEEK'S THEME
Living Stones and a Holy People, 1 Peter 2.2-10

Peter exhorts the believers to be like newborn babes, desiring God's spiritual milk through which they would grow up into their salvation, seeing that they had tasted that the Lord is good. We have come to Christ, God's chosen and precious Living Stone, we, like living stones, are being built up as a spiritual house to be God's holy priesthood offering spiritual sacrifices acceptable to God through Jesus Christ. We have the honor of resting on that foundation stone which God has laid in Zion, and since we believe in him we will never be put to shame.

Those who reject him, however – those refusing to believe in our Living Stone – have actually rejected the Cornerstone. For them, this Stone has become a stone of stumbling and a rock of offense. They who do not believe in him stumble, because they disobey the word, as Peter declares they were destined to do. But we who cling to Christ are a chosen race, a royal priesthood, a holy nation, a people for his own possession. We have been given the honor to proclaim the excellencies of God who called us out of darkness into his marvelous light. Once we were not a people, but now, we belong to God. Once we had not received mercy, now we are forgiven.

DAILY DEVOTIONAL GUIDE

PREPARING OUR HEARTS

Invocation: Our Prayer of Acclamation

Eternal and merciful God, the Lord who laid in Zion a tried and precious Cornerstone, grant us the wisdom to understand that we have been made living stones, being built up into your spiritual house, set apart to offer to you acceptable sacrifices and offerings of praise and surrender. We cling to your Son, Jesus of Nazareth, the Living Stone who is our Source and Strength. Open our eyes to see him more clearly today. In his name, amen.

Call to Worship

Blessed are you, O God: Father, Son, and Holy Spirit. And blessed is your Kingdom, both now and forever, Amen.

PRAISING OUR GOD

Te Deum Laudamus

You are God: we praise you; you are the Lord; we acclaim you; you are the eternal Father: All creation worships you. To you all angels, all the powers of heaven, Cherubim and Seraphim, sing in endless praise: Holy, holy, holy Lord, God of power and might, heaven and earth are full of your glory.

The glorious company of apostles praise you. The noble fellowship of prophets praise you. The white-robed army of martyrs praise you. Throughout the world the holy Church acclaims you; Father, of majesty unbounded, your true and only Son, worthy of all worship, and the Holy Spirit, advocate and guide.

You, Christ, are the king of glory, the eternal Son of the Father. When you became man to set us free you did not shun the Virgin's womb. You overcame the sting of death and opened the kingdom of heaven to all believers. You are seated at God's right hand in glory. We believe

that you will come and be our judge. Come then, Lord, and help your people, bought with the price of your own blood, and bring us with your saints to glory everlasting.

Praise and Thanksgiving (Songs and Prayers)

Gloria Patri
Glory be to the Father,
And to the Son and to the Holy Spirit:
As it was in the beginning,
Is now, and ever shall be,
World without end. Amen, amen.

LISTENING TO HIS VOICE

Chronological Reading for the Day
Sunday: 2 Kings 10.32-12.16; 2 Chron. 22.10-24.22 ✤ *Monday:* 2 Chron. 24.23-27; 2 Kings 12.17-13.25 ✤ *Tuesday:* 2 Kings 14.1-27; 15.1-5; 2 Chron. 25.1-26.21; Jon. 1-4 ✤ *Wednesday:* Amos 1-6 ✤ *Thursday:* Amos 7-9; 2 Kings 14.28-29; 15.6-29; 2 Chron. 26.22-23; Isa. 6 ✤ *Friday:* 2 Kings 15.32-16.9; 2 Chron. 27.1-28.15; Mic. 1; Isa. 7 ✤ *Saturday:* Isa. 8-11

Lectionary Readings
Psalm: Ps. 31.1-5, 15-16   *Acts*:* Acts 7.55-60
Gospel: John 14.1-14   *NT:* 1 Pet. 2.2-10

* During Eastertide, a reading from Acts is often sustituted for the lesson from the Hebrew Bible.

Reflection: Silence and/or Journaling

RESPONDING IN FAITH

The Apostles' Creed
I believe in God, the Father Almighty, Maker of heaven and earth;
and in Jesus Christ, his only Son, our Lord, who was conceived by the

Holy Spirit, born of the Virgin Mary, suffered under Pontius Pilate, was crucified, dead, and buried; he descended into hell; the third day he arose again from the dead; he ascended into heaven and sits on the right hand of God the Father Almighty; from thence he shall come to judge the quick and the dead.

I believe in the Holy Spirit, the holy catholic* church, the communion of saints, the forgiveness of sins, the resurrection of the body, and the life everlasting. Amen.

* In the Apostles' and Nicene Creeds, the term catholic refers to the Church's universality, through all ages and times, of all languages and peoples. It refers to no particular tradition or denominational expression (e.g., as in Roman Catholic).

Prayers of Confession
Let us now confess our sins to God and receive mercy and grace to help in our time of need.

Assurance of Pardon
Having faithfully confessed and renounced your sin, Christ also has been faithful to forgive your sins and to purify you from all unrighteousness. It is certain, that there is One who has spoken to the Father in your defense, Jesus Christ, the Righteous One who is the atoning sacrifice for our sins and for the sins of the whole world. His grace and peace are with you now. Amen.

Petitions and Supplications, Ending with The Lord's Prayer
Our Father which art in heaven, Hallowed be thy name. Thy kingdom come, Thy will be done in earth, as it is in heaven. Give us this day our daily bread. And forgive us our debts, as we forgive our debtors. And lead us not into temptation, but deliver us from evil: For thine is the kingdom, and the power, and the glory, for ever. Amen.

~ Matthew 6.9-13 (KJV)

Doxology (and/or closing song)

Praise God from whom all blessings flow;
Praise Him all creatures here below;
Praise Him above ye heavenly host;
Praise Father, Son and Holy Ghost. Amen.

DEPARTING TO SERVE

Benediction

Lord Jesus, who has made us, your people, into a chosen race and royal priesthood, weld our hearts together in common unity in order that we might glorify your Father through our works of surrender and faith. Fill us with power through the Holy Spirit, and grant us the privilege of hearing your voice even as we raise our voices to you in prayer and praise today. All that we have we offer to you today, as living sacrifices, for your glory. In your name we pray, amen.

Affirmation from the Psalms

In you, O LORD, do I take refuge; let me never be put to shame; in your righteousness deliver me! Incline your ear to me; rescue me speedily! Be a rock of refuge for me, a strong fortress to save me! For you are my rock and my fortress; and for your name's sake you lead me and guide me; you take me out of the net they have hidden for me, for you are my refuge. Into your hand I commit my spirit; you have redeemed me, O LORD, faithful God.

~ Psalm 31.1-5

Pray without Ceasing – Flash Prayer for the Day

Receive our offerings of praise and worship, O Savior and Living Stone, as we, your royal priesthood, offer acceptable sacrifices to God in your name.

FOR YOUR WEEKLY JOURNEY

Let God Arise! Seasonal Focus
To the Unknown God, Acts 17.22-31

Book Reading
DAILY: Extreme Devotion Writing Team, *Extreme Devotion*

DC Talk, The Voice of the Martyrs, *Jesus Freaks*

✤

SIXTH SUNDAY OF EASTER

May 25 - 31, 2014

For forty days after his resurrection, Jesus revealed himself alive to his disciples. On the fortieth day, he ascended to heaven to take his place as Lord and Christ at God's right hand. Ten days after this, on the fiftieth day after his resurrection, he would send to us the promise of the Father -- the Holy Spirit, the pledge of our salvation. Here we ponder the wonder of God's working, from Easter Sunday to the Spirit's descent at Pentecost.

THIS WEEK'S THEME
To the Unknown God, Acts 17.22-31

On Mars Hill in Athens, Paul preached one of his most famous sermons concerning the Lord Jesus Christ, identifying his God and Father as the "Unknown God" the Atheneans had been worshiping unaware. In his address Paul reviews for his audience God's true works in the past, who acted as creator of the universe, the maker of the nations, and source of human life, his offspring. He declared his works of the present, i.e., his desire to save all people, reaching out to humankind, calling all to repent and to turn from their idols to serve the living and true God. And finally, he announced God's work for the future, where one day he will judge the world through the One whom he has chosen, Jesus of Nazareth, whom he raised up from the dead.

DAILY DEVOTIONAL GUIDE

PREPARING OUR HEARTS

Invocation: Our Prayer of Acclamation

Eternal God, the Father Almighty, who as Creator and Maker is the source of life for all things and humankind, thank you for the testimony of the apostles regarding your true works in history, in the world, and the age to come. Grant us the wisdom to see and believe in your great works: you have made us, are willing to forgive us, and have called us to repent and believe in your Son, our Savior, Jesus Christ. We open our hearts to him this day, knowing that he is the One who will judge the world in righteousness. We give ourselves to you today. In his name we pray, amen.

Call to Worship

Blessed are you, O God: Father, Son, and Holy Spirit. And blessed is your Kingdom, both now and forever, Amen.

PRAISING OUR GOD

Te Deum Laudamus

You are God: we praise you; you are the Lord; we acclaim you; you are the eternal Father: All creation worships you. To you all angels, all the powers of heaven, Cherubim and Seraphim, sing in endless praise: Holy, holy, holy Lord, God of power and might, heaven and earth are full of your glory.

The glorious company of apostles praise you. The noble fellowship of prophets praise you. The white-robed army of martyrs praise you. Throughout the world the holy Church acclaims you; Father, of majesty unbounded, your true and only Son, worthy of all worship, and the Holy Spirit, advocate and guide.

You, Christ, are the king of glory, the eternal Son of the Father. When you became man to set us free you did not shun the Virgin's womb. You overcame the sting of death and opened the kingdom of heaven to all believers. You are seated at God's right hand in glory. We believe that you will come and be our judge. Come then, Lord, and help your people, bought with the price of your own blood, and bring us with your saints to glory everlasting.

Praise and Thanksgiving (Songs and Prayers)

Gloria Patri
Glory be to the Father,
And to the Son and to the Holy Spirit:
As it was in the beginning,
Is now, and ever shall be,
World without end. Amen, amen.

LISTENING TO HIS VOICE

Chronological Reading for the Day
Sunday: Isa. 12; 17; 2 Chron. 28.16-25; 29.1-2; 2 Kings 15.30-31; 16.10-18; 17.1-4; 18.1-8 ✤ *Monday:* Hos. 1-7 ✤ *Tuesday:* Hos. 8-14 ✤ *Wednesday:* Isa. 28; 1.1-20; 2 Kings 17.5-41; 18.9-12 ✤ *Thursday:* Isa. 1.21-5.30 ✤ *Friday:* 2 Kings 16.19-20; 2 Chron. 28.26-27; Isa. 13-16 ✤ *Saturday:* 2 Chron. 29.3-31.21

Lectionary Readings
Psalm: Ps. 66.8-20   *Acts*:* Acts 17.22-31
Gospel: John 14.15-21   *NT:* 1 Pet. 3.13-22

* During Eastertide, a reading from Acts is often sustituted for the lesson from the Hebrew Bible.

Reflection: Silence and/or Journaling

RESPONDING IN FAITH

The Apostles' Creed
I believe in God, the Father Almighty, Maker of heaven and earth; and in Jesus Christ, his only Son, our Lord, who was conceived by the Holy Spirit, born of the Virgin Mary, suffered under Pontius Pilate, was crucified, dead, and buried; he descended into hell; the third day he arose again from the dead; he ascended into heaven and sits on the right hand of God the Father Almighty; from thence he shall come to judge the quick and the dead.

I believe in the Holy Spirit, the holy catholic* church, the communion of saints, the forgiveness of sins, the resurrection of the body, and the life everlasting. Amen.

* In the Apostles' and Nicene Creeds, the term catholic refers to the Church's universality, through all ages and times, of all languages and peoples. It refers to no particular tradition or denominational expression (e.g., as in Roman Catholic).

Prayers of Confession
Let us now confess our sins to God and receive mercy and grace to help in our time of need.

Assurance of Pardon
Having faithfully confessed and renounced your sin, Christ also has been faithful to forgive your sins and to purify you from all unrighteousness. It is certain, that there is One who has spoken to the Father in your defense, Jesus Christ, the Righteous One who is the atoning sacrifice for our sins and for the sins of the whole world. His grace and peace are with you now. Amen.

Petitions and Supplications, Ending with The Lord's Prayer
Our Father which art in heaven, Hallowed be thy name. Thy kingdom come, Thy will be done in earth, as it is in heaven. Give us this day our daily bread. And forgive us our debts, as we forgive our debtors. And lead us not into temptation, but deliver us from evil: For thine is the kingdom, and the power, and the glory, for ever. Amen.

~ Matthew 6.9-13 (KJV)

Doxology (and/or closing song)
Praise God from whom all blessings flow;
Praise Him all creatures here below;
Praise Him above ye heavenly host;
Praise Father, Son and Holy Ghost. Amen.

DEPARTING TO SERVE

Benediction

In the name of Jesus of Nazareth, our Lord and King, we worship you, O God, the One whom the Atheneans of old called the "Unknown God." We know you to be the one, true God, the Creator of all things, and great Father who sent his Son to earth to redeem for yourself a remnant people destined to live with you forever in a new heaven and earth. We acknowledge you as our God and King. We love you. Abba, Father! In Jesus' name we pray, amen.

Affirmation from the Psalms

Come and hear, all you who fear God, and I will tell what he has done for my soul. I cried to him with my mouth, and high praise was on my tongue. If I had cherished iniquity in my heart, the Lord would not have listened. But truly God has listened; he has attended to the voice of my prayer. Blessed be God, because he has not rejected my prayer or removed his steadfast love from me!

~ Psalm 66.16-20

Pray without Ceasing – Flash Prayer for the Day

I acknowledge you, O God my Father, as my Creator and Redeemer, the One who sustains my soul and provides me with what I need to live, and to glorify you.

FOR YOUR WEEKLY JOURNEY

Let God Arise! Seasonal Focus
To the Unknown God, Acts 17.22-31

Book Reading
DAILY: Extreme Devotion Writing Team, *Extreme Devotion*

DC Talk, The Voice of the Martyrs, *Jesus Freaks*

Special Church Year Services
Ascension Day: Thursday, May 29, 2014

May 29, 2014

For forty days after his resurrection, Jesus revealed himself alive to his disciples. On the fortieth day, he ascended to heaven to take his place as Lord and Christ at God's right hand. Ten days after this, on the fiftieth day after his resurrection, he would send to us the promise of the Father -- the Holy Spirit, the pledge of our salvation. Here we ponder the wonder of God's working, from Easter Sunday to the Spirit's descent at Pentecost.

TODAY'S THEME
The Blessing of the Lord, Luke 24.44-5

After Jesus had risen from the dead, he appeared to his disciples and explained the relationship of his death to his resurrection. He instructed them that everything written about himself in the Law of Moses and the Prophets and the Psalms had to be fulfilled. He opened their minds to understand the Scriptures, and declared that, just as the Scripture foretold, the Christ would suffer and on the third day rise from the dead. The Word also testified that repentance and forgiveness of sins would be proclaimed in his name to all nations, beginning from Jerusalem. He testified that his disciples were witnesses of these things that were written in Scripture. He commanded them to stay in Jerusalem until they were clothed with power from on high, for he was about to send the promise of his Father upon them all.

After these things, the Lord Jesus led them out as far as Bethany, and lifting up his hands he blessed the apostles. And, it happened that, while he blessed them, he parted from them and was carried up into heaven. They worshiped the Lord, and returned to Jerusalem with great joy, and remained continually in the temple, blessing God.

DAILY DEVOTIONAL GUIDE

PREPARING OUR HEARTS

Invocation: Our Prayer of Acclamation
Be present, O Lord, to our supplications; that as we trust that the Saviour of mankind is seated with Thee in Thy Majesty, so we may feel that, according to His promise, He abideth with us unto the end of the world; through the same Jesus Christ our Lord. Amen.

~ Mozarabic Missal and Breviary (Wright, p. 59)

Call to Worship
Blessed are you, O God: Father, Son, and Holy Spirit. And blessed is your Kingdom, both now and forever, Amen.

PRAISING OUR GOD

Te Deum Laudamus
You are God: we praise you; you are the Lord; we acclaim you; you are the eternal Father: All creation worships you. To you all angels, all the powers of heaven, Cherubim and Seraphim, sing in endless praise: Holy, holy, holy Lord, God of power and might, heaven and earth are full of your glory.

The glorious company of apostles praise you. The noble fellowship of prophets praise you. The white-robed army of martyrs praise you. Throughout the world the holy Church acclaims you; Father, of majesty unbounded, your true and only Son, worthy of all worship, and the Holy Spirit, advocate and guide.

You, Christ, are the king of glory, the eternal Son of the Father. When you became man to set us free you did not shun the Virgin's womb. You overcame the sting of death and opened the kingdom of heaven to all believers. You are seated at God's right hand in glory. We believe that you will come and be our judge. Come then, Lord, and help your

*people, bought with the price of your own blood, and bring us with
your saints to glory everlasting.*

Praise and Thanksgiving (Songs and Prayers)

Gloria Patri
*Glory be to the Father,
And to the Son and to the Holy Spirit:
As it was in the beginning,
Is now, and ever shall be,
World without end. Amen, amen.*

LISTENING TO HIS VOICE

Chronological Reading for the Day
Isa. 1.21-5.30

Lectionary Readings
Psalm: Ps. 47   *Acts*:* Acts 1.1-11
Gospel: Luke 24.44-53   *NT:* Eph. 1.15-23

* During Eastertide, a reading from Acts is often sustituted for the lesson from the
Hebrew Bible.

Reflection: Silence and/or Journaling

RESPONDING IN FAITH

The Apostles' Creed
*I believe in God, the Father Almighty, Maker of heaven and earth;
and in Jesus Christ, his only Son, our Lord, who was conceived by the
Holy Spirit, born of the Virgin Mary, suffered under Pontius Pilate,
was crucified, dead, and buried; he descended into hell; the third day
he arose again from the dead; he ascended into heaven and sits on
the right hand of God the Father Almighty; from thence he shall come
to judge the quick and the dead.*

I believe in the Holy Spirit, the holy catholic* church, the communion of saints, the forgiveness of sins, the resurrection of the body, and the life everlasting. Amen.

* In the Apostles' and Nicene Creeds, the term catholic refers to the Church's universality, through all ages and times, of all languages and peoples. It refers to no particular tradition or denominational expression (e.g., as in Roman Catholic).

Prayers of Confession

Let us now confess our sins to God and receive mercy and grace to help in our time of need.

Assurance of Pardon

Having faithfully confessed and renounced your sin, Christ also has been faithful to forgive your sins and to purify you from all unrighteousness. It is certain, that there is One who has spoken to the Father in your defense, Jesus Christ, the Righteous One who is the atoning sacrifice for our sins and for the sins of the whole world. His grace and peace are with you now. Amen.

Petitions and Supplications, Ending with The Lord's Prayer

Our Father which art in heaven, Hallowed be thy name. Thy kingdom come, Thy will be done in earth, as it is in heaven. Give us this day our daily bread. And forgive us our debts, as we forgive our debtors. And lead us not into temptation, but deliver us from evil: For thine is the kingdom, and the power, and the glory, for ever. Amen.

~ Matthew 6.9-13 (KJV)

Doxology (and/or closing song)

Praise God from whom all blessings flow;
Praise Him all creatures here below;
Praise Him above ye heavenly host;
Praise Father, Son and Holy Ghost. Amen.

DEPARTING TO SERVE

Benediction

Saviour and Lord, Who, ascending into heaven, wast pleased to show Thyself in glory to the eyes of beholders, while Thou didst promise to come as our Judge in like manner as Thou hadst ascended; make us to welcome this feast-day of Thine Ascension with pure and devout hearts; that we may in such wise ascend continually in Thee to a better life, that when Thou comest to the judgement, we may see Thy face and not be confounded: through Thy mercy, O our God, Who art blessed, and dost live, and govern all things, world without end.

~ *Mozarabic Missal and Breviary* (Wright, p. 61)

Affirmation from the Psalms

Clap your hands, all peoples! Shout to God with loud songs of joy! For the LORD, the Most High, is to be feared, a great king over all the earth. He subdued peoples under us, and nations under our feet. He chose our heritage for us, the pride of Jacob whom he loves. Selah God has gone up with a shout, the LORD with the sound of a trumpet. Sing praises to God, sing praises! Sing praises to our King, sing praises! For God is the King of all the earth; sing praises with a psalm! God reigns over the nations; God sits on his holy throne. The princes of the peoples gather as the people of the God of Abraham. For the shields of the earth belong to God; he is highly exalted!

~ Psalm 47.1-9

Pray without Ceasing – Flash Prayer for the Day

Blessed be the Father, who gave his Son for the world, blessed be the Lord Jesus Christ, who reigns as King above, and blessed be the Holy Spirit, who clothes us with power from on high.

FOR YOUR WEEKLY JOURNEY

Let God Arise! Seasonal Focus
To the Unknown God, Acts 17.22-31

Book Reading
DAILY: Extreme Devotion Writing Team, *Extreme Devotion*

DC Talk, The Voice of the Martyrs, *Jesus Freaks*

June 1 - 7, 2014

For forty days after his resurrection, Jesus revealed himself alive to his disciples. On the fortieth day, he ascended to heaven to take his place as Lord and Christ at God's right hand. Ten days after this, on the fiftieth day after his resurrection, he would send to us the promise of the Father -- the Holy Spirit, the pledge of our salvation. Here we ponder the wonder of God's working, from Easter Sunday to the Spirit's descent at Pentecost.

THIS WEEK'S THEME
The High Priestly Prayer, John 17.1-11

In the Upper Room, before his passion and death, our Lord Jesus prayed as our high priest to God on behalf of the apostles and all believers. He lifted up his eyes to heaven, and asked his Father to glorify his Son that the Son might glorify him, for the hour of redemption had come. Jesus asked God to do this because he had given to him as the Son of God, authority over all flesh – to give eternal life to all whom the Father had given to him. Jesus declared this to be eternal life: to know the only true God, and Jesus Christ, the one whom the Father sent to the earth.

Jesus told the Father that he had glorified him on earth, having accomplished the work that he had given him to do. He asked the Father to glorify him in his own presence with the glory that he had with the Father before the world existed. Jesus declared that he had manifested God's name to the people whom he had given him out of the world; now the disciples knew that everything Jesus had was from God, and they had kept the Father's word.

Jesus prayed for his disciples, for those whom the Father had given him, and not for the world. Those who believed actually belonged to the Father, and to him, and he, the Lord Jesus, was glorified in them. Jesus declared that he would no longer be in the world, but they would be in the world, and he would soon be coming to the Lord. Jesus asked the Holy Father to keep them in his name, those whom he had given to Christ, in order that they might be one, even as he and his Father were one.

DAILY DEVOTIONAL GUIDE

PREPARING OUR HEARTS

Invocation: Our Prayer of Acclamation

Gracious God and Holy Father, to whom the Lord Jesus prayed on behalf of his apostles, thank you for the life and ministry of our high priest, Jesus, for us today. We know that he ever lives to make intercession on our account, and without his ministry for us we could neither stand nor survive in this world of evil and sin. Help us to yield to our Savior, to affirm that he is praying for us constantly before your throne, and that you still listen to his prayers on our behalf. He is still our High Priest before you. In his name we pray, amen.

Call to Worship

Blessed are you, O God: Father, Son, and Holy Spirit. And blessed is your Kingdom, both now and forever, Amen.

PRAISING OUR GOD

Te Deum Laudamus

You are God: we praise you; you are the Lord; we acclaim you; you are the eternal Father: All creation worships you. To you all angels, all the powers of heaven, Cherubim and Seraphim, sing in endless praise: Holy, holy, holy Lord, God of power and might, heaven and earth are full of your glory.

The glorious company of apostles praise you. The noble fellowship of prophets praise you. The white-robed army of martyrs praise you. Throughout the world the holy Church acclaims you; Father, of

majesty unbounded, your true and only Son, worthy of all worship, and the Holy Spirit, advocate and guide.

You, Christ, are the king of glory, the eternal Son of the Father. When you became man to set us free you did not shun the Virgin's womb. You overcame the sting of death and opened the kingdom of heaven to all believers. You are seated at God's right hand in glory. We believe that you will come and be our judge. Come then, Lord, and help your people, bought with the price of your own blood, and bring us with your saints to glory everlasting.

Praise and Thanksgiving (Songs and Prayers)

Gloria Patri
Glory be to the Father,
And to the Son and to the Holy Spirit:
As it was in the beginning,
Is now, and ever shall be,
World without end. Amen, amen.

LISTENING TO HIS VOICE

Chronological Reading for the Day
Sunday: Prov. 25-29 ✤ *Monday:* Prov. 30-31 ✤ *Tuesday:* Pss. 42-46 ✤ *Wednesday:* Pss. 47-49; 84-85; 87 ✤ *Thursday:* Pss. 1-2; 10; 33; 71; 91 ✤ *Friday:* Pss. 92-97 ✤ *Saturday:* Pss. 98-100; 102; 104

Lectionary Readings
Psalm: Ps. 68.1-10, 32-35   *Acts*:* Acts 1.6-14
Gospel: John 17.1-11   *NT:* 1 Pet. 4.12-14; 5.6-11

* During Eastertide, a reading from Acts is often sustituted for the lesson from the Hebrew Bible.

Reflection: Silence and/or Journaling

RESPONDING IN FAITH

The Apostles' Creed
*I believe in God, the Father Almighty, Maker of heaven and earth;
and in Jesus Christ, his only Son, our Lord, who was conceived by the
Holy Spirit, born of the Virgin Mary, suffered under Pontius Pilate,
was crucified, dead, and buried; he descended into hell; the third day
he arose again from the dead; he ascended into heaven and sits on
the right hand of God the Father Almighty; from thence he shall come
to judge the quick and the dead.*

I believe in the Holy Spirit, the holy catholic church, the communion
of saints, the forgiveness of sins, the resurrection of the body, and the
life everlasting. Amen.*

* In the Apostles' and Nicene Creeds, the term catholic refers to the Church's
universality, through all ages and times, of all languages and peoples. It refers to no
particular tradition or denominational expression (e.g., as in Roman Catholic).

Prayers of Confession
Let us now confess our sins to God and receive mercy and
grace to help in our time of need.

Assurance of Pardon
Having faithfully confessed and renounced your sin, Christ
also has been faithful to forgive your sins and to purify you
from all unrighteousness. It is certain, that there is One who
has spoken to the Father in your defense, Jesus Christ, the
Righteous One who is the atoning sacrifice for our sins and
for the sins of the whole world. His grace and peace are with
you now. Amen.

Petitions and Supplications, Ending with The Lord's Prayer
*Our Father which art in heaven, Hallowed be thy name. Thy kingdom
come, Thy will be done in earth, as it is in heaven. Give us this day our
daily bread. And forgive us our debts, as we forgive our debtors. And*

lead us not into temptation, but deliver us from evil: For thine is the kingdom, and the power, and the glory, for ever. Amen.

~ Matthew 6.9-13 (KJV)

Doxology (and/or closing song)

Praise God from whom all blessings flow;
Praise Him all creatures here below;
Praise Him above ye heavenly host;
Praise Father, Son and Holy Ghost. Amen.

DEPARTING TO SERVE

Benediction

Lord Jesus, we are humbled when we hear your tender words to the Father for the sake of your apostles and those who would believe in you through their words. We are overwhelmed by your grace and love, your sympathy and kindness, and ask that you would ever assure us of your ongoing high priestly ministry for us. Without your prayers and intercession, without your provision and help, we cannot make it in this life. We will ever trust in you. In your name we pray, amen.

Affirmation from the Psalms

God shall arise, his enemies shall be scattered; and those who hate him shall flee before him! As smoke is driven away, so you shall drive them away; as wax melts before fire, so the wicked shall perish before God! But the righteous shall be glad; they shall exult before God; they shall be jubilant with joy! Sing to God, sing praises to his name; lift up a song to him who rides through the deserts; his name is the LORD; exult before him! Father of the fatherless and protector of widows is God in his holy habitation. God settles the solitary in a home; he leads out the prisoners to prosperity, but the rebellious dwell in a parched land.

~ Psalm 68.1-6

Pray without Ceasing – Flash Prayer for the Day
O High Priest of God, who ever lives to make intercession for us as your people, represent us to the Father, for you know our need and our hearts.

FOR YOUR WEEKLY JOURNEY

Let God Arise! Seasonal Focus
To the Unknown God, Acts 17.22-31

Book Reading
DAILY: Extreme Devotion Writing Team, *Extreme Devotion*

DC Talk, The Voice of the Martyrs, *Jesus Freaks*

Our Corporate Disciplines
Concert of Prayer:
    Tuesday, June 3, 2014

June 8 - 14, 2014

For forty days after his resurrection, Jesus revealed himself alive to his disciples. On the fortieth day, he ascended to heaven to take his place as Lord and Christ at God's right hand. Ten days after this, on the fiftieth day after his resurrection, he would send to us the promise of the Father -- the Holy Spirit, the pledge of our salvation. Here we ponder the wonder of God's working, from Easter Sunday to the Spirit's descent at Pentecost.

THIS WEEK'S THEME
The Gifts of the Holy Spirit, 1 Corinthians 12.3-13
Paul spoke to the Corinthian believers concerning the gifts and graces of the Holy Spirit of the Lord. He said that no one who speaks in the Spirit of God ever says "Jesus is accursed!" Also, no one can actually claim "Jesus is Lord" except in the Holy Spirit. He said that although there were varieties of gifts, of service, and of activities, there was only the same Spirit, the same Lord, and the same God who empowers them all in everyone.

Paul claimed that God has given the manifestation of the Spirit to each believer for the common good. All the gifts, whatever they are, whether the utterance of wisdom or knowledge, faith, gifts of healing, miracles, prophecy, the ability to distinguish between spirits, kinds of tongues, or the interpretation of tongues – all these come from the Lord through the working of the same Spirit. Paul said that all of these manifold gifts are empowered by one and the same Spirit, who apportions to each one individually as he wills.

Paul compared the Christian community to the human body, which even though it is a single body, still possesses many different members, which function together for the good of the whole body. Jesus' people function like a body. In Christ and through the operations of one Spirit, we were all baptized into one body – Jews or Greeks, slaves or free – and all believers have been made to drink of one Spirit.

DAILY DEVOTIONAL GUIDE

PREPARING OUR HEARTS

Invocation: Our Prayer of Acclamation
O Holy Spirit of God, very God, who descended on Christ at the river Jordan and on the apostles in the upper chamber, we have sinned against heaven and before you; purify us again, we ask you, with your divine fire, and have mercy on us; for Christ's sake. Amen.

~ Nerses of Clajes (Oden, p. 135)

Call to Worship
Blessed are you, O God: Father, Son, and Holy Spirit. And blessed is your Kingdom, both now and forever, Amen.

PRAISING OUR GOD

Te Deum Laudamus
You are God: we praise you; you are the Lord; we acclaim you; you are the eternal Father: All creation worships you. To you all angels, all the powers of heaven, Cherubim and Seraphim, sing in endless praise: Holy, holy, holy Lord, God of power and might, heaven and earth are full of your glory.

The glorious company of apostles praise you. The noble fellowship of prophets praise you. The white-robed army of martyrs praise you. Throughout the world the holy Church acclaims you; Father, of majesty unbounded, your true and only Son, worthy of all worship, and the Holy Spirit, advocate and guide.

You, Christ, are the king of glory, the eternal Son of the Father. When you became man to set us free you did not shun the Virgin's womb. You overcame the sting of death and opened the kingdom of heaven

to all believers. You are seated at God's right hand in glory. We believe that you will come and be our judge. Come then, Lord, and help your people, bought with the price of your own blood, and bring us with your saints to glory everlasting.

Praise and Thanksgiving (Songs and Prayers)

Gloria Patri
Glory be to the Father,
And to the Son and to the Holy Spirit:
As it was in the beginning,
Is now, and ever shall be,
World without end. Amen, amen.

LISTENING TO HIS VOICE

Chronological Reading for the Day
Sunday: Pss. 105-106 ✦ *Monday:* Pss. 107; 111-114 ✦
Tuesday: Pss. 115-118 ✦ *Wednesday:* Ps. 119 ✦ *Thursday:*
Pss. 120-121; 123; 125-126 ✦ *Friday:* Pss. 128-130; 132;
134-135 ✦ *Saturday:* Pss. 136; 146-150

Lectionary Readings
Psalm: Ps. 104.24-34, 35b   *Acts*:* Acts 2.1-21
Gospel: John 20.19-23   *NT:* 1 Cor. 12.3b-13

* During Eastertide, a reading from Acts is often sustituted for the lesson from the Hebrew Bible.

Reflection: Silence and/or Journaling

RESPONDING IN FAITH

The Apostles' Creed
I believe in God, the Father Almighty, Maker of heaven and earth; and in Jesus Christ, his only Son, our Lord, who was conceived by the Holy Spirit, born of the Virgin Mary, suffered under Pontius Pilate,

was crucified, dead, and buried; he descended into hell; the third day he arose again from the dead; he ascended into heaven and sits on the right hand of God the Father Almighty; from thence he shall come to judge the quick and the dead.

I believe in the Holy Spirit, the holy catholic* church, the communion of saints, the forgiveness of sins, the resurrection of the body, and the life everlasting. Amen.

* In the Apostles' and Nicene Creeds, the term catholic refers to the Church's universality, through all ages and times, of all languages and peoples. It refers to no particular tradition or denominational expression (e.g., as in Roman Catholic).

Prayers of Confession

Let us now confess our sins to God and receive mercy and grace to help in our time of need.

Assurance of Pardon

Having faithfully confessed and renounced your sin, Christ also has been faithful to forgive your sins and to purify you from all unrighteousness. It is certain, that there is One who has spoken to the Father in your defense, Jesus Christ, the Righteous One who is the atoning sacrifice for our sins and for the sins of the whole world. His grace and peace are with you now. Amen.

Petitions and Supplications, Ending with The Lord's Prayer

Our Father which art in heaven, Hallowed be thy name. Thy kingdom come, Thy will be done in earth, as it is in heaven. Give us this day our daily bread. And forgive us our debts, as we forgive our debtors. And lead us not into temptation, but deliver us from evil: For thine is the kingdom, and the power, and the glory, for ever. Amen.

~ Matthew 6.9-13 (KJV)

Doxology (and/or closing song)
Praise God from whom all blessings flow;
Praise Him all creatures here below;
Praise Him above ye heavenly host;
Praise Father, Son and Holy Ghost. Amen.

DEPARTING TO SERVE

Benediction
O God the Holy Ghost, Sanctifier of the faithful, visit us, we pray Thee,
with Thy love and favour; enlighten our minds more and more with
the everlasting Gospel; graft in our hearts a love of the truth; increase
in us true religion; nourish us with all goodness, and of Thy great
mercy keep us in the same, O blessed Spirit, Whom with the Father
and Son together we worship and glorify as one God, world without
end. Amen.

~ *American Prayer Book,* AD 1789 (Fox, p. 130)

Affirmation from the Psalms
May the glory of the LORD endure forever; may the LORD rejoice in
his works, who looks on the earth and it trembles, who touches the
mountains and they smoke! I will sing to the LORD as long as I live;
I will sing praise to my God while I have being. May my meditation be
pleasing to him, for I rejoice in the LORD.

~ Psalm 104.31-34

Pray without Ceasing – Flash Prayer for the Day
Come, Holy Spirit, and demonstrate the wondrous, rich
grace of the Father through the gifts and expressions you
have given to God's people, to each and every one.

FOR YOUR WEEKLY JOURNEY

Let God Arise! Seasonal Focus
To the Unknown God, Acts 17.22-31

Book Reading
DAILY: Extreme Devotion Writing Team, *Extreme Devotion*

DC Talk, The Voice of the Martyrs, *Jesus Freaks*

Our Corporate Disciplines
Retreat, ending with Book Review:
    Wednesday, June 11, 2014

The Southern Steps of the Temple Mount
(possible location of many of Jesus' teachings,
as well as Peter's sermon at Pentecost)

The Holy Spirit Has Come to God's People

On *Pentecost* we commemorate the coming of the Holy Spirit to the people of God, the Church. Jesus Christ, the risen Lord, is now present with his people in the person of the Spirit of God in the midst of the assemblies of faith. Now during this season after Pentecost, we affirm the work of the holy Trinity on behalf of humankind. The love of the Father elects us to salvation, the grace of the Lord Jesus Christ has won us to God through his blood, and the Holy Spirit indwells the Church, helping and empowering us to represent and advance the Kingdom in the earth. On *Trinity Sunday*, we worship our Triune God: Father, Son, and Holy Spirit, and celebrate the mystery of God's revealed nature in three persons, expressed in their unity, equality, and diversity.

The Season after Pentecost is called *Ordinary Time* or *Kingdomtide*. During this time the Church considers the overarching theme of salvation history, the need for diligence in Christian discipleship, and focuses on the advance of the Kingdom to the ends of the earth. This is the longest season in the Church's calendar, having from twenty-three to twenty-eight Sundays, and lasting until Advent. During this time we, as believers and congregations, focus on the Church's maturity and multiplication and emphasize Christ's headship and the power of the Holy Spirit in the ministry of the apostles and through the body of Christ.

The phrase *Ordinary Time* ought not to be interpreted as "unimportant time." Rather, it should be understood in the sense of "counted or numbered days," i.e., like "ordinal" numbers – first, second, third. This has to do with the numbered Sundays of the year outside of the special seasons in the two cycles. These "ordinary" Sundays tend to emphasize Jesus' earthly life and ministry (in the first group of Ordinary Time between *Epiphany* and *Lent*), and his headship, harvest, and vigilance in light of Christ as our hope (in the larger group of Sundays in the second).

In a real sense, the Season after Pentecost emphasizes the most significant sign of the Kingdom's presence in this world: the coming of the Holy Spirit. As Peter recounted in his sermon so many years ago, God promised that in the last time the Spirit of God would be poured out on humankind, with all of the people of God prophesying, seeing visions, and dreaming dreams, both male and female. God's wonders would be seen in the earth, and the witness to God's salvation in Christ would be taken to the ends of the earth. Glory to God, we live in that age, the time of the presence of the heavenly dove and entrance of the Spirit into our world!

O, Heavenly Dove, Fill Your People with Your Power and Light
During this Season after Pentecost, we join with congregations worldwide to seek the power of the Spirit for our own transformation and the fruitfulness of our mission to the inner cities of America. Let us depend on the Holy Spirit, the One who has sealed us for the day of redemption, who indwells us and fills us with the presence and power of God for mission. Let us neither grieve nor quench him, but yield ourselves afresh to him for strength, grace, and wisdom. Only through the power of the Spirit can the cities of America be reached with the Gospel. Truly, if the cities of the world are won to Christ, it will not be by power nor by might, but by the Spirit of the Living God.

We desire to do all we can to help you fulfill the purpose of the Lord as you display Christ's love in the inner cities of

America. May God grant you grace and strength as you exalt Christ in the city where you live!

~ Refreshed by the living waters of the Spirit,
Rev. Dr. Don L. Davis

June 15 - 21, 2014

✠

TRINITY SUNDAY, FIRST SUNDAY AFTER PENTECOST

On Pentecost we commemorate the descent of the Holy Spirit to earth on Christ's believers, his infilling of the people of God, the Church. Through him, the third person of the Trinity, Jesus our Lord is now present with his people. The Spirit is the guarantee of the promised inheritance to come. We ponder the fullness and mystery of our God's person and work in our celebration on Trinity Sunday.

THIS WEEK'S THEME
Our Triune God, 2 Corinthians 13.11-14
Paul closed his message in his second epistle to the Corinthians by exhorting them, finally, to rejoice. He called them to aim for restoration, to comfort one another, to agree with one another, and to live in peace. He promised them, too, that the God of love and peace would be with them all. He closed his epistle with an acknowledgment of the working of our triune God, pronouncing a blessing, asking that the grace of the Lord Jesus Christ, the love of God, and the fellowship of the Holy Spirit be with them all. Paul's blessing provides insight into the working and leading of each of the members of the Trinity, not only for them, but for all the world.

DAILY DEVOTIONAL GUIDE

PREPARING OUR HEARTS

Invocation: Our Prayer of Acclamation
O LORD God, Father Almighty, bless and protect, through Thine Only Son, in the power of the Holy Spirit, Thy servants who are obedient to Thy majesty; that being free from fear of all enemies, they may continually rejoice in raising Thee; through the same Jesus Christ our Lord. Amen.

~ Gregorian Sacramentary (Wright, p. 65)

Call to Worship
Blessed are you, O God: Father, Son, and Holy Spirit. And blessed is your Kingdom, both now and forever, Amen.

PRAISING OUR GOD

Te Deum Laudamus
You are God: we praise you; you are the Lord; we acclaim you; you are the eternal Father: All creation worships you. To you all angels, all the powers of heaven, Cherubim and Seraphim, sing in endless praise: Holy, holy, holy Lord, God of power and might, heaven and earth are full of your glory.

The glorious company of apostles praise you. The noble fellowship of prophets praise you. The white-robed army of martyrs praise you. Throughout the world the holy Church acclaims you; Father, of majesty unbounded, your true and only Son, worthy of all worship, and the Holy Spirit, advocate and guide.

You, Christ, are the king of glory, the eternal Son of the Father. When you became man to set us free you did not shun the Virgin's womb. You overcame the sting of death and opened the kingdom of heaven to all believers. You are seated at God's right hand in glory. We believe that you will come and be our judge. Come then, Lord, and help your people, bought with the price of your own blood, and bring us with your saints to glory everlasting.

Praise and Thanksgiving (Songs and Prayers)

Gloria Patri
Glory be to the Father,
And to the Son and to the Holy Spirit:
As it was in the beginning,
Is now, and ever shall be,
World without end. Amen, amen.

LISTENING TO HIS VOICE

Chronological Reading for the Day
Sunday: Isa. 18-23 ❖ *Monday:* Isa. 24-27; ch.29 ❖ *Tuesday:*
Isa. 30-33 ❖ *Wednesday:* Isa. 34-35; Mic. 2-5 ❖ *Thursday:*
Mic. 6-7; 2 Chron. 32.1-8; 2 Kings 18.13-37; Isa. 36 ❖
Friday: 2 Kings 19; Isa. 37; 2 Chron. 32.9-23 ❖ *Saturday:*
2 Kings 20.1-19; Isa. 38-39; 2 Chron. 32.24-31

Lectionary Readings
Psalm: Ps. 8   *OT:* Gen. 1.1-2.4a
Gospel: Matt. 28.16-20   *NT:* 2 Cor. 13.11-13

Reflection: Silence and/or Journaling

RESPONDING IN FAITH

The Apostles' Creed
*I believe in God, the Father Almighty, Maker of heaven and earth;
and in Jesus Christ, his only Son, our Lord, who was conceived by the
Holy Spirit, born of the Virgin Mary, suffered under Pontius Pilate,
was crucified, dead, and buried; he descended into hell; the third day
he arose again from the dead; he ascended into heaven and sits on
the right hand of God the Father Almighty; from thence he shall come
to judge the quick and the dead.*

I believe in the Holy Spirit, the holy catholic church, the communion
of saints, the forgiveness of sins, the resurrection of the body, and the
life everlasting. Amen.*

* In the Apostles' and Nicene Creeds, the term catholic refers to the Church's
universality, through all ages and times, of all languages and peoples. It refers to no
particular tradition or denominational expression (e.g., as in Roman Catholic).

Prayers of Confession
Let us now confess our sins to God and receive mercy and
grace to help in our time of need.

Assurance of Pardon

Having faithfully confessed and renounced your sin, Christ also has been faithful to forgive your sins and to purify you from all unrighteousness. It is certain, that there is One who has spoken to the Father in your defense, Jesus Christ, the Righteous One who is the atoning sacrifice for our sins and for the sins of the whole world. His grace and peace are with you now. Amen.

Petitions and Supplications, Ending with The Lord's Prayer

Our Father which art in heaven, Hallowed be thy name. Thy kingdom come, Thy will be done in earth, as it is in heaven. Give us this day our daily bread. And forgive us our debts, as we forgive our debtors. And lead us not into temptation, but deliver us from evil: For thine is the kingdom, and the power, and the glory, for ever. Amen.

~ Matthew 6.9-13 (KJV)

Doxology (and/or closing song)

Praise God from whom all blessings flow;
Praise Him all creatures here below;
Praise Him above ye heavenly host;
Praise Father, Son and Holy Ghost. Amen.

DEPARTING TO SERVE

Benediction

Grant, O God, of your mercy, that we may come to everlasting life, and there beholding thy glory as it is, may equally say:
Glory to the Father who created us,
Glory to the Son who redeemed us,
Glory to the Holy Spirit who sanctified us.
Glory to the most high and undivided Trinity, whose works are inseparable, whose kingdom without end abides, from age to age forever. Amen.

~ Augustine (Oden, pp. 143-144)

Affirmation from the Psalms

O LORD, our Lord, how majestic is your name in all the earth! You have set your glory above the heavens. Out of the mouth of babies and infants, you have established strength because of your foes, to still the enemy and the avenger.

~ Psalm 8.1-2

Pray without Ceasing – Flash Prayer for the Day

Let the Father's love, and the Nazarene's amazing grace, and the sweet communion of the Holy Spirit be upon me this day, in all I do and say.

FOR YOUR WEEKLY JOURNEY

Let God Arise! Seasonal Focus

The Three Hebrew Boys, Daniel 3.1-30

Book Reading

DAILY: Extreme Devotion Writing Team, *Extreme Devotion*

DC Talk, The Voice of the Martyrs, *Jesus Freaks*

June 22 - 28, 2014 ✤ Proper 7

On Pentecost we commemorate the descent of the Holy Spirit to earth on Christ's believers, his infilling of the people of God, the Church. Through him, the third person of the Trinity, Jesus our Lord is now present with his people. The Spirit is the guarantee of the promised inheritance to come. We ponder the fullness and mystery of our God's person and work in our celebration on Trinity Sunday.

THIS WEEK'S THEME

We Will Not Bow: Pictures of Extreme Devotion, John 15.18-16.4

The Lord instructed the apostles that the world would hate them, but they should always remember that it had hated him before it hated them. He told them that if they had been of the world, the world would have loved them as its own. However, since they were not of the world, having been chosen out of the world, that is the reason the world hated them.

The Lord said, "A servant is not greater than his master." If they persecuted him, the Lord, they would also persecute them. And, if they kept Jesus' word, they would also keep the apostles' word. Those who reject the Lord know neither him nor the Father, and those who hate him as Lord also hate his Father. All of this causeless hatred of him would happen as predicted in Scripture, and the Holy Spirit would bear witness about him, and so would the apostles, having been with him since the beginning.

We who love Jesus must follow in the steps of those who offered him through their faith extreme devotion, the kind that led to persecution, suffering, and even death. Let us draw upon the example and pattern of those who yielded their all to God without qualification or condition. We can learn much from them, especially what it means to follow Jesus fully, to never turn back, and to give him our all, no matter what the price.

DAILY DEVOTIONAL GUIDE

PREPARING OUR HEARTS

Invocation: Our Prayer of Acclamation

Eternal God, our Father, Jesus reminded us that the servant is not greater than his master. As we sojourn in this world, we will wrestle with the principalities and powers who will tempt us to turn from you, abandon the faith, and yield to the lies and deception of the enemy. We declare, through the Spirit's power, that we will not bow, but offer instead through your Spirit extreme devotion. As the saints of old stood their ground, so we now, today, will stand up for the Savior, and represent the Kingdom well. In Jesus' name we pray, amen.

Call to Worship

Blessed are you, O God: Father, Son, and Holy Spirit. And blessed is your Kingdom, both now and forever, Amen.

PRAISING OUR GOD

Te Deum Laudamus

You are God: we praise you; you are the Lord; we acclaim you; you are the eternal Father: All creation worships you. To you all angels, all the powers of heaven, Cherubim and Seraphim, sing in endless praise: Holy, holy, holy Lord, God of power and might, heaven and earth are full of your glory.

The glorious company of apostles praise you. The noble fellowship of prophets praise you. The white-robed army of martyrs praise you. Throughout the world the holy Church acclaims you; Father, of majesty unbounded, your true and only Son, worthy of all worship, and the Holy Spirit, advocate and guide.

You, Christ, are the king of glory, the eternal Son of the Father. When you became man to set us free you did not shun the Virgin's womb. You overcame the sting of death and opened the kingdom of heaven

to all believers. You are seated at God's right hand in glory. We believe
that you will come and be our judge. Come then, Lord, and help your
people, bought with the price of your own blood, and bring us with
your saints to glory everlasting.

Praise and Thanksgiving (Songs and Prayers)

Gloria Patri
Glory be to the Father,
And to the Son and to the Holy Spirit:
As it was in the beginning,
Is now, and ever shall be,
World without end. Amen, amen.

LISTENING TO HIS VOICE

Chronological Reading for the Day
Sunday: Isa. 40-43 ✤ *Monday:* Isa. 44-48 ✤ *Tuesday:* Isa.
49-53 ✤ *Wednesday:* Isa. 54-57 ✤ *Thursday:* Isa. 58-62 ✤
Friday: Isa. 63-66; 2 Kings 20.20-21; 2 Chron. 32.32-33 ✤
Saturday: 2 Kings 21.1-22.2; 2 Chron. 33.1-34.7

Lectionary Readings
Psalm: Ps. 86.1-10, 16-17   *OT:* Gen. 21.8-21
Gospel: Matt. 10.24-39   *NT:* Rom. 6.1b-11

Reflection: Silence and/or Journaling

RESPONDING IN FAITH

The Apostles' Creed
I believe in God, the Father Almighty, Maker of heaven and earth;
and in Jesus Christ, his only Son, our Lord, who was conceived by the
Holy Spirit, born of the Virgin Mary, suffered under Pontius Pilate,
was crucified, dead, and buried; he descended into hell; the third day
he arose again from the dead; he ascended into heaven and sits on

the right hand of God the Father Almighty; from thence he shall come to judge the quick and the dead.

I believe in the Holy Spirit, the holy catholic* church, the communion of saints, the forgiveness of sins, the resurrection of the body, and the life everlasting. Amen.

* In the Apostles' and Nicene Creeds, the term catholic refers to the Church's universality, through all ages and times, of all languages and peoples. It refers to no particular tradition or denominational expression (e.g., as in Roman Catholic).

Prayers of Confession
Let us now confess our sins to God and receive mercy and grace to help in our time of need.

Assurance of Pardon
Having faithfully confessed and renounced your sin, Christ also has been faithful to forgive your sins and to purify you from all unrighteousness. It is certain, that there is One who has spoken to the Father in your defense, Jesus Christ, the Righteous One who is the atoning sacrifice for our sins and for the sins of the whole world. His grace and peace are with you now. Amen.

Petitions and Supplications, Ending with The Lord's Prayer
Our Father which art in heaven, Hallowed be thy name. Thy kingdom come, Thy will be done in earth, as it is in heaven. Give us this day our daily bread. And forgive us our debts, as we forgive our debtors. And lead us not into temptation, but deliver us from evil: For thine is the kingdom, and the power, and the glory, for ever. Amen.

~ Matthew 6.9-13 (KJV)

Doxology (and/or closing song)
Praise God from whom all blessings flow;
Praise Him all creatures here below;
Praise Him above ye heavenly host;
Praise Father, Son and Holy Ghost. Amen.

DEPARTING TO SERVE

Benediction

Lord Jesus, who maintained the good confession and never yielded to the abuse of evil, not even for a moment, work in us your disciples and warriors the same kind of heart and faith. Make us strong in the grace you displayed and granted to us when we first called upon your name, and strengthen us to never give in to the intimidation and lies of the enemy. We will remember you and your saints of old, and, with your help, we will never bow down to the idols of the world. In your name we pray, amen.

Affirmation from the Psalms

Turn to me and be gracious to me; give your strength to your servant, and save the son of your maidservant. Show me a sign of your favor, that those who hate me may see and be put to shame because you, LORD, have helped me and comforted me.

~ Psalm 86.16-17

Pray without Ceasing – Flash Prayer for the Day

O Lord Most High, who granted your apostles and saints the grace to withstand the onslaught of the enemy, grant us the grace to never bow down to the intimidation of the devil.

FOR YOUR WEEKLY JOURNEY

Let God Arise! Seasonal Focus

The Three Hebrew Boys, Daniel 3.1-30

Book Reading

DAILY: Extreme Devotion Writing Team, *Extreme Devotion*

DC Talk, The Voice of the Martyrs, *Jesus Freaks*

June 29 - July 5, 2014 ✠ Proper 8

On Pentecost we commemorate the descent of the Holy Spirit to earth on Christ's believers, his infilling of the people of God, the Church. Through him, the third person of the Trinity, Jesus our Lord is now present with his people. The Spirit is the guarantee of the promised inheritance to come. We ponder the fullness and mystery of our God's person and work in our celebration on Trinity Sunday.

THIS WEEK'S THEME
The Three Hebrew Boys, Daniel 3.1-30

King Nebuchadnezzar made an image of gold, which was approximately ninety feet high and nine feet wide, and set it up on the plain of Dura, in the province of Babylon. He gathered together all the senior leadership of the provinces for the dedication of the image, and ordered that when the music sounded, they were to fall down and worship the golden image that he, King Nebuchadnezzar, had set up. Whoever refused to fall down and worship were to be immediately cast into a burning fiery furnace.

It was reported to the king that the three Hebrew boys, Shadrach, Meshach, and Abednego had refused to bow. After offering them another chance to respond, the three declared that indeed their God was great, and could deliver if he saw fit. But, if on this occasion he decided not to act and deliver them, they still would never bow down to the idols of the king.

Furious, the king had the furnace heated seven times hotter than usual, and ordered the three thrown into the furnace. Yet, looking into the fire, the king noticed that the three men were unaffected by the flames, and that another man had joined them, one who looked like a divine being. At the king's urging, they exited the furnace, without any trace of the smell of smoke, and with no evidence of hurt of flame.

As a result, King Nebuchadnezzar issued a decree that imposed a death sentence on anyone who spoke against their God, and the three were promoted within the empire.

DAILY DEVOTIONAL GUIDE

PREPARING OUR HEARTS

Invocation: Our Prayer of Acclamation
Eternal God, our Father, you demonstrated your delivering power through the rescue of the three Hebrew boys who stood their ground and refused to bow down to the image of Nebuchadnezzar. You met them in the fire and sheltered them in the midst of the flame. In the same way, grant us the power and strength to refuse all invitations to idolatry and sin. Help us never to bow down to the empty idols and false gods of this world, but rather, give us the courage to be willing to endure suffering for the sake of Christ's name, whatever it may cost us. In his name we pray, amen.

Call to Worship
Blessed are you, O God: Father, Son, and Holy Spirit. And blessed is your Kingdom, both now and forever, Amen.

PRAISING OUR GOD

Te Deum Laudamus
You are God: we praise you; you are the Lord; we acclaim you; you are the eternal Father: All creation worships you. To you all angels, all the powers of heaven, Cherubim and Seraphim, sing in endless praise: Holy, holy, holy Lord, God of power and might, heaven and earth are full of your glory.

The glorious company of apostles praise you. The noble fellowship of prophets praise you. The white-robed army of martyrs praise you. Throughout the world the holy Church acclaims you; Father, of

majesty unbounded, your true and only Son, worthy of all worship, and the Holy Spirit, advocate and guide.

You, Christ, are the king of glory, the eternal Son of the Father. When you became man to set us free you did not shun the Virgin's womb. You overcame the sting of death and opened the kingdom of heaven to all believers. You are seated at God's right hand in glory. We believe that you will come and be our judge. Come then, Lord, and help your people, bought with the price of your own blood, and bring us with your saints to glory everlasting.

Praise and Thanksgiving (Songs and Prayers)

Gloria Patri
Glory be to the Father,
And to the Son and to the Holy Spirit:
As it was in the beginning,
Is now, and ever shall be,
World without end. Amen, amen.

LISTENING TO HIS VOICE

Chronological Reading for the Day
Sunday: Jer. 1-4 ✠ *Monday:* Jer. 5-6; 2 Kings 22.3-20; 2 Chron. 34.8-28 ✠ *Tuesday:* 2 Kings 23.1-28; 2 Chron. 34.29-35.19; Nah. 1-3 ✠ *Wednesday:* Hab. 1-3 ✠ *Thursday:* Zeph. 1-3; 2 Chron. 35.20-27; 2 Kings 23.29-30; Jer. 47-48 ✠ *Friday:* 2 Chron. 36.1-5; 2 Kings 23.31-24.4; Jer. 22.1-23; ch.26 ✠ *Saturday:* Jer. 25; 36; 45-46

Lectionary Readings
Psalm: Ps. 13   *OT:* Gen. 22.1-14
Gospel: Matt. 10.40-42   *NT:* Rom. 6.12-23

Reflection: Silence and/or Journaling

RESPONDING IN FAITH

The Apostles' Creed
I believe in God, the Father Almighty, Maker of heaven and earth; and in Jesus Christ, his only Son, our Lord, who was conceived by the Holy Spirit, born of the Virgin Mary, suffered under Pontius Pilate, was crucified, dead, and buried; he descended into hell; the third day he arose again from the dead; he ascended into heaven and sits on the right hand of God the Father Almighty; from thence he shall come to judge the quick and the dead.

I believe in the Holy Spirit, the holy catholic* church, the communion of saints, the forgiveness of sins, the resurrection of the body, and the life everlasting. Amen.

* In the Apostles' and Nicene Creeds, the term catholic refers to the Church's universality, through all ages and times, of all languages and peoples. It refers to no particular tradition or denominational expression (e.g., as in Roman Catholic).

Prayers of Confession
Let us now confess our sins to God and receive mercy and grace to help in our time of need.

Assurance of Pardon
Having faithfully confessed and renounced your sin, Christ also has been faithful to forgive your sins and to purify you from all unrighteousness. It is certain, that there is One who has spoken to the Father in your defense, Jesus Christ, the Righteous One who is the atoning sacrifice for our sins and for the sins of the whole world. His grace and peace are with you now. Amen.

Petitions and Supplications, Ending with The Lord's Prayer
Our Father which art in heaven, Hallowed be thy name. Thy kingdom come, Thy will be done in earth, as it is in heaven. Give us this day our daily bread. And forgive us our debts, as we forgive our debtors. And

lead us not into temptation, but deliver us from evil: For thine is the
kingdom, and the power, and the glory, for ever. Amen.

~ Matthew 6.9-13 (KJV)

Doxology (and/or closing song)
Praise God from whom all blessings flow;
Praise Him all creatures here below;
Praise Him above ye heavenly host;
Praise Father, Son and Holy Ghost. Amen.

DEPARTING TO SERVE

Benediction
Lord Jesus, who met the three Hebrew boys in the flames of
the fiery furnace and kept them safe from its torment and
effect, grant us the same courage and heart as we stand for
you today, in the place where you have us. Give us the grace
to never bow down to the false idols of our day, and grant
us the privilege of suffering for you, serving you with honor
and integrity of our hearts. We ask this in your name, amen.

Affirmation from the Psalms
How long, O LORD? Will you forget me forever? How long will you hide
your face from me? How long must I take counsel in my soul and have
sorrow in my heart all the day? How long shall my enemy be exalted
over me? Consider and answer me, O LORD my God; light up my eyes,
lest I sleep the sleep of death, lest my enemy say, "I have prevailed over
him," lest my foes rejoice because I am shaken. But I have trusted in
your steadfast love; my heart shall rejoice in your salvation. I will sing
to the LORD, because he has dealt bountifully with me.

~ Psalm 13.1-6

Pray without Ceasing – Flash Prayer for the Day
O Christ, who refused to give in to the lies of the devil, grant
us grace to never bow down to the idols and lies of the
enemy, here where we live, in this place.

FOR YOUR WEEKLY JOURNEY

Let God Arise! Seasonal Focus
The Three Hebrew Boys, Daniel 3.1-30

Book Reading
Dᴀɪʟʏ: Extreme Devotion Writing Team, *Extreme Devotion*

DC Talk, The Voice of the Martyrs, *Jesus Freaks*

July 6 - 12, 2014 ✠ Proper 9

On Pentecost we commemorate the descent of the Holy Spirit to earth on Christ's believers, his infilling of the people of God, the Church. Through him, the third person of the Trinity, Jesus our Lord is now present with his people. The Spirit is the guarantee of the promised inheritance to come. We ponder the fullness and mystery of our God's person and work in our celebration on Trinity Sunday.

THIS WEEK'S THEME
Jesus before Pilate, John 18.28-19.16; 1 Timothy 6.13-16
During his trial, Jesus was brought before Pilate, the Roman governor, to his headquarters in the early morning. Pilate called Jesus into his headquarters and asked him if he were, in fact, the King of the Jews. Jesus replied that his kingdom was not of this world, for, if it were, his servants would have been fighting to prevent his being delivered over to the Jews. Pilate asked again, "So you are a king?" Jesus answered, "You say that I am a king. For this purpose I was born and for this purpose I have come into the world – to bear witness to the truth. Everyone who is of the truth listens to my voice." Pilate then asked him, "What is truth?"

After this exchange, Pilate went back outside to the Jews, proclaiming that he found no guilt in Jesus. Pilate said then that he would release Jesus, the King of the Jews, but the crowds protested, asking rather for Barabbas, the robber. During the entire incident of shame, flogging, false accusation, merciless beating, and humiliation, Jesus never resisted nor recounted. He refused to give in to the lies of the sham trial, or the ill will and poisonous motive and action of the crowds. Christ Jesus, as Paul would later say, in giving his testimony before Pontius Pilate made the good confession – he did not bow to the suffering imposed upon him but remained faithful to the end.

DAILY DEVOTIONAL GUIDE

PREPARING OUR HEARTS

Invocation: Our Prayer of Acclamation

Gracious Father, your only begotten, Christ Jesus, made the good confession in the presence of Pontius Pilate, who recognized that Jesus was guilty of nothing. Our Lord did not seek to hide or run, or to justify himself before Pilate. Nor did Jesus answer his false, harsh accusers in the same way they lashed out at him. He did not change his testimony in order to win his own deliverance. Rather, he committed himself to your care, refused to run, and did not bow to the pressure and prospect of torture and murder. Reproduce the strength and faithfulness of our Lord in us, that we may glorify you when we are tested, even as he did. In his name we pray, amen.

Call to Worship

Blessed are you, O God: Father, Son, and Holy Spirit. And blessed is your Kingdom, both now and forever, Amen.

PRAISING OUR GOD

Te Deum Laudamus

You are God: we praise you; you are the Lord; we acclaim you; you are the eternal Father: All creation worships you. To you all angels, all the powers of heaven, Cherubim and Seraphim, sing in endless praise: Holy, holy, holy Lord, God of power and might, heaven and earth are full of your glory.

The glorious company of apostles praise you. The noble fellowship of prophets praise you. The white-robed army of martyrs praise you. Throughout the world the holy Church acclaims you; Father, of majesty unbounded, your true and only Son, worthy of all worship, and the Holy Spirit, advocate and guide.

You, Christ, are the king of glory, the eternal Son of the Father. When you became man to set us free you did not shun the Virgin's womb. You overcame the sting of death and opened the kingdom of heaven to all believers. You are seated at God's right hand in glory. We believe that you will come and be our judge. Come then, Lord, and help your people, bought with the price of your own blood, and bring us with your saints to glory everlasting.

Praise and Thanksgiving (Songs and Prayers)

Gloria Patri
Glory be to the Father,
And to the Son and to the Holy Spirit:
As it was in the beginning,
Is now, and ever shall be,
World without end. Amen, amen.

LISTENING TO HIS VOICE

Chronological Reading for the Day
Sunday: Jer. 19-20; Dan. 1 ✤ *Monday:* Dan. 2-3; Jer. 7.1-8.3 ✤ *Tuesday:* Jer. 8.4-11.23 ✤ *Wednesday:* Jer. 12-15 ✤ *Thursday:* Jer. 16-18; ch.35 ✤ *Friday:* Jer. 49.1-33; 22.24-23.32; 2 Kings 24.5-9; 2 Chron. 36.6-9 ✤ *Saturday:* Jer. 23.33-24.10; 29.1-31.14

Lectionary Readings
Psalm: Ps. 45.10-17   *OT:* Gen. 24.34-38, 42-49, 58-67
Gospel: Matt. 11.16-19, 25-30   *NT:* Rom. 7.15-25a

Reflection: Silence and/or Journaling

RESPONDING IN FAITH

The Apostles' Creed
I believe in God, the Father Almighty, Maker of heaven and earth; and in Jesus Christ, his only Son, our Lord, who was conceived by the

Holy Spirit, born of the Virgin Mary, suffered under Pontius Pilate, was crucified, dead, and buried; he descended into hell; the third day he arose again from the dead; he ascended into heaven and sits on the right hand of God the Father Almighty; from thence he shall come to judge the quick and the dead.

I believe in the Holy Spirit, the holy catholic* church, the communion of saints, the forgiveness of sins, the resurrection of the body, and the life everlasting. Amen.

* In the Apostles' and Nicene Creeds, the term catholic refers to the Church's universality, through all ages and times, of all languages and peoples. It refers to no particular tradition or denominational expression (e.g., as in Roman Catholic).

Prayers of Confession
Let us now confess our sins to God and receive mercy and grace to help in our time of need.

Assurance of Pardon
Having faithfully confessed and renounced your sin, Christ also has been faithful to forgive your sins and to purify you from all unrighteousness. It is certain, that there is One who has spoken to the Father in your defense, Jesus Christ, the Righteous One who is the atoning sacrifice for our sins and for the sins of the whole world. His grace and peace are with you now. Amen.

Petitions and Supplications, Ending with The Lord's Prayer
Our Father which art in heaven, Hallowed be thy name. Thy kingdom come, Thy will be done in earth, as it is in heaven. Give us this day our daily bread. And forgive us our debts, as we forgive our debtors. And lead us not into temptation, but deliver us from evil: For thine is the kingdom, and the power, and the glory, for ever. Amen.

~ Matthew 6.9-13 (KJV)

322 ⊕ The Season after Pentecost

Doxology (and/or closing song)

Praise God from whom all blessings flow;
Praise Him all creatures here below;
Praise Him above ye heavenly host;
Praise Father, Son and Holy Ghost. Amen.

DEPARTING TO SERVE

Benediction

Lord Jesus, who with honor and clarity testified to the truth
before Pilate, who was swayed by the crowd of accusers,
develop in us the same kind of courage and commitment you
displayed on that morning so many centuries ago. Bless us
with your mind and heart, and cause our love for you to
dominate every area of our lives, in order that we might reflect
your glory in this world, where we live, work, and play, for
your sake. Help us to stand for you, no matter what. In your
name we pray, amen.

Affirmation from the Psalms

Hear, O daughter, and consider, and incline your ear: forget your
people and your father's house, and the king will desire your beauty.
Since he is your lord, bow to him. The people of Tyre will seek your
favor with gifts, the richest of the people. All glorious is the princess in
her chamber, with robes interwoven with gold. In many-colored robes
she is led to the king, with her virgin companions following behind her.
With joy and gladness they are led along as they enter the palace of
the king. In place of your fathers shall be your sons; you will make
them princes in all the earth. I will cause your name to be remembered
in all generations; therefore nations will praise you forever and ever.

~ Psalm 45.10-17

Pray without Ceasing – Flash Prayer for the Day

Lord Jesus Christ, King and Lord of all, cause us in all things
to reflect the same lowliness and humility you displayed in
the presence of Pontius Pilate.

FOR YOUR WEEKLY JOURNEY

Let God Arise! Seasonal Focus
The Three Hebrew Boys, Daniel 3.1-30

Book Reading
DAILY: Extreme Devotion Writing Team, *Extreme Devotion*

DC Talk, The Voice of the Martyrs, *Jesus Freaks*

✠

FIFTH SUNDAY AFTER PENTECOST

July 13 - 19, 2014 ✠ Proper 10

On Pentecost we commemorate the descent of the Holy Spirit to earth on Christ's believers, his infilling of the people of God, the Church. Through him, the third person of the Trinity, Jesus our Lord is now present with his people. The Spirit is the guarantee of the promised inheritance to come. We ponder the fullness and mystery of our God's person and work in our celebration on Trinity Sunday.

THIS WEEK'S THEME
The Innocence of Abel, Genesis 4.1-16; Hebrews 11.4

Cain and Abel were the sons of Adam and Eve, Abel being a keeper of sheep, and Cain a gardener, a "worker of the ground." In the course of time, the brothers brought to the LORD an offering, Cain offering of the fruit of the ground, and Abel also of the firstborn of his flock and of their fat portions. And the LORD had regard for Abel and his offering, but not for Cain's, who in response became furious. The Lord, however, urged Cain to offer to him the kind of sacrifice he could accept.

Cain spoke to Abel his brother, and when they were in the field, in a fit of rage, Cain rose up against his brother Abel and killed him. When God inquired from Cain as to where his brother was, Cain said he didn't know, and argued that he wasn't his brother's keeper. Cain was cursed by the Lord to be a vagrant and a wanderer on the earth.

In the New Testament, Abel is viewed as the innocent, one who was murdered by his own brother purely on the basis of envy and rage. Hebrews testifies that by faith Abel offered to God a more acceptable sacrifice than Cain, through which sacrifice he was commended by God as righteous, God acknowledging him by accepting his gifts. Through Abel's faith, though he died at his brother's hand, he still speaks.

DAILY DEVOTIONAL GUIDE

PREPARING OUR HEARTS

Invocation: Our Prayer of Acclamation

Eternal God, Father of our Lord Jesus Christ, thank you for the example of innocent Abel who in lowliness and surrender offered to you a sacrifice which you accepted, and was murdered by his brother, out of anger and envy. You commended him, accepted his gifts, and allowed him to continue to speak, even though he died at Cain's hand. Make us like righteous Abel – obedient, faithful, and true, even if wrongly judged and despised. In Jesus' name, amen.

Call to Worship

Blessed are you, O God: Father, Son, and Holy Spirit. And blessed is your Kingdom, both now and forever, Amen.

PRAISING OUR GOD

Te Deum Laudamus

You are God: we praise you; you are the Lord; we acclaim you; you are the eternal Father: All creation worships you. To you all angels, all the powers of heaven, Cherubim and Seraphim, sing in endless praise: Holy, holy, holy Lord, God of power and might, heaven and earth are full of your glory.

The glorious company of apostles praise you. The noble fellowship of prophets praise you. The white-robed army of martyrs praise you. Throughout the world the holy Church acclaims you; Father, of majesty unbounded, your true and only Son, worthy of all worship, and the Holy Spirit, advocate and guide.

You, Christ, are the king of glory, the eternal Son of the Father. When you became man to set us free you did not shun the Virgin's womb. You overcame the sting of death and opened the kingdom of heaven to all believers. You are seated at God's right hand in glory. We believe

that you will come and be our judge. Come then, Lord, and help your
people, bought with the price of your own blood, and bring us with
your saints to glory everlasting.

Praise and Thanksgiving (Songs and Prayers)

Gloria Patri
Glory be to the Father,
And to the Son and to the Holy Spirit:
As it was in the beginning,
Is now, and ever shall be,
World without end. Amen, amen.

LISTENING TO HIS VOICE

Chronological Reading for the Day
Sunday: Jer. 31.15-40; 49.34-51.14 ✤ *Monday:* Jer. 51.15-58;
52.1-3a; 37.1-10; 2 Kings 24.10-20a; 2 Chron. 36.10-14;
1 Chron. 3.10-16 ✤ *Tuesday:* Jer. 37.11-38.28; Ezek. 1.1-3.15
✤ *Wednesday:* Ezek. 3.16-4.17; Jer. 27.1-28.17; 51.59-64 ✤
Thursday: Ezek. 5-9 ✤ *Friday:* Ezek. 10-13 ✤ *Saturday:*
Ezek. 14-16

Lectionary Readings
Psalm: Ps. 65.1-13   *OT:* Isa. 55.10-13
Gospel: Matt. 13.1-9, 18-23   *NT:* Rom. 8.1-11

Reflection: Silence and/or Journaling

RESPONDING IN FAITH

The Apostles' Creed
I believe in God, the Father Almighty, Maker of heaven and earth;
and in Jesus Christ, his only Son, our Lord, who was conceived by the
Holy Spirit, born of the Virgin Mary, suffered under Pontius Pilate,
was crucified, dead, and buried; he descended into hell; the third day
he arose again from the dead; he ascended into heaven and sits on

the right hand of God the Father Almighty; from thence he shall come to judge the quick and the dead.

I believe in the Holy Spirit, the holy catholic* church, the communion of saints, the forgiveness of sins, the resurrection of the body, and the life everlasting. Amen.

* In the Apostles' and Nicene Creeds, the term catholic refers to the Church's universality, through all ages and times, of all languages and peoples. It refers to no particular tradition or denominational expression (e.g., as in Roman Catholic).

Prayers of Confession

Let us now confess our sins to God and receive mercy and grace to help in our time of need.

Assurance of Pardon

Having faithfully confessed and renounced your sin, Christ also has been faithful to forgive your sins and to purify you from all unrighteousness. It is certain, that there is One who has spoken to the Father in your defense, Jesus Christ, the Righteous One who is the atoning sacrifice for our sins and for the sins of the whole world. His grace and peace are with you now. Amen.

Petitions and Supplications, Ending with The Lord's Prayer

Our Father which art in heaven, Hallowed be thy name. Thy kingdom come, Thy will be done in earth, as it is in heaven. Give us this day our daily bread. And forgive us our debts, as we forgive our debtors. And lead us not into temptation, but deliver us from evil: For thine is the kingdom, and the power, and the glory, for ever. Amen.

~ Matthew 6.9-13 (KJV)

Doxology (and/or closing song)

Praise God from whom all blessings flow;
Praise Him all creatures here below;
Praise Him above ye heavenly host;
Praise Father, Son and Holy Ghost. Amen.

DEPARTING TO SERVE

Benediction
Eternal God, your servant Abel fulfilled your will and became the object of his brother's hatred and rage, simply for obeying your word. Help us, dear Father, to never provoke others, to be humble and obedient to your command, to ever be responsive to you, with no sense of malice or harm offered to anyone. You are our strength and our defender; you will stand by us in our hour of trial, and enable us to honor you in the midst of difficulty. In the name of Jesus, we pray, amen.

Affirmation from the Psalms
Praise is due to you, O God, in Zion, and to you shall vows be performed. O you who hear prayer, to you shall all flesh come. When iniquities prevail against me, you atone for our transgressions. Blessed is the one you choose and bring near, to dwell in your courts! We shall be satisfied with the goodness of your house, the holiness of your temple!

~ Psalm 65.1-4

Pray without Ceasing – Flash Prayer for the Day
Teach us, Lord Jesus, to live by faith, like Abel, who offered to you in lowly obedience his acceptable sacrifice, though envied by Cain and murdered through his brother's rage.

FOR YOUR WEEKLY JOURNEY

Let God Arise! Seasonal Focus
The Three Hebrew Boys, Daniel 3.1-30

Book Reading
DAILY: Extreme Devotion Writing Team, *Extreme Devotion*

DC Talk, The Voice of the Martyrs, *Jesus Freaks*

Our Corporate Disciplines
Solitude and Silence, ending with Book Review:
    Wednesday, July 16, 2014

Christt Pantocrator (Christ Omnipotent)
Dome of St. Photina Church (built over Jacob's Well)

The Name above Every Name That Is Named

The Season after Pentecost is a season of recognition and affirmation of the headship and lordship of Jesus Christ. According to the Apostle Paul in his letter to the Ephesians, God the Father has displayed his immeasurable power to the world in raising his Son Jesus Christ from the dead. The same Jesus who was humiliated and abused in a sham Roman trial and Jewish Sanhedrin council proceeding has now been vindicated. Through his death and resurrection, Jesus the Nazarene has proven himself to be the one, true Son of God, the Christ and Lord of all.

Now, because of his obedience and sacrifice, God has highly magnified him and through his ascension has seated Jesus at his right hand in the heavenly places. This exalted status is unique and singular; he has been raised "far above all rule and authority and power and dominion, and above every name that is named, not only in this age but also in the one to come" (Eph. 1.21, ESV). In honor of his work as God's servant, the Father has put all things under his feet, and given Jesus Christ to be head over all things to his body, the Church, which is called "the fullness of him who fills all in all" (Eph. 1.23). The exaltation of Jesus Christ is appropriate and right; his is the only name under heaven given to humankind whereby they can be reconciled to God and forgiven of their sins (Acts 4.12).

The Already/Not Yet Kingdom: The Exaltation of Jesus Christ

During this unique season, we reflect and act in real time. We both ponder and live in that amazing "already/not yet" moment of Christ's reign between the sending of the Holy Spirit and his return at the Second Coming. During this season of God's calendar, we acknowledge and recognize Jesus' place in the universe. Given all authority in heaven and on earth, he now commands his people to go and make disciples of all nations (Matt. 28.18-19). Because our Lord is alive and exalted, we are empowered to accomplish his mandate of world evangelization, and serve as his ambassadors around the globe where people and nations still do not know him to be the Lord and Savior of the world. During this Season after Pentecost we extol him who has been given a name above every name, the same name that all tongues one day will confess and all knees one day will be made to bow to. Truly, Jesus Christ is Lord to the glory of God, the Father (Phil. 2.9-11).

According to Paul in 1 Corinthians 15, Jesus Christ must reign until God has put all of his enemies under his feet (cf. 15.25). As he whom God has exalted, Christ ever lives now to make intercession for his own (Heb. 7.25). As he whom God has honored, he alone is the head over all things to his people, leading and directing them as the Shepherd of their souls (1 Pet. 2.25). As he whom God has granted authority over all things, Jesus alone can provide for us the grace and strength to endure all that this world and its prince may do to thwart God's will (1 John 4.4).

Those of us committed to advancing the Kingdom of God in the cities of the world need to remind ourselves that things are not as they appear. On every hand God seems to be ignorant of the chaos around us, or worse, impotent to change the affairs in a world that seems to daily spin more and more out of control. Evil taunts righteousness in numerous societies that flail and wobble towards corruption, coasting without bearing or compass. In the face of such tragedies, let us worship God during this Season after Pentecost, and remember his holy Word: Jesus our Lord has been exalted at the Father's right hand, given a name above all names, and is the head of his people, directing his Church's affairs as we both show and tell the lost of the Good News of the Kingdom.

In the midst of despair and difficulty, we need never abandon our hope that, in spite of it all, God in Christ Jesus still commands the universe, and reigns in all the corridors of history. In all things, our Lord Christ alone will have the final say. The Ascension is our opportunity to confess that Christ is risen and exalted, and that God is still on the throne. This is the key to ministry, and this is the key to life.

He Must Reign until All His Enemies Are under His Feet
It turns out then that our remembrance during Ordinary Time is not that ordinary after all. During this Kingdomtide, let us affirm the truth that spans the centuries and binds all epochs of salvation history together. In Jesus Christ, God intends to rule and reign, and our Lord must now reign until all his enemies are under his feet. As we continue to worship and serve our Lord during this the longest season in the Church's calendar, let's remember as believers and congregations that the next season to follow is Advent: the return of the exalted Lord to the earth to complete the work he started on the Cross. Let us strive on toward maturity and multiplication in power of the Holy Spirit as the body of Christ in the world.

Join us as believers in Jesus Christ in giving glory to the Father for his exaltation of Christ, and let us strive in all our worship and service to give him the honor and praise he deserves. There is no other name under heaven given for us to be saved, and no other Lord in the universe who will reign and rule as God's sovereign King forever.

Let our knees gladly bow and our tongues joyfully confess that Jesus Christ is Lord, to the glory of God the Father. May we advance his kingdom reign in all that we are and say and do during this Season after Pentecost.

~ Standing in awe of the Risen and Exalted Lord,
Rev. Dr. Don L. Davis

July 20 - 26, 2014 ✢ Proper 11

During "Ordinary Time" (Kingdomtide), we consider God's saving acts through the unfolding of our days. As Christus Victor, Jesus is exalted at God's right hand, and he must reign until his enemies are put under his feet. He is the head of the body, the Church, and now he empowers his people to bear witness of his saving grace in the world.

THIS WEEK'S THEME
The Blood of Zechariah, 2 Chronicles 24.20-22; Matthew 23.29-36

During the reign of Joash, he called for the Temple to be repaired, but allowed Judah to return to idolatry. During his early years, Jehoiada the priest guided Joash, but later, he was influenced by wicked leaders in Judah. As the people began to worship idols again, the Spirit of God clothed Zechariah, the son of Jehoiada, who preached to the people for abandoning the Lord and turning to idols. He said to them, "Thus says God, 'Why do you break the commandments of the LORD, so that you cannot prosper? Because you have forsaken the LORD, he has forsaken you.'" The people conspired against Zechariah, and by command of Joash the king, they stoned him with stones in the court of the house of the LORD. So the king did not remember Jehoiada's kindness, but rather killed his son. This is the last martyr in the Hebrew Bible, as 2 Chronicles is the last book in the Hebrew Bible.

In condemning the hypocrisy of the scribes and Pharisees, Jesus put their murderous activity against God's spokespersons in the historical line of all those who shed the blood of the prophets. He promised to send them prophets and wise men and scribes, some whom they would kill and crucify, and others whom they would flog in their synagogues and persecute from town to town. This would occur in order that on them might come all the righteous blood shed on earth, from the blood of righteous Abel to the blood of Zechariah. All those things would come on that generation Jesus addressed.

DAILY DEVOTIONAL GUIDE

PREPARING OUR HEARTS

Invocation: Our Prayer of Acclamation

Gracious Father, who is mindful of the sacrifice and surrender of your saints around the world, thank you for the example of Zechariah. This brave prophet, who in the steps of his godly father, preached righteousness to the people and to the king, lost his life to proclaim your precious Word. Help us to stand for the truth, to be faithful in that righteous company of men and women who testified to your Gospel even though it cost them their lives. Help us to never shrink back, even in the face of those who refuse to hear your pleas for repentance. In Jesus' name we pray, amen.

Call to Worship

Blessed are you, O God: Father, Son, and Holy Spirit. And blessed is your Kingdom, both now and forever, Amen.

PRAISING OUR GOD

Te Deum Laudamus

You are God: we praise you; you are the Lord; we acclaim you; you are the eternal Father: All creation worships you. To you all angels, all the powers of heaven, Cherubim and Seraphim, sing in endless praise: Holy, holy, holy Lord, God of power and might, heaven and earth are full of your glory.

The glorious company of apostles praise you. The noble fellowship of prophets praise you. The white-robed army of martyrs praise you. Throughout the world the holy Church acclaims you; Father, of majesty unbounded, your true and only Son, worthy of all worship, and the Holy Spirit, advocate and guide.

You, Christ, are the king of glory, the eternal Son of the Father. When you became man to set us free you did not shun the Virgin's womb.

You overcame the sting of death and opened the kingdom of heaven to all believers. You are seated at God's right hand in glory. We believe that you will come and be our judge. Come then, Lord, and help your people, bought with the price of your own blood, and bring us with your saints to glory everlasting.

Praise and Thanksgiving (Songs and Prayers)

Gloria Patri
Glory be to the Father,
And to the Son and to the Holy Spirit:
As it was in the beginning,
Is now, and ever shall be,
World without end. Amen, amen.

LISTENING TO HIS VOICE

Chronological Reading for the Day
Sunday: Ezek. 17-19 ✠ *Monday:* Ezek. 20.1-22.16 ✠ *Tuesday:* Ezek. 22.17-24.14; 2 Kings 24.20b-25.2; Jer. 52.3b-5; 39.1 ✠ *Wednesday:* Ezek. 24.15-25.17; 29.1-16; 30.20-31.18; Jer. 34; ch.21 ✠ *Thursday:* Jer. 32-33; Ezek. 26 ✠ *Friday:* Ezek. 27-28; 2 Kings 25.3-7; Jer. 52.6-11; 39.2-10 ✠ *Saturday:* Jer. 39.11-18; 40.1-6; 52.12-27; 2 Kings 25.8-21; 2 Chron. 36.15-21

Lectionary Readings
Psalm: Ps. 86.11-17   *OT:* Isa. 44.6-8
Gospel: Matt. 13.24-30, 36-43   *NT:* Rom. 8.12-25

Reflection: Silence and/or Journaling

RESPONDING IN FAITH

The Apostles' Creed
I believe in God, the Father Almighty, Maker of heaven and earth; and in Jesus Christ, his only Son, our Lord, who was conceived by the

Holy Spirit, born of the Virgin Mary, suffered under Pontius Pilate, was crucified, dead, and buried; he descended into hell; the third day he arose again from the dead; he ascended into heaven and sits on the right hand of God the Father Almighty; from thence he shall come to judge the quick and the dead.

I believe in the Holy Spirit, the holy catholic* church, the communion of saints, the forgiveness of sins, the resurrection of the body, and the life everlasting. Amen.

* In the Apostles' and Nicene Creeds, the term catholic refers to the Church's universality, through all ages and times, of all languages and peoples. It refers to no particular tradition or denominational expression (e.g., as in Roman Catholic).

Prayers of Confession
Let us now confess our sins to God and receive mercy and grace to help in our time of need.

Assurance of Pardon
Having faithfully confessed and renounced your sin, Christ also has been faithful to forgive your sins and to purify you from all unrighteousness. It is certain, that there is One who has spoken to the Father in your defense, Jesus Christ, the Righteous One who is the atoning sacrifice for our sins and for the sins of the whole world. His grace and peace are with you now. Amen.

Petitions and Supplications, Ending with The Lord's Prayer
Our Father which art in heaven, Hallowed be thy name. Thy kingdom come, Thy will be done in earth, as it is in heaven. Give us this day our daily bread. And forgive us our debts, as we forgive our debtors. And lead us not into temptation, but deliver us from evil: For thine is the kingdom, and the power, and the glory, for ever. Amen.

~ Matthew 6.9-13 (KJV)

Doxology (and/or closing song)
Praise God from whom all blessings flow;
Praise Him all creatures here below;
Praise Him above ye heavenly host;
Praise Father, Son and Holy Ghost. Amen.

DEPARTING TO SERVE

Benediction
Gracious Savior, like the bold Zechariah who declared the word of God to those who ultimately took his life, create in us his valiant spirit. Give us the same prophetic voice he possessed, with the same heart and love for you he had, that we can represent you, and give you the same extreme devotion he offered. You are worthy of our praise. In your name we pray, amen.

Affirmation from the Psalms
Teach me your way, O LORD, that I may walk in your truth; unite my heart to fear your name. I give thanks to you, O Lord my God, with my whole heart, and I will glorify your name forever. For great is your steadfast love toward me; you have delivered my soul from the depths of Sheol. O God, insolent men have risen up against me; a band of ruthless men seeks my life, and they do not set you before them. But you, O Lord, are a God merciful and gracious, slow to anger and abounding in steadfast love and faithfulness.

~ Psalm 86.11-15

Pray without Ceasing – Flash Prayer for the Day
Savior, use us as your trumpet, sounding clear your word of hope and grace to all, even to those who turn their rejection of your offer into hatred and violence against us.

FOR YOUR WEEKLY JOURNEY

Let God Arise! Seasonal Focus
Daniel and the Lions' Den, Daniel 6.1-28

Book Reading
DAILY: Extreme Devotion Writing Team, *Extreme Devotion*

Howell, *Servants, Misfits, and Martyrs*

SEVENTH SUNDAY AFTER PENTECOST �֎

July 27 - August 2, 2014 �֎ Proper 12

During "Ordinary Time" (Kingdomtide), we consider God's saving acts through the unfolding of our days. As Christus Victor, Jesus is exalted at God's right hand, and he must reign until his enemies are put under his feet. He is the head of the body, the Church, and now he empowers his people to bear witness of his saving grace in the world.

THIS WEEK'S THEME
Herod Beheads John the Baptist, Matthew 14.1-12; 11.7-15
When Herod the tetrarch heard about the fame of Jesus, he commented to his servants mistakenly that Jesus was in fact John the Baptist who had been raised from the dead. He thought John to have been reincarnated in Jesus, working miracles through him. Previously Herod had seized John, bound him, and put him in prison at the bidding of Herodias, Herod's brother Philip's wife. John the Baptizer had preached against their arrangement, saying that it was not lawful for Herod to have his brother Philip's wife. For this, Herod wanted to put him to death, but feared the people, since they took John to be a prophet.

When Herod's birthday came, Herodias's daughter danced before the birthday company. Her dancing pleased Herod greatly, so much so that he promised with an oath to give her whatever she might ask. After consulting with her mother, she asked Herod to grant her the head of John the Baptist on a platter. Herod was sorry, yet, because of his oath and his guests, he commanded John's head to be given to her. John was beheaded in the prison, and his head was brought on a platter, and given to the girl, who brought it to her mother. John's disciples came, took his body, buried it, and went and told Jesus of the incident.

In commenting on John the Baptist, Jesus spoke of John as a prophet, yet someone who was more than a prophet. John in fact was the fulfillment of Malachi's prophecy, "Behold,

I send my messenger before your face, who will prepare your way before you." Jesus said that of all those who have been born of women there has arisen no one greater than John the Baptizer. Yet, the one who is least in the kingdom of heaven is greater than he. John stood for the truth, speaking it directly to all, regardless of station or rank, without flinching or compromise. He is a model of what it means to stand for the truth till the end.

DAILY DEVOTIONAL GUIDE

PREPARING OUR HEARTS

Invocation: Our Prayer of Acclamation
Eternal God, God of John the Baptizer, you sent him into the world to bear witness of the Light of the world, Jesus of Nazareth your Son. John refused to flinch in the face of power or threat, and stood by your word, at the cost of his own life. Grant us the wisdom and the strength to represent you and your Kingdom as John did. Make us both fierce and true for you, and only for you. In the name of Jesus we pray, amen.

Call to Worship
Blessed are you, O God: Father, Son, and Holy Spirit. And blessed is your Kingdom, both now and forever, Amen.

PRAISING OUR GOD

Te Deum Laudamus
You are God: we praise you; you are the Lord; we acclaim you; you are the eternal Father: All creation worships you. To you all angels, all the powers of heaven, Cherubim and Seraphim, sing in endless praise: Holy, holy, holy Lord, God of power and might, heaven and earth are full of your glory.

The glorious company of apostles praise you. The noble fellowship of prophets praise you. The white-robed army of martyrs praise you.

Throughout the world the holy Church acclaims you; Father, of majesty unbounded, your true and only Son, worthy of all worship, and the Holy Spirit, advocate and guide.

You, Christ, are the king of glory, the eternal Son of the Father. When you became man to set us free you did not shun the Virgin's womb. You overcame the sting of death and opened the kingdom of heaven to all believers. You are seated at God's right hand in glory. We believe that you will come and be our judge. Come then, Lord, and help your people, bought with the price of your own blood, and bring us with your saints to glory everlasting.

Praise and Thanksgiving (Songs and Prayers)

Gloria Patri
Glory be to the Father,
And to the Son and to the Holy Spirit:
As it was in the beginning,
Is now, and ever shall be,
World without end. Amen, amen.

LISTENING TO HIS VOICE

Chronological Reading for the Day
Sunday: Lam. 1-3 ✤ *Monday:* Lam. 4-5; Obad.; 2 Kings 25.22-26; Jer. 40.7-41.18 ✤ *Tuesday:* Jer. 42-44; Ezek. 33.21-33 ✤ *Wednesday:* Ezek. 34-36 ✤ *Thursday:* Ezek. 37-39; 32.1-16 ✤ *Friday:* Ezek. 32.17-33.20; Jer. 52.28-30; Ps. 137; 1 Chron. 4.24-5.17 ✤ *Saturday:* 1 Chron. 5.18-26; 6.3b-15, v.49; 7.1-8.28

Lectionary Readings

Psalm: Ps. 119.129-136	*OT:* Gen. 29.15-28
Gospel: Matt. 13.31-33, 44-52	*NT:* Rom. 8.26-39

Reflection: Silence and/or Journaling

Responding in Faith

The Apostles' Creed
I believe in God, the Father Almighty, Maker of heaven and earth; and in Jesus Christ, his only Son, our Lord, who was conceived by the Holy Spirit, born of the Virgin Mary, suffered under Pontius Pilate, was crucified, dead, and buried; he descended into hell; the third day he arose again from the dead; he ascended into heaven and sits on the right hand of God the Father Almighty; from thence he shall come to judge the quick and the dead.

I believe in the Holy Spirit, the holy catholic* church, the communion of saints, the forgiveness of sins, the resurrection of the body, and the life everlasting. Amen.

* In the Apostles' and Nicene Creeds, the term catholic refers to the Church's universality, through all ages and times, of all languages and peoples. It refers to no particular tradition or denominational expression (e.g., as in Roman Catholic).

Prayers of Confession
Let us now confess our sins to God and receive mercy and grace to help in our time of need.

Assurance of Pardon
Having faithfully confessed and renounced your sin, Christ also has been faithful to forgive your sins and to purify you from all unrighteousness. It is certain, that there is One who has spoken to the Father in your defense, Jesus Christ, the Righteous One who is the atoning sacrifice for our sins and for the sins of the whole world. His grace and peace are with you now. Amen.

Petitions and Supplications, Ending with The Lord's Prayer
Our Father which art in heaven, Hallowed be thy name. Thy kingdom come, Thy will be done in earth, as it is in heaven. Give us this day our daily bread. And forgive us our debts, as we forgive our debtors. And

lead us not into temptation, but deliver us from evil: For thine is the kingdom, and the power, and the glory, for ever. Amen.

~ Matthew 6.9-13 (KJV)

Doxology (and/or closing song)
Praise God from whom all blessings flow;
Praise Him all creatures here below;
Praise Him above ye heavenly host;
Praise Father, Son and Holy Ghost. Amen.

DEPARTING TO SERVE

Benediction
Eternal God, John the Baptizer lost his life because he testified for the truth. He was persecuted, imprisoned, and beheaded, solely because he stood for the truth and refused to compromise it, even if it meant his release from prison. Standing his ground, he offered himself up to you as a martyr for the truth. Reproduce in us the same kind of devotion that is both pure and extreme, the kind your servant John displayed, the kind of devotion that can stand in the face of opposition and speak truth to power without fear. In Jesus' name we pray, amen.

Affirmation from the Psalms
Your testimonies are wonderful; therefore my soul keeps them. The unfolding of your words gives light; it imparts understanding to the simple. I open my mouth and pant, because I long for your commandments. Turn to me and be gracious to me, as is your way with those who love your name. Keep steady my steps according to your promise, and let no iniquity get dominion over me. Redeem me from man's oppression, that I may keep your precepts. Make your face shine upon your servant, and teach me your statutes. My eyes shed streams of tears, because people do not keep your law.

~ Psalm 119.129-136

Pray without Ceasing – Flash Prayer for the Day
Dear Lord Jesus, whose mighty entrance was announced by John the Baptizer, help us keep the mind of John in all areas of our lives: we must decrease, so you can increase.

FOR YOUR WEEKLY JOURNEY

Let God Arise! Seasonal Focus
Daniel and the Lions' Den, Daniel 6.1-28

Book Reading
DAILY: Extreme Devotion Writing Team, *Extreme Devotion*

Howell, *Servants, Misfits, and Martyrs*

✠

EIGHTH SUNDAY AFTER PENTECOST

August 3 - 9, 2014 ✠ Proper 13

During "Ordinary Time" (Kingdomtide), we consider God's saving acts through the unfolding of our days. As Christus Victor, Jesus is exalted at God's right hand, and he must reign until his enemies are put under his feet. He is the head of the body, the Church, and now he empowers his people to bear witness of his saving grace in the world.

THIS WEEK'S THEME
Ruth's Devotion to Naomi, Ruth 1.1-18

The book of Ruth tells the story of a time in the days when the judges ruled, when famine arose. Elimelech, a man of Bethlehem in Judah, went to sojourn in the country of Moab, along with his wife, Naomi, and two sons. After some time, Elimelech died. The sons took Moabite wives, and after ten years, the sons also died.

After these things, Naomi arose with her daughters-in-law to return to Israel from Moab, hearing that the LORD had visited his people and given them food there. Naomi pressed her two daughters-in-law to return to Moab to their people and their gods, and look to their own futures. While the one daughter-in-law turned to return to Moab, Ruth clung to Naomi.

Willing to abandon her past to stay with Naomi, Ruth declared, "Do not urge me to leave you or to return from following you. For where you go I will go, and where you lodge I will lodge. Your people shall be my people, and your God my God. Where you die I will die, and there will I be buried. May the LORD do so to me and more also if anything but death parts me from you."

As a foreigner, a woman, and a widow, Ruth was entirely dependent on others for help. In her gleaning of the fields, she caught the notice of Boaz, who acted as a kinsman-redeemer for Ruth and Naomi. Later, Ruth would become Boaz's wife, and would have a child who would become an ancestor of David the king. Ruth's extreme, unconditional devotion to Naomi provides a clear example of what it means to give oneself over to another. Let us imitate Ruth's devotion to Naomi, a type of our devotion to the Lord. In the end, Ruth would become the great-grandmother of David, and thus an ancestor of our Lord Jesus Christ.

DAILY DEVOTIONAL GUIDE

PREPARING OUR HEARTS

Invocation: Our Prayer of Acclamation

Eternal God, thank you for the amazing fidelity and devotion that Ruth expressed toward Naomi. Ruth's heart revealed her willingness to cling to Naomi regardless of what it meant, where they went, or what was involved. Ruth is a clear testimony of what it means to be sold out for another person. Make us the kind of people who can be truly sold out to you, without condition or qualification, willing to go wherever you lead. In Jesus' name we pray, amen.

Call to Worship

Blessed are you, O God: Father, Son, and Holy Spirit. And blessed is your Kingdom, both now and forever, Amen.

PRAISING OUR GOD

Te Deum Laudamus

You are God: we praise you; you are the Lord; we acclaim you; you are the eternal Father: All creation worships you. To you all angels, all the powers of heaven, Cherubim and Seraphim, sing in endless praise: Holy, holy, holy Lord, God of power and might, heaven and earth are full of your glory.

The glorious company of apostles praise you. The noble fellowship of prophets praise you. The white-robed army of martyrs praise you. Throughout the world the holy Church acclaims you; Father, of

*majesty unbounded, your true and only Son, worthy of all worship,
and the Holy Spirit, advocate and guide.*

*You, Christ, are the king of glory, the eternal Son of the Father. When
you became man to set us free you did not shun the Virgin's womb.
You overcame the sting of death and opened the kingdom of heaven
to all believers. You are seated at God's right hand in glory. We believe
that you will come and be our judge. Come then, Lord, and help your
people, bought with the price of your own blood, and bring us with
your saints to glory everlasting.*

Praise and Thanksgiving (Songs and Prayers)

Gloria Patri
*Glory be to the Father,
And to the Son and to the Holy Spirit:
As it was in the beginning,
Is now, and ever shall be,
World without end. Amen, amen.*

LISTENING TO HIS VOICE

Chronological Reading for the Day
Sunday: 1 Chron. 8.29-9.1a; Dan. 4; Ezek. 40 ✤ *Monday:*
Ezek. 41-43 ✤ *Tuesday:* Ezek. 44-46 ✤ *Wednesday:* Ezek.
47-48; 29.17-30.19; 2 Kings 25.27-30; Jer. 52.31-34 ✤
Thursday: Dan. 7-8; ch.5 ✤ *Friday:* Dan. 6; 9; 2 Chron.
36.22-23; Ezra 1; 1 Chron. 3.17-19a ✤ *Saturday:* Ezra 2.1-4.5;
1 Chron. 3.19b-24

Lectionary Readings
Psalm: Ps. 145.8-9, 14-21   *OT:* Gen. 32.22-31
Gospel: Matt. 14.13-21   *NT:* Rom. 9.1-5

Reflection: Silence and/or Journaling

RESPONDING IN FAITH

The Apostles' Creed

I believe in God, the Father Almighty, Maker of heaven and earth; and in Jesus Christ, his only Son, our Lord, who was conceived by the Holy Spirit, born of the Virgin Mary, suffered under Pontius Pilate, was crucified, dead, and buried; he descended into hell; the third day he arose again from the dead; he ascended into heaven and sits on the right hand of God the Father Almighty; from thence he shall come to judge the quick and the dead.

I believe in the Holy Spirit, the holy catholic* church, the communion of saints, the forgiveness of sins, the resurrection of the body, and the life everlasting. Amen.

* In the Apostles' and Nicene Creeds, the term catholic refers to the Church's universality, through all ages and times, of all languages and peoples. It refers to no particular tradition or denominational expression (e.g., as in Roman Catholic).

Prayers of Confession

Let us now confess our sins to God and receive mercy and grace to help in our time of need.

Assurance of Pardon

Having faithfully confessed and renounced your sin, Christ also has been faithful to forgive your sins and to purify you from all unrighteousness. It is certain, that there is One who has spoken to the Father in your defense, Jesus Christ, the Righteous One who is the atoning sacrifice for our sins and for the sins of the whole world. His grace and peace are with you now. Amen.

Petitions and Supplications, Ending with The Lord's Prayer

Our Father which art in heaven, Hallowed be thy name. Thy kingdom come, Thy will be done in earth, as it is in heaven. Give us this day our daily bread. And forgive us our debts, as we forgive our debtors. And

lead us not into temptation, but deliver us from evil: For thine is the kingdom, and the power, and the glory, for ever. Amen.

~ Matthew 6.9-13 (KJV)

Doxology (and/or closing song)
Praise God from whom all blessings flow;
Praise Him all creatures here below;
Praise Him above ye heavenly host;
Praise Father, Son and Holy Ghost. Amen.

DEPARTING TO SERVE

Benediction
Lord Jesus, whose disciples reflected the same kind of extreme devotion to you as Ruth demonstrated to Naomi, reproduce in us the same kind of fidelity, loyalty, and commitment. Forgive us when we forget what it means to be devoted to you. Cleanse us and protect us from our shallowness and distraction, and re-center our lives on you, on your people, and on your mission. Give to us Ruth's heart for you. In your name we pray, amen.

Affirmation from the Psalms
The LORD is gracious and merciful, slow to anger and abounding in steadfast love. The LORD is good to all, and his mercy is over all that he has made.

~ Psalm 145.8-9

Pray without Ceasing – Flash Prayer for the Day
Lord Jesus Christ, make us unconditionally available to you, to do whatever you demand, to go wherever you lead, and connect our whole persons and possibilities to you.

FOR YOUR WEEKLY JOURNEY

Let God Arise! Seasonal Focus
Daniel and the Lions' Den, Daniel 6.1-28

Book Reading
DAILY: Extreme Devotion Writing Team, *Extreme Devotion*

Howell, *Servants, Misfits, and Martyrs*

August 10 - 16, 2014 ✠ Proper 14

During "Ordinary Time" (Kingdomtide), we consider God's saving acts through the unfolding of our days. As Christus Victor, Jesus is exalted at God's right hand, and he must reign until his enemies are put under his feet. He is the head of the body, the Church, and now he empowers his people to bear witness of his saving grace in the world.

THIS WEEK'S THEME
Daniel and the Lions' Den, Daniel 6.1-28
During the time of the Babylonian captivity, King Darius set over his kingdom 120 satraps (administrators) to manage his entire kingdom, with three high officials over them, Daniel being one of the three, to whom the 120 gave account in stewarding the king's affairs. Daniel became distinguished above all the other officials and leaders, and the king planned on setting him over the whole kingdom.

The officials and the satraps sought to find some reason for complaint against Daniel in regard to his conduct and the kingdom, but they found none, for Daniel was blameless. His detractors could find no error or fault in him. Seeing that they could not find anything in his behavior to warrant a complaint against him, they determined to use his devotion to God as the means to undermine him before the king.

So, the officials tricked Darius into issuing a decree preventing anyone for a thirty-day period to pray to any god or man besides the king. The sentence for disobeying this decree would mean the fate of being thrown into the lions' den. After hearing of the decree, Daniel continued his discipline of praying three times each day. In the same way that he had done before, he knelt down, faced Jerusalem, and prayed to God. The leaders caught him, told Darius, and insisted on the sentence being carried out. Although Darius loved Daniel and tried to save him, he could not revoke his decree, and so, at sundown, he had Daniel thrown into the lions' den.

After an uneasy night without eating or sleeping, Darius at dawn ran to the lions' den. He asked Daniel if his God had intervened and protected him. Daniel replied, "My God sent his angel and shut the lions' mouths, and they have not harmed me, because I was found blameless before him; and also before you, O king, I have done no harm." King Darius released Daniel, arrested those who had falsely accused Daniel, and threw them (with their wives and children) into the den meant for Daniel. They were slaughtered by the lions quickly. Darius then issued a decree that all people should both fear and reverence the God of Daniel.

Daniel's story reveals the power of the constancy of faith in the face of compromise. In spite of the prospect of death, he refused to be intimidated, and left himself in the hands of the Lord.

DAILY DEVOTIONAL GUIDE

PREPARING OUR HEARTS

Invocation: Our Prayer of Acclamation
Eternal God, our Father, you visited Daniel that night in the lions' den, shutting the mouths of these wild beasts, and protecting his life from the treacherous plan of the officials. You gave him the heart and determination to stand true to you in the face of known danger. He refused to compromise, even at the risk of his very life. God, rework that kind of passion in your servants today, making us the kind of people who do not shrink back, whatever the cost. In Jesus' name we pray, amen.

Call to Worship
Blessed are you, O God: Father, Son, and Holy Spirit. And blessed is your Kingdom, both now and forever, Amen.

PRAISING OUR GOD

Te Deum Laudamus

You are God: we praise you; you are the Lord; we acclaim you; you are the eternal Father: All creation worships you. To you all angels, all the powers of heaven, Cherubim and Seraphim, sing in endless praise: Holy, holy, holy Lord, God of power and might, heaven and earth are full of your glory.

The glorious company of apostles praise you. The noble fellowship of prophets praise you. The white-robed army of martyrs praise you. Throughout the world the holy Church acclaims you; Father, of majesty unbounded, your true and only Son, worthy of all worship, and the Holy Spirit, advocate and guide.

You, Christ, are the king of glory, the eternal Son of the Father. When you became man to set us free you did not shun the Virgin's womb. You overcame the sting of death and opened the kingdom of heaven to all believers. You are seated at God's right hand in glory. We believe that you will come and be our judge. Come then, Lord, and help your people, bought with the price of your own blood, and bring us with your saints to glory everlasting.

Praise and Thanksgiving (Songs and Prayers)

Gloria Patri

Glory be to the Father,
And to the Son and to the Holy Spirit:
As it was in the beginning,
Is now, and ever shall be,
World without end. Amen, amen.

LISTENING TO HIS VOICE

Chronological Reading for the Day

Sunday: Dan. 10-12; Ezra 4.24-5.1 ✠ *Monday:* Hag. 1-2; Zech. 1-5; Ezra 5.2 ✠ *Tuesday:* Zech. 6-8; Ezra 5.3-6.14a ✠

Wednesday: Zech. 9-14 ✤ *Thursday:* Ezra 6.14b-22; 4.6; Esther 1-4 ✤ *Friday:* Esther 5-10 ✤ *Saturday:* Ezra 4.7-23; ch.7-8

Lectionary Readings

Psalm: Ps. 85.8-13   *OT:* Gen. 37.1-4, 12-28
Gospel: Matt. 14.22-33   *NT:* Rom. 10.5-15

Reflection: Silence and/or Journaling

RESPONDING IN FAITH

The Apostles' Creed

I believe in God, the Father Almighty, Maker of heaven and earth; and in Jesus Christ, his only Son, our Lord, who was conceived by the Holy Spirit, born of the Virgin Mary, suffered under Pontius Pilate, was crucified, dead, and buried; he descended into hell; the third day he arose again from the dead; he ascended into heaven and sits on the right hand of God the Father Almighty; from thence he shall come to judge the quick and the dead.

I believe in the Holy Spirit, the holy catholic* church, the communion of saints, the forgiveness of sins, the resurrection of the body, and the life everlasting. Amen.

* In the Apostles' and Nicene Creeds, the term catholic refers to the Church's universality, through all ages and times, of all languages and peoples. It refers to no particular tradition or denominational expression (e.g., as in Roman Catholic).

Prayers of Confession

Let us now confess our sins to God and receive mercy and grace to help in our time of need.

Assurance of Pardon

Having faithfully confessed and renounced your sin, Christ also has been faithful to forgive your sins and to purify you from all unrighteousness. It is certain, that there is One who has spoken to the Father in your defense, Jesus Christ, the

Righteous One who is the atoning sacrifice for our sins and for the sins of the whole world. His grace and peace are with you now. Amen.

Petitions and Supplications, Ending with The Lord's Prayer
Our Father which art in heaven, Hallowed be thy name. Thy kingdom come, Thy will be done in earth, as it is in heaven. Give us this day our daily bread. And forgive us our debts, as we forgive our debtors. And lead us not into temptation, but deliver us from evil: For thine is the kingdom, and the power, and the glory, for ever. Amen.

~ Matthew 6.9-13 (KJV)

Doxology (and/or closing song)
Praise God from whom all blessings flow;
Praise Him all creatures here below;
Praise Him above ye heavenly host;
Praise Father, Son and Holy Ghost. Amen.

Departing to Serve

Benediction
Master and King, Lord Jesus Christ, who sent your angel and shut the lions' mouths, so that they did no harm to your servant Daniel, grant us the confidence to know that you are the Sovereign Lord, the King of kings, and Lord of lords. You are the Son of God, our Lord, who directs our steps and fights our battles as we trust in you. Let us never be ashamed of the Gospel or afraid to represent your will, for you are still the Savior from the lions who prey after us each day. We will ever trust in you. In your name we pray, amen.

Affirmation from the Psalms

Let me hear what God the LORD will speak, for he will speak peace to his people, to his saints; but let them not turn back to folly. Surely his salvation is near to those who fear him, that glory may dwell in our land.

~ Psalm 85.8-13

Pray without Ceasing – Flash Prayer for the Day

Lord Jesus, give us the grace and the will to be like Daniel, who, even in the face of deception, trickery, and threats, kept constant in your will and way.

FOR YOUR WEEKLY JOURNEY

Let God Arise! Seasonal Focus

Daniel and the Lions' Den, Daniel 6.1-28

Book Reading

DAILY: Extreme Devotion Writing Team, *Extreme Devotion*

Howell, *Servants, Misfits, and Martyrs*

Our Corporate Disciplines

In-Service, ending with Book Review:
    Wednesday, August 13, 2014

✠

TENTH SUNDAY AFTER PENTECOST

August 17 - 23, 2014 ✠ Proper 15

During "Ordinary Time" (Kingdomtide), we consider God's saving acts through the unfolding of our days. As Christus Victor, Jesus is exalted at God's right hand, and he must reign until his enemies are put under his feet. He is the head of the body, the Church, and now he empowers his people to bear witness of his saving grace in the world.

THIS WEEK'S THEME
Paul's Defense before Agrippa, Acts 26.1-32

Having been harassed and falsely accused by various Jewish groups, Paul found himself making his defense before Agrippa, a high ranking official in the Roman empire. While Paul had already made a defense of his life and ministry to the lesser official Festus, so he now directed his comments to Agrippa, who would hear Paul's defense and provide consult for Festus.

In classic oratorical fashion (i.e., by motioning and movement of the hand), Paul gave his introductory, complimentary remarks, and explained his commitment and distinction in his early life as a devout Jew. He explained to Agrippa his incredible zeal in opposing all things associated with Jesus of Nazareth, and gave an overview of his conversion in his journey to Damascus. He summarized his commission he had received from Christ, his appointment to be a servant and a witness. Jesus had called him to be delivered from the Jews and from the Gentiles, in order to open their eyes so that they might turn from darkness to light and from the power of Satan to God, that they might receive forgiveness of sins and a place among those who are sanctified by faith in him.

Paul commented that he was not disobedient to this heavenly vision, but declared in Damascus, in Jerusalem, and through-out all the region of Judea, even too, to the Gentiles, that all should turn to God through Jesus Christ. He testified that it was for this reason he was seized and why others sought to kill him. He explained that he had been detained merely because he was testifying to what the prophets and Moses said would come to pass. Their message was that the Messiah would suffer, rise from the dead, and then be proclaimed to both Jews and Gentiles alike.

Although Festus accused Paul of being insane because of his great learning, Paul assured him that he was in fact sane, speaking true and rational words. He addressed Agrippa directly, suggesting that he knew that Agrippa was well aware of the truth, and the testimony of the prophets. King Agrippa mildly protested, dismissing Paul's short attempt to persuade him to be a Christian. Still, Paul said, "Whether short or long, I would to God that not only you but also all who hear me this day might become such as I am – except for these chains."

Paul was stalwart in testifying of Jesus of Nazareth as the Christ, although he was hounded and harassed from various groups throughout his entire ministry life. He did not waver, and he did not quit. He was given over to one thing – to testify of the Gospel of Jesus Christ to all who had never heard.

DAILY DEVOTIONAL GUIDE

PREPARING OUR HEARTS

Invocation: Our Prayer of Acclamation

Eternal God, our Lord, many centuries ago you revealed your Son and his salvation to the angry, legalistic young man who would become an apostle of the Lord, and wind up giving his life for the Nazarene. You encountered him on the road to Damascus and turned him from being a blasphemer and persecutor to a herald and an ambassador. He honored you in his life and ministry, and today we still read the writings you inspired through him for your people. Remind us that you are the God who can transform an assassin into an apostle, and reveal to those who hated you what they must endure for you as you win them and aid them. In Jesus' name we pray, amen.

Call to Worship

Blessed are you, O God: Father, Son, and Holy Spirit. And blessed is your Kingdom, both now and forever, Amen.

PRAISING OUR GOD

Te Deum Laudamus

You are God: we praise you; you are the Lord; we acclaim you; you are the eternal Father: All creation worships you. To you all angels, all the powers of heaven, Cherubim and Seraphim, sing in endless praise: Holy, holy, holy Lord, God of power and might, heaven and earth are full of your glory.

The glorious company of apostles praise you. The noble fellowship of prophets praise you. The white-robed army of martyrs praise you. Throughout the world the holy Church acclaims you; Father, of majesty unbounded, your true and only Son, worthy of all worship, and the Holy Spirit, advocate and guide.

You, Christ, are the king of glory, the eternal Son of the Father. When you became man to set us free you did not shun the Virgin's womb. You overcame the sting of death and opened the kingdom of heaven to all believers. You are seated at God's right hand in glory. We believe that you will come and be our judge. Come then, Lord, and help your people, bought with the price of your own blood, and bring us with your saints to glory everlasting.

Praise and Thanksgiving (Songs and Prayers)

Gloria Patri

Glory be to the Father,
And to the Son and to the Holy Spirit:
As it was in the beginning,
Is now, and ever shall be,
World without end. Amen, amen.

LISTENING TO HIS VOICE

Chronological Reading for the Day
Sunday: Ezra 9-10; Neh. 1-2 ✠ *Monday:* Neh. 3.1-5.13;
6.1-7.3 ✠ *Tuesday:* Neh. 7.4-8.18 ✠ *Wednesday:* Neh. 9-10
✠ *Thursday:* 1 Chron. 9.1b-34; Neh. 11-12 ✠ *Friday:*
Neh. 13; 5.14-19; Mal. 1-4 ✠ *Saturday:* Joel 1-3

Lectionary Readings
Psalm: Ps. 133   *OT:* Gen. 45.1-15
Gospel: Matt. 15.10-28   *NT:* Rom. 11.1-2a, 29-32

Reflection: Silence and/or Journaling

RESPONDING IN FAITH

The Apostles' Creed
*I believe in God, the Father Almighty, Maker of heaven and earth;
and in Jesus Christ, his only Son, our Lord, who was conceived by the
Holy Spirit, born of the Virgin Mary, suffered under Pontius Pilate,
was crucified, dead, and buried; he descended into hell; the third day
he arose again from the dead; he ascended into heaven and sits on
the right hand of God the Father Almighty; from thence he shall come
to judge the quick and the dead.*

I believe in the Holy Spirit, the holy catholic church, the communion
of saints, the forgiveness of sins, the resurrection of the body, and the
life everlasting. Amen.*

* In the Apostles' and Nicene Creeds, the term catholic refers to the Church's
universality, through all ages and times, of all languages and peoples. It refers to no
particular tradition or denominational expression (e.g., as in Roman Catholic).

Prayers of Confession
Let us now confess our sins to God and receive mercy and
grace to help in our time of need.

Assurance of Pardon

Having faithfully confessed and renounced your sin, Christ also has been faithful to forgive your sins and to purify you from all unrighteousness. It is certain, that there is One who has spoken to the Father in your defense, Jesus Christ, the Righteous One who is the atoning sacrifice for our sins and for the sins of the whole world. His grace and peace are with you now. Amen.

Petitions and Supplications, Ending with The Lord's Prayer

Our Father which art in heaven, Hallowed be thy name. Thy kingdom come, Thy will be done in earth, as it is in heaven. Give us this day our daily bread. And forgive us our debts, as we forgive our debtors. And lead us not into temptation, but deliver us from evil: For thine is the kingdom, and the power, and the glory, for ever. Amen.

~ Matthew 6.9-13 (KJV)

Doxology (and/or closing song)

Praise God from whom all blessings flow;
Praise Him all creatures here below;
Praise Him above ye heavenly host;
Praise Father, Son and Holy Ghost. Amen.

DEPARTING TO SERVE

Benediction

Lord Jesus, who met the wild and out-of-control Saul of Tarsus on the road to Damascus, meet us and transform us, from the inside out, as you did to your servant Paul. Create in us a heart that is easily turned from our own self-interests to those things that bring you pleasure and honor. Above all, grant that we will never be ashamed of the suffering and loss associated with service to your high and holy name. Let death work in us, so your life may be seen through us, for your name's sake. Amen.

Affirmation from the Psalms

Behold, how good and pleasant it is when brothers dwell in unity!
It is like the precious oil on the head, running down on the beard,
on the beard of Aaron, running down on the collar of his robes! It
is like the dew of Hermon, which falls on the mountains of Zion!
For there the LORD has commanded the blessing, life forevermore.

~ Psalm 133.1-3

Pray without Ceasing – Flash Prayer for the Day

Lord Jesus, give us a heart that is both fierce and steadfast, that is calm and resolute, a heart like your servant Paul, whom you transformed from a blasphemer into an apostle of the Lord.

FOR YOUR WEEKLY JOURNEY

Let God Arise! Seasonal Focus
Daniel and the Lions' Den, Daniel 6.1-28

Book Reading
DAILY: Extreme Devotion Writing Team, *Extreme Devotion*

Howell, *Servants, Misfits, and Martyrs*

Our Corporate Disciplines
Concert of Prayer:
    Saturday, August 23, 2014

Harvest field, West Bank

The Harvest Is Great, but the Laborers Are Few

During the Season after Pentecost we engage in mission to
the world. The risen and exalted Christ has given his people
the commission to make disciples of all nations, to spread
the Gospel of salvation to the ends of the earth. In Matthew
9.37-38 Jesus said to his disciples, "The harvest is plentiful,
but the workers are few. Therefore beseech the Lord of the
harvest to send out workers into his harvest." He exhorted
them to lift up their eyes and simply look to the fields of
harvest, the teeming millions of the nations who need to
know of God's grace in the Son of God. The harvest is ripe,
and the fields are white; the peoples of the world are truly
ready for harvest (John 4.34-35).

The call to mission is a call to obedience and perseverance.
We are called to share the apostolic heart, its clarity, passion,
and vision. Christ has revealed to us that the harvest of souls
is vast, the judgment that the lost face is inevitable, and the
time is urgent. The opportunity for millions to hear of God's
love in Christ has been given to God's messengers. They are
called to proclaim to the very ends of the earth, to cross the
barriers of race, culture, and class in order to prophesy
deliverance in Christ, new hope of eternal salvation, and
the certainty of divine judgment. These truths, when em-
braced and believed, produced a kind of internal urgency in
the heart of the apostles, and can do the same in us.

The Season after Pentecost, therefore, is a time of urgency
and readiness. No time can be wasted, no opportunity should
be ignored, and no prospect overlooked. Our understanding
of the harvest's fullness and ripeness, when combined with a
deep sense of the shortage of workers, should produce in us
an overwhelming burden to share the Gospel with the lost,

and to hazard our lives to go to the ends of the earth in order to tell those who have not heard the good news of salvation. This is a season of preparation, of mobilization, of engagement, and of courage. If we truly come to see and understand what the apostles saw and understood, then we, like them, will be moved to share and go even as they did.

**Pray to the Lord of the Harvest to
Send Forth Laborers into His Harvest**
Even though the workers are few, the harvest is great, and the time is short, we can be hopeful during this season of the Church Year. Jesus asserts that the harvest is his own, he who is called the "Lord of the harvest." It is neither ours to possess nor ours alone to superintend. Neither the enemy nor God's workers are possessors of the harvest. It belongs to Christ alone.

The breadth of the harvest and its Gospel is mind boggling, indeed: It is universal, including the "entire creation" (Mark 16.15-16). It involves every person, with offers to be made to every man, woman, boy, and girl who does not know the Lord Jesus as their personal Savior (Col. 1.27-29). It crosses all barriers of race and clan, the Gospel itself being a dynamic power to be proclaimed to every person and which can save all who hear and believe, not only the Jew but also the Gentile (Rom. 1.16-17). The Gospel is to be proclaimed to every single person beginning from Jerusalem, to Judea, in Samaria, and to the very ends of the earth (Acts 1.8), covering all nations, kindreds, peoples, and tongues who will one day worship Christ (Rev. 7.9-11). Every one of Adam's condemned race, all who are currently under the power of the prince of the air, can hear, believe, and be delivered by faith in the Gospel (Rom. 5; Eph. 2.2; Col. 1.13; 3.5-7).

During this season, therefore, let us exalt the risen Christ as Head of the Church, and the Holy Spirit as the anointing power who is given to us in order to fulfill his commission in the world. Let us, during this season, pray for courage to share the Gospel with our family and friends, and let us strive to be used of God in order to do all we can to help God's messengers cross barriers of culture and class with the message of reconciliation. Let us contribute our time and treasure to persuade as many people as we can to become obedient disciples of Jesus of Nazareth, now the exalted Lord of all. Let us pray that all who believe will too become joyful members of his Church, living in community with the saints, and fleshing out in their lives God's kingdom power.

The next season we celebrate is Advent, the coming of the Lord. Let us labor with all the strength he gives us, declaring unashamedly that Jesus Christ is the Victor over all sin and the forces of evil. He alone is the true King who will return in power and reign as Lord in his Kingdom. Then the ancient words will be fulfilled: the knowledge of the Lord will cover the earth even as the waters cover the sea. Until then, let us proclaim Jesus as both Lord and Christ. To him be glory evermore!

~ Praying for laborers for the Lord's harvest,
Rev. Dr. Don L. Davis

✠

ELEVENTH SUNDAY AFTER PENTECOST

August 24 - 30, 2014 ✠ Proper 16

As Lord of the harvest, Jesus has commissioned his Church during this age to go and make disciples of all nations. During this season after Pentecost, let us obey Christ's command and share the Gospel to the ends of the earth, gathering in the harvest of souls so ripe for reaping. As Christ's hands and feet in the world, let us both show and tell of his salvation to a dying and hurting world. This is a season of harvest.

THIS WEEK'S THEME
Esther Promises to Help, Esther 4.1-17
Haman, who served as prime minister of King Ahasuerus's empire, held great contempt for Mordecai, who sat at the palace gates, and publicly refused to bow down to Haman. Knowing that Mordecai was of the Jewish people, Haman set a plan to not only take Mordecai's life, but also to kill all the Jews in the king's empire. After making a proposal to the king, Haman received his permission to put his treacherous plot into action, who offered to fund the entire plan with a payment of 10,000 talents (about 375 tons) of silver, although the king refused the offer of money.

With the king's permission, his scribes were summoned on the thirteenth day of the first month, and an edict, according to Haman's plan, was written to the king's officials and leaders from over all the provinces and to the officials of all the peoples, to every province in its own script and every people in its own language. The edict was written in the king's name, sealed with his own signet ring. The letters contained the instruction to destroy, to kill, and to annihilate all Jews, young and old, women and children in a single day, the thirteenth day of Adar, the twelfth month, and to plunder their goods. A copy of this document was to be issued as a decree in every province, to be shared as a proclamation to all the peoples, who were charged to be ready for that day.

When Mordecai learned about these plans, he mourned deeply and informed Esther to use her royal office to help deliver the Jews, her people, and herself. Esther reminded Mordecai that to enter into the king's presence without being summoned was to invite a death sentence. Mordecai replied to Esther, "Do not think to yourself that in the king's palace you will escape any more than all the other Jews. For if you keep silent at this time, relief and deliverance will rise for the Jews from another place, but you and your father's house will perish. And who knows whether you have not come to the kingdom for such a time as this?"

Facing the possibility of death, and knowing what was at stake in her going to the king, Esther replied to Mordecai, to gather all the Jews in Susa to fast for three days and nights, as she and her young women would also do. She said, "Then I will go to the king, though it is against the law, and if I perish, I perish." Esther risked her life to stand in the gap on behalf of her people, expressing extreme devotion to God and to her own people.

DAILY DEVOTIONAL GUIDE

PREPARING OUR HEARTS

Invocation: Our Prayer of Acclamation

Eternal God, God of Queen Esther and her cousin Mordecai, you are the sovereign God who controls all things, who sees everything, and works out the events of history according to your will. At a time when your people were in peril, and a young woman had to risk everything in order to stand for their defense, you granted Esther the courage and strength to defend your people. She surrendered to you in fasting and prayer, and then put herself in a position to represent you and her people against evil. Grant us that same courage, that we may, fortified by your grace, stand strong in the face of evil, and move forward, trusting you with the outcome. You are the Lord. In Jesus' name we pray, amen.

Call to Worship
Blessed are you, O God: Father, Son, and Holy Spirit. And blessed is your Kingdom, both now and forever, Amen.

PRAISING OUR GOD

Te Deum Laudamus
You are God: we praise you; you are the Lord; we acclaim you; you are the eternal Father: All creation worships you. To you all angels, all the powers of heaven, Cherubim and Seraphim, sing in endless praise: Holy, holy, holy Lord, God of power and might, heaven and earth are full of your glory.

The glorious company of apostles praise you. The noble fellowship of prophets praise you. The white-robed army of martyrs praise you. Throughout the world the holy Church acclaims you; Father, of majesty unbounded, your true and only Son, worthy of all worship, and the Holy Spirit, advocate and guide.

You, Christ, are the king of glory, the eternal Son of the Father. When you became man to set us free you did not shun the Virgin's womb. You overcame the sting of death and opened the kingdom of heaven to all believers. You are seated at God's right hand in glory. We believe that you will come and be our judge. Come then, Lord, and help your people, bought with the price of your own blood, and bring us with your saints to glory everlasting.

Praise and Thanksgiving (Songs and Prayers)

Gloria Patri
Glory be to the Father,
And to the Son and to the Holy Spirit:
As it was in the beginning,
Is now, and ever shall be,
World without end. Amen, amen.

LISTENING TO HIS VOICE

Chronological Reading for the Day
Sunday: Mark 1.1; Luke 1.1-38; 3.23b-38; John 1.1-18;
Matt. 1.1-17 ✠ *Monday:* Luke 1.39-2.40; Matt. 1.18-25 ✠
Tuesday: Matt. 2-3; Luke 2.41-3.18; 3.21-22; Mark 1.2-11 ✠
Wednesday: Mark 1.12-13; Matt. 4.1-11; Luke 4.1-15; John
1.19-2.25 ✠ *Thursday:* John 3.1-4.45; Luke 3.19-20 ✠
Friday: Mark 1.14-39; Matt. 4.12-25; 8.14-17; Luke 3.23a;
4.16-44; John 4.46-54 ✠ *Saturday:* Luke 5; Mark 1.40-2.22;
Matt. 8.1-4; 9.1-17

Lectionary Readings
Psalm: Ps. 124   *OT:* Exod. 1.8-2.10
Gospel: Matt. 16.13-20   *NT:* Rom. 12.1-8

Reflection: Silence and/or Journaling

RESPONDING IN FAITH

The Apostles' Creed
*I believe in God, the Father Almighty, Maker of heaven and earth;
and in Jesus Christ, his only Son, our Lord, who was conceived by the
Holy Spirit, born of the Virgin Mary, suffered under Pontius Pilate,
was crucified, dead, and buried; he descended into hell; the third day
he arose again from the dead; he ascended into heaven and sits on
the right hand of God the Father Almighty; from thence he shall come
to judge the quick and the dead.*

I believe in the Holy Spirit, the holy catholic church, the communion
of saints, the forgiveness of sins, the resurrection of the body, and the
life everlasting. Amen.*

* In the Apostles' and Nicene Creeds, the term catholic refers to the Church's
universality, through all ages and times, of all languages and peoples. It refers to no
particular tradition or denominational expression (e.g., as in Roman Catholic).

Prayers of Confession

Let us now confess our sins to God and receive mercy and grace to help in our time of need.

Assurance of Pardon

Having faithfully confessed and renounced your sin, Christ also has been faithful to forgive your sins and to purify you from all unrighteousness. It is certain, that there is One who has spoken to the Father in your defense, Jesus Christ, the Righteous One who is the atoning sacrifice for our sins and for the sins of the whole world. His grace and peace are with you now. Amen.

Petitions and Supplications, Ending with The Lord's Prayer

Our Father which art in heaven, Hallowed be thy name. Thy kingdom come, Thy will be done in earth, as it is in heaven. Give us this day our daily bread. And forgive us our debts, as we forgive our debtors. And lead us not into temptation, but deliver us from evil: For thine is the kingdom, and the power, and the glory, for ever. Amen.

~ Matthew 6.9-13 (KJV)

Doxology (and/or closing song)

Praise God from whom all blessings flow;
Praise Him all creatures here below;
Praise Him above ye heavenly host;
Praise Father, Son and Holy Ghost. Amen.

DEPARTING TO SERVE

Benediction

Eternal God, the Lord who saved the Jews from the mad plan of Haman through Esther's intercession, grant us the same mind to risk everything, to put ourselves in the fray for the sake of rescuing the vulnerable and voiceless, that you may, through your Spirit and leading, use us for your glory. Do again what you did through Esther, through us, and for your glory. In Jesus' name, amen.

Affirmation from the Psalms

If it had not been the LORD who was on our side – let Israel now say – if it had not been the LORD who was on our side when people rose up against us, then they would have swallowed us up alive, when their anger was kindled against us; then the flood would have swept us away, the torrent would have gone over us; then over us would have gone the raging waters. Blessed be the LORD, who has not given us as prey to their teeth! We have escaped like a bird from the snare of the fowlers; the snare is broken, and we have escaped! Our help is in the name of the LORD, who made heaven and earth.

~ Psalm 124.1-8

Pray without Ceasing – Flash Prayer for the Day

Grant us grace, Lord Jesus, to never shrink back in the evil time, but risk everything in order that those who are vulnerable and under threat of death may be saved and delivered from evil.

FOR YOUR WEEKLY JOURNEY

Let God Arise! Seasonal Focus
The Stoning of Stephen, Acts 7.1-60

Book Reading
DAILY: Extreme Devotion Writing Team, *Extreme Devotion*

Howell, *Servants, Misfits, and Martyrs*

Our Corporate Disciplines
Concert of Prayer:
Tuesday, August 26, 2014

August 31 - September 6, 2014 ✠ Proper 17

As Lord of the harvest, Jesus has commissioned his Church during this age to go and make disciples of all nations. During this season after Pentecost, let us obey Christ's command and share the Gospel to the ends of the earth, gathering in the harvest of souls so ripe for reaping. As Christ's hands and feet in the world, let us both show and tell of his salvation to a dying and hurting world. This is a season of harvest.

THIS WEEK'S THEME
Paul and Silas in Prison, Acts 16.16-40

While in Philippi, a leading city of the district of Macedonia and a Roman colony, Paul and Silas for many days were followed by a slave girl with a spirit of divination. When Paul cast it out in Jesus' name, her owners seized them and drug them to the magistrates before the rulers. They accused them as Jews who were disturbing their city, advocating customs that were not lawful for them as Romans to accept or practice. The crowd attacked them, with the magistrates tearing off Paul and Silas' garments, had them beat them with rods with "many blows." They were thrown into prison, to be kept safely by the jailer there.

As a result of this order, the jailer put them into the inner prison, fastening their feet in the stocks. Around midnight Paul and Silas were praying and singing hymns to God, with the prisoners listening to them. In the midst of their devotion, suddenly a great earthquake struck, shaking the very foundations of the prison. And immediately, all the doors of the prison were opened, and everyone's bonds were unfastened.

When the jailer awakened and saw the prison doors open, he drew his sword to kill himself, supposing that the prisoners had escaped. Paul cried out with a loud voice for the jailer to not harm himself for they were all present! The jailer called for light, rushed in, and with trembling and fear, fell down before Paul and Silas. He brought them out, asked them what he needed to do to be saved, and was told to believe in the Lord Jesus, and he and his household would be saved. Paul and Silas shared the Gospel with his household that same hour of the night, they were all baptized, they all rejoiced in God, and they tended to Paul and Silas's wounds, and provided food for them.

At daylight, the magistrates sent the police, saying, "Let those men go." The jailer reported this to Paul, but Paul said, "They have beaten us publicly, uncondemned, men who are Roman citizens, and have thrown us into prison; and do they now throw us out secretly? No! Let them come themselves and take us out." This was reported to the magistrates, who became afraid after hearing that they were Roman citizens. The magistrates came, apologized to them, and asked them to leave the city.

Paul and Silas demonstrated the kind of extreme devotion that, when they were unjustly beaten and abused, they worshiped God with unbroken fear. They prayed and sang to God, the same Lord who heard their pleas, who also delivered them, saved others, and exposed those who sought to hurt them.

DAILY DEVOTIONAL GUIDE

PREPARING OUR HEARTS

Invocation: Our Prayer of Acclamation

Great God and deliverer of all those who cling to you, thank you for the mercy and power you demonstrated on behalf of Paul and Silas in the Philippian jail. Through their simple faith, expressed in prayer and singing to you around midnight in the inner prison there, you acknowledged their devotion and rescued them. The great earthquake and the loosing of their bonds symbolizes your power to deliver everyone who gives their lives to you without condition. Through their devotion you saved the Philippian jailer and his household. Do the same thing through us, for your sake, amen.

Call to Worship
Blessed are you, O God: Father, Son, and Holy Spirit. And blessed is your Kingdom, both now and forever, Amen.

PRAISING OUR GOD

Te Deum Laudamus
You are God: we praise you; you are the Lord; we acclaim you; you are the eternal Father: All creation worships you. To you all angels, all the powers of heaven, Cherubim and Seraphim, sing in endless praise: Holy, holy, holy Lord, God of power and might, heaven and earth are full of your glory.

The glorious company of apostles praise you. The noble fellowship of prophets praise you. The white-robed army of martyrs praise you. Throughout the world the holy Church acclaims you; Father, of majesty unbounded, your true and only Son, worthy of all worship, and the Holy Spirit, advocate and guide.

You, Christ, are the king of glory, the eternal Son of the Father. When you became man to set us free you did not shun the Virgin's womb. You overcame the sting of death and opened the kingdom of heaven to all believers. You are seated at God's right hand in glory. We believe that you will come and be our judge. Come then, Lord, and help your people, bought with the price of your own blood, and bring us with your saints to glory everlasting.

Praise and Thanksgiving (Songs and Prayers)

Gloria Patri

Glory be to the Father,
And to the Son and to the Holy Spirit:
As it was in the beginning,
Is now, and ever shall be,
World without end. Amen, amen.

LISTENING TO HIS VOICE

Chronological Reading for the Day

Sunday: John 5; Mark 2.23-3.6; Matt. 12.1-21; Luke 6.1-11 ✤
Monday: Mark 3.7-19; Luke 6.12-36; Matt. 5.1-6.4 ✤
Tuesday: Matt. 6.5-7.29; Luke 6.37-49 ✤ *Wednesday:* Matt.
8.5-13; ch.11; Luke 7 ✤ *Thursday:* Luke 8.1-8, vv.19-21;
Mark 3.20-4.20; Matt. 12.22-13.9 ✤ *Friday:* Matt. 13.10-52;
8.23-27; Luke 8.9-18, vv.22-25; Mark 4.21-41 ✤ *Saturday:*
Mark 5; Matt. 8.28-34; 9.18-26; Luke 8.26-56

Lectionary Readings

Psalm: Ps. 105.1-6, 23-26, 45b *OT:* Exod. 3.1-15
Gospel: Matt. 16.21-28 *NT:* Rom. 12.9-21

Reflection: Silence and/or Journaling

RESPONDING IN FAITH

The Apostles' Creed

I believe in God, the Father Almighty, Maker of heaven and earth;
and in Jesus Christ, his only Son, our Lord, who was conceived by the
Holy Spirit, born of the Virgin Mary, suffered under Pontius Pilate,
was crucified, dead, and buried; he descended into hell; the third day
he arose again from the dead; he ascended into heaven and sits on
the right hand of God the Father Almighty; from thence he shall come
to judge the quick and the dead.

I believe in the Holy Spirit, the holy catholic* church, the communion of saints, the forgiveness of sins, the resurrection of the body, and the life everlasting. Amen.

* In the Apostles' and Nicene Creeds, the term catholic refers to the Church's universality, through all ages and times, of all languages and peoples. It refers to no particular tradition or denominational expression (e.g., as in Roman Catholic).

Prayers of Confession
Let us now confess our sins to God and receive mercy and grace to help in our time of need.

Assurance of Pardon
Having faithfully confessed and renounced your sin, Christ also has been faithful to forgive your sins and to purify you from all unrighteousness. It is certain, that there is One who has spoken to the Father in your defense, Jesus Christ, the Righteous One who is the atoning sacrifice for our sins and for the sins of the whole world. His grace and peace are with you now. Amen.

Petitions and Supplications, Ending with The Lord's Prayer
Our Father which art in heaven, Hallowed be thy name. Thy kingdom come, Thy will be done in earth, as it is in heaven. Give us this day our daily bread. And forgive us our debts, as we forgive our debtors. And lead us not into temptation, but deliver us from evil: For thine is the kingdom, and the power, and the glory, for ever. Amen.

~ Matthew 6.9-13 (KJV)

Doxology (and/or closing song)
Praise God from whom all blessings flow;
Praise Him all creatures here below;
Praise Him above ye heavenly host;
Praise Father, Son and Holy Ghost. Amen.

Departing to Serve

Benediction

Lord Jesus Christ, who watched over your servants Paul and Silas when they were unjustly beaten and abused for delivering the young slave girl from the spirit of divination, let us never reject the reproach associated with your name and Gospel. Help us, like them, to maintain perspective in the midst of hardship and abuse, when we stand for you and receive persecution and misunderstanding. You see us, and will aid us, as we wait on you. In your name, we pray, amen.

Affirmation from the Psalms

Oh give thanks to the LORD; call upon his name; make known his deeds among the peoples! Sing to him, sing praises to him; tell of all his wondrous works! Glory in his holy name; let the hearts of those who seek the LORD rejoice! Seek the LORD and his strength; seek his presence continually! Remember the wondrous works that he has done, his miracles, and the judgments he uttered, O offspring of Abraham, his servant, children of Jacob, his chosen ones!

~ Psalm 105.1-6

Pray without Ceasing – Flash Prayer for the Day

Let our prayers and songs be lifted up to you, Lord Jesus, even in the midst of the worst conditions, and let us ever wait on you to move on our behalf.

FOR YOUR WEEKLY JOURNEY

Let God Arise! Seasonal Focus
The Stoning of Stephen, Acts 7.1-60

Book Reading
DAILY: Extreme Devotion Writing Team, *Extreme Devotion*

Howell, *Servants, Misfits, and Martyrs*

✠

THIRTEENTH SUNDAY AFTER PENTECOST

September 7 - 13, 2014 ✠ Proper 18

As Lord of the harvest, Jesus has commissioned his Church during this age to go and make disciples of all nations. During this season after Pentecost, let us obey Christ's command and share the Gospel to the ends of the earth, gathering in the harvest of souls so ripe for reaping. As Christ's hands and feet in the world, let us both show and tell of his salvation to a dying and hurting world. This is a season of harvest.

THIS WEEK'S THEME
Jeremiah Imprisoned for the Truth, Jeremiah 20.1-13
When Jeremiah came from a town where the LORD had sent him to prophesy, he came and stood in the court of the LORD's house, and said to the people: "Thus says the LORD of hosts, the God of Israel, behold, I am bringing upon this city and upon all its towns all the disaster that I have pronounced against it, because they have stiffened their neck, refusing to hear my words." Pashhur the priest and chief officer in the house of the LORD, heard Jeremiah prophesying these things. Upon hearing Jeremiah, he beat him, and put him in the stocks that were in the upper Benjamin Gate of the house of the LORD.

On the next day, when Pashhur released Jeremiah from the stocks, Jeremiah prophesied then against Pashhur! Jeremiah told him that the LORD no longer calls you Pashhur, but Terror on Every Side. Jeremiah prophesied from the LORD that God would make Pashhur a terror to himself and to all his friends. They would fall by the sword of their enemies while he looked on, and the LORD would give all Judah into the hand of the king of Babylon. He would carry them captive to Babylon, strike them down with the sword, and plunder their wealth. Passhur himself and all his house would also go into captivity to Babylon, where he would both die and be buried, along with all his friends, to whom he had falsely prophesied.

When Jeremiah contemplated the high price he was paying for bearing witness to the truth, and pondered not mentioning or speaking the LORD's name any longer, he said there was in his heart as it were a burning fire shut up in his bones, and he grew tired and weary trying to hold it in. No matter what he did, he could not hold it in. When his persecutors sought to destroy him, God like a dread warrior defended him, for the LORD delivered him from the hand of evildoers.

Regardless of the price we must pay for living true to God's word and telling the truth to others, we ought never compromise his word. Those who prophesy falsely may seek to persecute us, but they cannot overcome the truth. Though speaking and prophesying the truth carries with it the weight of certain persecution, God will stand with those who stand for him.

DAILY DEVOTIONAL GUIDE

PREPARING OUR HEARTS

Invocation: Our Prayer of Acclamation

Eternal God and our Father, you granted Jeremiah your holy word, and he prophesied the truth of your word to those who abused and persecuted him. Your word is living and active, and try as he could to ignore, the prophet could not hold it in. Reproduce in us this same unction and anointing, this same burden and burning, that we, like Jeremiah, may testify of your truth without shame or fear. May your name be exalted in every place where you send us. In your name amen.

Call to Worship

Blessed are you, O God: Father, Son, and Holy Spirit. And blessed is your Kingdom, both now and forever, Amen.

PRAISING OUR GOD

Te Deum Laudamus

You are God: we praise you; you are the Lord; we acclaim you; you are the eternal Father: All creation worships you. To you all angels, all the powers of heaven, Cherubim and Seraphim, sing in endless praise: Holy, holy, holy Lord, God of power and might, heaven and earth are full of your glory.

The glorious company of apostles praise you. The noble fellowship of prophets praise you. The white-robed army of martyrs praise you. Throughout the world the holy Church acclaims you; Father, of majesty unbounded, your true and only Son, worthy of all worship, and the Holy Spirit, advocate and guide.

You, Christ, are the king of glory, the eternal Son of the Father. When you became man to set us free you did not shun the Virgin's womb. You overcame the sting of death and opened the kingdom of heaven to all believers. You are seated at God's right hand in glory. We believe that you will come and be our judge. Come then, Lord, and help your people, bought with the price of your own blood, and bring us with your saints to glory everlasting.

Praise and Thanksgiving (Songs and Prayers)

Gloria Patri

Glory be to the Father,
And to the Son and to the Holy Spirit:
As it was in the beginning,
Is now, and ever shall be,
World without end. Amen, amen.

LISTENING TO HIS VOICE

Chronological Reading for the Day

Sunday: Matt. 9.27-10.42; 13.53-58; Mark 6.1-13; Luke 9.1-6
✦ *Monday:* Luke 9.7-17; Mark 6.14-56; Matt. 14; John 6.1-21

✠ *Tuesday:* John 6.22-71; Mark 7.1-23; Matt. 15.1-20 ✠
Wednesday: Mark 7.24-8.21; Matt. 15.21-16.12 ✠ *Thursday:*
Mark 8.22-9.13; Matt. 16.13-17.13; Luke 9.18-36 ✠ *Friday:*
Mark 9.14-50; Matt. 17.14-18.35; Luke 9.37-50 ✠ *Saturday:*
John 7.1-8.20; Luke 9.51-62; Matt. 8.18-22

Lectionary Readings

Psalm: Ps. 149   *OT:* Exod. 12.1-14
Gospel: Matt. 18.15-20   *NT:* Rom. 13.8-14

Reflection: Silence and/or Journaling

RESPONDING IN FAITH

The Apostles' Creed
*I believe in God, the Father Almighty, Maker of heaven and earth;
and in Jesus Christ, his only Son, our Lord, who was conceived by the
Holy Spirit, born of the Virgin Mary, suffered under Pontius Pilate,
was crucified, dead, and buried; he descended into hell; the third day
he arose again from the dead; he ascended into heaven and sits on
the right hand of God the Father Almighty; from thence he shall come
to judge the quick and the dead.*

I believe in the Holy Spirit, the holy catholic church, the communion
of saints, the forgiveness of sins, the resurrection of the body, and the
life everlasting. Amen.*

* In the Apostles' and Nicene Creeds, the term catholic refers to the Church's
universality, through all ages and times, of all languages and peoples. It refers to no
particular tradition or denominational expression (e.g., as in Roman Catholic).

Prayers of Confession
Let us now confess our sins to God and receive mercy and
grace to help in our time of need.

Assurance of Pardon

Having faithfully confessed and renounced your sin, Christ also has been faithful to forgive your sins and to purify you from all unrighteousness. It is certain, that there is One who has spoken to the Father in your defense, Jesus Christ, the Righteous One who is the atoning sacrifice for our sins and for the sins of the whole world. His grace and peace are with you now. Amen.

Petitions and Supplications, Ending with The Lord's Prayer

Our Father which art in heaven, Hallowed be thy name. Thy kingdom come, Thy will be done in earth, as it is in heaven. Give us this day our daily bread. And forgive us our debts, as we forgive our debtors. And lead us not into temptation, but deliver us from evil: For thine is the kingdom, and the power, and the glory, for ever. Amen.

~ Matthew 6.9-13 (KJV)

Doxology (and/or closing song)

Praise God from whom all blessings flow;
Praise Him all creatures here below;
Praise Him above ye heavenly host;
Praise Father, Son and Holy Ghost. Amen.

DEPARTING TO SERVE

Benediction

Eternal God, whose Word is both living and active, sharper than any two-edged sword, and is able to penetrate to the very dividing of soul and spirit, thank you for the anointing you give us who believe in you. We are continuing in the word of Jesus, and we have come to know the truth, and the truth is setting us free. Make us channels and vessels of your word, willing to testify and speak your word to everyone to whom you send us, regardless of the price. Your words are the joy and delight of our hearts. In Jesus' name we pray, amen.

Affirmation from the Psalms

Praise the LORD! Sing to the LORD a new song, his praise in the assembly of the godly! Let Israel be glad in his Maker; let the children of Zion rejoice in their King! Let them praise his name with dancing, making melody to him with tambourine and lyre! For the LORD takes pleasure in his people; he adorns the humble with salvation. Let the godly exult in glory; let them sing for joy on their beds. Let the high praises of God be in their throats and two-edged swords in their hands, to execute vengeance on the nations and punishments on the peoples, to bind their kings with chains and their nobles with fetters of iron, to execute on them the judgment written! This is honor for all his godly ones. Praise the LORD!

~ Psalm 149.1-9

Pray without Ceasing – Flash Prayer for the Day

Let your word be within us today as a burning and anointing, Lord Jesus, and may we express that Word without holding anything back, allowing others to hear your word through us as you desire them to hear it.

FOR YOUR WEEKLY JOURNEY

Let God Arise! Seasonal Focus
The Stoning of Stephen, Acts 7.1-60

Book Reading
DAILY: Extreme Devotion Writing Team, *Extreme Devotion*

Howell, *Servants, Misfits, and Martyrs*

Our Corporate Disciplines
Prayer and Fasting, ending with Book Review:
Wednesday, September 10, 2014

September 14 - 20, 2014 ✠ Proper 19

As Lord of the harvest, Jesus has commissioned his Church during this age to go and make disciples of all nations. During this season after Pentecost, let us obey Christ's command and share the Gospel to the ends of the earth, gathering in the harvest of souls so ripe for reaping. As Christ's hands and feet in the world, let us both show and tell of his salvation to a dying and hurting world. This is a season of harvest.

THIS WEEK'S THEME
The Stoning of Stephen, Acts 7.1-60

In the early church, Stephen was one of the seven deacons of the Christian community in Jerusalem. He was full of grace and power, and was doing great wonders and signs among the people. When some leaders of the synagogue rose up and disputed with Stephen, they could not withstand the wisdom that the Spirit had given to him, and through which he was speaking. They falsely accused him of speaking blasphemous words against Moses and God, stirred up the people and elders, who then seized him and took him before the Sanhedrin, the Jewish council.

Stephen addressed the council, rehearsing the entire history of God's people in the Hebrew Scriptures, making the point that possessing the Temple does not automatically guarantee nearness to God, or receptivity to his word. He argued boldly that Israel was favored by the LORD before possessing either the Tabernacle or the Temple, seen through Abraham, Joseph, and Moses.

Futhermore, Israel proved to be unfaithful to God even after they engaged in worship in both the Tabernacle and the Temple! The children of Israel rebelled during the period of the Tabernacle, the first Temple period, and even after the exile. They were rebellious, murdered the Messiah, and disobeyed God's law. He summarized his argument with this conclusion: "You stiff-necked people, uncircumcised in heart and ears, you always resist the Holy Spirit. As your fathers did, so do you. Which of the prophets did your fathers not persecute? And they killed those who announced beforehand the coming of the Righteous One, whom you have now betrayed and murdered, you who received the law as delivered by angels and did not keep it."

When the members of the Council heard Stephen they became enraged, but he, full of the Holy Spirit, gazed into heaven and saw the glory of God, and Jesus standing at the right hand of God. Stephen said in the Council's presence, "Behold, I see the heavens opened, and the Son of Man standing at the right hand of God." They cried out loudly, stopped their ears, and rushed together at Stephen. They drug him out of the city, and there stoned him. The young Saul of Tarsus kept the garments of those who stoned him.

As the members were stoning Stephen, he called out, "Lord Jesus, receive my spirit," and falling to his knees he cried out loudly, "Lord, do not hold this sin against them." After saying this, Stephen fell asleep – he died.

Stephen was full of the Holy Spirit when he gave his extended message on the spiritual fitness of the Council. He neither sugar-coated nor amended his address; seeing the impact of his words on the members, he undoubtedly saw that they would not judge rightly and repent at his truth before them. In the midst of their hatred and rejection, he gazed into heaven and sought the deliverance and comfort that heaven alone can provide. Extreme devotion to God is effective because it fixes its gaze on the heavenly realm, a gaze that, whether we live or die, is never in vain.

DAILY DEVOTIONAL GUIDE

PREPARING OUR HEARTS

Invocation: Our Prayer of Acclamation

God, the Father Almighty, God of your servant Stephen, thank you for granting through your Holy Spirit the wisdom, grace, and clarity that Stephen gave in his address to the Council. You worked many signs and wonders through him, and yet, after he testified to the truth to the members of the Council, he paid the ultimate price of devotion, his own martyrdom before you. You granted him the vision of the risen and ascended Christ, and heard his dying request for mercy to those who took his life. We stand in awe of your work in Stephen; do the same in us, as we trust in you. In Jesus' name, amen.

Call to Worship

Blessed are you, O God: Father, Son, and Holy Spirit. And blessed is your Kingdom, both now and forever, Amen.

PRAISING OUR GOD

Te Deum Laudamus

You are God: we praise you; you are the Lord; we acclaim you; you are the eternal Father: All creation worships you. To you all angels, all the powers of heaven, Cherubim and Seraphim, sing in endless praise: Holy, holy, holy Lord, God of power and might, heaven and earth are full of your glory.

The glorious company of apostles praise you. The noble fellowship of prophets praise you. The white-robed army of martyrs praise you. Throughout the world the holy Church acclaims you; Father, of majesty unbounded, your true and only Son, worthy of all worship, and the Holy Spirit, advocate and guide.

You, Christ, are the king of glory, the eternal Son of the Father. When you became man to set us free you did not shun the Virgin's womb. You overcame the sting of death and opened the kingdom of heaven to all believers. You are seated at God's right hand in glory. We believe that you will come and be our judge. Come then, Lord, and help your people, bought with the price of your own blood, and bring us with your saints to glory everlasting.

Praise and Thanksgiving (Songs and Prayers)

Gloria Patri
Glory be to the Father,
And to the Son and to the Holy Spirit:
As it was in the beginning,
Is now, and ever shall be,
World without end. Amen, amen.

LISTENING TO HIS VOICE

Chronological Reading for the Day
Sunday: John 8.21-59; Luke 10.1-11.13 ✤ *Monday:* Luke 11.14-12.34 ✤ *Tuesday:* Luke 12.35-13.21; John 9 ✤ *Wednesday:* John 10; Luke 13.22-14.24 ✤ *Thursday:* Luke 14.25-17.10; John 11.1-37 ✤ *Friday:* John 11.38-57; Luke 17.11-18.8 ✤ *Saturday:* Luke 18.9-30; Mark 10.1-31; Matt. 19

Lectionary Readings
Psalm: Ps. 114 *OT:* Exod. 15.1b-11, 20-21
Gospel: Matt. 18.21-35 *NT:* Rom. 14.1-12

Reflection: Silence and/or Journaling

RESPONDING IN FAITH

The Apostles' Creed

I believe in God, the Father Almighty, Maker of heaven and earth; and in Jesus Christ, his only Son, our Lord, who was conceived by the Holy Spirit, born of the Virgin Mary, suffered under Pontius Pilate, was crucified, dead, and buried; he descended into hell; the third day he arose again from the dead; he ascended into heaven and sits on the right hand of God the Father Almighty; from thence he shall come to judge the quick and the dead.

I believe in the Holy Spirit, the holy catholic* church, the communion of saints, the forgiveness of sins, the resurrection of the body, and the life everlasting. Amen.

* In the Apostles' and Nicene Creeds, the term catholic refers to the Church's universality, through all ages and times, of all languages and peoples. It refers to no particular tradition or denominational expression (e.g., as in Roman Catholic).

Prayers of Confession

Let us now confess our sins to God and receive mercy and grace to help in our time of need.

Assurance of Pardon

Having faithfully confessed and renounced your sin, Christ also has been faithful to forgive your sins and to purify you from all unrighteousness. It is certain, that there is One who has spoken to the Father in your defense, Jesus Christ, the Righteous One who is the atoning sacrifice for our sins and for the sins of the whole world. His grace and peace are with you now. Amen.

Petitions and Supplications, Ending with The Lord's Prayer

Our Father which art in heaven, Hallowed be thy name. Thy kingdom come, Thy will be done in earth, as it is in heaven. Give us this day our daily bread. And forgive us our debts, as we forgive our debtors. And

*lead us not into temptation, but deliver us from evil: For thine is the
kingdom, and the power, and the glory, for ever. Amen.*

~ Matthew 6.9-13 (KJV)

Doxology (and/or closing song)

Praise God from whom all blessings flow;
Praise Him all creatures here below;
Praise Him above ye heavenly host;
Praise Father, Son and Holy Ghost. Amen.

DEPARTING TO SERVE

Benediction

Lord Most High, God of Abraham, Isaac and Jacob, thank
you for your faithful revelation through the history of your
people Israel. You have never wavered in your love for
humankind, even when we, in disobedience and neglect,
failed to acknowledge your goodness and grace. You are the
God who forgives and blesses those who truly do not deserve
your mercy. Grant us the wisdom to stay near to you, and,
like your servant Stephen, to always fix our gaze on the
heavenly realm, for it is there our life and help comes from.
In your name we pray, amen.

Affirmation from the Psalms

*When Israel went out from Egypt, the house of Jacob from a people of
strange language, Judah became his sanctuary, Israel his dominion.
The sea looked and fled; Jordan turned back. The mountains skipped
like rams, the hills like lambs. What ails you, O sea, that you flee? O
Jordan, that you turn back? O mountains, that you skip like rams? O
hills, like lambs? Tremble, O earth, at the presence of the Lord, at the
presence of the God of Jacob, who turns the rock into a pool of water,
the flint into a spring of water.*

~ Psalm 114.1-8

Pray without Ceasing – Flash Prayer for the Day

Cause us to gaze into the heavens, Lord Jesus, and see you standing there, ascended and glorified at the Father's right hand – you will reign until all your enemies have been subdued.

FOR YOUR WEEKLY JOURNEY

Let God Arise! Seasonal Focus

The Stoning of Stephen, Acts 7.1-60

Book Reading

DAILY: Extreme Devotion Writing Team, *Extreme Devotion*

Howell, *Servants, Misfits, and Martyrs*

September 21 - 27, 2014 ✛ Proper 20

As Lord of the harvest, Jesus has commissioned his Church during this age to go and make disciples of all nations. During this season after Pentecost, let us obey Christ's command and share the Gospel to the ends of the earth, gathering in the harvest of souls so ripe for reaping. As Christ's hands and feet in the world, let us both show and tell of his salvation to a dying and hurting world. This is a season of harvest.

THIS WEEK'S THEME
Jehoshaphat Prays to God, 2 Chronicles 20.1-32

Jehoshaphat was a king of Judah who reigned at a time when a vast army of Moabites, Ammonites, and Meunites, Israel's enemies, threatened to attack. When Jehoshaphat heard the news, he was afraid and set his face to seek the LORD, proclaiming a fast throughout all Judah. All the people of Judah and its cities assembled to seek help from the LORD, with Jehoshaphat standing in the assembly of Judah and Jerusalem, in the house of the LORD, before the new court.

Jehoshaphat prayed to the LORD, God of his fathers, affirming that he alone was God in heaven, the ruler over all the kingdoms of the nations, in whose hand are power and might, so that none is able to withstand him. He reviewed God's mighty acts of deliverance, and reminded God of his promise to hear their prayer from that sanctuary when they were in need.

At the end of his petition, Jehoshaphat prayed, "O our God, will you not execute judgment on them? For we are powerless against this great horde that is coming against us. We do not know what to do, but our eyes are on you." And all Judah stood there before the LORD, with their little ones, their wives, and their children. At that precise moment, the Spirit of the LORD came upon a Levite

named Jahaziel who prophesied that the LORD would win
for them a great victory. In a spirit of faith and confidence,
Jeshoshaphat led the people in worship before the LORD,
"with a very loud voice."

They all rose early the next morning and went out into the
wilderness of Tekoa. Jehoshaphat appointed singers to lead
the attack before the army of the LORD, and when they
began to sing and praise, the LORD set an ambush against
the people of Ammon, Moab, and Mount Seir, who had
come against Judah. These rival nations were all routed,
and yielded an abundant plunder for the people of Judah.
After three whole days of collecting the plunder, the people
assembled in the Valley of Beracah (Blessing), and gave
thanks to the LORD. They marched back to Jerusalem with
praise, songs, and music.

In the midst of trial and when danger threatens, we express
extreme devotion to the LORD when we praise him, which is
a tangible expression of our trust and confidence in him.

DAILY DEVOTIONAL GUIDE

PREPARING OUR HEARTS

Invocation: Our Prayer of Acclamation
Eternal God and Lord of history, you heard the petition of
your servant Jehoshaphat, who affirmed the words of the
prophet who said, "Do not be afraid and do not be dismayed
at this great horde, for the battle is not yours but God's."
Truly, in every great trial we face, or every difficult experience
we encounter, we must learn to trust in you, your word,
and the testimony of your prophets, apostles, and your Son.
Only then can we succeed or overcome. The battle is not
ours, but yours, and we will win only if we cling to you
alone. In Jesus' name we pray, amen.

Call to Worship
Blessed are you, O God: Father, Son, and Holy Spirit. And blessed is your Kingdom, both now and forever, Amen.

PRAISING OUR GOD

Te Deum Laudamus
You are God: we praise you; you are the Lord; we acclaim you; you are the eternal Father: All creation worships you. To you all angels, all the powers of heaven, Cherubim and Seraphim, sing in endless praise: Holy, holy, holy Lord, God of power and might, heaven and earth are full of your glory.

The glorious company of apostles praise you. The noble fellowship of prophets praise you. The white-robed army of martyrs praise you. Throughout the world the holy Church acclaims you; Father, of majesty unbounded, your true and only Son, worthy of all worship, and the Holy Spirit, advocate and guide.

You, Christ, are the king of glory, the eternal Son of the Father. When you became man to set us free you did not shun the Virgin's womb. You overcame the sting of death and opened the kingdom of heaven to all believers. You are seated at God's right hand in glory. We believe that you will come and be our judge. Come then, Lord, and help your people, bought with the price of your own blood, and bring us with your saints to glory everlasting.

Praise and Thanksgiving (Songs and Prayers)

Gloria Patri
Glory be to the Father,
And to the Son and to the Holy Spirit:
As it was in the beginning,
Is now, and ever shall be,
World without end. Amen, amen.

LISTENING TO HIS VOICE

Chronological Reading for the Day
Sunday: Matt. 20; Mark 10.32-52; Luke 18.31-19.27 ✠
Monday: Mark 14.3-9; 11.1-11; Matt. 26.6-13; 21.1-11; John
12.1-36; Luke 19.28-44 ✠ *Tuesday:* John 12.37-50; Mark
11.12-33; Matt. 21.12-27; Luke 19.45-20.8 ✠ *Wednesday:*
Matt. 21.28-22.33; Mark 12.1-27; Luke 20.9-40 ✠ *Thursday:*
Mark 12.28-44; Matt. 22.34-23.39; Luke 20.41-21.4 ✠
Friday: Mark 13.1-31; Matt. 24.1-35; Luke 21.5-33 ✠
Saturday: Mark 13.32-37; Matt. 24.36-25.46; Luke 21.34-38

Lectionary Readings
Psalm: Ps. 145.1-8   *OT:* Exod. 16.2-15
Gospel: Matt. 20.1-16   *NT:* Phil. 1.21-30

Reflection: Silence and/or Journaling

RESPONDING IN FAITH

The Apostles' Creed
*I believe in God, the Father Almighty, Maker of heaven and earth;
and in Jesus Christ, his only Son, our Lord, who was conceived by the
Holy Spirit, born of the Virgin Mary, suffered under Pontius Pilate,
was crucified, dead, and buried; he descended into hell; the third day
he arose again from the dead; he ascended into heaven and sits on
the right hand of God the Father Almighty; from thence he shall come
to judge the quick and the dead.*

I believe in the Holy Spirit, the holy catholic church, the communion
of saints, the forgiveness of sins, the resurrection of the body, and the
life everlasting. Amen.*

* In the Apostles' and Nicene Creeds, the term catholic refers to the Church's
universality, through all ages and times, of all languages and peoples. It refers to no
particular tradition or denominational expression (e.g., as in Roman Catholic).

Prayers of Confession
Let us now confess our sins to God and receive mercy and grace to help in our time of need.

Assurance of Pardon
Having faithfully confessed and renounced your sin, Christ also has been faithful to forgive your sins and to purify you from all unrighteousness. It is certain, that there is One who has spoken to the Father in your defense, Jesus Christ, the Righteous One who is the atoning sacrifice for our sins and for the sins of the whole world. His grace and peace are with you now. Amen.

Petitions and Supplications, Ending with The Lord's Prayer
Our Father which art in heaven, Hallowed be thy name. Thy kingdom come, Thy will be done in earth, as it is in heaven. Give us this day our daily bread. And forgive us our debts, as we forgive our debtors. And lead us not into temptation, but deliver us from evil: For thine is the kingdom, and the power, and the glory, for ever. Amen.

~ Matthew 6.9-13 (KJV)

Doxology (and/or closing song)
Praise God from whom all blessings flow;
Praise Him all creatures here below;
Praise Him above ye heavenly host;
Praise Father, Son and Holy Ghost. Amen.

DEPARTING TO SERVE

Benediction
Lord Jesus, through the Cross you have ended the Curse, forgiven our sin, routed the devil and his minions, and ended our fear of death and the grave. You have overcome! Teach us, dear Savior, then, to place the choir before the army, to offer praise and thanksgiving before the battle, and to affirm the truth regardless of how things may look or appear. In all

things, you have shown us that "the battle is not yours but God's." Develop in us a mindset and lifestyle of praise that truly testifies that no weapon formed against us shall prosper, for we have placed our trust in you alone. In your name we pray, amen.

Affirmation from the Psalms

I will extol you, my God and King, and bless your name forever and ever. Every day I will bless you and praise your name forever and ever. Great is the LORD, and greatly to be praised, and his greatness is unsearchable. One generation shall commend your works to another, and shall declare your mighty acts. On the glorious splendor of your majesty, and on your wondrous works, I will meditate. They shall speak of the might of your awesome deeds, and I will declare your greatness. They shall pour forth the fame of your abundant goodness and shall sing aloud of your righteousness. The LORD is gracious and merciful, slow to anger and abounding in steadfast love.

~ Psalm 145.1-8

Pray without Ceasing – Flash Prayer for the Day

O Lord, with Jehoshaphat we declare, "Believe in the LORD your God, and you will be established; believe his prophets, and you will succeed."

FOR YOUR WEEKLY JOURNEY

Let God Arise! Seasonal Focus

The Stoning of Stephen, Acts 7.1-60

Book Reading

DAILY: Extreme Devotion Writing Team, *Extreme Devotion*

Howell, *Servants, Misfits, and Martyrs*

Western Wall

Ordinary Time in the Church Year
Is Anything But Ordinary Time

As the dawn follows night, so our Lord will surely appear in power and glory to gather his own to himself, to make an end of war and sin, and to restore creation under God's will. This is a season of the hope of Christ's soon return.

The Season after Pentecost (Kingdomtide) is a season of celebration, recognizing Christ's headship; a season of soul winning, affirming our role as laborers in Christ's harvest; and a season of expectation, grounded in the hope of Christ's return. In one sense, this Season after Pentecost is anything but what it is usually referred to in Church-Year-celebrating circles: "Ordinary Time."

Dan Connors in his wonderful little book, *The Liturgical Year*, explains the meaning of "ordinary" in this designation of the Church Year's final season.

> *The word 'ordinary' in Ordinary Time doesn't mean ordinary in the usual sense. Remember "ordinal" numbers – first, second, third? That's what 'ordinary' refers to here. The numbered Sundays of the year outside of the special seasons. Yet ordinary time does seem rather ordinary, it doesn't bring any strong images to mind the way the other seasons do. In fact, the Sundays of Ordinary Time don't all fall during the same time of the year. To understand Ordinary Time, we need to understand the Church Year as a whole. We need to remember the essential meaning of all the other seasons and then think about the rhythms of time.*

~ Dan Connors. *The Liturgical Year.*
Mystic, CT: Twenty-Third Publications, 2005, p. 39.

At the Coming of Christ, God Will Make an End of War and Sin, and Restore His Creation to Himself

The rhythms of time, of all time, will consummate with the coming of Jesus Christ at his return. Christians throughout the ages have yearned for the time when God will consummate his plan of salvation with the revelation of his Son at the end of this age. The darkness and shadow of this tragic human story, the Fall's dread and ugly curse, the costly punishment for our original foreparents' and our own willful disobedience – death – will finally be overcome. The glory of God is destined to fill all heaven and earth, and God's own dear warrior-Son will put all enemies of the Father under his feet. This is our hope and our future!

Nothing could be more encouraging to us in the midst of a dark, foreboding, and confused world system than knowing that God the Father has set a time in his own sovereign will to shine his light into every dark crack of this world, and bring an end to this long, hard night of sin and sorrow and death. Truly, as the dawn follows night, so our Lord will surely appear in power and glory to gather his own to himself, to make an end of war and sin, and to restore creation under God's will. The Season after Pentecost is a season of hope, the hope of a restored earth, a new humanity, and a consummated King-dom. Only Christ can restore this creation, and we recall and remember this during this season, the season of hope of Christ's soon return.

At the end of this remarkable time of expectation, we celebrate two feast days which underscore the remarkable character of our hope in the soon return of Christ. *All Saints Day* is our time as believers to remember those martyrs and saints, those heroes of the faith who came before us. It is also a time to especially recall and remember those who gave up their lives for the sake of Christ and the Gospel. We affirm that the Church is the body of Christ, and that the living

Savior now lives and is seen in the world through the words and deeds of his people (John 14.12; Heb. 11; Rev. 17.6).

The second feast day at the end of this season, the *Feast of Christ the King* (also called the *Feast of the Reign of Christ*), is the last Sunday of this season, and the last one before Advent. According to Scripture, our Lord Jesus Christ will return and finish the work he began on the Cross, to judge the world and save his own. The *Feast of Christ the King* points to that day when the kingdom of this world will become the kingdom of our Lord and of his Christ, who will reign forever and ever (Rev. 11.15ff.). How appropriate to end the season after the coming of the Holy Spirit with a feast which honors the future reign of our risen Savior, the true Lord who one day will reign alone and supreme!

May our hearts' cry resound with the prayers of the saints of the ages in saying, "Maranatha!" Even so, Lord Jesus, come soon!

~ Awaiting that Great Day,
Rev. Dr. Don L. Davis

✠

SIXTEENTH SUNDAY AFTER PENTECOST

September 28 - October 4, 2014 ✠ Proper 21

The Season after Pentecost is likewise the season before Advent -- it is a season of the blessed hope. As we declare Jesus' return in every Communion celebration, so we confess that he will assuredly appear in power and glory to complete God's salvation for the world. He will come in power to rescue his own, to make an end of war and sin, and to restore creation under God's will.

THIS WEEK'S THEME
Elijah and the Prophets of Baal, 1 Kings 18.17-46
After prophesying against Ahab for abandoning the LORD for the Baals of the land, Elijah challenged Ahab to send and gather all Israel to Mount Carmel, along with the 450 prophets of Baal and the 400 prophets of Asherah who ate at Jezebel's table. Once Ahab, the 850 prophets, and the people gathered at Mount Carmel, Elijah challenged the people to follow the LORD God or Baal. Silent before him, Elijah ordered the people to let two bulls be given to he and the false prophets, which would be cut in pieces, laid on wood, without fire on altars. They would call on the name of their god, and Elijah would call on the name of the LORD. Whoever answered by fire would be declared to be God.

The prophets of Baal chose one bull, prepared it first, and called on the name of their god without putting fire to the sacrifice. Having called on their god to respond from morning until noon, there was neither voice nor answer. Elijah mocked their efforts as they limped around their altar, and they continued to cry aloud, cutting themselves with swords and lances until they bled. And even after midday passed, their ravings produced neither voice nor answer; no one paid attention.

After this vain show, Elijah told the people to come near, and he repaired the LORD's altar that had been thrown down. He then took twelve stones according to the number of Jacob's

sons, and he built an altar in the name of the LORD. He
made a trench around the altar, put the wood in order, cut
the bull in pieces, and laid it on the wood. He commanded
people to fill four jars with water, and to pour them upon
the burnt offering and on the wood. He had them do this a
second, and third time, which made the water run around
the altar, filling the trench with water. Elijah prayed a prayer
to the LORD to let it be known that he was God in Israel,
and that he indeed was the LORD's servant.

Following his prayer, the fire of the LORD fell and consumed
the burnt offering, the wood, the stones, the dust, and even
licked up the water that was in the trench. The people saw it,
fell on their faces and said, "The LORD, he is God; the LORD,
he is God." Elijah told the people to seize the prophets of
Baal, and to let not even one of them escape. The prophets
were seized, and Elijah brought them down to the brook
Kishon and slaughtered them there.

With courage and boldness, Elijah withstood Ahab and the
prophets of Baal. Against impossible odds and in the darkest
of times, God shows himself strong on behalf of those who
represent him. He is the God who vindicates himself through
his servants, and demonstrates his power on his behalf
through their faithful representation.

DAILY DEVOTIONAL GUIDE

PREPARING OUR HEARTS

Invocation: Our Prayer of Acclamation

God of Elijah, God and Father of our Lord Jesus Christ,
who rains fire on altars smothered and drenched in water
on the wood and the trench, demonstrate your faithfulness
to us as we stand before others on your behalf. Though
we are apparently outnumbered and overwhelmed, give
us the calm assurance of faith, that you are a God who

cannot lie, and who always demonstrates himself as King and LORD to all who call on you in faith. In Jesus' name, amen.

Call to Worship
Blessed are you, O God: Father, Son, and Holy Spirit. And blessed is your Kingdom, both now and forever, Amen.

PRAISING OUR GOD

Te Deum Laudamus
You are God: we praise you; you are the Lord; we acclaim you; you are the eternal Father: All creation worships you. To you all angels, all the powers of heaven, Cherubim and Seraphim, sing in endless praise: Holy, holy, holy Lord, God of power and might, heaven and earth are full of your glory.

The glorious company of apostles praise you. The noble fellowship of prophets praise you. The white-robed army of martyrs praise you. Throughout the world the holy Church acclaims you; Father, of majesty unbounded, your true and only Son, worthy of all worship, and the Holy Spirit, advocate and guide.

You, Christ, are the king of glory, the eternal Son of the Father. When you became man to set us free you did not shun the Virgin's womb. You overcame the sting of death and opened the kingdom of heaven to all believers. You are seated at God's right hand in glory. We believe that you will come and be our judge. Come then, Lord, and help your people, bought with the price of your own blood, and bring us with your saints to glory everlasting.

Praise and Thanksgiving (Songs and Prayers)

Gloria Patri

Glory be to the Father,
And to the Son and to the Holy Spirit:
As it was in the beginning,
Is now, and ever shall be,
World without end. Amen, amen.

LISTENING TO HIS VOICE

Chronological Reading for the Day

Sunday: Mark 14.1-2, vv.10-26; Matt. 26.1-5, vv.14-30; Luke 22.1-30; John 13.1-30 ✦ *Monday:* John 13.31-15.17; Mark 14.27-31; Matt. 26.31-35; Luke 22.31-38 ✦ *Tuesday:* John 15.18-17.26 ✦ *Wednesday:* John 18.1-24; Mark 14.32-52; Matt. 26.36-56; Luke 22.39-53 ✦ *Thursday:* Mark 14.53-15.1; Matt. 26.57-27.10; Luke 22.54-71; John 18.25-27 ✦ *Friday:* Mark 15.2-20; Matt. 27.11-31; Luke 23.1-25; John 18.28-19.16 ✦ *Saturday:* Mark 15.21-41; Matt. 27.32-56; Luke 23.26-49; John 19.17-37

Lectionary Readings

Psalm: Ps. 78.1-4, 12-16   *OT:* Exod. 17.1-7
Gospel: Matt. 21.23-32   *NT:* Phil. 2.1-13

Reflection: Silence and/or Journaling

RESPONDING IN FAITH

The Apostles' Creed

I believe in God, the Father Almighty, Maker of heaven and earth; and in Jesus Christ, his only Son, our Lord, who was conceived by the Holy Spirit, born of the Virgin Mary, suffered under Pontius Pilate, was crucified, dead, and buried; he descended into hell; the third day he arose again from the dead; he ascended into heaven and sits on the right hand of God the Father Almighty; from thence he shall come to judge the quick and the dead.

I believe in the Holy Spirit, the holy catholic* church, the communion of saints, the forgiveness of sins, the resurrection of the body, and the life everlasting. Amen.

* In the Apostles' and Nicene Creeds, the term catholic refers to the Church's universality, through all ages and times, of all languages and peoples. It refers to no particular tradition or denominational expression (e.g., as in Roman Catholic).

Prayers of Confession

Let us now confess our sins to God and receive mercy and grace to help in our time of need.

Assurance of Pardon

Having faithfully confessed and renounced your sin, Christ also has been faithful to forgive your sins and to purify you from all unrighteousness. It is certain, that there is One who has spoken to the Father in your defense, Jesus Christ, the Righteous One who is the atoning sacrifice for our sins and for the sins of the whole world. His grace and peace are with you now. Amen.

Petitions and Supplications, Ending with The Lord's Prayer

Our Father which art in heaven, Hallowed be thy name. Thy kingdom come, Thy will be done in earth, as it is in heaven. Give us this day our daily bread. And forgive us our debts, as we forgive our debtors. And lead us not into temptation, but deliver us from evil: For thine is the kingdom, and the power, and the glory, for ever. Amen.

~ Matthew 6.9-13 (KJV)

Doxology (and/or closing song)

Praise God from whom all blessings flow;
Praise Him all creatures here below;
Praise Him above ye heavenly host;
Praise Father, Son and Holy Ghost. Amen.

DEPARTING TO SERVE

Benediction

Lord Jesus Christ, holy Son of God, grant us the courage and strength to stand up for you in the face of ridicule and shame. Grant us the ability to stand for you even when we are outnumbered and overwhelmed, when we are hounded and considered illegitimate, or stupid, or foolish. Help us to never shrink back from representing your interests and your Kingdom, whatever opposition we face, or wherever you lead us. Make us strong in your strength, for your glory. In your name we pray, amen.

Affirmation from the Psalms

Give ear, O my people, to my teaching; incline your ears to the words of my mouth! I will open my mouth in a parable; I will utter dark sayings from of old, things that we have heard and known, that our fathers have told us. We will not hide them from their children, but tell to the coming generation the glorious deeds of the LORD, and his might, and the wonders that he has done.

~ Psalm 78.1-4

Pray without Ceasing – Flash Prayer for the Day

Grant us courage to hold our ground, O God, even in the face of many who resist your name and glory.

FOR YOUR WEEKLY JOURNEY

Let God Arise! Seasonal Focus

The Apostles Arrested and Beaten, Acts 5.12-42

Book Reading

DAILY: Extreme Devotion Writing Team, *Extreme Devotion*

Howell, *Servants, Misfits, and Martyrs*

SEVENTEENTH SUNDAY AFTER PENTECOST ✠

October 5 - 11, 2014 ✠ Proper 22

The Season after Pentecost is likewise the season before Advent -- it is a season of the blessed hope. As we declare Jesus' return in every Communion celebration, so we confess that he will assuredly appear in power and glory to complete God's salvation for the world. He will come in power to rescue his own, to make an end of war and sin, and to restore creation under God's will.

THIS WEEK'S THEME
Elisha and the Chariots of Fire, 2 Kings 6.8-23

On several different occasions the LORD gave Elisha insight ahead of time of the king of Aram's (Syria) plans to attack and overwhelm Israel. In each case, Elisha warned the king of Israel of the king of Aram's intention to attack, and the king of Israel overcame each threat. After learning that Elisha was the one who forewarned Israel's king, the king of Aram sent his army to find Elisha and arrest him. The king sent horses, chariots, and a great army, which came during the night, and surrounded the place where Elisha was.

Early the next morning, Elisha's servant saw the Aramean army surrounding the home of his master, became afraid, and went into a panic. Elisha reassured his servant saying, "Do not be afraid, for those who are with us are more than those who are with them." After this Elisha prayed, "O LORD, please open his eyes that he may see." So the LORD opened his eyes, he saw, and behold, the mountain was full of horses and chariots of fire all around Elisha.

As the Syrians came down against him, Elisha prayed to the LORD to strike them with blindness, and so they were! Elisha led the Syrians to the city of Samaria, and when the king of Israel saw them, he asked if he should kill them. Elisha told him no, but rather ordered the king to feed them and to send them home, which the king did. On this, the Syrians ended their raid on the Israelites.

Extreme devotion counts on God doing more than what is physically observable. For the one who trusts in the Lord, nothing is as it appears to be. We are commanded to walk by faith and not by sight – by the word of the Lord and not how things appear to the naked eye.

DAILY DEVOTIONAL GUIDE

PREPARING OUR HEARTS

Invocation: Our Prayer of Acclamation
LORD Most High, the God who answered the prophet's prayers and enabled his servant to see the forces of God on the mountain, help us to see all that you supply those who trust in you. Grant to us the spirit of wisdom and revelation in the knowledge of you, in order that we might behold all the wonderful provision you have supplied to those who trust in you. In Jesus, your Son's name, amen.

Call to Worship
Blessed are you, O God: Father, Son, and Holy Spirit. And blessed is your Kingdom, both now and forever, Amen.

PRAISING OUR GOD

Te Deum Laudamus
You are God: we praise you; you are the Lord; we acclaim you; you are the eternal Father: All creation worships you. To you all angels, all the powers of heaven, Cherubim and Seraphim, sing in endless praise: Holy, holy, holy Lord, God of power and might, heaven and earth are full of your glory.

The glorious company of apostles praise you. The noble fellowship of prophets praise you. The white-robed army of martyrs praise you. Throughout the world the holy Church acclaims you; Father, of majesty unbounded, your true and only Son, worthy of all worship, and the Holy Spirit, advocate and guide.

You, Christ, are the king of glory, the eternal Son of the Father. When you became man to set us free you did not shun the Virgin's womb. You overcame the sting of death and opened the kingdom of heaven to all believers. You are seated at God's right hand in glory. We believe that you will come and be our judge. Come then, Lord, and help your people, bought with the price of your own blood, and bring us with your saints to glory everlasting.

Praise and Thanksgiving (Songs and Prayers)

Gloria Patri
Glory be to the Father,
And to the Son and to the Holy Spirit:
As it was in the beginning,
Is now, and ever shall be,
World without end. Amen, amen.

LISTENING TO HIS VOICE

Chronological Reading for the Day
Sunday: Mark 15.42-16.11; Matt. 27.57-28.15; Luke 23.50-24.12; John 19.38-20.18 ✠ *Monday:* Luke 24.13-49; Mark 16.12-18; John 20.19-21.25; Matt. 28.16-20 ✠ *Tuesday:* Mark 16.19-20; Luke 24.50-53; Acts 1-2 ✠ *Wednesday:* Acts 3-5 ✠ *Thursday:* Acts 6.1-8.1a ✠ *Friday:* Acts 8.1b-9.43 ✠ *Saturday:* Acts 10-12

Lectionary Readings
Psalm: Ps. 19   *OT:* Exod. 20.1-4, 7-9, 12-20
Gospel: Matt. 21.33-46   *NT:* Phil. 3.4b-14

Reflection: Silence and/or Journaling

RESPONDING IN FAITH

The Apostles' Creed

I believe in God, the Father Almighty, Maker of heaven and earth; and in Jesus Christ, his only Son, our Lord, who was conceived by the Holy Spirit, born of the Virgin Mary, suffered under Pontius Pilate, was crucified, dead, and buried; he descended into hell; the third day he arose again from the dead; he ascended into heaven and sits on the right hand of God the Father Almighty; from thence he shall come to judge the quick and the dead.

I believe in the Holy Spirit, the holy catholic* church, the communion of saints, the forgiveness of sins, the resurrection of the body, and the life everlasting. Amen.

* In the Apostles' and Nicene Creeds, the term catholic refers to the Church's universality, through all ages and times, of all languages and peoples. It refers to no particular tradition or denominational expression (e.g., as in Roman Catholic).

Prayers of Confession

Let us now confess our sins to God and receive mercy and grace to help in our time of need.

Assurance of Pardon

Having faithfully confessed and renounced your sin, Christ also has been faithful to forgive your sins and to purify you from all unrighteousness. It is certain, that there is One who has spoken to the Father in your defense, Jesus Christ, the Righteous One who is the atoning sacrifice for our sins and for the sins of the whole world. His grace and peace are with you now. Amen.

Petitions and Supplications, Ending with The Lord's Prayer

Our Father which art in heaven, Hallowed be thy name. Thy kingdom come, Thy will be done in earth, as it is in heaven. Give us this day our daily bread. And forgive us our debts, as we forgive our debtors. And lead us not into temptation, but deliver us from evil: For thine is the kingdom, and the power, and the glory, for ever. Amen.

~ Matthew 6.9-13 (KJV)

Doxology (and/or closing song)
Praise God from whom all blessings flow;
Praise Him all creatures here below;
Praise Him above ye heavenly host;
Praise Father, Son and Holy Ghost. Amen.

DEPARTING TO SERVE

Benediction
Lord Jesus, who opened the eyes of the blind during your divine ministry here on the earth, grant to us, your children, the ability to see things as you do. Teach us to continue in your Word, and so come to understand and know the truth, the same truth that will set us free and give us the strength to stand for you. In your name we pray, amen.

Affirmation from the Psalms
The law of the LORD is perfect, reviving the soul; the testimony of the LORD is sure, making wise the simple; the precepts of the LORD are right, rejoicing the heart; the commandment of the LORD is pure, enlightening the eyes; the fear of the LORD is clean, enduring forever; the rules of the LORD are true, and righteous altogether. More to be desired are they than gold, even much fine gold; sweeter also than honey and drippings of the honeycomb. Moreover, by them is your servant warned; in keeping them there is great reward.

~ Psalm 19.7-11

Pray without Ceasing – Flash Prayer for the Day
Open our eyes that we might come to see things, as it were, from your divine point of view. Grant us eyes that we may see the truth, and so believe in you.

FOR YOUR WEEKLY JOURNEY

Let God Arise! Seasonal Focus
The Apostles Arrested and Beaten, Acts 5.12-42

Book Reading
DAILY: Extreme Devotion Writing Team, *Extreme Devotion*

Howell, *Servants, Misfits, and Martyrs*

Our Corporate Disciplines
Retreat, ending with Book Review:
  Wednesday, October 8, 2014

October 12 - 18, 2014 ✠ Proper 23

The Season after Pentecost is likewise the season before Advent -- it is a season of the blessed hope. As we declare Jesus' return in every Communion celebration, so we confess that he will assuredly appear in power and glory to complete God's salvation for the world. He will come in power to rescue his own, to make an end of war and sin, and to restore creation under God's will.

THIS WEEK'S THEME
Micaiah Prophesies against Ahab, 1 Kings 22.1-40
During a fight where the kings of Judah and Israel collaborated, they decided to consult the prophets as to their prospects of victory. King Jehoshaphat of Judah and King Ahab of Israel agreed to an alliance, a partnership confirmed by the prophets of Ahab, about 400 in all, which assured the two kings of victory on the battlefield. At Jehoshaphat's request, a prophet of the LORD is also consulted before they entered the fight.

Micaiah, a prophet of the LORD, was brought before King Ahab and asked if Israel would be victorious in the fight. At the beginning, Micaiah agrees with the other prophets, but after Ahab orders him to tell the truth, Micaiah tells what he actually saw. He spoke of a vision where he saw the Israelites scattered like sheep because their shepherd (King Ahab) had been killed. He also spoke of a vision of the LORD allowing a spirit to inspire Ahab's prophets to tell lies to him!

While Ahab's prophets protested Micaiah's visions, Micaiah advised the king to wait, to not attack, and to see if his prophecies were, in fact, the truth. The king told the people to seize Micaiah, to put him in prison, and feed him with meager rations of bread and water until he returned in peace!

So both kings decided to lead their armies into battle, with King Ahab disguising himself so as to avoid being detected as the king, while Jehoshaphat wore his royal garb. The Syrians saw Jehoshaphat and chased him, but called off the hunt when they realized it was not Ahab. An enemy arrow was let go, shot without regard to a particular target, and it struck King Ahab, which took his life. Later, the dogs licked up his blood just as the prophet Elijah and Micaiah foretold.

Even though Micaiah suffered greatly for speaking the truth to Ahab, he never wavered but only said to him what the LORD had revealed to him. With boldness and clarity, Micaiah spoke truth to power, regardless of the consequences. We should do the same.

DAILY DEVOTIONAL GUIDE

PREPARING OUR HEARTS

Invocation: Our Prayer of Acclamation

Eternal God our Father, God of the prophet Micaiah, who spoke your word with clarity and boldness even though it cost him greatly, grant us the strength and the will to tell the truth to power, even if it proves inconvenient or dangerous. Remind us that your Word never returns to you void, and that your Spirit empowers everyone who tells the truth in your name. In Jesus' name, amen.

Call to Worship

Blessed are you, O God: Father, Son, and Holy Spirit. And blessed is your Kingdom, both now and forever, Amen.

PRAISING OUR GOD

Te Deum Laudamus

You are God: we praise you; you are the Lord; we acclaim you; you are the eternal Father: All creation worships you. To you all angels, all the powers of heaven, Cherubim and Seraphim, sing in endless praise:

Holy, holy, holy Lord, God of power and might, heaven and earth are full of your glory.

The glorious company of apostles praise you. The noble fellowship of prophets praise you. The white-robed army of martyrs praise you. Throughout the world the holy Church acclaims you; Father, of majesty unbounded, your true and only Son, worthy of all worship, and the Holy Spirit, advocate and guide.

You, Christ, are the king of glory, the eternal Son of the Father. When you became man to set us free you did not shun the Virgin's womb. You overcame the sting of death and opened the kingdom of heaven to all believers. You are seated at God's right hand in glory. We believe that you will come and be our judge. Come then, Lord, and help your people, bought with the price of your own blood, and bring us with your saints to glory everlasting.

Praise and Thanksgiving (Songs and Prayers)

Gloria Patri
Glory be to the Father,
And to the Son and to the Holy Spirit:
As it was in the beginning,
Is now, and ever shall be,
World without end. Amen, amen.

LISTENING TO HIS VOICE

Chronological Reading for the Day
Sunday: Acts 13-14 ✠ *Monday:* Gal. 1.1-4.7 ✠ *Tuesday:* Gal. 4.8-6.18; Acts 15 ✠ *Wednesday:* Acts 16.1-18.3 ✠ *Thursday:* 1 Thess. 1-5 ✠ *Friday:* 2 Thess. 1-3; Acts 18.4-28 ✠ *Saturday:* Acts 19.1-20; 1 Cor. 1-3

Lectionary Readings
Psalm: Ps. 106.1-6, 19-23   *OT:* Exod. 32.1-14
Gospel: Matt. 22.1-14   *NT:* Phil. 4.1-9

Reflection: Silence and/or Journaling

RESPONDING IN FAITH

The Apostles' Creed

I believe in God, the Father Almighty, Maker of heaven and earth; and in Jesus Christ, his only Son, our Lord, who was conceived by the Holy Spirit, born of the Virgin Mary, suffered under Pontius Pilate, was crucified, dead, and buried; he descended into hell; the third day he arose again from the dead; he ascended into heaven and sits on the right hand of God the Father Almighty; from thence he shall come to judge the quick and the dead.

I believe in the Holy Spirit, the holy catholic* church, the communion of saints, the forgiveness of sins, the resurrection of the body, and the life everlasting. Amen.

* In the Apostles' and Nicene Creeds, the term catholic refers to the Church's universality, through all ages and times, of all languages and peoples. It refers to no particular tradition or denominational expression (e.g., as in Roman Catholic).

Prayers of Confession

Let us now confess our sins to God and receive mercy and grace to help in our time of need.

Assurance of Pardon

Having faithfully confessed and renounced your sin, Christ also has been faithful to forgive your sins and to purify you from all unrighteousness. It is certain, that there is One who has spoken to the Father in your defense, Jesus Christ, the Righteous One who is the atoning sacrifice for our sins and for the sins of the whole world. His grace and peace are with you now. Amen.

Petitions and Supplications, Ending with The Lord's Prayer

Our Father which art in heaven, Hallowed be thy name. Thy kingdom come, Thy will be done in earth, as it is in heaven. Give us this day our daily bread. And forgive us our debts, as we forgive our debtors. And

lead us not into temptation, but deliver us from evil: For thine is the kingdom, and the power, and the glory, for ever. Amen.

~ Matthew 6.9-13 (KJV)

Doxology (and/or closing song)

Praise God from whom all blessings flow;
Praise Him all creatures here below;
Praise Him above ye heavenly host;
Praise Father, Son and Holy Ghost. Amen.

Departing to Serve

Benediction

Lord Jesus Christ, who made the good confession before Pontius Pilate, who spoke the truth directly with power and clarity to all you addressed, anoint us that we may do the same. Protect us from fear and shame, and grant us the courage to stand for you, always affirming the truth of your word in all we do and say. Give us the spirit of Micaiah, to tell to others what you have revealed to us. In your name we pray, amen.

Affirmation from the Psalms

Praise the LORD! Oh give thanks to the LORD, for he is good, for his steadfast love endures forever! Who can utter the mighty deeds of the LORD, or declare all his praise? Blessed are they who observe justice, who do righteousness at all times! Remember me, O LORD, when you show favor to your people; help me when you save them, that I may look upon the prosperity of your chosen ones, that I may rejoice in the gladness of your nation, that I may glory with your inheritance.

~ Psalm 106.1-5

Pray without Ceasing – Flash Prayer for the Day
Give us the strength to tell the truth, to never compromise your Word, even if it means persecution or misunderstanding. Teach us to speak the truth to power, always in love.

FOR YOUR WEEKLY JOURNEY

Let God Arise! Seasonal Focus
The Apostles Arrested and Beaten, Acts 5.12-42

Book Reading
DAILY: Extreme Devotion Writing Team, *Extreme Devotion*

Howell, *Servants, Misfits, and Martyrs*

WEEK
47

NINETEENTH SUNDAY AFTER PENTECOST

October 19 - 25, 2014 ✠ Proper 24

The Season after Pentecost is likewise the season before Advent -- it is a season of the blessed hope. As we declare Jesus' return in every Communion celebration, so we confess that he will assuredly appear in power and glory to complete God's salvation for the world. He will come in power to rescue his own, to make an end of war and sin, and to restore creation under God's will.

THIS WEEK'S THEME
The Apostles Arrested and Beaten, Acts 5.12-42

Luke's record of the early church in Acts reveals that many signs and wonders were regularly done by the apostles among the people. The people revered them, holding them in high esteem, and did not join them. And multitudes of believers were being added to the Lord, both men and women. Many sick people and demon-possessed from towns around Jerusalem were gathering there in Jerusalem, and came to the apostles, who healed them.

Filled with jealously and envy, the high priest and the Sadducees arrested the apostles and put them in the public prison. During the night an angel appeared, and released the apostles, telling them, "Go and stand in the temple and speak to the people all the words of this Life." At daybreak, then, they reentered the temple and began to teach. Now, the high priest and his associates called the Council together, the senate of the people, and ordered the officials at the prison to have them brought to the gathering.

Of course, when the officers came, they did not find them in the prison, so they returned and reported as much to the chief priests. Someone alerted the officers that the apostles were in the temple teaching the people, and the officials had them brought to the gathering (but not by force, for they were afraid of being stoned by the people).

Having been brought before the Council, the high priest questioned them, reminding them that they were strictly charged not to teach in Jesus' name, and yet, they had filled Jerusalem with their teaching, intending to bring "this man's blood" upon them. Peter and the apostles explained their mission, saying, "We must obey God rather than men." They again testified concerning Jesus as Leader and Savior, as the Messiah who would grant repentance to Israel and the forgiveness of sins. They testified that they were witnesses to his death and resurrection, and so was the Holy Spirit, whom the Father was granting to those who obeyed him.

Enraged with a desire to kill the apostles, the high priest and the officials were counseled by the respected Pharisee Gamaliel to leave these men alone, for if their teaching was merely on their own, it would soon come to nothing. However, if what the apostles were saying was from God, no one would be able stop them. So the Council, having again called in the apostles, beat them, charging them not to speak in the name of Jesus. After being released, the apostles rejoiced that they were counted worthy to suffer dishonor for Jesus' name. And every day, wherever they were, the apostles continued to teach and preach that the Messiah was Jesus.

Extreme devotion to Christ is often times associated with the testimony of the Gospel concerning his mission in the world. It is an honor to suffer dishonor for bearing witness to the name of Jesus.

DAILY DEVOTIONAL GUIDE

PREPARING OUR HEARTS

Invocation: Our Prayer of Acclamation

Eternal God our Father, the God of the Lord Jesus, thank you for the commitment of the apostles, who counted it an honor to bear the shame of speaking in the name of Jesus of Nazareth. Help us to overcome the fear of other people, and to stand true and clear, representing him with boldness and integrity, for his name is great and worthy of praise. In his name we pray, amen.

Call to Worship

Blessed are you, O God: Father, Son, and Holy Spirit. And blessed is your Kingdom, both now and forever, Amen.

PRAISING OUR GOD

Te Deum Laudamus

You are God: we praise you; you are the Lord; we acclaim you; you are the eternal Father: All creation worships you. To you all angels, all the powers of heaven, Cherubim and Seraphim, sing in endless praise: Holy, holy, holy Lord, God of power and might, heaven and earth are full of your glory.

The glorious company of apostles praise you. The noble fellowship of prophets praise you. The white-robed army of martyrs praise you. Throughout the world the holy Church acclaims you; Father, of majesty unbounded, your true and only Son, worthy of all worship, and the Holy Spirit, advocate and guide.

You, Christ, are the king of glory, the eternal Son of the Father. When you became man to set us free you did not shun the Virgin's womb. You overcame the sting of death and opened the kingdom of heaven to all believers. You are seated at God's right hand in glory. We believe that you will come and be our judge. Come then, Lord, and help your people, bought with the price of your own blood, and bring us with your saints to glory everlasting.

Praise and Thanksgiving (Songs and Prayers)

Gloria Patri

Glory be to the Father,
And to the Son and to the Holy Spirit:
As it was in the beginning,
Is now, and ever shall be,
World without end. Amen, amen.

LISTENING TO HIS VOICE

Chronological Reading for the Day

Sunday: 1 Cor. 4-7 ✤ *Monday:* 1 Cor. 8.1-11.1 ✤ *Tuesday:* 1 Cor. 11.2-13.13 ✤ *Wednesday:* 1 Cor. 14-15 ✤ *Thursday:* 1 Cor. 16; Acts 19.21-20.6 ✤ *Friday:* Rom. 1-3 ✤ *Saturday:* Rom. 4-6

Lectionary Readings

Psalm: Ps. 99
Gospel: Matt. 22.15-22

OT: Exod. 33.12-23
NT: 1 Thess. 1.1-10

Reflection: Silence and/or Journaling

RESPONDING IN FAITH

The Apostles' Creed

I believe in God, the Father Almighty, Maker of heaven and earth; and in Jesus Christ, his only Son, our Lord, who was conceived by the Holy Spirit, born of the Virgin Mary, suffered under Pontius Pilate, was crucified, dead, and buried; he descended into hell; the third day he arose again from the dead; he ascended into heaven and sits on the right hand of God the Father Almighty; from thence he shall come to judge the quick and the dead.

I believe in the Holy Spirit, the holy catholic* church, the communion of saints, the forgiveness of sins, the resurrection of the body, and the life everlasting. Amen.

* In the Apostles' and Nicene Creeds, the term catholic refers to the Church's universality, through all ages and times, of all languages and peoples. It refers to no particular tradition or denominational expression (e.g., as in Roman Catholic).

Prayers of Confession

Let us now confess our sins to God and receive mercy and grace to help in our time of need.

Assurance of Pardon

Having faithfully confessed and renounced your sin, Christ also has been faithful to forgive your sins and to purify you from all unrighteousness. It is certain, that there is One who has spoken to the Father in your defense, Jesus Christ, the Righteous One who is the atoning sacrifice for our sins and for the sins of the whole world. His grace and peace are with you now. Amen.

Petitions and Supplications, Ending with The Lord's Prayer

Our Father which art in heaven, Hallowed be thy name. Thy kingdom come, Thy will be done in earth, as it is in heaven. Give us this day our daily bread. And forgive us our debts, as we forgive our debtors. And lead us not into temptation, but deliver us from evil: For thine is the kingdom, and the power, and the glory, for ever. Amen.

~ Matthew 6.9-13 (KJV)

Doxology (and/or closing song)

Praise God from whom all blessings flow;
Praise Him all creatures here below;
Praise Him above ye heavenly host;
Praise Father, Son and Holy Ghost. Amen.

DEPARTING TO SERVE

Benediction

Lord Jesus Christ, our Lord and Savior, grant to us the same mind as that of the apostles, who determined to speak your message with clarity, and represent your mission boldly. They stood their ground for you, even in the face of religious leaders who ordered them to do otherwise, and who punished them with beatings and stripes. Help us never to waver or be ashamed, to stand strong and clear, and to declare with love and respect your Gospel message, which carries the words of eternal life for those who believe. In your name we pray, amen.

Affirmation from the Psalms

The LORD reigns; let the peoples tremble! He sits enthroned upon the cherubim; let the earth quake! The LORD is great in Zion; he is exalted over all the peoples. Let them praise your great and awesome name! Holy is he! The King in his might loves justice. You have established equity; you have executed justice and righteousness in Jacob. Exalt the LORD our God; worship at his footstool! Holy is he!

~ Psalm 99.1-5

Pray without Ceasing – Flash Prayer for the Day

Show us the worth and weight of the name of Jesus, the highest name in this world and the one to come.

FOR YOUR WEEKLY JOURNEY

Let God Arise! Seasonal Focus

The Apostles Arrested and Beaten, Acts 5.12-42

Book Reading

DAILY: Extreme Devotion Writing Team, *Extreme Devotion*

Howell, *Servants, Misfits, and Martyrs*

The Church of All Nations, with Christian cemetery below, Mount of Olives, Jerusalem

After the longest season of the Church Year, our calendar ends
with three significant days of remembrance and readiness.
On October 31 we commemorate the protestant reformation
of the church (*Reformation Day*), and on November 1 we
anticipate the gathering of all believers together at his throne,
while remembering his martyrs and generations gone by (*All
Saints Day*). On the last Sunday before Advent, we celebrate
the *Feast of Christ the King* (also called the *Feast of the Reign
of Christ*) which points to that day when the kingdom of this
world will become the kingdom of our Lord and of his Christ.

Reformation Day *(semper reformanda)*

Reformation Day is the Christian festival day celebrated on
October 31 to mark the Reformation, and is observed largely
by Protestant mainline churches, and in particular, by both
Lutheran and some Reformed churches. During the time of
1516–17, Johann Tetzel, a friar of the Dominican order and
official commissioner of the Pope for indulgences, was given
the assignment to go to Germany and to raise money through
the sale of indulgences to rebuild St. Peter's Basilica in Rome.

On October 31, 1517, Martin Luther, an Augustinian monk,
wrote to Albrecht, Archbishop of Mainz and Magdeburg,
levying his argument against the scandal surrounding the
sale and purchase of indulgences (a Roman Catholic practice
to shorten terms of dead loved ones in Purgatory). Luther
enclosed in his letter to Archbishop Albrecht a copy of his
case entitled "Disputation of Martin Luther on the Power and
Efficacy of Indulgences," a document which later came to be
referred to as *The 95 Theses*. Luther probably did not intend
for his views to be taken as undermining the church; he more
probably viewed his letter as a reasoned scholarly, spiritual

objection to these kinds of church allowances. Nevertheless, the thrust of Luther's argument came to be seen as a direct challenge to the pope's authority and policies, and this simple act would become the touchstone of sweeping changes in the life of the Church.

Luther's nailing his letter to the door of the Schlosskirche (known as the Castle Church) in Wittenberg has been marked as the initial spark that ignited the movement known as the Reformation. Even a contemporary of Luther, Philip Melanchthon, would write in 1546 that Luther's writing and posting of his arguments against indulgence was a seminal event in the Reformation's start. While this has been debated in some scholarly circles, it is clear that *The 95 Theses* would go on to be published from Latin into German, and copied much throughout Europe, aided remarkably by the dawning of the printing press. It would set in motion a series of events which would effect the Church's faith and practice, even to the present day.

We at TUMI recognize this festival, even though it is not broadly celebrated as the other feast days in the Christian calendar. We are unashamedly Protestant in that, while we affirm the unity of the one, holy, catholic, and apostolic church, we recognize the significance and authority of the prophetic and apostolic testimony of the Scriptures, and reference to the Word of God as ultimate authority in all matters of Christian faith and practice. The church must ever be open to the Holy Spirit-inspired Scriptures, manifesting a willingness to be corrected, directed, and reformed (*"ecclesia semper reformands, semper reformanda"*: "the church is always reformed, always reforming"). To be open to Christ is to be ever open to responding to his leadership among us, as Head and Lord of the church.

Bruce Epperly succinctly summarizes the heart of the Reformer's desire for a faith anchored in Scripture, faith, grace, and Christ, all for the glory of God alone. "As they sought to articulate their reforming faith, the Reformers affirmed "five solas" – *sola scriptura, sola fides, sola gratia, solus Christus, soli Deo Gloria*. These "*solas*" expressed the contours of Reformation faith while not narrowly defining its meaning. To be faithful to the Reformed spirit, each of these must be constantly updated to respond to God's call in a constantly changing universe."[1]

Confessing the Communion of Saints: All Saints Day
The remembrance of *All Saints Day* calls the Church to recognize the singular, universal, and potent communion of saints who have believed in and followed Christ through the ages. With its special remembrance of the martyrs historically and within contemporary society, the focus of *All Saints Day* enables us to never forget the organic unity we share with all believers everywhere throughout all time. We are spiritually, theologically, and eschatologically linked: We sup at the same Table, hold fast to the same Word, preach to the lost the same Gospel, and wait for the same return of the exalted King, the Lord Jesus Christ.

All Saints Day is our time as believers to remember our membership in the one, holy, catholic (universal), and apostolic Church, the same company of which Christ is head, and which awaits his glorious return in power. We share both DNA and destiny with those martyrs and saints, those heroes of the faith who came before us. Of special importance, *All Saints Day* is a time to recall and remember those who gave up their lives for the sake of Christ and the Gospel. In celebrating this feast we gladly affirm that the Church is the body of Christ, and that the living Savior now lives and is seen in the world through the words and deeds

---

[1] Bruce Epperly, "A Church Always Reforming: Reflections on Reformation Day." *http://www.patheos.com/Resources/Additional-Resources/Church-Always-Reforming-Bruce-Epperly-10-24-2011.html*, Oct. 23, 2011.

of his people (John 14.12; Heb. 11; Rev. 17.6), and through all who through time have clung to him by faith.

To whet your appetite on the riches available to those interested in spending time considering the discipleship of the saints, both ancient and modern, please read a synopsis of some of the heroes and heroines of the faith in our *Saints, Martyrs, and Other Luminaries of the Faith* (located at *www.tumi.org/annual*).

Awaiting the Arrival of our Lord: The Feast of Christ the King

According to the testimony of Scripture, our Lord will return and finish the work he began on the Cross, judging the world, saving his own, and making a final end to evil and sin.

The third feast day at the end of this season, the *Feast of Christ the King* (also called the *Feast of the Reign of Christ*) is the last Sunday of this season, and the final one before Advent. The hope of the saints throughout the ages is that the Lord Jesus will return to rightfully claim this world as his own, to establish in fullness the reign of God, restoring creation to its edenic glory, and putting down evil, once and for all. The *Feast of Christ the King* points to that day when the kingdom of this world will become the kingdom of our Lord and of his Christ, who will reign forever and ever (Rev. 11.15ff.). How appropriate to end the season after the coming of the Holy Spirit with a feast which honors the future reign of our risen Savior, the true Lord who one day will reign alone and supreme!

One, Undivided Church: For All the Saints

William W. How and Ralph Vaughan Williams created a marvelous lyrical poem that summarizes and highlights the glorious communion and unity we share with all true believers in Jesus Christ who hold the hope of the new heavens and earth in their hearts, and who long to see the Lord soon. It is entitled *For All the Saints*, and is considered a classic hymn outlining the amazing perseverance of the martyrs and believers who have held true in their witness to Christ and his Kingdom.

For All the Saints

For all the saints, who from their labors rest,
Who Thee by faith before the world confessed,
Thy Name, O Jesus, be forever blessed. Alleluia, Alleluia!

Thou wast their Rock, their Fortress and their Might;
Thou, Lord, their Captain in the well-fought fight;
Thou, in the darkness drear, their one true Light. Alleluia, Alleluia!

For the Apostles' glorious company,
Who bearing forth the Cross o'er land and sea,
Shook all the mighty world, we sing to Thee: Alleluia, Alleluia!

For the Evangelists, by whose blest word,
Like fourfold streams, the garden of the Lord,
Is fair and fruitful, be Thy Name adored. Alleluia, Alleluia!

For Martyrs, who with rapture-kindled eye,
Saw the bright crown descending from the sky,
And seeing, grasped it, Thee we glorify. Alleluia, Alleluia!

O blest communion, fellowship divine!
We feebly struggle; they in glory shine.
All are one in Thee, for all are Thine. Alleluia, Alleluia!

O may Thy soldiers, faithful, true and bold,
Fight as the saints who nobly fought of old,
And win with them the victor's crown of gold. Alleluia, Alleluia!

And when the strife is fierce, the warfare long,
Steals on the ear the distant triumph song,
And hearts are brave, again, and arms are strong. Alleluia, Alleluia!

The golden evening brightens in the west;
Soon, soon to faithful warriors comes their rest;
Sweet is the calm of paradise the blessed. Alleluia, Alleluia!

But lo! there breaks a yet more glorious day;
The saints triumphant rise in bright array;
The King of glory passes on His way. Alleluia, Alleluia!

From earth's wide bounds, from ocean's farthest coast,
Through gates of pearl streams in the countless host,
And singing to Father, Son and Holy Ghost: Alleluia, Alleluia!

~ Words: William W. How.
Music: Sine Nomine. Ralph Vaughan Williams.
© Public Domain.

As sojourners of the Way, we must ever be open to hear and respond to the living voice of God in the Spirit, the Word of God preached in the Church. It is in this spirit of meekness, lowliness, and humility that we celebrate the dramatic impact of the Reformation on the church, and its ongoing legacy for mission, discipleship, and spiritual formation today. We remember our membership, with all the saints through the ages, in the one, holy, catholic (universal), and apostolic Church of which Christ is the head. And, we share with those saints, the hope throughout the ages that the Lord Jesus will return in power and establish his kingdom reign. To live by faith is to have this hope and do nothing less than be responsive to the risen Christ as he directs his people into his good, perfect, and acceptable will.

~ Anticipating the reign of the ages
Rev. Dr. Don L. Davis

October 26 - November 1, 2014 ✠ Proper 25

According to God's holy promise, the saints of Christ will dine at the marriage supper of the Lamb, a feast of love and communion with the risen Lord and Savior himself. The Feast of Christ the King, the last Sunday before Advent, anticipates the day when Christ will reign supreme, and the saints of God will never again leave the presence of their Lord.

THIS WEEK'S THEME
Deborah Defeats Sisera, Judges 4.1-22

After the judge Ehud died, the people of Israel again did what was evil in the LORD's sight. The LORD sold them into the hand of Jabin, king of Canaan, whose commander was named Sisera. God's people cried to the LORD for help, for Sisera had 900 chariots of iron and he oppressed Israel cruelly for twenty years.

Deborah was judging Israel at this time, and she was a prophetess. She summoned and informed Barak that he had been chosen to gather an army of 10,000 men to fight the general of Jabin's army and win. Barak agreed to go, only if Deborah would accompany him. She agreed to go but warned him that, nevertheless, the road on which he would go would not lead to his victory, for the LORD would sell Sisera into the hand of a woman.

Warriors from the tribes of Zebulun, Naptali, Ephraim, Benjamin, and Issachur joined Barak's army, whose forces quickly engaged Sisera in battle at Mount Tabor and the Kishon River. Deborah told Barak to get up and get ready, for the LORD that day would give Sisera into his hand, going out before him into the fight. Barak went down from Mount Tabor, attacked with 10,000 men following him, and the LORD himself routed Sisera and all his chariots and all his army. Realizing that he had lost, Sisera got down from his chariot and fled away on foot. (Barak pursued the chariots and annihilated the entire army of Sisera; not even a single man was left).

Sisera fled away on foot to the tent of Jael, the wife of a man who was at peace with Jabin, Sisera's leader. Inviting Sisera into her tent, he entered, and she covered him with a rug. After receiving from Jael some milk and asking her to stand guard at the tent, he fell asleep from weariness. Jael took a tent peg, with a hammer in her hand, and going softly to Sisera, she drove the peg into his temple until it went down into the ground while he was lying fast asleep from weariness. So he died. While Barak was pursuing Sisera, Jael went out to meet him, telling him that the man he was seeking was in her tent. Barak entered her tent, and saw Sisera lying there, dead, with the tent peg in his temple.

God is not a respecter of persons. He calls and uses both men and women to be his messengers and servants. Extreme acts of devotion are not limited to those whom we consider naturally gifted. God uses everyone who makes himself or herself available to him.

DAILY DEVOTIONAL GUIDE

PREPARING OUR HEARTS

Invocation: Our Prayer of Acclamation

Eternal God, our Father Almighty, God of Abraham and Sarah, God of Joshua and Deborah, thank you that you are the God who calls and empowers both men and women to represent your Son and his Kingdom. You reveal in your Word that you do not respect persons, but will use anyone who yields their lives to you in total surrender. Make us the kind of people who offer you everything, and thus, are used by you to do your will. In Jesus' name, amen.

Call to Worship

Blessed are you, O God: Father, Son, and Holy Spirit. And blessed is your Kingdom, both now and forever, Amen.

PRAISING OUR GOD

Te Deum Laudamus

You are God: we praise you; you are the Lord; we acclaim you; you are the eternal Father: All creation worships you. To you all angels, all the powers of heaven, Cherubim and Seraphim, sing in endless praise: Holy, holy, holy Lord, God of power and might, heaven and earth are full of your glory.

The glorious company of apostles praise you. The noble fellowship of prophets praise you. The white-robed army of martyrs praise you. Throughout the world the holy Church acclaims you; Father, of majesty unbounded, your true and only Son, worthy of all worship, and the Holy Spirit, advocate and guide.

You, Christ, are the king of glory, the eternal Son of the Father. When you became man to set us free you did not shun the Virgin's womb. You overcame the sting of death and opened the kingdom of heaven to all believers. You are seated at God's right hand in glory. We believe that you will come and be our judge. Come then, Lord, and help your people, bought with the price of your own blood, and bring us with your saints to glory everlasting.

Praise and Thanksgiving (Songs and Prayers)

Gloria Patri

Glory be to the Father,
And to the Son and to the Holy Spirit:
As it was in the beginning,
Is now, and ever shall be,
World without end. Amen, amen.

LISTENING TO HIS VOICE

Chronological Reading for the Day
Sunday: Rom. 7-9 ✤ *Monday:* Rom. 10-13 ✤ *Tuesday:* Rom. 14-16 ✤ *Wednesday:* 2 Cor. 1.1-6.13 ✤ *Thursday:* 2 Cor. 6.14-10.18 ✤ *Friday:* 2 Cor. 11-13 ✤ *Saturday:* Acts 20.7-21.36

Lectionary Readings
Psalm: Ps. 90.1-6, 13-17   *OT:* Deut. 34.1-12
Gospel: Matt. 22.34-46   *NT:* 1 Thess. 2.1-8

Reflection: Silence and/or Journaling

RESPONDING IN FAITH

The Apostles' Creed
I believe in God, the Father Almighty, Maker of heaven and earth; and in Jesus Christ, his only Son, our Lord, who was conceived by the Holy Spirit, born of the Virgin Mary, suffered under Pontius Pilate, was crucified, dead, and buried; he descended into hell; the third day he arose again from the dead; he ascended into heaven and sits on the right hand of God the Father Almighty; from thence he shall come to judge the quick and the dead.

I believe in the Holy Spirit, the holy catholic* church, the communion of saints, the forgiveness of sins, the resurrection of the body, and the life everlasting. Amen.

* In the Apostles' and Nicene Creeds, the term catholic refers to the Church's universality, through all ages and times, of all languages and peoples. It refers to no particular tradition or denominational expression (e.g., as in Roman Catholic).

Prayers of Confession
Let us now confess our sins to God and receive mercy and grace to help in our time of need.

Assurance of Pardon

Having faithfully confessed and renounced your sin, Christ also has been faithful to forgive your sins and to purify you from all unrighteousness. It is certain, that there is One who has spoken to the Father in your defense, Jesus Christ, the Righteous One who is the atoning sacrifice for our sins and for the sins of the whole world. His grace and peace are with you now. Amen.

Petitions and Supplications, Ending with The Lord's Prayer

Our Father which art in heaven, Hallowed be thy name. Thy kingdom come, Thy will be done in earth, as it is in heaven. Give us this day our daily bread. And forgive us our debts, as we forgive our debtors. And lead us not into temptation, but deliver us from evil: For thine is the kingdom, and the power, and the glory, for ever. Amen.

~ Matthew 6.9-13 (KJV)

Doxology (and/or closing song)

Praise God from whom all blessings flow;
Praise Him all creatures here below;
Praise Him above ye heavenly host;
Praise Father, Son and Holy Ghost. Amen.

DEPARTING TO SERVE

Benediction

Lord Jesus Christ, Son of God and Savior, thank you for showing us in your company that you call both men and women to your side, to serve as your servants and messengers. You called James and John, and you used Mary Magdalene and Martha. You do not discriminate with those whom you call and use, and for that, we are grateful. Cause us to know and understand this, and look for your work in the lives of all who call on you, regardless of their gender or background. In your name we pray, amen.

Affirmation from the Psalms

Lord, you have been our dwelling place in all generations. Before the mountains were brought forth, or ever you had formed the earth and the world, from everlasting to everlasting you are God. You return man to dust and say, "Return, O children of man!" For a thousand years in your sight are but as yesterday when it is past, or as a watch in the night. You sweep them away as with a flood; they are like a dream, like grass that is renewed in the morning: in the morning it flourishes and is renewed; in the evening it fades and withers.

~ Psalm 90.1-6

Pray without Ceasing – Flash Prayer for the Day

Thank you, Savior and King, that you empower all, whether male or female, whether Jew or Greek, whether slave or free, who yield their lives into your hands.

FOR YOUR WEEKLY JOURNEY

Let God Arise! Seasonal Focus

The Great Multitude to Come, Rev. 7.9-17

Book Reading

DAILY: Extreme Devotion Writing Team, *Extreme Devotion*

Howell, *Servants, Misfits, and Martyrs*

Special Church Year Services

Reformation Day: Friday, October 31, 2014
All Saints Day: Saturday, November 1, 2014

October 31, 2014

According to God's holy promise, the saints of Christ will dine at the marriage supper of the Lamb, a feast of love and communion with the risen Lord and Savior himself. The Feast of Christ the King, the last Sunday before Advent, anticipates the day when Christ will reign supreme, and the saints of God will never again leave the presence of their Lord.

TODAY'S THEME
The Truth Shall Set You Free, John 8.31-36

In training his disciples, those Jews who had recently believed on him, the Lord declared that if they were to abide in his Word, they would truly prove to be his disciples. And they would know the truth, and that the truth would set them free. Some of those who heard his words doubted him, and answered that they, as Jews, were themselves the very offspring of Abraham, and thus had never been enslaved to anyone. They asked him, "How is it that you say, 'You will become free'?"

On hearing their question and knowing their minds, Jesus replied "Truly, truly, I say to you, everyone who practices sin is a slave to sin. The slave does not remain in the house forever; the son remains forever. So if the Son sets you free, you will be free indeed."

On this Reformation day let us affirm that the truth of our Lord Jesus Christ, his Word, foretold by the prophets and testified by his own apostles, remains the very truth that sets those who believe free. We are his disciples because we cling to his Word, the word of life concerning Jesus of Nazareth. This word was given to the Father through the inspiration of the Holy Spirit, who led the writers of the Scriptures to give us the true Word of God, the very foundation of our faith.

DAILY DEVOTIONAL GUIDE

PREPARING OUR HEARTS

Invocation: Our Prayer of Acclamation
O God, who has given us the great and saving truths of your gospel: grant us, we ask you, to live amid these things, to mediate on them and to see them; for one who goes on seeking, finds. Help us, therefore, to learn those things on earth, the knowledge of which shall abide with us in heaven. Grant this for Jesus Christ's sake. Amen.

~ Jerome (Oden, p. 91

Call to Worship
Blessed are you, O God: Father, Son, and Holy Spirit. And blessed is your Kingdom, both now and forever, Amen.

PRAISING OUR GOD

Te Deum Laudamus
You are God: we praise you; you are the Lord; we acclaim you; you are the eternal Father: All creation worships you. To you all angels, all the powers of heaven, Cherubim and Seraphim, sing in endless praise: Holy, holy, holy Lord, God of power and might, heaven and earth are full of your glory.

The glorious company of apostles praise you. The noble fellowship of prophets praise you. The white-robed army of martyrs praise you. Throughout the world the holy Church acclaims you; Father, of majesty unbounded, your true and only Son, worthy of all worship, and the Holy Spirit, advocate and guide.

You, Christ, are the king of glory, the eternal Son of the Father. When you became man to set us free you did not shun the Virgin's womb. You overcame the sting of death and opened the kingdom of heaven

to all believers. You are seated at God's right hand in glory. We believe that you will come and be our judge. Come then, Lord, and help your people, bought with the price of your own blood, and bring us with your saints to glory everlasting.

Praise and Thanksgiving (Songs and Prayers)

Gloria Patri
Glory be to the Father,
And to the Son and to the Holy Spirit:
As it was in the beginning,
Is now, and ever shall be,
World without end. Amen, amen.

LISTENING TO HIS VOICE

Chronological Reading for the Day
2 Cor. 11-13

Lectionary Readings
Psalm: Ps. 46   OT: Jer. 31.31-34
Gospel: John 8.31-36   NT: Rom. 3.19-28

Reflection: Silence and/or Journaling

RESPONDING IN FAITH

The Apostles' Creed
I believe in God, the Father Almighty, Maker of heaven and earth; and in Jesus Christ, his only Son, our Lord, who was conceived by the Holy Spirit, born of the Virgin Mary, suffered under Pontius Pilate, was crucified, dead, and buried; he descended into hell; the third day he arose again from the dead; he ascended into heaven and sits on the right hand of God the Father Almighty; from thence he shall come to judge the quick and the dead.

I believe in the Holy Spirit, the holy catholic* church, the communion of saints, the forgiveness of sins, the resurrection of the body, and the life everlasting. Amen.

* In the Apostles' and Nicene Creeds, the term catholic refers to the Church's universality, through all ages and times, of all languages and peoples. It refers to no particular tradition or denominational expression (e.g., as in Roman Catholic).

Prayers of Confession

Let us now confess our sins to God and receive mercy and grace to help in our time of need.

Assurance of Pardon

Having faithfully confessed and renounced your sin, Christ also has been faithful to forgive your sins and to purify you from all unrighteousness. It is certain, that there is One who has spoken to the Father in your defense, Jesus Christ, the Righteous One who is the atoning sacrifice for our sins and for the sins of the whole world. His grace and peace are with you now. Amen.

Petitions and Supplications, Ending with The Lord's Prayer

Our Father which art in heaven, Hallowed be thy name. Thy kingdom come, Thy will be done in earth, as it is in heaven. Give us this day our daily bread. And forgive us our debts, as we forgive our debtors. And lead us not into temptation, but deliver us from evil: For thine is the kingdom, and the power, and the glory, for ever. Amen.

~ Matthew 6.9-13 (KJV)

Doxology (and/or closing song)

Praise God from whom all blessings flow;
Praise Him all creatures here below;
Praise Him above ye heavenly host;
Praise Father, Son and Holy Ghost. Amen.

DEPARTING TO SERVE

Benediction

O God Almighty, Father of our Lord Jesus Christ, grant us, we pray thee, to be grounded and settled in the truth, by the coming down of the Holy Spirit into our hearts. That which we know not, . . . reveal; that which is wanting in us, . . . fill up; that which we know, . . . confirm, and keep us blameless in thy service; through the same Jesus Christ our Lord. Amen.

~ Clement (Oden, p. 233)

Affirmation from the Psalms

God is our refuge and strength, a very present help in trouble. Therefore we will not fear though the earth gives way, though the mountains be moved into the heart of the sea, though its waters roar and foam, though the mountains tremble at its swelling. Selah. There is a river whose streams make glad the city of God, the holy habitation of the Most High. God is in the midst of her; she shall not be moved; God will help her when morning dawns.

~ Psalm 46.1-11

Pray without Ceasing – Flash Prayer for the Day

Dear Savior Jesus, help us to abide in your Word, and thus come to know the truth, the only truth that can set us free from sin, the curse, and the grave.

FOR YOUR WEEKLY JOURNEY

Let God Arise! Seasonal Focus

The Great Multitude to Come, Rev. 7.9-17

Book Reading

DAILY: Extreme Devotion Writing Team, *Extreme Devotion*

Howell, *Servants, Misfits, and Martyrs*

November 1, 2014

According to God's holy promise, the saints of Christ will dine at the marriage supper of the Lamb, a feast of love and communion with the risen Lord and Savior himself. The Feast of Christ the King, the last Sunday before Advent, anticipates the day when Christ will reign supreme, and the saints of God will never again leave the presence of their Lord.

TODAY'S THEME
The Great Multitude to Come, Revelation 7.9-17

In one of the visions John the apostle received on the isle of Patmos, he looked, and saw a great multitude that no one could number, from every nation, from all tribes and peoples and languages, standing before the throne and before the Lamb. This multitude was clothed in white robes, with palm branches in their hands, and they cried out with a loud voice, saying, "Salvation belongs to our God who sits on the throne, and to the Lamb!"

John testified that while he viewed this sight all the angels were standing around the throne, along with the Elders and the four living creatures he had observed in his vision of the throne room. These Elders and four living creatures fell, too, on their faces before the throne and worshiped God, saying, "Amen! Blessing and glory and wisdom and thanksgiving and honor and power and might be to our God forever and ever! Amen."

In the midst of this vision, one of the elders addressed John, saying to him, "Who are these, clothed in white robes, and from where have they come?" John answered, "Sir, you know." The elder answered that this multitude were those ones who came out of the great tribulation. They had washed their robes and made them white in the blood of the Lamb. The elder said that these therefore are before the throne of God, serving him day and night in his temple. The one who sat on the throne would shelter them with his presence, and they would never hunger any more, neither would they thirst anymore, for the sun would never strike them, nor any scorching heat.

The elder declared that the Lamb himself in the midst of the throne would be their shepherd, and he would guide them to springs of living water, and God would wipe away every tear from their eyes. This is the vision of God's redeemed company, the saints of God who make up that great multitude of the redeemed to come.

DAILY DEVOTIONAL GUIDE

PREPARING OUR HEARTS

Invocation: Our Prayer of Acclamation
Almighty and everlasting God, Who adornest the sacred body of Thy Church by the confessions of the holy Martyrs; grant us, we pray Thee, that both by their doctrines and their pious example, we may follow after what is pleasing in Thy sight; through Jesus Christ our Lord. Amen.

~ Leonine Sacramentary (Bright, p. 68)

Call to Worship
Blessed are you, O God: Father, Son, and Holy Spirit. And blessed is your Kingdom, both now and forever, Amen.

PRAISING OUR GOD

Te Deum Laudamus
You are God: we praise you; you are the Lord; we acclaim you; you are the eternal Father: All creation worships you. To you all angels, all the powers of heaven, Cherubim and Seraphim, sing in endless praise: Holy, holy, holy Lord, God of power and might, heaven and earth are full of your glory.

The glorious company of apostles praise you. The noble fellowship of prophets praise you. The white-robed army of martyrs praise you. Throughout the world the holy Church acclaims you; Father, of majesty unbounded, your true and only Son, worthy of all worship, and the Holy Spirit, advocate and guide.

You, Christ, are the king of glory, the eternal Son of the Father. When you became man to set us free you did not shun the Virgin's womb. You overcame the sting of death and opened the kingdom of heaven to all believers. You are seated at God's right hand in glory. We believe that you will come and be our judge. Come then, Lord, and help your people, bought with the price of your own blood, and bring us with your saints to glory everlasting.

Praise and Thanksgiving (Songs and Prayers)

Gloria Patri
Glory be to the Father,
And to the Son and to the Holy Spirit:
As it was in the beginning,
Is now, and ever shall be,
World without end. Amen, amen.

LISTENING TO HIS VOICE

Chronological Reading for the Day
Acts 20.7-21.36

Lectionary Readings
Psalm: Ps. 34.1-10, 22   *OT:* Rev. 7.9-17
Gospel: Matt. 5.1-12   *NT:* 1 John 3.1-3

Reflection: Silence and/or Journaling

RESPONDING IN FAITH

The Apostles' Creed
I believe in God, the Father Almighty, Maker of heaven and earth; and in Jesus Christ, his only Son, our Lord, who was conceived by the Holy Spirit, born of the Virgin Mary, suffered under Pontius Pilate, was crucified, dead, and buried; he descended into hell; the third day he arose again from the dead; he ascended into heaven and sits on the right hand of God the Father Almighty; from thence he shall come to judge the quick and the dead.

I believe in the Holy Spirit, the holy catholic* church, the communion of saints, the forgiveness of sins, the resurrection of the body, and the life everlasting. Amen.

* In the Apostles' and Nicene Creeds, the term catholic refers to the Church's universality, through all ages and times, of all languages and peoples. It refers to no particular tradition or denominational expression (e.g., as in Roman Catholic).

Prayers of Confession
Let us now confess our sins to God and receive mercy and grace to help in our time of need.

Assurance of Pardon
Having faithfully confessed and renounced your sin, Christ also has been faithful to forgive your sins and to purify you from all unrighteousness. It is certain, that there is One who has spoken to the Father in your defense, Jesus Christ, the Righteous One who is the atoning sacrifice for our sins and for the sins of the whole world. His grace and peace are with you now. Amen.

Petitions and Supplications, Ending with The Lord's Prayer
Our Father which art in heaven, Hallowed be thy name. Thy kingdom come, Thy will be done in earth, as it is in heaven. Give us this day our daily bread. And forgive us our debts, as we forgive our debtors. And

*lead us not into temptation, but deliver us from evil: For thine is the
kingdom, and the power, and the glory, for ever. Amen.*

~ Matthew 6.9-13 (KJV)

Doxology (and/or closing song)
Praise God from whom all blessings flow;
Praise Him all creatures here below;
Praise Him above ye heavenly host;
Praise Father, Son and Holy Ghost. Amen.

DEPARTING TO SERVE

Benediction
*O Almighty God, who hast knit together thine elect in one communion
and fellowship, in the mystical body of thy Son Christ our Lord: Grant
us grace so to follow thy blessed Saints in all virtuous and godly living,
that we may come to those unspeakable joys which thou hast prepared for those who unfeignedly love thee; through the same thy Son
Jesus Christ our Lord. Amen.*

~ *Book of Common Prayer*, England Revised (1928) (Suter, p. 65)

Affirmation from the Psalms
*I will bless the LORD at all times; his praise shall continually be in my
mouth. My soul makes its boast in the LORD; let the humble hear and
be glad. Oh, magnify the LORD with me, and let us exalt his name
together! I sought the LORD, and he answered me and delivered me
from all my fears. Those who look to him are radiant, and their faces
shall never be ashamed. This poor man cried, and the LORD heard him
and saved him out of all his troubles. The angel of the LORD encamps
around those who fear him, and delivers them. Oh, taste and see that
the LORD is good! Blessed is the man who takes refuge in him! Oh, fear
the LORD, you his saints, for those who fear him have no lack! The
young lions suffer want and hunger; but those who seek the LORD
lack no good thing.*

~ Psalm 34.1-10

Pray without Ceasing – Flash Prayer for the Day
We bless your holy name, O God and our Savior, awaiting with great expectation for the time of your coming again. Gather together your own, and grant us favor to be included in that number, for your sake.

FOR YOUR WEEKLY JOURNEY

Let God Arise! Seasonal Focus
The Great Multitude to Come, Rev. 7.9-17

Book Reading
DAILY: Extreme Devotion Writing Team, *Extreme Devotion*

Howell, *Servants, Misfits, and Martyrs*

✠

TWENTY-FIRST SUNDAY AFTER PENTECOST

November 2 - 8, 2014 ✠ Proper 26

According to God's holy promise, the saints of Christ will dine at the marriage supper of the Lamb, a feast of love and communion with the risen Lord and Savior himself. The Feast of Christ the King, the last Sunday before Advent, anticipates the day when Christ will reign supreme, and the saints of God will never again leave the presence of their Lord.

THIS WEEK'S THEME
James Is Killed with the Sword, Acts 12.1-5

At the beginning of the Jesus movement growing in Jerusalem, King Herod had the Apostle James killed. He laid, as the Acts of the Apostles testifies, "violent hands" on some who belonged to the church. Early on in the movement, he killed James the brother of John with the sword, and, seeing that it pleased the Jews to kill James, he then proceeded to arrest Peter as well. When Herod had seized Peter, he put him in prison, delivering him over to four squads of soldiers to guard him, intending after the Passover to bring him out to the people. So Peter was kept in the prison, but the gathering of believers offered earnest prayer for him to God. On the eve of his trial, God sent an angel to him, which loosened his chains and opened the prison doors on his behalf.

While it may not be clear why the Lord would allow James to be killed so early in his ministry, being a notable and devoted disciple of Jesus, we can still trust that God knows well what his will is for us. In giving the Lord the extreme devotion he deserves, let us not seek to outmaneuver or outwit the Lord in his disposing of all things. We are his servants, and he is our Lord; he knows what is best for us, and his methods and timing are always right, whether we understand them all – or not.

DAILY DEVOTIONAL GUIDE

PREPARING OUR HEARTS

Invocation: Our Prayer of Acclamation

God of the Apostle James, who followed intimately our Lord during his earthly ministry, we thank you for your gracious and good will. We readily admit that your ways of wisdom are beyond us, and that we cannot always comprehend your divine reasons for the works that you allow and accomplish. Still, we believe in you with all our hearts, and our devotion will always be extreme enough to cling to you regardless of what occurs or what we understand. You, O God, are truly Lord, and we trust in you. In Jesus' name, amen.

Call to Worship

Blessed are you, O God: Father, Son, and Holy Spirit. And blessed is your Kingdom, both now and forever, Amen.

PRAISING OUR GOD

Te Deum Laudamus

You are God: we praise you; you are the Lord; we acclaim you; you are the eternal Father: All creation worships you. To you all angels, all the powers of heaven, Cherubim and Seraphim, sing in endless praise: Holy, holy, holy Lord, God of power and might, heaven and earth are full of your glory.

The glorious company of apostles praise you. The noble fellowship of prophets praise you. The white-robed army of martyrs praise you. Throughout the world the holy Church acclaims you; Father, of majesty unbounded, your true and only Son, worthy of all worship, and the Holy Spirit, advocate and guide.

You, Christ, are the king of glory, the eternal Son of the Father. When you became man to set us free you did not shun the Virgin's womb. You overcame the sting of death and opened the kingdom of heaven

to all believers. You are seated at God's right hand in glory. We believe that you will come and be our judge. Come then, Lord, and help your people, bought with the price of your own blood, and bring us with your saints to glory everlasting.

Praise and Thanksgiving (Songs and Prayers)

Gloria Patri
Glory be to the Father,
And to the Son and to the Holy Spirit:
As it was in the beginning,
Is now, and ever shall be,
World without end. Amen, amen.

LISTENING TO HIS VOICE

Chronological Reading for the Day
Sunday: Acts 21.37-23.35 ✤ *Monday:* Acts 24-26 ✤ *Tuesday:* Acts 27-28 ✤ *Wednesday:* Eph. 1-3 ✤ *Thursday:* Eph. 4-6 ✤ *Friday:* Col. 1-2 ✤ *Saturday:* Col. 3-4

Lectionary Readings
Psalm: Ps. 107.1-7, 33-37   *OT:* Mic. 3.5-12
Gospel: Matt. 23.1-12   *NT:* 1 Thess. 2.9-13

Reflection: Silence and/or Journaling

RESPONDING IN FAITH

The Apostles' Creed
I believe in God, the Father Almighty, Maker of heaven and earth; and in Jesus Christ, his only Son, our Lord, who was conceived by the Holy Spirit, born of the Virgin Mary, suffered under Pontius Pilate, was crucified, dead, and buried; he descended into hell; the third day he arose again from the dead; he ascended into heaven and sits on the right hand of God the Father Almighty; from thence he shall come to judge the quick and the dead.

I believe in the Holy Spirit, the holy catholic* church, the communion of saints, the forgiveness of sins, the resurrection of the body, and the life everlasting. Amen.

* In the Apostles' and Nicene Creeds, the term catholic refers to the Church's universality, through all ages and times, of all languages and peoples. It refers to no particular tradition or denominational expression (e.g., as in Roman Catholic).

Prayers of Confession

Let us now confess our sins to God and receive mercy and grace to help in our time of need.

Assurance of Pardon

Having faithfully confessed and renounced your sin, Christ also has been faithful to forgive your sins and to purify you from all unrighteousness. It is certain, that there is One who has spoken to the Father in your defense, Jesus Christ, the Righteous One who is the atoning sacrifice for our sins and for the sins of the whole world. His grace and peace are with you now. Amen.

Petitions and Supplications, Ending with The Lord's Prayer

Our Father which art in heaven, Hallowed be thy name. Thy kingdom come, Thy will be done in earth, as it is in heaven. Give us this day our daily bread. And forgive us our debts, as we forgive our debtors. And lead us not into temptation, but deliver us from evil: For thine is the kingdom, and the power, and the glory, for ever. Amen.

~ Matthew 6.9-13 (KJV)

Doxology (and/or closing song)

Praise God from whom all blessings flow;
Praise Him all creatures here below;
Praise Him above ye heavenly host;
Praise Father, Son and Holy Ghost. Amen.

DEPARTING TO SERVE

Benediction

Lord Jesus, who leads your children step by step in your perfect will, grant us the wisdom and patience to trust in you, to follow you wherever you lead, to take whatever you give, to let go whatever you take away, and to affirm the truth however things look. Regardless of what we see and know, we cling to you alone, for you are our hope and our strength. We love you, dear Savior; bless us as we trust in you. In your name, amen.

Affirmation from the Psalms

Oh give thanks to the LORD, for he is good, for his steadfast love endures forever! Let the redeemed of the LORD say so, whom he has redeemed from trouble and gathered in from the lands, from the east and from the west, from the north and from the south. Some wandered in desert wastes, finding no way to a city to dwell in; hungry and thirsty, their soul fainted within them. Then they cried to the LORD in their trouble, and he delivered them from their distress. He led them by a straight way till they reached a city to dwell in.

~ Psalm 107.1-7

Pray without Ceasing – Flash Prayer for the Day

In sunshine or rain, during clear skies or in the midst of the storm, we will ever trust you, O God, our shield and help, for you are worthy of our praise and our hope.

FOR YOUR WEEKLY JOURNEY

Let God Arise! Seasonal Focus
The Great Multitude to Come, Rev. 7.9-17

Book Reading
DAILY: Extreme Devotion Writing Team, *Extreme Devotion*

Howell, *Servants, Misfits, and Martyrs*

✚

TWENTY-SECOND SUNDAY AFTER PENTECOST

November 9 - 15, 2014 ✚ Proper 27

According to God's holy promise, the saints of Christ will dine at the marriage supper of the Lamb, a feast of love and communion with the risen Lord and Savior himself. The Feast of Christ the King, the last Sunday before Advent, anticipates the day when Christ will reign supreme, and the saints of God will never again leave the presence of their Lord.

THIS WEEK'S THEME
John Is Exiled to Patmos, Revelation 1.9-19

The Apostle John, our brother and partner, as he says, "in the tribulation and the kingdom and the patient endurance that are in Jesus" was exiled to the island called Patmos on account of the word of God and the testimony of Jesus. His brother, James, had been killed some years earlier by king Herod, and he John, found himself under state custody for his role in declaring the Good News of Jesus of Nazareth.

At the beginning of his book written to the seven churches regarding Christ's return, John testified that he was in the Spirit on the Lord's day, and he heard behind him a loud voice like a trumpet which said, "Write what you see in a book and send it to the seven churches, to Ephesus and to Smyrna and to Pergamum and to Thyatira and to Sardis and to Philadelphia and to Laodicea." When John turned to see the voice that was speaking to him, he saw seven golden lampstands, and in the midst of these he saw one who was like a son of man.

This amazing figure was clothed with a long robe and with a golden sash around his chest. The hairs of his head were white, like white wool, white as snow. His eyes were like a flame of fire, and this person's feet were like burnished bronze, refined in a furnace. His voice was like the roar of many waters, and he held seven stars in his right hand. From this figure's mouth came a sharp two-edged sword, and his face was like the sun shining in full strength.

John testifies that when he saw him, he fell at his feet as though he was a dead man. This person, however, laid his right hand on John and said to him, "Fear not, I am the first and the last, and the living one. I died, and behold I am alive forevermore, and I have the keys of Death and Hades." This person, the glorified Jesus, commanded John to write the things he had seen, those things that were taking place, and those things that would happen in the future.

For James the son of Zebedee and John the brother of James (those whom the Lord gave the name "Boanerges," that is, Sons of Thunder [Mark 3.17]), extreme devotion included martyrdom, on the one hand, and exile, on the other. Their lives were marked by persecution and death, from ruthless leaders who viewed their misery and suffering as either politically expedient or necessary. Their lives shone like a beacon of what true devotion to the Savior looks like. They both were willing to pay the extreme sacrifice for being unconditionally available to God. May we, like them, yield ourselves to God to serve however he wills, for his glory.

DAILY DEVOTIONAL GUIDE

PREPARING OUR HEARTS

Invocation: Our Prayer of Acclamation

Eternal God, God and Father of our Lord Jesus Christ, grant us the honor of serving you like the sons of Zebedee, James and John, who accompanied the Lord during his most private encounters of grace and healing with others. As they witnessed the glory of the Son of God, so did they also suffer at the hands of ungodly men, merely for living in obedience to the Gospel. Help us never to underestimate the price of walking intimately with your Son, so, whether by martyrdom or exile (or whatever your will demands) we will be ever ready to totally surrender to your call. In Jesus' name, amen.

Call to Worship

Blessed are you, O God: Father, Son, and Holy Spirit. And blessed is your Kingdom, both now and forever, Amen.

PRAISING OUR GOD

Te Deum Laudamus

You are God: we praise you; you are the Lord; we acclaim you; you are the eternal Father: All creation worships you. To you all angels, all the powers of heaven, Cherubim and Seraphim, sing in endless praise: Holy, holy, holy Lord, God of power and might, heaven and earth are full of your glory.

The glorious company of apostles praise you. The noble fellowship of prophets praise you. The white-robed army of martyrs praise you. Throughout the world the holy Church acclaims you; Father, of majesty unbounded, your true and only Son, worthy of all worship, and the Holy Spirit, advocate and guide.

You, Christ, are the king of glory, the eternal Son of the Father. When you became man to set us free you did not shun the Virgin's womb. You overcame the sting of death and opened the kingdom of heaven to all believers. You are seated at God's right hand in glory. We believe that you will come and be our judge. Come then, Lord, and help your people, bought with the price of your own blood, and bring us with your saints to glory everlasting.

Praise and Thanksgiving (Songs and Prayers)

Gloria Patri

Glory be to the Father,
And to the Son and to the Holy Spirit:
As it was in the beginning,
Is now, and ever shall be,
World without end. Amen, amen.

LISTENING TO HIS VOICE

Chronological Reading for the Day
Sunday: Philem.; Phil. 1-4 ✤ *Monday:* James 1-3 ✤ *Tuesday:* James 4-5; 1 Tim. 1-2 ✤ *Wednesday:* 1 Tim. 3-6 ✤ *Thursday:* Titus 1-3 ✤ *Friday:* 2 Tim. 1-4 ✤ *Saturday:* Heb. 1.1-4.13

Lectionary Readings
Psalm: Ps. 70   *OT:* Amos 5.18-24
Gospel: Matt. 25.1-13   *NT:* 1 Thess. 4.13-18

Reflection: Silence and/or Journaling

RESPONDING IN FAITH

The Apostles' Creed
I believe in God, the Father Almighty, Maker of heaven and earth; and in Jesus Christ, his only Son, our Lord, who was conceived by the Holy Spirit, born of the Virgin Mary, suffered under Pontius Pilate, was crucified, dead, and buried; he descended into hell; the third day he arose again from the dead; he ascended into heaven and sits on the right hand of God the Father Almighty; from thence he shall come to judge the quick and the dead.

I believe in the Holy Spirit, the holy catholic* church, the communion of saints, the forgiveness of sins, the resurrection of the body, and the life everlasting. Amen.

* In the Apostles' and Nicene Creeds, the term catholic refers to the Church's universality, through all ages and times, of all languages and peoples. It refers to no particular tradition or denominational expression (e.g., as in Roman Catholic).

Prayers of Confession
Let us now confess our sins to God and receive mercy and grace to help in our time of need.

Assurance of Pardon

Having faithfully confessed and renounced your sin, Christ also has been faithful to forgive your sins and to purify you from all unrighteousness. It is certain, that there is One who has spoken to the Father in your defense, Jesus Christ, the Righteous One who is the atoning sacrifice for our sins and for the sins of the whole world. His grace and peace are with you now. Amen.

Petitions and Supplications, Ending with The Lord's Prayer

Our Father which art in heaven, Hallowed be thy name. Thy kingdom come, Thy will be done in earth, as it is in heaven. Give us this day our daily bread. And forgive us our debts, as we forgive our debtors. And lead us not into temptation, but deliver us from evil: For thine is the kingdom, and the power, and the glory, for ever. Amen.

~ Matthew 6.9-13 (KJV)

Doxology (and/or closing song)

Praise God from whom all blessings flow;
Praise Him all creatures here below;
Praise Him above ye heavenly host;
Praise Father, Son and Holy Ghost. Amen.

Departing to Serve

Benediction

Lord Jesus, who called the fisherman's boys to your side as your disciples, James and John, you foresaw what they would endure for your name's sake. You are the righteous Shepherd, who leads your own step by step into your perfect way. Help us to trust you no matter what we encounter or must endure. Enable us to be ever ready to cling to you, to love you, and to never leave your side, for in you alone do we have hope. Take us where you need us to go. In your name we pray, amen.

Affirmation from the Psalms

Make haste, O God, to deliver me! O LORD, make haste to help me! Let them be put to shame and confusion who seek my life! Let them be turned back and brought to dishonor who delight in my hurt! Let them turn back because of their shame who say, "Aha, Aha!" May all who seek you rejoice and be glad in you! May those who love your salvation say evermore, "God is great!" But I am poor and needy; hasten to me, O God! You are my help and my deliverer; O LORD, do not delay!

~ Psalm 70.1-5

Pray without Ceasing – Flash Prayer for the Day

Whether in life or death, make us ever ready to surrender to your embrace and your leading. We will follow you wherever you lead, and never turn back.

FOR YOUR WEEKLY JOURNEY

Let God Arise! Seasonal Focus

The Great Multitude to Come, Rev. 7.9-17

Book Reading

DAILY: Extreme Devotion Writing Team, *Extreme Devotion*

Howell, *Servants, Misfits, and Martyrs*

Our Corporate Disciplines

Solitude and Silence, ending with Book Review:
    Wednesday, November 12, 2014

November 16 - 22, 2014 ✣ Proper 28

According to God's holy promise, the saints of Christ will dine at the marriage supper of the Lamb, a feast of love and communion with the risen Lord and Savior himself. The Feast of Christ the King, the last Sunday before Advent, anticipates the day when Christ will reign supreme, and the saints of God will never again leave the presence of their Lord.

THIS WEEK'S THEME
The White-Robed Army of the Martyrs, Hebrews 11.32-40, Psalm 116.10-19

The history of the martyrs and saints is a profound and amazing catalogue of the most stout-hearted people this world has ever known. The writer of the book of Hebrews covered a smattering of this amazing roster, and he ran out of time to mention all that are included in the sacred Scriptures. He suggested that time would fail him to speak of the mighty acts of Barak, Samson, Jephthah, of David and Samuel and the prophets.

These men and women, who lived lives of extreme devotion to God, accomplished great things for the Lord, and, in the words of the writer, they "through faith conquered kingdoms, enforced justice, obtained promises, stopped the mouths of lions, quenched the power of fire, escaped the edge of the sword, were made strong out of weakness, became mighty in war, put foreign armies to flight."

He told, in passing only, of how those whose extreme devotion resulted in both miracle and misery. He spoke of "women who received back their dead by resurrection. Some were tortured, refusing to accept release, so that they might rise again to a better life. Others suffered mocking and flogging, and even chains and imprisonment. They were stoned, they were sawn in two, they were killed with the sword. They went about in skins of sheep and goats, destitute, afflicted, mistreated – of whom the world was not worthy – wandering about in deserts and mountains, and in dens and caves of the earth."

To cap this amazing testimony off, the writer suggested that these amazing saints who gave their all to God, were commended through their faith. Nevertheless, none of them received what they were promised, because God's plan was to provide something better for us. Incredibly, this amazing list of saints could not receive their full reward apart from us!

May we, as the psalmist declared, believe in our hearts and so affirm that salvation and grace come only from the name of the LORD. Knowing that it is impossible to render to the LORD back again what his benefits have provided us, let us then grant to him our full surrender, our unconditional availability to be and do all that he asks of us.

For those who have paid the ultimate price and sacrifice for their love of the Lord, let us remember that in the sight of the Lord, their death is precious. The white-robed army of martyrs will be rewarded in the city whose maker and builder is God. Inspired by them, we will lift up the cup of salvation and call on the name of the LORD.

DAILY DEVOTIONAL GUIDE

PREPARING OUR HEARTS

Invocation: Our Prayer of Acclamation

Eternal God, we are moved to tears as we consider your dear people, who over the centuries gave their all and best to glorify your name, even unto death. Like them, we desire to live lives of extreme devotion, of perseverance and faithfulness, to glorify you, whether by life or by death. Dear Father, make us the kind of people that bring pleasure to your heart. In Jesus' name we pray, amen.

Call to Worship

Blessed are you, O God: Father, Son, and Holy Spirit. And blessed is your Kingdom, both now and forever, Amen.

PRAISING OUR GOD

Te Deum Laudamus

You are God: we praise you; you are the Lord; we acclaim you; you are the eternal Father: All creation worships you. To you all angels, all the powers of heaven, Cherubim and Seraphim, sing in endless praise: Holy, holy, holy Lord, God of power and might, heaven and earth are full of your glory.

The glorious company of apostles praise you. The noble fellowship of prophets praise you. The white-robed army of martyrs praise you. Throughout the world the holy Church acclaims you; Father, of majesty unbounded, your true and only Son, worthy of all worship, and the Holy Spirit, advocate and guide.

You, Christ, are the king of glory, the eternal Son of the Father. When you became man to set us free you did not shun the Virgin's womb. You overcame the sting of death and opened the kingdom of heaven to all believers. You are seated at God's right hand in glory. We believe that you will come and be our judge. Come then, Lord, and help your people, bought with the price of your own blood, and bring us with your saints to glory everlasting.

Praise and Thanksgiving (Songs and Prayers)

Gloria Patri

*Glory be to the Father,
And to the Son and to the Holy Spirit:
As it was in the beginning,
Is now, and ever shall be,
World without end. Amen, amen.*

LISTENING TO HIS VOICE

Chronological Reading for the Day
Sunday: Heb. 4.14-7.28 ✤ *Monday:* Heb. 8-10 ✤ *Tuesday:* Heb. 11-13 ✤ *Wednesday:* 1 Pet. 1-2 ✤ *Thursday:* 1 Pet. 3-5 ✤ *Friday:* 2 Pet. 1-3 ✤ *Saturday:* 1 John 1-3

Lectionary Readings
Psalm: Ps. 123

Gospel: Matt. 25.14-30

OT: Judg. 4.1-7

NT: 1 Thess. 5.1-11

Reflection: Silence and/or Journaling

RESPONDING IN FAITH

The Apostles' Creed
I believe in God, the Father Almighty, Maker of heaven and earth; and in Jesus Christ, his only Son, our Lord, who was conceived by the Holy Spirit, born of the Virgin Mary, suffered under Pontius Pilate, was crucified, dead, and buried; he descended into hell; the third day he arose again from the dead; he ascended into heaven and sits on the right hand of God the Father Almighty; from thence he shall come to judge the quick and the dead.

I believe in the Holy Spirit, the holy catholic* church, the communion of saints, the forgiveness of sins, the resurrection of the body, and the life everlasting. Amen.

* In the Apostles' and Nicene Creeds, the term catholic refers to the Church's universality, through all ages and times, of all languages and peoples. It refers to no particular tradition or denominational expression (e.g., as in Roman Catholic).

Prayers of Confession
Let us now confess our sins to God and receive mercy and grace to help in our time of need.

Assurance of Pardon

Having faithfully confessed and renounced your sin, Christ also has been faithful to forgive your sins and to purify you from all unrighteousness. It is certain, that there is One who has spoken to the Father in your defense, Jesus Christ, the Righteous One who is the atoning sacrifice for our sins and for the sins of the whole world. His grace and peace are with you now. Amen.

Petitions and Supplications, Ending with The Lord's Prayer

Our Father which art in heaven, Hallowed be thy name. Thy kingdom come, Thy will be done in earth, as it is in heaven. Give us this day our daily bread. And forgive us our debts, as we forgive our debtors. And lead us not into temptation, but deliver us from evil: For thine is the kingdom, and the power, and the glory, for ever. Amen.

~ Matthew 6.9-13 (KJV)

Doxology (and/or closing song)

Praise God from whom all blessings flow;
Praise Him all creatures here below;
Praise Him above ye heavenly host;
Praise Father, Son and Holy Ghost. Amen.

Departing to Serve

Benediction

Lord Jesus, who will personally acknowledge and reward each one who paid the final price for devotion to you, create in us the kind of heart and soul that honors you alone. Like your saints and martyrs, purify us from every base motive and low intention, and raise within us a new love for you and your Kingdom, the kind of love that will honor you through every valley of death we must face. We thank you for our brothers and sisters, the martyrs, who gave you their all. Make us like them – faithful till the end. In your name, amen.

Affirmation from the Psalms

To you I lift up my eyes, O you who are enthroned in the heavens! Behold, as the eyes of servants look to the hand of their master, as the eyes of a maidservant to the hand of her mistress, so our eyes look to the LORD our God, till he has mercy upon us. Have mercy upon us, O LORD, have mercy upon us, for we have had more than enough of contempt. Our soul has had more than enough of the scorn of those who are at ease, of the contempt of the proud.

~ Psalm 123.1-4

Pray without Ceasing – Flash Prayer for the Day

Keep us ever mindful of that assembly of the faithful who paid the ultimate price to bring you glory and honor in their lives. Make us like them, for your sake.

FOR YOUR WEEKLY JOURNEY

Let God Arise! Seasonal Focus

The Great Multitude to Come, Rev. 7.9-17

Book Reading

DAILY: Extreme Devotion Writing Team, *Extreme Devotion*

Howell, *Servants, Misfits, and Martyrs*

✠

REIGN OF CHRIST THE KING

November 23 - 29, 2014 ✠ Proper 29

According to God's holy promise, the saints of Christ will dine at the marriage supper of the Lamb, a feast of love and communion with the risen Lord and Savior himself. The Feast of Christ the King, the last Sunday before Advent, anticipates the day when Christ will reign supreme, and the saints of God will never again leave the presence of their Lord.

THIS WEEK'S THEME
The King Who Is a Shepherd, Ezekiel 34. 11-16, 20-24

In testifying of the future kingdom of his reign, the Lord GOD says that he, himself, will search for his sheep, seeking them out. Just as a shepherd searches to find his flock when they have become scattered, so the Lord promises to seek his own sheep, and to rescue them from all places where they have been scattered, "on a day of clouds and thick darkness."

Furthermore, the Lord promises that he will bring them out from the peoples and gather his own from the nations, bringing them into their own place. He himself will feed them on the mountains of Israel, by the ravines, and in all the inhabited places of the country, with good pasture, good grazing land, feeding on the mountains of Israel. The Lord declares, "I myself will be the shepherd of my sheep, and I myself will make them lie down, declares the Lord GOD. I will seek the lost, and I will bring back the strayed, and I will bind up the injured, and I will strengthen the weak, and the fat and the strong I will destroy. I will feed them in justice."

In the day when the reign of God is consummated, he will rescue his flock, and they will no longer be a prey. And the LORD God promises to set up over them one shepherd, his servant David, who will feed them, be their shepherd, and be prince among them. And the Lord God will be their God.

This is the hope of the saints through the ages – the forever kingdom of God, when Christ, the risen and exalted Lord, will return to earth, put evil down, and establish forever the kingdom reign of God in the earth. The LORD seals it with his own promise, which the prophet Ezekiel declared, "And I, the LORD, will be their God, and my servant David shall be prince among them. I am the LORD; I have spoken."

DAILY DEVOTIONAL GUIDE

PREPARING OUR HEARTS

Invocation: Our Prayer of Acclamation
Almighty and everlasting God, whose will it is to restore all things in your well-beloved Son, the King of kings and Lord of Lords; Mercifully grant that the peoples of the earth, divided and enslaved by sin, may be freed and brought together under his most gracious rule; who lives and reigns with you and the Holy Spirit, one God, now and for ever. Amen.

~ Book of Common Prayer (Tickle, p. 242)

Call to Worship
Blessed are you, O God: Father, Son, and Holy Spirit. And blessed is your Kingdom, both now and forever, Amen.

PRAISING OUR GOD

Te Deum Laudamus
You are God: we praise you; you are the Lord; we acclaim you; you are the eternal Father: All creation worships you. To you all angels, all the powers of heaven, Cherubim and Seraphim, sing in endless praise: Holy, holy, holy Lord, God of power and might, heaven and earth are full of your glory.

The glorious company of apostles praise you. The noble fellowship of prophets praise you. The white-robed army of martyrs praise you. Throughout the world the holy Church acclaims you; Father, of

majesty unbounded, your true and only Son, worthy of all worship, and the Holy Spirit, advocate and guide.

You, Christ, are the king of glory, the eternal Son of the Father. When you became man to set us free you did not shun the Virgin's womb. You overcame the sting of death and opened the kingdom of heaven to all believers. You are seated at God's right hand in glory. We believe that you will come and be our judge. Come then, Lord, and help your people, bought with the price of your own blood, and bring us with your saints to glory everlasting.

Praise and Thanksgiving (Songs and Prayers)

Gloria Patri
Glory be to the Father,
And to the Son and to the Holy Spirit:
As it was in the beginning,
Is now, and ever shall be,
World without end. Amen, amen.

LISTENING TO HIS VOICE

Chronological Reading for the Day
Sunday: 1 John 4-5; 2 John 1; 3 John 1 ✤ *Monday:* Jude 1; Rev. 1-2 ✤ *Tuesday:* Rev. 3-6 ✤ *Wednesday:* Rev. 7-10 ✤ *Thursday:* Rev. 11-14 ✤ *Friday:* Rev. 15-18 ✤ *Saturday:* Rev. 19-22

Lectionary Readings
Psalm: Ps. 100   *OT:* Ezek. 34.11-16, 20-24
Gospel: Matt. 25.31-46   *NT:* Eph. 1.15-23

Reflection: Silence and/or Journaling

RESPONDING IN FAITH

The Apostles' Creed

I believe in God, the Father Almighty, Maker of heaven and earth; and in Jesus Christ, his only Son, our Lord, who was conceived by the Holy Spirit, born of the Virgin Mary, suffered under Pontius Pilate, was crucified, dead, and buried; he descended into hell; the third day he arose again from the dead; he ascended into heaven and sits on the right hand of God the Father Almighty; from thence he shall come to judge the quick and the dead.

I believe in the Holy Spirit, the holy catholic* church, the communion of saints, the forgiveness of sins, the resurrection of the body, and the life everlasting. Amen.

* In the Apostles' and Nicene Creeds, the term catholic refers to the Church's universality, through all ages and times, of all languages and peoples. It refers to no particular tradition or denominational expression (e.g., as in Roman Catholic).

Prayers of Confession

Let us now confess our sins to God and receive mercy and grace to help in our time of need.

Assurance of Pardon

Having faithfully confessed and renounced your sin, Christ also has been faithful to forgive your sins and to purify you from all unrighteousness. It is certain, that there is One who has spoken to the Father in your defense, Jesus Christ, the Righteous One who is the atoning sacrifice for our sins and for the sins of the whole world. His grace and peace are with you now. Amen.

Petitions and Supplications, Ending with The Lord's Prayer

Our Father which art in heaven, Hallowed be thy name. Thy kingdom come, Thy will be done in earth, as it is in heaven. Give us this day our daily bread. And forgive us our debts, as we forgive our debtors. And

lead us not into temptation, but deliver us from evil: For thine is the kingdom, and the power, and the glory, for ever. Amen.

~ Matthew 6.9-13 (KJV)

Doxology (and/or closing song)
Praise God from whom all blessings flow;
Praise Him all creatures here below;
Praise Him above ye heavenly host;
Praise Father, Son and Holy Ghost. Amen.

DEPARTING TO SERVE

Benediction
Stir up, O Lord, your power, and come; mercifully fulfill that which you have promised to your church unto the end of the world! Amen.

~ The Gelasian Sacramentary (Oden, p. 263)

Affirmation from the Psalms
Make a joyful noise to the LORD, all the earth! Serve the LORD with gladness! Come into his presence with singing! Know that the LORD, he is God! It is he who made us, and we are his; we are his people, and the sheep of his pasture. Enter his gates with thanksgiving, and his courts with praise! Give thanks to him; bless his name! For the LORD is good; his steadfast love endures forever, and his faithfulness to all generations.

~ Psalm 100.1-5

Pray without Ceasing – Flash Prayer for the Day
Come, good and princely Shepherd, and reign over your sheep, in that place the Father has prepared for those who love him.

FOR YOUR WEEKLY JOURNEY

Let God Arise! Seasonal Focus
The Great Multitude to Come, Rev. 7.9-17

Book Reading
DAILY: Extreme Devotion Writing Team, *Extreme Devotion*

Howell, *Servants, Misfits, and Martyrs*

Special Church Year Services
Thanksgiving Day: Thursday, November 27, 2014

THANKSGIVING DAY

November 27, 2014

According to God's holy promise, the saints of Christ will dine at the marriage supper of the Lamb, a feast of love and communion with the risen Lord and Savior himself. The Feast of Christ the King, the last Sunday before Advent, anticipates the day when Christ will reign supreme, and the saints of God will never again leave the presence of their Lord.

TODAY'S THEME
Praise the God of Our Salvation, Psalm 65

In Psalm 65 the psalmist gave thanks to God, giving praise in Zion, affirming that to God alone shall our vows be performed. He is worthy, for he is the one who hears prayer, the one to whom all flesh will come. He deserves praise, for he alone forgives sin and atones for our transgressions. He deserves our thanks, for in his mercy he chooses to bring us near to his presence, allowing us to dwell in his courts, to be satisfied with the goodness of his house, and the holiness of his temple.

We offer him thanks for he is the one who formed the mountains by his strength, who stills the roaring of the seas and its waves, and silences the tumult of the people. He is worthy of our thanks, for those who dwell at the ends of the earth stand in awe at his amazing signs and works. He is the one who establishes the going out of the morning and the evening to shout for joy.

As creator and king, he visits the earth, watering and greatly enriching it, making his river full of water, providing grain and making bountiful harvests and lush pastures. Let the hills and the meadows acknowledge him, along with all creation, for our God is God – who provides all creation with his providential care and blessing. Let us acknowledge our God, the God and Father of our Lord Jesus Christ, as the Lord, who blesses us with every blessing, for his glory's sake.

DAILY DEVOTIONAL GUIDE

PREPARING OUR HEARTS

Invocation: Our Prayer of Acclamation
May God the Father bless us. May Christ the Son take care of us. The Holy Spirit enlighten us all the days of our life. The Lord be our defender and keeper of body and soul both now and for ever and to the ages of ages. Amen.

~ An Ancient Blessing (Oden, p. 232)

Call to Worship
Blessed are you, O God: Father, Son, and Holy Spirit. And blessed is your Kingdom, both now and forever, Amen.

PRAISING OUR GOD

Te Deum Laudamus
You are God: we praise you; you are the Lord; we acclaim you; you are the eternal Father: All creation worships you. To you all angels, all the powers of heaven, Cherubim and Seraphim, sing in endless praise: Holy, holy, holy Lord, God of power and might, heaven and earth are full of your glory.

The glorious company of apostles praise you. The noble fellowship of prophets praise you. The white-robed army of martyrs praise you. Throughout the world the holy Church acclaims you; Father, of majesty unbounded, your true and only Son, worthy of all worship, and the Holy Spirit, advocate and guide.

You, Christ, are the king of glory, the eternal Son of the Father. When you became man to set us free you did not shun the Virgin's womb. You overcame the sting of death and opened the kingdom of heaven to all believers. You are seated at God's right hand in glory. We believe that you will come and be our judge. Come then, Lord, and help your people, bought with the price of your own blood, and bring us with your saints to glory everlasting.

Praise and Thanksgiving (Songs and Prayers)

Gloria Patri
Glory be to the Father,
And to the Son and to the Holy Spirit:
As it was in the beginning,
Is now, and ever shall be,
World without end. Amen, amen.

LISTENING TO HIS VOICE

Chronological Reading for the Day
Rev. 11-14

Lectionary Readings
Psalm: Ps. 65   *OT:* Deut. 8.7-18
Gospel: Luke 17.11-19   *NT:* 2 Cor. 9.6-15

Reflection: Silence and/or Journaling

RESPONDING IN FAITH

The Apostles' Creed
I believe in God, the Father Almighty, Maker of heaven and earth;
and in Jesus Christ, his only Son, our Lord, who was conceived by the
Holy Spirit, born of the Virgin Mary, suffered under Pontius Pilate,
was crucified, dead, and buried; he descended into hell; the third day
he arose again from the dead; he ascended into heaven and sits on
the right hand of God the Father Almighty; from thence he shall come
to judge the quick and the dead.

I believe in the Holy Spirit, the holy catholic* church, the communion
of saints, the forgiveness of sins, the resurrection of the body, and the
life everlasting. Amen.

* In the Apostles' and Nicene Creeds, the term catholic refers to the Church's
universality, through all ages and times, of all languages and peoples. It refers to no
particular tradition or denominational expression (e.g., as in Roman Catholic).

Prayers of Confession
Let us now confess our sins to God and receive mercy and grace to help in our time of need.

Assurance of Pardon
Having faithfully confessed and renounced your sin, Christ also has been faithful to forgive your sins and to purify you from all unrighteousness. It is certain, that there is One who has spoken to the Father in your defense, Jesus Christ, the Righteous One who is the atoning sacrifice for our sins and for the sins of the whole world. His grace and peace are with you now. Amen.

Petitions and Supplications, Ending with The Lord's Prayer
Our Father which art in heaven, Hallowed be thy name. Thy kingdom come, Thy will be done in earth, as it is in heaven. Give us this day our daily bread. And forgive us our debts, as we forgive our debtors. And lead us not into temptation, but deliver us from evil: For thine is the kingdom, and the power, and the glory, for ever. Amen.

~ Matthew 6.9-13 (KJV)

Doxology (and/or closing song)
Praise God from whom all blessings flow;
Praise Him all creatures here below;
Praise Him above ye heavenly host;
Praise Father, Son and Holy Ghost. Amen.

Departing to Serve

Benediction
We ask not of you, O Father, silver and gold, honor and glory, nor the pleasures of the world, but grant us grace to seek your kingdom and your righteousness, and add to us things necessary for the body and for this life. Behold, O Lord, our desire; may it be pleasing in your sight. We present our petition to you through our Lord Jesus Christ, who is at your right hand, our mediator and advocate, through whom you

sought us that we might seek you; your Word, through whom you made us and all things; your only begotten Son, through whom you called us to adoption, who intercedes with you for us, and in whom are hid all the treasures of wisdom and knowledge; to him, with yourself and the Holy Spirit, be all honor, praise and glory, now and forever. Amen.

~ Augustine (Oden, p. 237)

Affirmation from the Psalms

Praise is due to you, O God, in Zion, and to you shall vows be performed. O you who hear prayer, to you shall all flesh come. When iniquities prevail against me, you atone for our transgressions. Blessed is the one you choose and bring near, to dwell in your courts! We shall be satisfied with the goodness of your house, the holiness of your temple! By awesome deeds you answer us with righteousness, O God of our salvation, the hope of all the ends of the earth and of the farthest seas.

~ Psalm 65.1-5

Pray without Ceasing – Flash Prayer for the Day

Eternal God, Father Almighty, thank you for the abundant favor you pour upon the earth, and on our lives, for your glory. No other name can save; no one else blesses us like you.

FOR YOUR WEEKLY JOURNEY

Let God Arise! Seasonal Focus

The Great Multitude to Come, Rev. 7.9-17

Book Reading

DAILY: Extreme Devotion Writing Team, *Extreme Devotion*

Howell, *Servants, Misfits, and Martyrs*